PRAISE FOR *CHRISTIAN LIFE*

I'm always interested in what Kelly Kapic writes, and his *Christian Life* exceeds my usual high expectations! One key reason is the originality and conventionality of his approach, which yields "a theology of Christian life [that] will feel fresh and vibrant yet also somewhat familiar" to us. So we are well acquainted with traditional topics such as love, grace, worship of and communion with the triune God, the gospel of Jesus Christ, the church, and Christian rituals. At the same time, a freshness emerges as discussions exhibit cultural awareness without becoming contextually bound, presentations are corporately oriented as well as personally appropriated, and directives stimulate a faith that is both catholic and particular. Be sure to read this book!

—*Gregg R. Allison, Professor of Christian Theology,*
The Southern Baptist Theological Seminary

At a time when Christian life, worship, and ecclesial identity are often reduced to polarized options, Kelly Kapic offers a theologically rich and pastorally grounded vision of communion with the triune God as the source, means, and end of life in Christ. Through Christ's prophetic, priestly, and kingly work and the Spirit's enlivening presence, we are called to worship and to lives poured out in love for God, neighbor, and creation. Saturated with Scripture and drawing deeply from the wisdom of the historic Christian faith, this book is a beacon amid today's troubled waters—abounding in theological insight, pastoral clarity, and joy.

—*J. Todd Billings, Girod Research Professor of Reformed Theology,*
Western Theological Seminary, Holland, MI

What does it mean to be a Christian? The answer of Kelly Kapic is both simple and profound: Christian life is the grateful response to the love of the triune God and is anchored in the church as worshiping community. This theology has far-reaching implications, especially for modern evangelicals whose spirituality is often experience-centered and individualistic. But it is not just a book for evangelicals. Its balanced approach and ecumenical breadth would appeal to Christians of other traditions. This book is such a delight. Over and over I felt like shouting "Amen and Amen."

—*Simon Chan, former Earnest Lau Professor of Systematic Theology*
at Trinity Theological College, Singapore

One of the most pressing tasks for Christians of every generation is to articulate the tangible difference Christ makes to our lives. Kelly Kapic's *Christian Life* displays in dazzling detail the shape of Christian life as a response to what God has done and is doing in Christ, the Righteous One, who serves as both the object and leader of Christian worship. A work of a theologian par excellence operating at the height of his powers, you will find yourself comforted, convicted, and encouraged to pursue a life of communion with God rooted in our union with Christ. I cannot recommend it highly enough.

—***Daniel Lee Hill,*** *Assistant Professor of Christian Theology, George W. Truett Theological Seminary, Baylor University*

Gathering the jewels of scriptural teaching as well as a glittering array of sources across the centuries, Kapic gives us here a masterpiece. Deconstructing familiar dichotomies, this is the most edifying exploration of the Christian life I have seen in a long time. Let Kapic show you the riches of Christ for you and in his body, the church.

—***Michael Horton,*** *J. Gresham Machen Professor of Theology and Apologetics, Westminster Seminary California*

The richness of Christian life is on display in this marvelous work of Reformed theological scholarship. Kapic writes about what he knows—and so this book is filled with the humility of love, with a liturgical sensibility, with the Spirit's power in uniting us to Christ our Savior, and with a realistic and vibrant appreciation of the church. There is much here for all Christians and for all who are seeking true life!

—***Matthew Levering,*** *James N. Jr. and Mary D. Perry Chair of Theology, Mundelein Seminary*

This alert and elegant theology of Christian life begins and ends in the right place: with the life and love of God the Holy Trinity. In light of God's goodness and grace, Kelly Kapic offers a rich theological vision—both Reformed and catholic—of Christian life as life in communion with God and with one another in Christ and by the Spirit. Highly recommended.

—***Matthew Mason,*** *Assistant Director, Pastors' Academy, London*

Kelly Kapic's *Christian Life* lays out, as winsomely as finite words can convey, the enormity of the triune God's love for us and our invitation to respond. How wonderfully fitting, then, that a book about the whole of Christian life being an act of worship would draw readers to that same end.

—***Christa McKirland,*** *Dean of Faculty and Lecturer, Systematic Theology, Carey Baptist College, New Zealand*

This wonderful book is brimming with theological insight and pastoral guidance. Animated by the conviction that the Christian life is a response to God's love, Kelly Kapic sets forth a comprehensive theological vision that trains readers to receive and embrace life in communion with God. A wise and timely study.

—*Adam Neder,* *Associate Dean, Professor of Theology,*
Belmont University

Kelly Kapic's book offers a rich and thought-provoking reflection on the foundations of Christian life, grounded in Scripture and in a capacious, generous, and ecumenical appropriation of Christian theological traditions.

—*Barbara Pitkin,* *Senior Lecturer in Religious Studies,*
Stanford University

"What a relief! We have long needed such an account of Christian life: resting in the threefold work of the triune God, responding to grace, reconciling law and gospel. This book is more than just the next clever theological program. Kapic is clever enough to know how to keep out of the way and let the big, central doctrines do the work."

—*Fred Sanders,* *Torrey Honors College,*
Biola University

There is a temptation for works on humanity and the Christian life to focus on the negatives, such as our sin or fallenness—and these are certainly part of the story. However, in Kelly Kapic's volume on the Christian life, he gets to the root of it all: the love of God toward humanity. This book is a deeply biblical and soundly theological reflection on the triune God's love and how this love shapes Christian life and worship. Kapic's ability to move between theology and doxology is masterful and should be a model for others.

—*Brandon D. Smith,* *Chair of the Hobbs School of Theology and Ministry*
and Associate Professor of Theology and Early Christianity,
Oklahoma Baptist University

Often both underdeveloped and amorphous, the doctrine of the Christian life is reinvigorated by Kapic through his vision of God's self-giving love. Weaving together theology and a call to worship, Kapic's account of the Christian life refuses to divide doctrine from doxology, the individual from the ecclesial, or the objective from the subjective. Here is a rigorous and robust articulation of life in Christ giving a clarion call to respond to the God of love.

—*Kyle Strobel,* *Director of the Institute for Spiritual Formation,*
Talbot School of Theology, Biola University

We have long needed an entryway to show that the Christian life is holistic—not one-sidedly about learning doctrine or about practices, not merely about one local expression or another, and not merely about prioritizing the present over the past or vice versa. In the most accessible volume in the New Studies in Dogmatics series yet, Kapic shows us in holistic ways that the Christian life is about responding to the love of God, doing justice to the corporate yet personal, catholic yet particular, and reasoned and embodied nature of what it means to live in light of God's mercies. This book is no mere exposition but also an invitation for life in communion with God.

—*N. Gray Sutanto, Associate Professor of Systematic Theology, Reformed Theological Seminary*

Courses in human flourishing attract hundreds of college students, but a good life is hard to find, much less define. Kelly Kapic sets forth a theological thesis that is as comprehensive as it is concise: The good life, for which men and women were created, is a God-centered life, a life that returns God's love for us by loving God and everything that God has created. *Christian Life* is chock full of biblical, historical, and doctrinal direction for wise living with and right worship of the triune God.

—*Kevin J. Vanhoozer, Research Professor of Systematic Theology, Trinity Evangelical Divinity School*

Christian existence is a response to God's love. Yet this response is also God's grace, led by Jesus himself and shaped in us by his Spirit. Our communion with God flows from our union with Christ. Against this backdrop, Kelly Kapic triangulates Christology, the individual, and the church community to situate the arc of Christian life in the worship of the *totus Christus*. This is a dogmatically serious treatise, brimming with insight. Kapic seamlessly joins depth and clarity, doctrine and doxology, to illuminate the liturgy of Christian living for all Christ's people. His book is a gift to both church and academy.

—*Tyler R. Wittman, Associate Professor of Christian Theology, New Orleans Baptist Theological Seminary*

NEW STUDIES IN DOGMATICS

CHRISTIAN LIFE

SERIES EDITORS

Michael Allen, John Dyer Trimble Professor of Systematic Theology and Academic Dean, Reformed Theological Seminary, Orlando, Florida, USA

Scott R. Swain, President and James Woodrow Hassell Professor of Systematic Theology, Reformed Theological Seminary, Orlando, Florida, USA

ADVISORY BOARD

John B. Webster, † Professor of Divinity, St. Mary's College, University of St. Andrews, Scotland, UK

Kevin J. Vanhoozer, Research Professor of Systematic Theology, Trinity Evangelical Divinity School, Deerfield, Illinois, USA

Katherine Sonderegger, Professor of Theology, Virginia Theological Seminary, Alexandria, Virginia, USA

Henri Blocher, Professor of Systematic Theology, Faculté Libre de Théologie Évangélique, Vaux-sur-Seine, France

ZONDERVAN EDITORIAL ADVISOR

Katya Covrett, Vice President and Publisher, Zondervan Academic

NEW STUDIES IN DOGMATICS

CHRISTIAN LIFE

KELLY M. KAPIC

MICHAEL ALLEN AND SCOTT R. SWAIN,
GENERAL EDITORS

ZONDERVAN ACADEMIC

Christian Life
Copyright © 2025 by Kelly M. Kapic

Published by Zondervan, 3950 Sparks Drive SE, Suite 101, Grand Rapids, MI 49546, USA. Zondervan is a registered trademark of The Zondervan Corporation, L.L.C., a wholly owned subsidiary of HarperCollins Christian Publishing, Inc.

Requests for information should be addressed to customercare@harpercollins.com.

Zondervan titles may be purchased in bulk for educational, business, fundraising, or sales promotional use. For information, please email SpecialMarkets@Zondervan.com.

Library of Congress Cataloging-in-Publication Data

Names: Kapic, Kelly M., 1972- author | Allen, Michael, 1981- editor | Swain, Scott R. editor
Title: Christian life / Kelly M. Kapic ; Michael Allen and Scott R. Swain, general editors.
Description: Grand Rapids, Michigan : Zondervan Academic, [2025] | Series: New studies in dogmatics | Includes index.
Identifiers: LCCN 2025025127 (print) | LCCN 2025025128 (ebook) | ISBN 9780310523581 paperback | ISBN 9780310523598 ebook
Subjects: LCSH: Christian life
Classification: LCC BV4501.3 .K36 2025 (print) | LCC BV4501.3 (ebook) | DDC 248.4--dc23/eng/20250813
LC record available at https://lccn.loc.gov/2025025127
LC ebook record available at https://lccn.loc.gov/2025025128

Unless otherwise noted, Scripture quotations are taken from the ESV® Bible (The Holy Bible, English Standard Version®). Copyright © 2001 by Crossway, a publishing ministry of Good News Publishers. Used by permission. All rights reserved. • Scripture quotations marked NIV are taken from The Holy Bible, New International Version®, NIV®. Copyright © 1973, 1978, 1984, 2011 by Biblica, Inc.® Used by permission of Zondervan. All rights reserved worldwide. www.Zondervan.com. The "NIV" and "New International Version" are trademarks registered in the United States Patent and Trademark Office by Biblica, Inc.® • Scripture quotations marked NRSVue are taken from the New Revised Standard Version Updated Edition. Copyright © 2021 National Council of Churches of Christ in the United States of America. Used by permission. All rights reserved worldwide. • Scripture quotations marked CSB® are taken from the Christian Standard Bible®. Copyright © 2017 by Holman Bible Publishers. Used by permission. Christian Standard Bible® and CSB® are federally registered trademarks of Holman Bible Publishers. • Scripture quotations marked NASB are taken from the (NASB®) New American Standard Bible®. Copyright © 1960, 1971, 1977, 1995, 2020 by The Lockman Foundation. Used by permission. All rights reserved. www.lockman.org.

Any internet addresses (websites, blogs, etc.) and telephone numbers in this book are offered as a resource. They are not intended in any way to be or imply an endorsement by Zondervan, nor does Zondervan vouch for the content of these sites and numbers for the life of this book.

All rights reserved. No part of this publication may be reproduced, stored in a retrieval system, or transmitted in any form or by any means—electronic, mechanical, photocopy, recording, or any other—except for brief quotations in printed reviews, without the prior permission of the publisher.

Without limiting the exclusive rights of any author, contributor or the publisher of this publication, any unauthorized use of this publication to train generative artificial intelligence (AI) technologies is expressly prohibited. HarperCollins also exercise their rights under Article 4(3) of the Digital Single Market Directive 2019/790 and expressly reserve this publication from the text and data mining exception.

HarperCollins Publishers, Macken House, 39/40 Mayor Street Upper, Dublin 1, D01 C9W8, Ireland (https://www.harpercollins.com)

Cover design: Micah Kandros Design
Interior design: Kait Lamphere and Denise Froehlich

$PrintCode

To Jonathan and Juliette.
May God's life and love continue to animate
and guide your life together.
We are so grateful for you two.

The Christian Faith revolves about two main doctrines: the divinity of the Trinity and the humanity of Christ.
—THOMAS AQUINAS[1]

Thesis:
Christian life is a response to the love of God.

Expanded Dogmatic Statement:
A theology of Christian life is framed in terms of divine and human agency.

Not only did the triune God first love us, but the incarnate Son also first loved God for us.

We respond to God's love as those who have been united to Christ by the Spirit.

---

1. Thomas Aquinas, *Aquinas's Shorter Summa: St. Thomas Aquinas's Own Concise Version of His Summa Theologica* (Manchester: Sophia Institute, 1993), 215.

CONTENTS

Series Preface 13
Acknowledgments. 15

PART 1: Setting the Stage
1. Why We Need a Theology of Christian Life 21

PART 2: God to Us: Divine Agency—the Triune God's Love
2. Love: The Fountain of God's Love 55
3. Grace: The Coming of God's Love 91
4. Fellowship: The Connection to God's Love. 125

PART 3: Interlude
5. The Law-Gospel Distinction: Framing the Human
   Response to God 153

PART 4: Us to God: Human Agency—Responding to God's Love
6. Messiah: The Foundation of Christian Life 181
7. Ego: The Drama of Christian Life. 219
8. Ecclesia I: The Context of Christian Life. 253
9. Ecclesia II: Corporate Worship as the Arc of Christian Life . . 283

Conclusion 319
Scripture Index 321
Subject Index 330

SERIES PREFACE

New Studies in Dogmatics follows in the tradition of G. C. Berkouwer's classic series, Studies in Dogmatics, in seeking to offer concise, focused treatments of major topics in dogmatic theology that fill the gap between introductory theology textbooks and advanced theological monographs. Dogmatic theology, as understood by editors and contributors to the series, is a conceptual representation of scriptural teaching about God and all things in relation to God. The source of dogmatics is Holy Scripture; its scope is the summing up of all things in Jesus Christ; its setting is the communion of the saints; and its end is the conversion, consolation, and instruction of creaturely wayfarers in the knowledge and love of the triune God until that knowledge and love is consummated in the beatific vision.

The series wagers that the way forward in constructive theology lies in a program of renewal through retrieval. This wager follows upon the judgment that much modern theology exhibits "a stubborn tendency to grow not higher but to the side," to borrow Alexander Solzhenitsyn's words from another context. Though modern theology continues to grow in a number of areas of technical expertise and interdisciplinary facility (especially in both the exegetical and historical domains), this growth too often displays a sideways drift rather than an upward progression in relation to theology's subject matter, scope, and source, and in fulfilling theology's end. We believe the path toward theological renewal in such a situation lies in drawing more deeply upon the resources of Holy Scripture in conversation with the church's most trusted teachers (ancient, medieval, and modern) who have sought to fathom Christ's unsearchable riches. In keeping with this belief, authors from a broad evangelical constituency will seek in this series to retrieve the riches of Scripture and tradition for constructive dogmatics. The purpose of retrieval is neither simple repetition of past theologians nor repristination of an earlier phase in church history; Christianity, at any rate, has no golden age east of Eden and short of the kingdom of God.

CHRISTIAN LIFE

Properly understood, retrieval is an inclusive and enlarging venture, a matter of tapping into a vital root and, in some cases, of relearning a lost grammar of theological discourse, all for the sake of equipping the church in its contemporary vocation to think and speak faithfully and fruitfully about God and God's works.

While the specific emphases of individual volumes will vary, each volume will display (1) awareness of the "state of the question" pertaining to the doctrine under discussion; (2) attention to the patterns of biblical reasoning (exegetical, biblical-theological, etc.) from which the doctrine emerges; (3) engagement with relevant ecclesiastical statements of the doctrine (creedal, conciliar, confessional), as well as with leading theologians of the church; and (4) appreciation of the doctrine's location within the larger system of theology, as well as of its contribution to Christian piety and practice.

Our prayer is that by drawing upon the best resources of the past and with an awareness of both perennial and proximate challenges to Christian thought and practice in the present, New Studies in Dogmatics will contribute to a flourishing theological culture in the church today. Soli Deo Gloria.

MICHAEL ALLEN AND SCOTT R. SWAIN

ACKNOWLEDGMENTS

I long ago gave up the myth of the solitary scholar who comes up with everything on their own—that image is generally untrue, plus, believing it often fosters arrogance and isolation rather than gratitude and shalom. While I cannot imagine trying to untangle all of the influences that have helped shape me, nor will I ever be able to adequately thank all who have and continue to pour into my life and inspire my thinking, I nevertheless find so much joy in mentioning at least some of those have been so vital to me while writing this particular book.

Because of the encouragement and vision of Michael Allen, Scott Swain, and Katya Covrett, I agreed to write this volume back in 2014. I am so grateful for their patience and willingness to let the idea swirl around in my mind and grow through my research and conversations over the last ten years. While completing other projects, this one continued to capture my imagination in fresh and unexpected ways, so I experimented with various possibilities in terms of the structure and vision of the book. Only through much time spent reading, in conversations, and often trying out material on different audiences did I eventually land on a structure and overall vision that felt right and faithful. Where I ended is not where I thought I would be when I began, but I am so grateful I had the years to allow the material to develop in organic and stimulating ways. While I hope readers will find it fresh and useful, I leave that to their judgment, but for now, I am grateful to finally send this book out into the world.

Along this journey, many have proven so helpful. Back in 2016, I remember sitting in a creative studio with my dear friends Jay Green and Jeffrey Morton as I started to form my ideas of what became the "three-corded rope" (Messiah, ecclesia, and ego), asking my friends to help me create the visuals for these ideas (we were working with 3-D models) and how they relate together in corporate worship and Christian life. I also benefited from Dan Treier's graciousness in switching deadlines with me so his New Studies in Dogmatics volume would come out before mine. Dan is not only a superb theologian but also an excellent human being. Other authors in the series have also been deep encouragements at different points.

Thanks to an invitation from Christopher Green in 2018, I went to Australia to deliver some early explorations on this topic at a Theology Connect conference. In 2022, I was invited to give the Annual Moore College lectures in Sydney, Australia. I laid out the first half of my book on a Theology of Christian life in that setting. Principal Mark Thompson and the entire faculty and staff were incredible hosts for that week, and I have such happy memories of that time together.

Throughout the process of my research and writing, many scholars willingly discussed ideas with me in person, chatted on Zoom, or otherwise spoke into my work. While I cannot name them all, I would like to mention the following, knowing each deserves far more than just being named: John Witvliet, Donald K. McKim, Rob Rayburn (who generously gave me his own copy of J.-J. von Allmen's hard-to-find classic volume on worship!), Miroslav Volf, Matt Jenson, Fred Sanders, Mickey Mattox, Chuck DeGroat, Tom Schwanda, Adam Johnson, Paul C. H. Lim, Peter C. Orr, Andrew M. Leslie, Brian Fikkert, Daphne Haddad, Steve Corbett, Russell Mask, Brannon Ellis, and Todd Billings. Members of my department also provided insights and much-needed wisdom: Scott Jones, Hans Madueme, Clift Ward, Emmie Thompson, Herb Ward, Luke Irwin, Jeff Dryden, and Dan MacDougal. A particular thanks to Ty Kieser, David Barr, John Clark, Jonathan Bailes, Joey Sherrard, and John Yates (my patron saint of editing!), who, representing various theological traditions, institutions, and specializations, all read through the entire manuscript to give final corrections, feedback, and encouragement. Susan Anderson, Charity Chaney, Alayna Bradberry all served as my work-study assistants for part of the time I was working on this volume, and each offered not just help and wise feedback but also needed encouragement and grace. A large adult Sunday School class at Lookout Mountain Presbyterian Church also graciously engaged with early forms of this material, raising fantastic questions and helping me better understand more of the practical implications of these ideas. I'm also deeply grateful for my Zondervan editors David McNutt and Matthew Estel—you two diligently improved the final product.

Parallel to my research for this project, I have also been involved in research funded by the John Templeton Foundation. While that work

ACKNOWLEDGMENTS

was often not directly related to the volume you hold in your hands, there inevitably was some overlap and mutually enriching themes developed. Therefore, I would like to express my deepest thanks for the subtle and profound ways the team and work influenced me. Accordingly, I would like to thank both the team as well as a few particular individuals who helped us/me along the way: Elizabeth Hall, Jason McMartin, Crystal Park, Eric Silverman, Jamie Aten, Laura Rosemary Shannonhouse, Robert C. Roberts, Alexis Abernethy, Gerald L. Sittser, Jonathan Pennington, and Adam A. Neder.

Furthermore, the support and reassurance of a few people stand out in terms of making this work possible: Norris† and Billie Little (we miss you, Norris, more than we can say!), Jim and Martha Seneff (your calls and support have meant so much), Derek and Wendy Halverson, Jeff and Lynn Hall, Brad and Kelli Voyles, Collin and Elizabeth Messer, Everett and Stephanie Pierce, and many others I cannot name here.

Finally, my family. Tabitha, thank you for consistently pointing me to Christ and modeling a life of sacrificial service toward others. With over three decades of marriage behind us, I can't wait to see how the future unfolds. Margot, your joy, energy, and vision are life-giving; you are such a gift to me and countless others. Jonathan and Juliette, I dedicate this book to you as you begin your married life together. You two are so fun together, and seeing your hearts develop a rich love for God, his people, and his world is a great joy. May your shared life always be animated by the love, grace, and fellowship of God, the God who delights in you and invites you to participate in the motions and movements of his generosity and kindness. May you two always have the courage of faith, the perseverance of hope, and the center of love guiding your lives together.

PART 1

SETTING THE STAGE

CHAPTER 1

WHY WE NEED A THEOLOGY OF CHRISTIAN LIFE

It is worship of God alone that renders [humans] higher than the brutes.
—JOHN CALVIN[1]

Christian worship is the most momentous, the most urgent, the most glorious action that can take place in human life.
—KARL BARTH[2]

Christian life has the fundamental character of communion with God, which is nourished in the soil of worship. In this book we will explore why we need a *theology* of Christian life and how that theology and our lives can enrich each other in a faithful way. To situate such a theology within the landscape of Christian thought and practice, let's begin with some questions.

OPENING QUESTIONS

We begin with a question that quickly unearths many others: *How do we live a Christian life?*

Notice the particular words we take for granted here. Let's begin

---

1. John Calvin, *Institutes of the Christian Religion*, ed. John T. McNeill, trans. Ford Lewis Battles, vol. 1, Library of Christian Classics (Louisville: Westminster John Knox, 2011), 1.3.3, p. 47.
2. Cited by J.-J. von Allmen, *Worship: Its Theology and Practice* (New York: Oxford University Press, 1965), 13.

with what it means to *live*. What does it mean to *live* as a Christian? Non-Christians live and breathe, so what differentiates Christians here? Is this mostly a description of distinct morals, or does Christian living include more than growth in virtue? We hear about the Christian *faith*, so how do faith and action relate—are they the same, utterly different, or do they interact? Is Christian living more about a mental attitude, or does embodied action matter? How does Christian living relate to emotions and experience? To my self-perception? To my neighbors or even the earth?

What makes it *Christian* in the first place? How is Christian life different from other forms of spirituality? What does it mean to be *Christian*, or like Christ, or followers of Christ? Why is it so important that this living is done "in Christ"?

Furthermore, *who* is the "we" doing this living? Are we talking about an individual, a community, or both? Western readers tend to view the "we" as a batch of individuals rather than as a body in which each "I" has identity in communion with the whole. But we can hold that view only when we forget that Christians belong to Christ's body, united not only to him but also to each other *because* we are united to Christ. As the church, we have been engrafted into Israel, and so we are united with God's people throughout all history (cf. Gal 3). Christian life is therefore a community-oriented life. But who are these people—just my local church, or my denomination, or does it also include the global church and the variety of Christian traditions through the ages? How can I even begin to comprehend that, given all the disagreements and differences?

How should *I*, as the particular person I am, understand this communal manner of living in Christ? The communal nature of our being excludes both isolation and a restricted focus on my internal world. The *other* must matter. Isn't there more to Christian life than an extended examination of the *I* (the ego)? If we begin with the *I*, does that distort the whole venture before we even get started?

Finally, what is *life*? We speak of eternal life, of life in the Spirit, of new life. How do we make sense of the Christian paradox that *true life comes through death*? Is our goal to live or to die? How do we understand this as good news? A theology of Christian life will inevitably raise questions about human flourishing, so it will need to have clear relevance both to this world and to our future life in glory. How then do *life* and *flourishing* relate to seemingly stunting biblical principles, such as self-denial and self-control? How might this life relate to tradition and suffering, community and convictions?

We must avoid restricting our questions to abstract concerns: We must deal with concrete matters also. Surely one's worldly context—country, family, church, sex, color, caste—affects the ways one puts faith into action. For example, our background, language, and experiences all inevitably inform how we read and apply the Bible.[3] How then do we navigate between the universal and the singular so we don't confuse unity with uniformity? A faithful theology of Christian life must create space for practices that are normative for everyone as well as space for particular, contextual differences within the body of Christ. We must not make what is historically contingent normative, nor should we ignore what is enduring and essential for all settings. God is consistent in his character and his call on our lives in a way that transcends our particularities without belittling them.

All of us are tempted to universalize bits of our own particular circumstances without realizing it; this risks distorting a vision of the kingdom that could otherwise work as a backdrop for a theology of Christian life. On the other hand, some of us will be so captivated by an abstractly idealized vision of the kingdom of God that our words will hardly resonate with people as they face such earthly problems as the need to eat and sleep, to live in complicated marriages and exhausting jobs, to handle gritty real-world troubles rather more than they are called to assemble theological constructs. We need a theology of Christian life that faithfully represents God and how he relates to his people through time and space, even in different cultures and historical epochs. And it must do this without diminishing or denying the goodness of our differences, our unique stories, or our everyday challenges.

Imagine four people walking into a bar: a Brazilian Pentecostal, an American nondenominational evangelical, a devout Greek Orthodox believer from Athens, and a Dutch Calvinist from Amsterdam.

---

3. For some helpful examples of how context often does shape hermeneutics, see, e.g., Elizabeth Mburu, *African Hermeneutics* (Plateau State, Nigeria: HippoBooks, 2019), Esau McCaulley, *Reading While Black: African American Biblical Interpretation as an Exercise in Hope* (Downers Grove, IL: IVP Academic, 2020); E. Randolph Richards and Brandon J. O'Brien, *Misreading Scripture with Western Eyes: Removing Cultural Blinders to Better Understand the Bible* (Downers Grove, IL: InterVarsity Press, 2012); Timothy C. Tennent, *Theology in the Context of World Christianity: How the Global Church Is Influencing the Way We Think About and Discuss Theology* (Grand Rapids: Zondervan, 2007); and Stephen T. Pardue, *Why Evangelical Theology Needs the Global Church* (Grand Rapids: Baker Academic, 2023).

Who buys? Or maybe they just debate whether to go into the bar in the first place. This sounds facetious, even flippant, but it illustrates a genuine and important goal for a theology of Christian life, namely, that it be broad enough to make space for our real and unpredictable life in the kingdom of God (encompassing the globe and different Christian traditions) yet particular enough that it is genuinely *Christian*, biblically saturated, and existentially satisfying. The four church groups mentioned above are real enough, as are tensions over questions like those about alcohol: Shouldn't we aim to have a theology of Christian life robust enough to handle questions like the one above, whether as the beginning of a joke or of a serious discussion? I believe it is possible, even if it isn't easy, given the pressures to become either overly focused and narrow or overly broad and vague: One extreme eventually pulls up the wheat with the tares, while the other waters down the wine so much that its benefit and joy are lost and you're not even sure if it *is* wine anymore.

What are we to do?

I wanted us to begin by pondering these basic questions about Christian life because otherwise we might start too quickly, thinking we know more than we do, confusing assumptions with verified facts, biases with wisdom, and the repetition of vogue words with real knowledge. Only with greater self-awareness will we begin to appreciate that many factors shape our assumptions about Christian life and we don't even realize it. Only by slowing down, by recognizing and examining assumptions, can we see things in fresh ways, which is necessary for a constructive, faithful, and lively theology.

OLD OR NEW?

I propose a path forward that may appear novel to some but wholly expected to others. My hope is that this approach to a theology of Christian life will feel fresh and vibrant yet also somewhat familiar, as if you have had similar thoughts before. In any case, I hope it provides a useful tool for more deeply understanding and experiencing our faith. Ideally, two things will happen together: (1) Our theology will become more textured and reflective of the deep things of God, and (2) our experience will become richer, testifying to what has always been true but not always recognized. Let me explain the dynamic of this path with a relevant example.

WHY WE NEED A THEOLOGY OF CHRISTIAN LIFE

When I begin teaching undergraduates about the Trinity, they often go through a somewhat predictable series of responses. As I lay out just how vital it is for Christians to be robustly Trinitarian, it often stirs them with unexpected excitement, and then they start to realize that Trinitarian doctrine states what is at the core of being Christian. To be Christian is to be Trinitarian: It is *that* important. Father, Son, and Spirit is who God *is*! Then I raise concerns about ways we have been tempted to lose our Trinitarian emphasis or orientation or downplay its importance and relevance. This sadly resonates with many of them. As stimulating as it appears to them and as much as they grow concerned about the possible neglect of Trinitarian doctrine in their lives and churches, they start to worry: Is it true? Is it that bad? And how do we fix it? "I've never heard about Gregory of Nazianzus until now, and most believers don't know the words *ousia* and *hypostasis*. I've heard a few prooftexts, but now they don't seem to hold up as well as I had thought." More concerns and questions emerge. "Wait, was the church I grew up in not Trinitarian? Am I not Trinitarian? Does this mean I'm not really Christian?" They become genuinely concerned because, although they have always nominally affirmed the Christian belief that God is triune, it now occurs to them that they are not sure what that means. So does their lack of clarity mean they don't believe, and does their inability to articulate a carefully constructed philosophical explanation mean that they are not Trinitarian, or even not Christian?

At this point, it becomes vital to help them see what has always been there for most of them, but they failed to appreciate: They and the church are indeed Trinitarian; they just were not very conscious of it.[4] My goal is to raise their consciousness and then deepen and enrich it. Experientially, very few of us become "Trinitarian" because we study the doctrine. Most don't come to believe that God is triune from carefully digging into a word study or gathering all the biblical texts together on the topic and working through them. Nor do they become so because they read Augustine's *De Trinitate* or Aquinas's detailed treatment in the *Summa*. They don't know who John Owen and Karl Barth are, and they have never read Richard Bauckham or Larry Hurtado's exegetical and historical studies. So how are they and their churches Trinitarian in our day without all this background? Is it all a sham?

---

4. Cf. Fred Sanders, *The Deep Things of God: How the Trinity Changes Everything*, 2nd ed. (Wheaton, IL: Crossway, 2017).

SETTING THE STAGE

Let me bring you in on a secret: The way most people become Trinitarian—and this is true from the earliest apostles and disciples to Christians in Sri Lanka today, for women and men, young and old, rich and poor, educated and illiterate—is that *we experience the life-giving power of the Spirit who unites us to the crucified and risen Savior as we learn to rest in the deep love of the Father*. People *become* Trinitarian because they *experience* the Trinity. No matter how nervous that may make Presbyterians like me, it's still true. It is both a gift and a calling by God.[5]

In the twentieth century Michael Polanyi argued at great length that we "know more than we can tell." He called this "tacit knowledge."[6] This was his way of saying our inability to articulate a truth doesn't mean we don't know it. You probably can't explain the physics of riding a bicycle, but that doesn't mean you don't know how to ride one. Or, as we were hinting above, just because people can't fully explain the Trinity or haven't studied the doctrine in depth doesn't mean they don't "know" the Trinity. Here theology and experience come together.

While I cannot here unpack the Christian theory of *lex orandi, lex credendi*—"the law of prayer is the law of belief"—for our purposes right now, we simply must acknowledge that there is a real sense in which all Christians might have intuitions not just about the Trinity but also about a theology of Christian life that they absorb merely by entering into the life of faith and worshiping with God's people. This shapes and informs us in ways we often don't realize, and in these dynamics we can see the action of God's Spirit. It is also, however, a warning that distorted church practices or proclamations can misshape how believers understand Christian life.

This dynamic of tacit knowing will be important in our theology of Christian life. The human experiences of corporately worshiping the triune God shape our understanding and our lives in deep ways, often without us recognizing it. Why? Because *God* is doing the shaping. This takes us back to theology. Social phenomena also have important theological aspects. I will argue that *absorbing a theology of Christian life*

---

5. Cf. James Buckley and David Yeago, in the context of renewed ecclesial attention to the Trinity, observe that "in accounting for Christian trinitarianism, one is up against the deep structures of Christian identity, with that which is constitutive of what is 'Christian' in a profound and epistemically basic way." *Knowing the Triune God: The Work of the Spirit in the Practices of the Church*, ed. James J. Buckley and David S. Yeago (Grand Rapids: Eerdmans, 2001), 15.

6. Michael Polanyi, *The Tacit Dimension* (1966; repr., Chicago: University of Chicago Press, 2009), 4–5.

simply by being part of the gathered Christian worshiping community is part of God's design, and his Spirit uses our communal worship to conform us more and more into the image of the Son. The soil in which our growth in Christ normally occurs is worship, especially corporate worship by the gathered people of God, whether that happens in a tiny house church in Nepal, a cathedral in Italy, a megachurch in Korea, or a neighborhood congregation in Nebraska. But to see this more clearly, let's lay out the argument of this book in brief.

THE ARGUMENT IN BRIEF

I hope to bring great news to ministers and congregants alike: Thanks to Scripture, tradition, and experience, you already have all you need to understand the shape and form of Christian life. *We don't need new or better ideas; we need to recognize what is already true and already in our lives.* The goal here is not novelty but depth, not innovation but communion and love. And because that has always been God's intent as well as the way he works, he didn't create a situation where only those with a high IQ or vast doctrinal training can understand a theology of Christian life. This is for all of God's people.

Let me now lay out the basic theme of this book, beginning with its overall thesis. Although it will need a great deal of unpacking, here is the working argument.

> **Overall thesis of the book:**
> Christian life is a response to the love of God.
>
> **A brief outline of the argument:**
> Christian life has the fundamental character of communion with the triune God, a communion that grows out of love and is nourished by worship. Communion reflects God's nature, original intentions for creation, and ongoing work of re-creation. In this light, we will begin by spending three chapters exploring love, grace, and fellowship. These three terms point to the three divine persons and the work of the one God. Christians are those who enjoy the love of the Father through the grace of the incarnate Son in the fellowship of the Holy Spirit.
>
> In sum, Christian life is a response to the life and love of God

as it flows from God toward us, drawing us back into communion with the Creator. When we examine this love against the backdrop of the biblical story, we discover that it doesn't merely bring an emotional change in us nor only have consequences for our relationship with God. Instead, flowing from the triune God's inner life, this love constitutes God's working plan for shalom and his response to the problems that sin introduces. God's love draws us back into communion with him, and receiving his love enables us to love our neighbors and the rest of creation. As sinners, we receive God's love and enter his kingdom not by our natural standing or faithfulness but by Christ working in and for us. Jesus the Messiah is the gift of God: As Mediator between God and humanity, the incarnate Son is God's grace given to us. He is not only God, worthy of worship, but also our Priest, King, and Prophet who leads our worship. In theology as in worship, we must always see that Christ is central to Christian life. We enjoy life, love, and fellowship now with God by the Holy Spirit, the eternal divine person who is the bond of love between the Father and Son, so even now the same Spirit is the bond of love connecting us and God in Christ.

Built on this Trinitarian foundation, we pause for a necessary interlude to explore how best to understand the "law" and "gospel" distinction, since in this space we live and respond to God's love and grace. Seeking to avoid common mistakes that undermine a healthy theology of Christian life, we aim to uphold both the full significance of the person and work of Christ while also affirming the goodness of God's creation and commandments, all anchored in God's goodness and his vision of shalom, communion, and love. Gaining a proper view of this law-gospel dynamic is key as we turn to properly orienting a human response to God.

In the last section of the book, we explore positive human response to God's love. Here we must hold together the christological, personal, and ecclesial. Building on what was already noted in section one, we dive deeper into the significance of the Messiah as the center and leader of human response to God. Jesus's faithfulness in life, death, resurrection, and ongoing heavenly intercession is the basis for our Christian life. I (ego), therefore, freely respond to God's love because I am united to Christ and his people, liberated now from the dominion of sin. Rather than a privatized vision, a believer's new life in Christ is organically and necessarily connected to the community of faith. The ecclesia—a community of worship—shapes, sustains, and invigorates Christian life. Such worship, however, is not so much about a feeling or whim but is based on general practices passed on through generations and millennia.

We therefore conclude by considering the importance of Christian rituals that remind us of the vital importance of the institutional church even as we recognize the limits of such practices. From there, we turn our attention more specifically to the centrality of corporate worship: Christian life reflects and is shaped by the basic contours of the arc of corporate worship, which moves in the rhythm of call and response:

- calling invites coming;
- proclamation provokes faith, prayer, and praise;
- Eucharist grounds and enables our gratitude made manifest in offerings;
- the peace of Christ enables us to live in peace with our neighbor; and
- benediction frees and sends us out in love to sacrificially serve a broken and hurting world.

In this liturgical and theological conversation, God reveals himself through the calling, proclamation, Eucharist, passing of the peace, and benediction. By our union with Christ, he also joins us to Christ's own human response of coming; of faith, prayers, and praises; of peace making; of offerings; and even of going out into the world.

This theological and liturgical flow of Christian life has a threefold dynamic: It is christologically driven (the centrality of the Messiah), it emphasizes the corporate (God's people, ecclesia, both ancient Israel and the historic and continuing universal church), and it includes the particular and personal (me, ego). Christ both presents and represents God to us and us to God, and only in him by the Spirit do we have new life. In this way, God in Christ, by his Spirit, extends his love, grace, and fellowship to us, bringing the fresh waters of forgiveness, reconciliation, and purpose as he enables us to participate in his loving work in the church and world.

Readers will likely notice that throughout this volume I refer to "a theology of Christian life" rather than "a theology of *the* Christian life." I wrestled through the idea of whether or not to use an article (*a* or *the*) before *Christian life*. As my theology worked itself out, I started to rethink this common construction. Too many theologies of Christian life fuse culture and theology in unhealthy ways, for example, imposing certain cultural assumptions as if they were universally required. Christian life is not defined by any particular culture or historical moment, so in many ways it will look different in different settings. Furthermore, using an article (*a* or *the*) before *Christian life* often unintentionally smuggles individualistic assumptions into the discussion. The simple phrase *Christian life* brings some useful ambiguity. My hope is that this construction will help us remember that Christian life is always communal as well as personal, always our participation, by the work of the Holy Spirit, in Christ's own life. *Christian* life is, therefore, not just my life, but life in communion with God and all his people. This larger communion that God creates and upholds in and among his people is Christian life, a life in the Son and by the Spirit. A theology of Christian life thus requires that we speak chiefly about God and not merely about ourselves. My hope is that we will find a way to speak clearly about its distinctiveness (Christian life versus other types of life) and avoid any tyrannical insistence on homogeneity (by suggesting there is only one pattern for Christian life).

Finally, before we start unpacking my thesis in the following chapters, I would like us to pause and consider some problems posed by a handful of false dichotomies that surface far too often in our theological discussions.

AVOIDING FALSE DICHOTOMIES

One reason I have become convinced that we need a theology of Christian life in our day is that too often we are offered forms of spirituality that assert false dichotomies. That is, they take one principle or insight and oppose it against others that are just as true but seem to compete with the chosen one. It isn't a matter of opposing truth to falsehood so much as an inability to see how two true ideas relate. We should hold together what God does not want separated. Here as we begin, we can examine a few of them, preparing us to recognize and avoid them as we construct a theology of Christian life. The trick is to ask where we can legitimately choose *and* rather than *or* when discussing these ideas:

- objective *and* subjective
- catholic *and* particular
- transcendence *and* immanence
- Trinitarian *and* Christ-centered
- representation *and* imitation

Each of these could fill a chapter, but a brief look at them can help us to avoid rejecting one where we should be affirming both. After this, we will be ready to jump into the love of God, the grace of Christ, and the fellowship of the Holy Spirit, followed by the second half of the book, where we speak of human response to God. As we proceed throughout the whole book, we will address the biggest tension we face in unpacking a theology of Christian life, which is navigating questions related to agency (divine and human). The entire book will be unpacking this relationship while trying to avoid a false dichotomy that would make us pick between them or to pit them against each other in an inappropriate manner. But for now, we start with these five potential false dichotomies, which, if not recognized, could take us in problematic directions.

Objective and Subjective

Part of the challenge of living a Christian life is developing a healthy appreciation for its objective and subjective aspects. For our purposes, *objective* refers to realities outside of us that are true regardless of what we think or feel, whereas *subjective* refers to our internal world, the experience of our emotions, mind, and will. The first focuses on an external inventory—what is true "out there." This includes not simply what is happening that we see with our eyes but also what is true about God, about his presence and character—all of that is objective and not subjective. The second focuses on an internal inventory—what is true "inside" me that notices and processes perceptions, finds words, uses logic to solve a problem (sometimes we call that "reasoning"), applies subconscious intuitions to evaluate circumstances (sometimes we call that "feelings"), and so on. Those internal processes respond to worship, determining whether it is merely empty ritual and detached cognitive affirmations or something deeper that penetrates the heart, mind, and soul.

Like other conscious experiences, corporate worship involves subjective responses to objective factors. On the one hand, sometimes we're most aware of what's going on around us: greeting our friends, finding the children, following the music and words of a new hymn, contemplating the content of a sermon, deciding whether to put cash or a check in the collection plate, and so forth. Beyond these easily observable external factors, however, is God's own presence, his promises, his glory. The power, knowledge, and love of the *I Am* are not dependent upon our subjective feelings or awareness—they are always just true of him. On the other hand, sometimes we are also aware of our internal responses to the service: noticing how glad we are to see our friends, resolving to be less irritated when our children are inconveniently energetic, trying to hold in tears when deeply stirred by a song, giving a little more because we're moved by gratitude for God's gifts. Sometimes our emotions kick in, sometimes the theology of the service energizes our minds, sometimes both, sometimes neither. How important are our internal responses? Not just in terms of corporate worship (which is central) but to our daily lives?

The answer to the last two questions probably depends on your ecclesial tradition and personality. Some people will answer, "Jesus calls us to respond to him from the heart. If I'm not hearing him and following him, then something is wrong." Others will answer, "Jesus is no less true and faithful and present if the music was sloppy, no one spoke to me, and the sermon was as engaging as reading the Paris phone book." One perspective might resonate with you more than the other, but in that case the other might need more attention than it currently receives. Either way, we are often very nervous about the "other side," whatever that is for us. Here, as in many other situations, we need to affirm both dimensions of worship, although some seasons and situations call us to emphasize one aspect more because it has been lost or compromised in our community or personal experience. For example, a faith that advocates "heart religion" but ignores systematic injustice in its midst fails at loving our neighbor, just as an activist version of the faith that ignores personal repentance fails at loving God. We need both, so we need to contemplate the function of both the objective and subjective in theology and practice.

WHY WE NEED A THEOLOGY OF CHRISTIAN LIFE

I'll never forget a unique occasion in which I found myself, with a few other Christian scholars, sitting atop a skyscraper in Atlanta, overlooking the city and enjoying adult beverages and an engaging conversation. Vulnerable conversations are not the norm for academics, including Christian authors, which makes their occurrence that much more valuable. But in this setting, these folks from different backgrounds said a lot that deeply resonated with me but also caused me to listen with fresh ears. In particular, one of the gentlemen was a leading and highly respected scholar of the great Reformer Martin Luther. As a younger person, this scholar had been a big fan of Luther, especially certain aspects of his personality that seemed to reinforce evangelical forms of piety that had been important to him as a young man. His particular evangelical background put great emphasis on personal encounter, on decision, on passion and repentance, all of which animated his life. He saw all of that, in one form or another, in various parts of Luther. But as the years moved on and his life experiences and disappointments piled up, as his own ideas became more complicated, the piety that once resonated with him started to just feel exhausting. He also began to appreciate other sides of Luther's theology and biography that he had known about but hadn't given due attention to because his background as an evangelical had led him to focus so heavily on subjective experience. Luther handled his own existential crisis, in part, by learning to value what was objectively true, what was outside of himself. This scholar's questions about experience and theology merged together, and, to make a very complicated story far too simple, he converted to Roman Catholicism. A Luther scholar! Yes, there are several famous Luther scholars who became Eastern Orthodox or Roman Catholic. That may surprise some, but let's just say that there are very good scholars who will point out that Luther had far more in common with medieval Catholic piety and faith than he might have with certain expressions of contemporary evangelicalism. But that is not my point. Here is the story he told us that I will never forget, as best as I can recall and reconstruct it.

"I just got so tired of going to church and feeling like I needed to get myself into some emotional state," he explained. "There was so much pressure to feel certain things, to believe at some visceral level whatever I was supposed to be experiencing in the service. I didn't need just to sing the songs, but I was required to feel them. I didn't need just to be there, making public confession, but I needed to *feel* God's love in that moment.

So much pressure. It was exhausting. Especially during difficult times in my life." So, eventually, his journey took him to Roman Catholic services, which he described as liberating and meaningful. "I just had to show up. I didn't have to get myself into an emotional state, I didn't have to pretend, I didn't have to feel everything in order for those things to be true and meaningful. I loved how it didn't emphasize my internal world but something outside of me. The priests were leading the worship, and I was there to affirm and simply receive the Eucharist. I was there to witness, not to make things happen. I was not there to convince God I was serious enough in my faith. God was a gift to be received, not a magical genie my internal state needed to conjure up in order to have him work his magic on me and for me." That, at least, is roughly how I heard him that evening.

In this context, *subjective* points toward the experiential, toward the internal and psychological, while *objective* indicates something true outside of us. This person believed his Christian life had become deformed because there was so much emphasis on the subjective that he temporarily lost sight of the objective reality of God and his work. The good of Luther's call to personal faith had been distorted, changed from a helpful insight into a crushing new expectation or, one might even say, a new "work." The spotlight had turned from God to the believer's internal world, and the emotional pressure was crushing this person.

The irony here, as he himself was aware, is that Luther knew this problem well, which was one of the reasons he raised questions about Rome in the first place. While it is true that Luther was passionate and called people to have personal faith, he valued the doctrine of justification so highly because it teaches us to find our security outside ourselves in the finished work of Christ. Jesus's righteousness is often described by Luther as "alien" or "foreign" to us because it originates *extra nos* (outside of us) and is not contingent upon our current feelings or even personal obedience. Concepts like alien or foreign righteousness became central for Luther because they took the burden off his own inadequacies and unsteady internal world, teaching him instead to rely on Jesus the Messiah. He could stand secure before God not by constantly conducting internal investigations but by trusting Christ, who was crucified for us. Ironically, this Luther scholar left the Protestant world and turned to Rome because his experience in the evangelical world had—in his estimation—completely lost sight of the objectivity of the risen Christ and was putting all its weight on the subjectivity of our internal response. He found this in a more sacramentally driven spirituality. Strangely, the same kind of disquiet that slowly pushed Luther away from Rome was roughly what turned this scholar back to Rome.

On the other hand, one can tell countless stories of people who grew up in heavily formal liturgical settings, whether Roman Catholic (like myself), Eastern Orthodox, or something else, and who report that until they joined a charismatic church in Mexico City or started attending a nondenominational church in their neighborhood, faith never seemed "real" to them. Somehow the objective affirmations about God never seemed to move to the personal, leaving their hearts apathetic or unengaged. The priests were active, and the rituals beautiful, but too often the experience seemed more like a visit to a museum than responsive worship before the personal Lord who brings conviction, forgiveness, and transformation. Then, through some experience and engagement outside of these structures, they became convinced that Christianity was not simply a historic religion but a vibrant faith that moved to the center of their lives. Their hearts were, as John Wesley famously said, "strangely warmed." Emphasizing subjective responses to various forms, whether application-heavy preaching or praise music, these more informal traditions often stir hearts and provoke committed devotion. So those who had been soaked in objectively valid worship had nevertheless not been subjectively engaged by it and found this personal emphasis on a call to response—on personal faith and the present action of God—to be life-giving.

So what should we emphasize: the objective—what is simply true outside of us—or the subjective—calling people to respond holistically with their minds, wills, and affections?

Some traditions, such as the Eastern Orthodox, faithfully emphasize the objective reality of worship and that we come to God not as those who force his hand but as witnesses to a heavenly mystery happening in front of and around us. Orthodox places of worship often have their ceilings painted with blues and whites like clouds and feature images of the prophets and apostles on the walls because they are affirming to the local worshiping community that the true glories of worship are happening in the heavens even now. Their local corporate worship is an opportunity for the congregation to have their hearts and minds enlightened and even raised up to this eternal reality so that they might participate in the heavenly praise. Whether they feel it or not, the heavens are bursting with praise, and the congregation is encouraged to join in.

At their best, traditions like this engage the subjectivity of the worshipers and do not merely state objective fact. But we celebrants and congregants are deeply flawed, so we frequently fail to engage or be engaged by others when we should. We can coldly state, or coldly fail to hear, affirmations of objective truth. As a result, when our hearts and minds are not engaged, we often feel disconnected, and Christianity starts to be treated as just another identity marker linked to one's ethnicity or family heritage or culture rather than as the living faith that requires personal response to the risen and ascended King.

Other traditions, like charismatics and Baptists, can place heavy weight on calls for personal response, emphasizing each person's need to trust God fully. Raised hands, belting voices, and earnest hearts often characterize these congregations, stirring people's emotions and giving them hope and energy. Active congregation members look forward to Sunday gatherings where they receive a boost through corporate worship, especially with an emphasis on song and prayer. In these settings praise is often seen as a weapon against the enemies of faith and as a refreshment for the soul. These traditions value emotional expression, personal commitment, and confirmation of deep faith. At their best, they understand all of these subjective responses within the context of the objective goodness and holiness of God, which are not dependent upon our subjective responses. But we celebrants and congregants are deeply flawed, so our focus on people's enthusiastic responses can distort our appreciation for the objective presence and power of our Lord, sometimes lost in the haze of emotionalism or even manipulation. When life starts to go sideways, when our own minds and hearts fail us, once-strong believers may find themselves on the outside, unable to muster the feelings that once strengthened them and became the mark of identifying with the rest of the congregation. When the positive emotions and energy fade, they not only question their faith but start to wonder whether Christianity has always just been an emotional crutch or if it is something real, and they become unsure about God himself.

These pictures, in their attempt to speak in concrete terms, obviously rely on hasty generalizations and stereotypes. I have employed these pictures of corporate worship because our theology of Christian life is, in fact, anchored in the church. Objectively, the church is created from

WHY WE NEED A THEOLOGY OF CHRISTIAN LIFE

the love of God, secure through the grace of Christ, and sealed by the fellowship of the Holy Spirit. When corporate worship functions well and we connect well to it, when our churches value and address the objective and subjective aspects of Christian life, then we also might be more able to receive good theology there. For these reasons we must later briefly examine how our church services help or hinder our theology and our practices. We want our corporate worship to convey a faithful theology of Christian life to us, a life that subjectively engages the objective realities of our present and powerful Lord.

Catholic and Particular

Similar to the objective-subjective dynamic is the relationship between the catholic and particular in our theology of Christian life. As many readers will know, *catholic* means universal. One of the reasons many believers who are not Roman Catholic have found Catholicism hard to accept is that, in their opinion, it seems to assume the universal for what is a very particular expression of the faith. Does its "Roman" identity actually undermine its essential catholicity?[7] Debates that split East and West were not merely about the filioque clause but also included frustrations about how we are to understand the catholic nature of Christianity.

Lest we imagine this is merely a tension between the titans like Orthodoxy and Roman Catholicism, there is plenty of drama within Protestantism about who is "in" and who is "out." Northern Methodists grow frustrated with the Southern Baptists, while old-school Presbyterians scratch their heads at megachurches. Having said that, many people in places like the United States attend a local church without being aware of its denominational history or distinctive beliefs. While there was a time when Christian families who moved from one town to another would immediately find their denomination's local church there, now American Christians often care more about a local church's singing style or kids' programs than they do about creedal affirmations. Ecclesial fidelity means less than it did a century or two ago.

Theologians often refer to four characteristics as marks of the true

---

7. *Roman Catholic* is, therefore, a kind of oxymoron. However, it may be worth reminding us that *Roman Catholic* is a label that Protestants attribute to Catholics, not one that they (generally) use for themselves. They believe they are simply Catholic, though that preferred naming is paired with Roman particularism in both theology and practice. It is crucial to appreciate both how they self-identify and also how others have consistently identified them.

church, namely that it is *one, holy, catholic,* and *apostolic.* The phrase appears in the Nicene Creed (*mian hagian katholikēn kai apostolikēn ekklēsian*) and partly in the earlier Apostles' Creed ("holy catholic Church," *sanctam ecclesiam catholicam*), so it has become a useful starting point for describing the church, and we will refer briefly to it here.

At some level, the organic, living, connected, united body of Christ reflects these four adjectives despite significant differences among local expressions of the faith. Jesus prayed that his people would be *one* just as he and his Father are *one* (John 17:11, 21; cf. 10:30), so we are not allowed to dismiss church unity as if it were not a proper concern of Christian life. Our divisions, most especially those that prevent us from sharing the Lord's Supper together, are a painful contradiction of that unity. Consequently, the church is required to yearn for the union of God's people, even when genuine and serious disagreements occur among us. The unity of the body of Christ is somehow a reality that transcends racial, economic, geographical, and historical differences. It even transcends our divisions. Although the true church even now, despite its disobedience, participates in the oneness of its Lord, the current circumstances of our multiple divisions reflect both our sin and the work still ahead of us. While Christian life must, therefore, acknowledge the reality of serious disagreement within the body, we also must learn to appreciate the even deeper reality of our connectedness in Christ.

Furthermore, God's church is *holy* (Eph 5:25–27; 1 Pet 2:9–10) because the holy God dwells in and with his people, both individually and collectively (John 14:23; 1 Cor 3:16; Eph 2:19–22). His people are holy because we belong to him, because he has sought us and made us his, transforming us and reconciling us to himself, making us Christ's ambassadors of reconciliation (2 Cor 5:20). As the "called out" ones who have been made "saints," the church finds its identity within God's love, transformed to be "holy and blameless before him" as his adopted children (Rom 1:7; Eph 1:3–5). God's people are "members of the household of God," both corporately and individually, joined together in Christ and grown "into a holy temple in the Lord" (Eph 2:19–21). God is holy, and so his church is holy.

Catholic claims that the faith of the church is the same faith around the globe and throughout time because the same Lord is the object of that faith. That faith is therefore universal, or "*katholikos*" in Greek, applying to the whole. A truly catholic church must have space for the

Ethiopian court official (Acts 8:26–40), Tabitha the charitable disciple from Joppa (Acts 9:36–43), Cornelius the Roman centurion (Acts 10), and Lydia of Thyatira the Greek businesswoman (Acts 16:14–15). In our catholic worship, we join the ongoing worship of the God of Abraham and Isaac, of Mary and Matthew, for he is the God of the living rather than the dead (Matt 22:31–32). It is universal in its breadth, claiming that all who truly call on Jesus as Lord and believe God raised him from the dead belong to him and are therefore organically connected to all other saints around the world (Rom 10:9–10 // Joel 2:32; Matt 24:14; Luke 24:47).

Finally, God's church is based on the *apostolic* witness, which is shorthand for the full testimony of the apostles and prophets given in Scripture, with Christ as the "cornerstone" (e.g., Eph 2:20; 4:11–12; 2 Cor 12:12; 2 Tim 3:16; 4:1–6). From Genesis through Revelation, all of Scripture testifies to Christ as sent from the Father in the power of the Spirit (e.g., Luke 24:25–27; 1 Pet 1:10–12). As Kevin Vanhoozer states, at a minimum "apostolicity means that a church in whatever place and time must be in line with the apostles if it is to be considered genuinely Christian."[8] There may be serious debate about church polity and how ecclesiology relates to the canon of Scripture, but ultimately all of church life—even its heated disagreements—is shaped, sustained, and upheld by the sacred Scriptures, which are the apostolic witness (cf. 1 Cor 15:3). Thus, as part of the church, God's people belong to this one, holy, catholic, apostolic church and are called to be faithful to it and to its Lord no matter the tradition, denomination, geographical location, and heritage. And while we could analyze these four adjectives much more carefully, our level of generality here is both necessary and hopeful.

These adjectives don't mean that all Christians will agree on everything—we surely do not. Real disagreements must be allowed and even honored because they are a means of growth and because we will all stand before the risen King, both as individuals and together. Our consciences and attempts to be faithful matter. So even though I'm a Reformed theologian, which is deeply meaningful to me and guides me in countless ways, my ultimate allegiance is to Christ and his kingdom, and his bride (Rev 19:7–9; 22:2, 17) is clearly larger than what could possibly be contained within the Reformed tradition. Thus a theology

---

8. Kevin J. Vanhoozer, *Biblical Authority After Babel: Retrieving the Solas in the Spirit of Mere Protestant Christianity* (Grand Rapids: Brazos, 2016), 92.

of Christian life, even an explicitly Reformed theology of Christian life, must make sense beyond the Reformed tradition. Therefore, as part of the body of Christ, I must uphold the catholic nature of our faith, which moves beyond the mere local or denominational. By local here, we mean both geographical and peculiar characteristics or practices. Dutch Reformed Christians in Grand Rapids are not exactly the same as Korean Presbyterians in Seoul. Across the globe, Baptists can differ greatly, as do different expressions of post–Vatican II Roman Catholicism, which can now reflect the kind of variety that used to be attributed only to Protestants.

This emphasis on the catholic nature of our faith, however, does not eliminate the need for particularity. Seeking to be catholic is not the same as what modernity has imagined to be "universal religion." We are not looking for a generic religion or unknown deity because we bow the knee before Jesus the Messiah who reigns over heaven and earth (Phil 2:10). So while we must be united in our confession of the triune God and his salvific work in the world, we are not required to agree exactly on how he accomplishes that work and what are all the implications of it. We need not name all those differences and why they exist. People have often died over these divisions, and to this day families and communities can experience deep splits over theological distinctives. It would be a lie to claim that these differences don't matter. Having said that, I am not a "Reformed" Christian because I am trying to *add* something to Christianity but because this expression names a tradition that characterizes my attempts to be faithful in understanding Scripture and applying the faith to the life of the church and world. When others call themselves Anabaptists, part of the Assemblies of God, or Anglican, these labels similarly serve as shorthand for a similarly distinctive attempt at faithfulness. The differences between these traditions or expressions of the faith matter, and sometimes they matter a lot. Nothing I have said thus far is meant to undermine those traditions or to make people think they must give up their particularity to be part of the catholic church. Instead, I hope we will see that there is no need—nor is it even possible—to be *catholic* apart from our particularity. Catholicity means that our particularity must not undermine the most cherished and central unity of the church: We worship the triune God who reconciled sinful humanity to himself through the incarnate Son and in the power of his given Spirit. And by this affirmation of particularity within a larger catholicity, our theology of Christian life will seek to honor both the historical and the contemporary. We look to the past and the present, honoring the universal while creating space for the particular.

In this spirit, I hope to lay out a theology of Christian life that can be truly catholic without denying space for legitimate particularity and difference. In a sense, I would love to eventually see others write follow-up volumes to this one, where they take and expound the basic approach I will lay out here and then show how their own tradition further unpacks the Christian faith and life in distinctive and helpful ways. I think of this volume as trying to offer a catholic theology of Christian life, and I would find profound joy in seeing Methodist, Presbyterian, Eastern Orthodox, Roman Catholic, and Episcopalian theologians and pastors build upon (and/or modify) this as they employ the very distinctive particularities that make their tradition decidedly faithful or helpful. For example, while I will talk about "calling" and "coming" in this book, I do not seek to settle all the debates between the traditions on how exactly that works out. Attentive readers will inevitably find times when my particularly Reformed assumptions and biases guide my decisions more clearly than at others, but do know that my goal here is actually to be as catholic as I can be, even as I seek to honor particularity. Some readers will inevitably wish I tightened the framework more in accord with my own theological tradition, while others will be irked when they believe I have let too many of my Protestant or Reformed ideas govern my framework. That, however, is a debate I leave for others. Here I simply tell you my goal, and I will let you decide how faithfully I have carried out that task.

Transcendence and Immanence

A faithful theology of Christian life will necessarily be realistic. It will acknowledge who God is according to his revelation of himself, and that means it will declare both his transcendence and immanence. Divine immanence is God's activity of dwelling among his people and acting within his creation; divine transcendence refers to God's otherness and his superiority over creation even as he loves and cares for it. Again, for various reasons, as traditions and as individuals, we are prone to attend more to one or the other of these attributes, which can easily distort both our understanding of God and, consequently, our conception of Christian life.

SETTING THE STAGE

A classic text that holds together both transcendence and immanence is Isaiah 57:15:

> For thus says the high and lofty one
>   who inhabits eternity, whose name is Holy:
> I dwell in the high and holy place
>   and also with those who are contrite and humble in spirit,
> to revive the spirit of the humble
>   and to revive the heart of the contrite. (NRSVue)

This text clearly affirms that God is the holy and exalted one who inhabits eternity and that this same God is present to and concerned for the needy and broken, inclined toward those who cry out to him for forgiveness and hope. You will notice that the prophet unites pictures of distance with those of closeness. But we sometimes forget that unity. For example, what happens when pastors try to correct congregations that treat our holy God too casually, as if he were a celestial Santa Claus? In response, these pastors may resort to language that makes God appear unreachably distant and ceaselessly demanding. But that misses the point of transcendence.

Transcendence and immanence are less about God's physical location (near or far) than about the qualities of his being and action. God is always present and active, but he is also and always *God* and not his creation. This is why John of Damascus, for example, as he led the church's confession of God, emphasized what is often called "negative theology" by reminding us that God is "the *un*created, the *un*original, the *im*mortal, the boundless, the eternal, the *im*material . . . the *in*visible, the *in*conceivable."[9] John is not denying the events of revelation, but he knows that as we approach God, we will be tempted to treat him like other objects of our knowledge, trying to fit him into concepts we are comfortable with, trying to domesticate him and put him in a box, as it were. God is holy, majestic, sovereign, all-wise, beyond comprehension, even as he is gloriously present, active, tender, abounding with compassion, and truly knowable. If we lose sight of God's action of claiming us for himself as his very own people, we can fall into what Colin Gunton

---

9. John of Damascus, *The Orthodox Faith*, in *John of Damascus: Writings*, trans. Frederic H. Chase Jr. (Washington, DC: Catholic University of America Press, 1958), I.14, p. 201, emphasis added.

called a "platonically conceived otherness" that hides God behind the adjectives of his otherness, and thus treats him as a divinity who remains ever outside of the gift of his own self-revelation.[10] So rather than pick between God's transcendence and immanence, or between his incomprehensibility and knowability, we must examine and affirm them both by looking at how they relate to each other.

Believers often are tempted to split up the persons of the Trinity, which is never a good move. Consider how this relates to misconceptions of transcendence and immanence. For example, we simultaneously conceive of the Father as being really far away (remember "high and lofty" from Isaiah 57:15) and of the Spirit as being near or even in us (Rom 8:9). But this misunderstands God as well as the word *transcendence*.

It misunderstands God by forgetting that *holy* is the most common title given to the Spirit (e.g., Isa 63:10–11; Matt 1:18–20; 3:11; 12:32; 28:19; John 14:26; 20:22; Acts 1:5, 8; 2:4, 33, 38; cf. 2 Esdr 14:22). The persons of God are not divided: the Holy Spirit is the presence of God with us in his fullness.

Also, transcendence as applied to God does not mean the location of his being but the manner of it. Isaiah 6, for example, shows the presence of God's transcendence: He is near to the prophet—there in the temple—and yet he is the one in whom we live and move and have our being (Acts 17:28). He upholds the universe, so it cannot contain him. The presence of that transcendence puts the kind of strain on the universe that causes the prophet and the temple to tremble and the angels to turn their faces away. The Spirit's work with and in us should also inform our view of how God is both transcendent and immanent.

The God who is other, who is holy, is present with his creation and orders it (e.g., Gen 1:2; Job 33:4; Ps 104:30) and even makes his abode in us by his Holy Spirit (e.g., Isa 63:11; Ezek 36:27; Rom 8:11–15; 1 Cor 3:16; 6:19; 2 Cor 6:16; 2 Tim 1:14; 1 John 2:27). The Spirit is not an element of creation nor simply an attribute of God, but as the Nicene Creed affirms, the Spirit is the "Lord and Giver of Life," who "with the Father and Son is worshiped and glorified." The Spirit is holy and other than us—transcendent—yet this Spirit is at the same time God's present

---

10. Colin E. Gunton, *The Promise of Trinitarian Theology*, 2nd ed. (Edinburgh: T&T Clark, 1997), 194. Do note that when Gunton attacks Augustine along these lines he is often barking up the wrong tree. I also don't think a social trinitarian model is the answer. However, I do think Gunton's underlying concerns remain legitimate and quite important.

action and transforming power—immanent. Thus the Son is with us by his Spirit even now as he reigns and rules in the heavenly places (e.g., Acts 2:38; Rom 8:9–11; Gal 4:6).

An incident in the New Testament further illustrates the combination of transcendence and immanence. Luke 5 portrays crowds gathered around Jesus at Lake Gennesaret (5:1). Using a small boat as a speaking platform, he floats just offshore to bring God's word to all those within hearing. After finishing teaching, which he is clearly gifted at—thus the crowds!—Jesus turns to the professional fisherman, Simon, and says, "Put out into the deep and let down your nets for a catch" (5:4). One can only imagine the irritated tone that Simon had in his voice when he responded by reminding Jesus that all the real fishermen had already been out all night, including Simon, and their efforts yielded "nothing" (5:5). "But at your word I will let down the nets," he retorts, seemingly annoyed and maybe even passive-aggressively trying to put Jesus in his place: While he may be a gifted teacher, he knows nothing about fishing. But as readers know well, the lowered nets quickly fill and soon cannot contain all the fish that are there to be caught. At this point one might expect Simon to be delighted, to let his excited imagination begin to consider all the profits he could get: Maybe now with Jesus at his side, he can make magical things happen. Isn't this good news? But instead of responding with celebration, "when Simon Peter saw it, he fell down at Jesus' knees, saying, 'Depart from me, for I am a sinful man, O Lord'" (5:8). This man in front of Simon clearly transcends the nature of other people Simon knows.

In the early part of the twentieth century, Rudolf Otto used the phrase *mysterium tremendum* ("terrifying mystery") in his *Idea of the Holy*. It refers to a presence sensed as "wholly other" that provokes both a strange sense of attraction and a desire to flee, as well as the conviction that this presence is beyond our comprehension.[11] While John Webster is right to encourage us to avoid allowing a general phenomenology of holiness rather than exegesis of the Scriptures to ground our theology of holiness,[12] Otto's observations do have some usefulness within exegesis. Why is Peter suddenly talking about his sinfulness when all they had been doing was fishing? Because rather than encountering an abstract

---

11. Rudolf Otto, *The Idea of the Holy: An Inquiry into the Non-Rational in the Idea of the Divine and Its Relation to the Rational*, trans. John W. Harvey (Oxford: Oxford University Press, 1950), 30.

12. John Webster, *Holiness* (Grand Rapids: Eerdmans, 2003), 18–19.

concept of "the holy," Simon encounters the physical presence of the holy Son of God, and that presence brings with it a frightening sense of transcendent mystery. For at least a moment, his eyes are opened to greater realities than he had imagined. Simon, like Isaiah standing in God's presence in the temple (Isa 6), suddenly knows this person right there in his boat to be beyond the everyday, a "beyond" that makes demands and will change him. But this "beyond" is not vague; it is a particular person and it is of God—thus it drives him also to awareness that his own sinfulness is completely inconsistent with this presence. Despite this, he also feels drawn to this presence, this holy man in front of him, prostrating himself instead of running away, addressing Jesus instead of curling into a ball. To borrow somewhat cautiously again from Otto, Simon senses both awe-fullness and attraction.[13] Simon and others are "astonished" at not just the surprise catch but also the one who orchestrated it. And Simon is beyond astonished: He is *afraid*. Jesus, of course, understands what is happening and transforms the moment of terrifying mystery into the mystery of union. He pulls Simon into his fellowship by pulling him into his ministry, saying, "Do not be afraid; from now on you will be catching men" (5:10). After getting settled on the shore, Jesus collects Simon's companions also. The text says, "They left everything and followed him" (5:11). Simon's encounter with Jesus exposes Simon's sinfulness by convincing him that Jesus is somehow God's presence among them. By the end of the Gospels, it becomes clear that Jesus is both truly human and truly one with the Father and thus worthy of worship (John 20:28). God and Human. Jesus is the embodiment both of God's relation to his created world (immanence) and of divine perfection (transcendence).

A faithful theology of Christian life will avoid pitting divine transcendence against immanence. Instead, while constantly reminding ourselves that God is God and we are not, we will also remember that the one God knows us, reveals himself to us, cares for us, and rescues us from our own sin and the dysfunctions of the world. When we ignore transcendence, God too easily gets absorbed into and distorted by our cultural moment. When we ignore immanence, we treat God as if he were a distant deity far removed from our lives, making our tears or delights, our obedience or rebellion, our fears or hopes all

---

13. Otto, *The Idea of the Holy*, esp. 12–24.

basically irrelevant to this apathetic or unable God. By affirming that the biblical God is transcendent and immanent, other and present, holy and loving, we also affirm that these adjectives in no way conflict but rather reinforce each other.

Trinitarian and Christ-Centered

Since this is a *theology* of Christian life, we must make sure the foundation and goal of our vision remain God himself. The Creator is also the Redeemer, who is also the Sustainer (e.g., 1 Chron 16:23–30). God alone is the worthy object of our worship (Matt 4:10). Consistently the Scriptures show that people respond with awe and worship to the presence of God (e.g., Exod 3:3–4; Deut 5:3–5; Isa 6:1). This worship includes praise, repentance, adoration, forgiveness, and joy (e.g., Gen 32:30; Job 42:1–6; Ps 34:8; Jer 31:34). But only God is to be treated in this way (e.g., Exod 20:3): Idols are a danger not only because they are unworthy of worship but because we become like what we worship (e.g., Pss 115:8; 135:18). Consequently, while God calls us to be conformed to the image of the good and loving God, worshiping an idol starts us down the path of becoming *de*formed in the image of a false deity.

The New Testament displays useful and fresh connections between worship, Christ, and us. Chapter 3 on the Mediator and chapter 6 on Messiah will both explore this in more detail, but we should affirm a few things here. First, the New Testament clearly considers Jesus to be none other than the presence of God, as when Thomas calls him, "My Lord and my God" (John 20:28). In his apocalyptic vision, John responds to the appearance of Jesus by falling at his feet in worship, even as Jesus encourages John not to be afraid (Rev 1:17). This is strongly contrasted with occasions when people treat an angel or a human messenger who is not God as an object of worship; those bowing are consistently corrected and told to stand up since the messengers are fellow servants rather than the Lord himself (e.g., Col 2:18; Rev 22:8–9). Only the one Lord is to be worshiped and served, no matter what the tempter tries to make us believe (e.g., Matt 4:9–10; Luke 4:7–8). The New Testament treats Jesus as the divine presence in human flesh, and thus he is worthy of praise and worship, unlike angels or even great heroes.

This brings us to the second point: Because the New Testament acknowledges Jesus to be truly Immanuel (God with us), Christian worship of God has a Christ-centered nature. This is both justified and required in light of God's self-revelation in Christ so that we direct worship now both *through* the Son and *to* the Son. The later chapters will deal with this dynamic in greater detail, but here we simply repeat the words of Paul: "For there is one God and one mediator between God and mankind, the man Christ Jesus" (1 Tim 2:5 NIV). The incarnate Christ is both God's self-revelation to us and humanity's representative before God. Too often we pick between these.

The goal of God-centeredness must concretely take into account God's nature as he has revealed himself and not stop at abstract ideas of divinity. A God-centered Christian theology, therefore, must be Trinitarian in form, method, and content. Further, since God reveals himself specifically and ultimately in Jesus Christ, "God-centered" also concretely means Christ-centered. To know the Father, we look to the Son who comes from the bosom of the Father (John 1:18), truly revealing God (1 John 2:14) as he lays down his life for God's sheep (John 10:14–15). For the Father and the Son are one (John 10:30; 17:11, 21). Furthermore, the Holy Spirit is always the Spirit of Christ (Rom 8:9–11; 1 Pet 1:11), and so the Spirit consistently and truly draws us to the incarnate Lord (1 John 4:2). This Christ-centered dynamic does not belittle the Spirit of the Son but ascribes him his due glory and honor, for only by the Spirit does this communion with God occur (e.g., Gal 4:6; Phil 1:19; 3:3). For there are not three gods, but one God: Father, Son, and Spirit. Therefore, into this triune name alone are we baptized (Matt 28:19). Accordingly, the best Reformed views of the beatific vision, as exemplified by John Owen, managed to uphold this Christ-centeredness even in the eschaton.[14]

Revelation and salvation are often characterized as occurring *from* the Father *through* the Son *in* the Spirit, and we return in faith, worship, and praise as we are moved *by* the Spirit *through* the Son *to* the Father (cf. Heb 2:11). One God worthy of worship. This one God who is active in creation is the same God who does the work of new creation—one God caring for his church and world (e.g., 1 Cor 8:6). And this one God promises that he will reshape his people by his Spirit, remaking them more and more in his image, which means the image of Christ (2 Cor 4:4; Col 1:15–17), who is "the radiance of the glory of God and

---

14. Suzanne McDonald, "Beholding the Glory of God in the Face of Jesus Christ: John Owen and the 'Reforming' of the Beatific Vision," in *The Ashgate Research Companion to John Owen's Theology*, ed. Mark Jones and Kelly M. Kapic (Burlington: Ashgate, 2012), 141–58.

the exact imprint of his nature" (Heb 1:3). Paul captures much of what we are getting at here when he describes the congregation's worship in this way: "There is one body and one Spirit, just as you were called to the one hope of your calling, one Lord, one faith, one baptism, one God and Father of all, who is above all and through all and in all" (Eph 4:4–6 NRSVue). God alone is worthy of worship, and this God is the triune Lord. And as we worship God, we find that worship *and our lives* necessarily start to have a Christ-centered nature to them.

The adjectives *Trinitarian* and *Christ-centered* as applied to worship and Christian life do not contradict each other. The Trinity is not some abstract, formless "threeness" but specifically this Father, this Son, this Spirit in this eternal fellowship as this eternal God. Even more specifically, God reveals himself in Christ, and our worship of the one God is a participation in (and not merely alongside or around) the incarnate Son's worship of the Father.

Representation and Imitation

A final pair of ideas we should understand as related and not contradictory I will call *representation* and *imitation*.

Older debates about the atonement commonly presented a tension between what was sometimes called the "moral influence theory" and various forms of substitutionary atonement. Moral influence theories appeared to argue that the main significance of Jesus's death on the cross was that he modeled a life of love directed toward others. His exemplary death liberated us to follow his example in our own lives. This theory became a call to imitate Christ. Sometimes this was labeled a "subjective" view of the atonement because it chiefly concerned a moral change within us.[15] Those who disagreed with this said that the atonement was not about changing our internal moral landscape, claiming instead that Christ in some way represented sinful humanity as our substitute, dealt with the problem of sin and judgment, and thus brought the consequence of forgiveness and restoration. This was

---

15. I agree with more recent assessments that not only raise questions about the fairness of such categorization and treatment of historical figures like Abelard, who was clearly more nuanced than this, and I also agree with those who see this approach as more of a consequence of atonement rather than a proper theory that explains the work of Jesus on the cross. Cf. Graham A. Cole, *God the Peacemaker: How Atonement Brings Shalom* (Downers Grove, IL: InterVarsity Press, 2009), 242–44; Robert Letham, *The Work of Christ* (Downers Grove, IL: InterVarsity Press, 1993), 152.

sometimes described as an "objective" theory of the atonement because it accomplished something outside of us.[16] Current scholarship on the atonement, however, is hesitant about employing narrowly defined boxes like these to explain this great mystery: It's a mistake to accept approaches to theology that flatten out a question in terms of a single biblical image or idea and downplay or ignore other, equally important biblical images and themes.

We can find relief and a path forward by remembering that the Bible is aware that the world is a complex place, that God is infinitely complex, and that God has mercy on his followers in our attempts to hear him. Regarding our example of atonement theology, relief comes in remembering that we have time to listen to the range of biblical motifs used to describe the atonement and examine the value of each one as we try to describe the fullness of Christ and his atoning work.[17] Rather than choosing among them (for there are several), a faithful account must make space for all the imagery and the range of these biblical ideas, including such motifs as *Christus Victor*, the battlefield, the marketplace, reconciliation, redemption, healing, new creation, kingdom, and sacrifice.[18]

As with the atonement debate, shaping a theology of Christian life will lead us into areas that we would like to simplify into one or two elements, but doing so will not produce results faithful to the Scriptures. So we will be confronted by ideas that, at least initially, seem to be in tension with each other. We don't like that kind of tension. We will be tempted to demand a quick answer when we ought to dwell in the tension as a way of waiting on God. If he shows us a way out of the tension, then well and good. If not, we must not in our haste dismiss difficult elements of the Scriptures. One case in point is our dual affirmation (1) that Christ is our head or representative, acting for us, and

---

16. For a classic example and summary of this language and approach, see Louis Berkhof, *Systematic Theology* (Grand Rapids: Eerdmans, 1941), 373–75.

17. See, e.g., Colin E. Gunton, *The Actuality of Atonement: A Study of Metaphor, Rationality and the Christian Tradition* (London: T&T Clark, 1988); Ben Pugh, *Atonement Theories: A Way Through the Maze* (Eugene, OR: Cascade, 2014); Alan Spence, *The Promise of Peace: A Unified Theory of Atonement* (London: T&T Clark, 2006).

18. Recent attempts, besides those mentioned above, include Joshua M. McNall, *The Mosaic of Atonement: An Integrated Approach to Christ's Work* (Grand Rapids: Zondervan Academic, 2019); Jeremy R. Treat, *The Crucified King: Atonement and Kingdom in Biblical and Systematic Theology* (Grand Rapids: Zondervan Academic, 2014). For an excellent and more comprehensive resource, see Adam J. Johnson, ed., *T&T Clark Companion to Atonement* (London: Bloomsbury, 2017).

(2) that our human agency matters as we are called to participate in the life of Christ as his body.[19]

Pursuing these two ideas, we will examine what was expected to be our true and faithful response to God, the effects of sin and rebellion on us as they relate to that response, and the fulfillment of that response in the incarnate Son of God, Jesus of Nazareth. He has become the embodiment of faithful human response, the keeper of the covenant that we—collectively or individually—could not keep. This leads us to see that the whole of Jesus's life of faithfulness—not just his death on the cross—matters to our life and salvation. Thus our life in Christ is genuinely grace upon grace from first to last, for at each point in our lives where we turn from God, Jesus as our representative has turned to the Father. We are safe in Christ, secure in the salvation he achieved on our behalf, and we are kept by his Spirit.

In addition, we also examine the character and function of human agency, showing that while Christ has "done it all" in the sense of completely accomplishing our rescue, this does not undermine our agency but establishes it. This takes us to the "law" and "gospel" dynamic. While faith is a gift of God, it is we who believe, not God who believes for us. While God does not need our obedience in order to love us, we who are made alive in Christ are called to participate actively in the Spirit's work in and through the body of Christ. There are "good works" he prepared in advance for us to do (Eph 2:10). Even as Christ is our representative, we don't need to shy away from the consistent biblical calls to faith, obedience, sacrifice, love, and acts of mercy. Christ is our representative who frees us to participate in his life and love, not to undermine our energy and action. Imitating Christ is the appropriate and right pattern for Christian life.

To focus on representation and ignore participation risks diminishing the countless Scriptures that call us to follow after Christ, imitating his sacrificial life and death. To focus on participation and ignore representation risks reducing the gospel to mere activism or efforts of moral improvement, undermining the countless Scriptures that proclaim the

---

19. For growing literature on "agency" in contemporary theological, biblical, and philosophical discussions, see, e.g., William J. Abraham, *Divine Agency and Divine Action*, vol. 1, *Exploring and Evaluating the Debate* (New York: Oxford University Press, 2018); John M. G. Barclay and Simon J. Gathercole, eds., *Divine and Human Agency in Paul and His Cultural Environment*, TTCBS (New York: T&T Clark, 2008); Ty Kieser, *Theandric and Triune: John Owen and Christological Agency*, Studies in Systematic Theology (New York: T&T Clark, 2024).

work of Christ, who did what we cannot do and reconciled heaven and earth. But when believers hold both ideas together, they are both secure and active, humble and confident, repentant and service-oriented, gracious and truthful.

Christ is our great representative, our head who enables us to follow him in his life of faith, hope, and love.

CONCLUSION

We began this chapter by slowing down to ask some basic questions about how we live a Christian life. The treatment here isn't especially new, but it establishes a starting place that allows us to overcome many denominational, historical, and geographical boundaries, partly by emphasizing what Christians have in common and partly by showing that some of our divisions are rooted in false dichotomies. From this point onward, I will argue that the theological foundation for Christian life is God's love, grace, and fellowship. In light of this foundation, we can make sense of how to relate the law and gospel. Once that is understood, we can unpack how Christian life is a response to the love of God: a response embodied in the Messiah who leads the worship, a response that is personal and particular even as it is necessarily framed within a community of faith, and a response that is thus ecclesial in orientation, most especially captured in corporate worship. Learning to recognize the arc of Christian life modeled and strengthened in corporate worship, we follow a movement from calling to benediction, all in Christ and as part of his body. With this preliminary work now behind us, we can turn our focus to the love of God.

PART 2

GOD TO US

Divine Agency—
the Triune God's Love

CHRISTIAN LIFE IS A RESPONSE TO THE LOVE OF GOD.

> *The grace of the Lord Jesus Christ and the love of God and the fellowship of the Holy Spirit be with you all.*
> —2 CORINTHIANS 13:14

CHAPTER 2

LOVE

The Fountain of God's Love

Embrace love which is God, and embrace God with love.
—AUGUSTINE[1]

The longing for the greatest, the first and the ultimate on the human side is addressed by this love made known to us in Christ Jesus, our Lord. He manifests, makes present and communicates the knowledge of a love that is beyond knowing. (Eph 3:19) This love "drove" him, so to speak, to identify with his opposites, sin and damnation, out of love for the sinners and the damned. (2 Cor 5:21 and Gal 3:14) In so doing he "realigns" all reality in a new rapport.
—THOMAS NORRIS[2]

So we have come to know and to believe the love that God has for us. God is love, and whoever abides in love abides in God, and God abides in him.
—1 JOHN 4:16

---

1. Augustine, *On the Trinity (De Trinitate)*, ed. John E. Rotelle, trans. Edmund Hill, in The Works of Saint Augustine: A Translation for the 21st Century (New York: New City, 1991), 8.12, p. 253.
2. Thomas J. Norris, *The Trinity: Life of God, Hope for Humanity; Toward a Theology of Communion* (Hyde Park, NY: New City, 2009), 80.

SURPRISINGLY HARD QUESTIONS

When my children were young, I would normally put them to bed with a brief passage from Scripture and a prayer. But as many parents know, when the lights are off and the parent starts to leave the room, then little kids want to talk. They will do anything to put off bedtime. And my kids quickly figured out that if they wanted to talk about God, it would be hard for me to ever leave. Kids are clever that way. But one evening when I was walking out of my children's bedroom, after having just kissed them both goodnight, I didn't immediately want to turn around when my little boy said, "Papa, I have a question." I loved his questions, but I was exhausted and just wanted to go downstairs and watch television. But I could tell from Jonathan's voice this was not manufactured; something was deeply bothering him that night. As I turned around, he went on, "I don't know if I love God." Well, now he had my attention. He tried to explain. "I know I love you and Mama. But I don't think I love God. What does it even mean to love God?" Whatever his exact next words were, it was clear he was saying, "I don't know what it means for God to love me, and I don't know what it would mean for me to love God." He was wrestling with good theological questions.

Such questions are clearly relevant not just to an elementary school kid but to all of us, whether six or sixty-six, whether professional theologians or laity. In fact, I think we clergy and theologians move too quickly beyond such basics, assuming we understand what we are saying, while in truth we are sometimes far from clear about the basics. Too often we assume what should be stated and take for granted what should be savored, often misunderstanding it ourselves. One sign that such a dullness has taken hold is that the good news no longer stirs us with its goodness; another is that we reduce Christian life to a moment of decision without making sense of the extended time between conversion and death. Questions about God loving us and us loving God are, in one sense, easily answered, and in another sense, there are not enough pages to explain the depth and wonder of the truth. To borrow and further modify an early-church image sometimes applied to describe the gospel of John, this love is shallow enough for a lamb to walk in and deep enough for an elephant to swim in.[3] In this

---

3. This line has been modified and used in different ways throughout church history, but it seems to have been initially drawn from Pope Gregory, quoted in John Moorhead, *Gregory the Great* (New York: Routledge, 2005), 21, 45.

chapter, we will explore the idea of love to make sure our minds are not trapped in dead cliché but renewed in a fresh and lively examination of these ideas. While I hope to conclude this chapter with an answer that makes sense to a six-year-old, we will dive deeply into the mystery of divine love and the goodness of the Creator on the way there. The rigor in our work is not meant for a child to follow but to help us better understand the layered depth behind simple childlike answers. It will, in fact, take nothing less than heaven and earth coming together to answer the child's question.

LOVE: WHERE THE DIVINE AND HUMAN MEET

To theologically and pastorally answer these questions about love and to see why it is a good place to start our discussion of Christian life, let me remind you of the overall thesis of this book: *Christian life is a response to the love of God.* This thesis indicates the proper basis, goal, and method for a theology of Christian life.

Unpacking this thesis will occupy the rest of the chapter and book, as we look at its meaning and significance for creation, the incarnation, our relationship with God, and the priority and place of corporate worship. But this basic thesis states the ground and context for whatever else we say.

To explain the content and relevance of that thesis, this chapter sets up a framework of six affirmations, each serving to situate the larger thesis:

1. God is love.
2. Creation is the overflow of God's love.
3. The purpose of creation, with humanity at the center, includes its reflection of and participation in God's love. When this is happening, we call it "shalom."
4. Sin disrupts and disorders love, thus rupturing the communion of the creation with its Creator and distorting the nature of the created order.
5. The incarnate Son is both the embodiment and object of divine love.
6. Loving the incarnate Christ necessarily means loving God and his creation.

Love can be understood as the beginning, middle, and end of Christian life. This is because it not only constitutes the original purposes for creation but describes the triune God himself. Love also points us forward to eschatological expectations, helping us in our fallen world to know and desire a fullness that is to come but is not yet fully realized. God's love informs our present as those who in faith have been reconciled to the Creator: That is, God's grace even now enables us to participate in the kingdom of heaven—a kingdom in which love and shalom break into this broken and rebellious world.

Four simple words can therefore capture the message of this book: love, grace, fellowship, and worship. After laying the theological groundwork in this chapter, we will spend the remaining chapters explaining more fully how God's grace is found in Jesus the Mediator who uniquely centers Christian life and how the Holy Spirit draws us into communion with God so that we might experience and be energized by love. Finally, the book will conclude with reflections on how we rightly frame human response to God (the law-gospel dynamic) and how corporate worship shapes and energizes our lives of faith. We will emerge with a theology of Christian life that not only is biblically sound but also (I hope) resonates throughout time and across cultures, ecclesial traditions, and personal experiences. But first, we must make sure we understand why and how love is where the divine and the human meet.

AFFIRMATION 1

God is love.

Part of what is distinctive about Christianity is that we believe God *is* love (1 John 4:8, 16). It's not that God is theoretically or intermittently loving. Nor is God merely capable of love. The truth is boundlessly better than that. Love is who God is! From all eternity, one God pulsating in Trinitarian love: God perfectly satisfied, whole, and complete.

When John claims that God *is love*, how can love be used to properly describe a deity who is one? Does not love require an other for this expression even to make sense? Here we see a distinctive fundamental Christian claim. Other ancient and modern religions occasionally claim their deity can express love or act lovingly toward creatures, but this doesn't mean that the god is *in essence* love, but only that a time or circumstance comes when the deity expresses love toward another, normally an inferior. In the case of such a deity, love therefore has a beginning: It is not eternal nor necessary. Properly speaking, only when acting in a charitable or beneficial manner can the god then be described as loving. To become loving or express love, the deity needs an object of love outside itself. Love is thus something that the god occasionally *does* but not what or who the god *is*. But this differs from the apostle John's confession. According to orthodox Christian confession, the one God *is love*, and that is distinctly possible because that God is triune: Father, Son, and Holy Spirit. God does not need creation to become love or to be loving, for love is what he is and does before he ever creates. As John Webster comments, "The Holy Trinity is perfect blessedness in himself in the absence of creatures."[4] And this blessedness is the perfection of love.

One of the most robust explorations of this proposition was made by Augustine in the fourth century. Augustine attributes a triadic nature to love when he writes, "Love means someone loving and something loved with love. There you are with three, the lover, what is being loved, and love."[5] He will eventually argue that God is love, and this is possible only *because* God is eternally triune. This triune doctrine does not contradict the ancient Christian doctrine of God's simplicity or oneness or unity because it, in fact, establishes that unity on the basis of God's *being* as love.[6] Augustine comments, "For love is not loved unless it is already loving something, because where nothing is being loved there is no love."[7] From statements like this the Augustinian tradition developed the shorthand of describing God as Lover (Father), Beloved (Son), and Love (Spirit). The Spirit, who is the love "common to Father and Son . . . is their very commonness or communion, consubstantial and coeternal." Augustine makes the following allowance in language and imagery: "Call this friendship, if it helps, but a better word for it is charity. And this too is substance because God is substance, and God *is charity* [*charity* comes from the Latin *caritas*, which means 'love'] (1 John

---

4. John Webster, *God Without Measure: Working Papers in Christian Theology*, 2 vols. (London: Bloomsbury T&T Clark, 2016), 1:89.

5. Augustine, *On the Trinity*, 8.14, p. 255.

6. From all eternity, this one God is always and never less or more than Father, Son, and Spirit. "Therefore there are not more than three; one loving him who is from him, and one loving him from whom he is, and love itself. If this is not anything, how is it that God is love?" Augustine, *On the Trinity*, 6.7, p. 210.

7. Augustine, *On the Trinity*, 9.2, p. 272. Later in that same section he adds, "Take away lover and there is no love; take away love and there is no lover."

4:8, 16)."[8] In other words, John's claim does not imply the existence of three independent separate beings or gods, which would be a form of tritheism. Instead, Augustine shows that love is the mode of God's unity as three eternal and divine persons.

How are we to make sense of this mystery, proclaimed by the church in the East and West, while avoiding the many easy missteps? Here are the creedal basics as succinctly as I can put them in my own words:

> God is one; the Father is God, the Son is God, and the Holy Spirit is God; the Father is not the Son, and the Son is not the Father, and the Father and Son are not the Spirit, and so on; the Father proceeds from none, while the Son is eternally begotten by the Father as his exact Image and Word, and the Spirit eternally proceeds from the Father [and the Son];[9] the three persons are distinguished by relations, not by nature: one God, three persons; God is to be worshiped and glorified, and each divine person is thus rightly worshiped, adored, and glorified.

While we must sidestep the linguistic misunderstandings and various debates between the Greek and Latin churches, what was basically agreed upon was that this one God has three "subsistences" or "hypostases." In more commonly used language, God is one being in three persons.

One consequence of this affirmation is that divine attributes (i.e., what is always and necessarily true of God) are not true merely of any one divine person but of God himself as God. God is holy. God is life. God is love. The only thing that distinguishes the persons in eternity is their relations with one another: None is more divine than the others, nor are the attributes broken up according to persons. One should not imagine the Son is love, but not the Father or Spirit; nor that the Father alone is life, or the Spirit alone is omniscient. Whatever is true of God as God must also be true of each divine person—this is why we must say that the divine persons are *homoousios* (having the same essence or nature) with one another.[10]

---

8. Augustine, *On the Trinity*, 6.7, p. 209, emphasis original.

9. We will not here debate the *filioque* clause but simply use these brackets to note it is the one area of the creed that is contested within the universal church. For those who want an in-depth study of the history and theology of this topic, see A. Edward Siecienski, *The Filioque: A History of Doctrinal Controversy* (Oxford: Oxford University Press, 2010).

10. As we will explore more fully in a later chapter, this is what is behind the Nicene claim that Jesus, who is truly God, is nothing less than "God from God, light from light, true God from true God."

Such matters provoked the entire Arian controversy. Augustine affirms that the Father is light and wisdom, the Son is light and wisdom, and the Spirit is light and wisdom, but also that there are not three lights or three wisdoms, but one light, one wisdom: "Because in their case *to be* is the same as to be wise, Father and Son and Holy Spirit are one being. Nor with them is *to be* anything else than to be God."[11] God simply is. And the God who is, *is* Father, Son, and Spirit. This triune God *is* eternally holy, *is* eternally wise, *is* eternally almighty, and *is* eternally love. For our purposes, we will concentrate on the question of love, since it serves as a test case and will help shape our view of creation and Christian life.

As with all God's other perfections, love is not an attribute of one particular divine person (e.g., the Son) *as* that person, but of God as God. God *is* love, which describes the eternal relations of the three divine persons. The Father who comes from none *eternally* begets the Son as the object of his love, and as the image of the Father, the Son *eternally* reflects that love, and in this sharing there is the person of the Spirit, who is *eternally* the mutual bond of love between the Father and Son. Three persons, one essence. God is love: The Father loves the Son in the Spirit.[12]

Divine attributes do not work against one another, so we must not describe them as though there were tension between them. By concentrating on love, therefore, we do not belittle or ignore the other attributes, but we look at God from this particular angle for now. When we move to look at the justice or wisdom of God, for example, we are looking at the same object (God himself, who is love in all his being and activity) but from a different angle. But I do believe there is something especially helpful about concentrating on love in our treatment of Christian life, especially since Jesus repeatedly calls our attention to a twofold pattern of love—love of God and love of neighbor—as our guide for living. Obviously a faithful rendering of biblical love must never ignore or deny other divine attributes: After all, they inform

---

11. Augustine, *On the Trinity*, 7.6, p. 224, emphasis added. There are real similarities to the Athanasian creed, commonly assumed to have been written around the fifth century.

12. Jumping from above to below, while reflecting on human creatures made in God's image—which will become more important later in our discussion—Augustine observes the threefold nature of love wherein you have "the lover, and what is being loved, and love.... For love is not loved unless it is already loving something, because where nothing is being loved there is no love." Augustine, *On the Trinity*, 9.2, p. 272. This earthly experience is taken by Augustine as a vague but true shadow of the heavenly reality, so that the triune nature of God is the necessary truth that illumines that confession that God, *in himself*, is love.

and orient our understanding of love and they tell us about God.[13] Yet this attribute does often appear to take center stage for Jesus. "We love because he first loved us" (1 John 4:19).

According to Augustine, love can take center stage for an understanding of God because none of the other attributes can be understood apart from love, especially from our human perspective. This might help make sense of why we, as made in God's image, can best understand all the virtues as "a form of love." Tarsicius J. Van Bavel explains Augustine's reasoning: "Temperance is love which knows how to protect its integrity and is dedicated wholly to what is loved. Fortitude is love that is capable of enduring much for the sake of the beloved. Justice is love which does not desire to retain for itself the good things of life but knows how to share them equally. Prudence is love that knows how to discern what will benefit and what will harm it."[14] Centuries after Augustine, Thomas Aquinas built on these ideas in his memorable discussion of the virtues.[15] All of these expressions of love, in one way or another, point us to the God who is love.

What, then, is our connection with love and its resulting virtues? We do not generate virtues any more than we generate our own lives. Rather, just as our lives are a matter of participating in the life of Christ (Gal 2:20; Col 3:3), so too do we participate in his character. We will unpack this much more fully in a later chapter on the Holy Spirit. For now, we should never forget that the virtues point beyond themselves, finding their source and their return in God himself. God is love, and his love is always a just love, a wise love, a powerful love, a holy love. God's wisdom, goodness, and power all make sense in light of divine love. Infinite power *apart* from God's holy love, for example, could easily describe an all-powerful demon. Further, the relation of God's attributes to each other tells us that God's love is never ignorant or unjust—for God to be ignorant or unjust would be unloving. Let's bring this entire discussion back to where we started: We must begin with God himself, understanding that God *is* love. This is not a small "part"

---

13. Cf. H. Richard Niebuhr, who rightly warned against certain forms of "religious liberalism" that not only magnified the virtue of Jesus's love, but seemed to pit it against other virtues one finds in Jesus and the Gospels; this often led to problematic reductionism. Niebuhr, *Christ and Culture* (New York: Harper & Row, 1951), 15–29.

14. Tarsicius J. van Bavel, "Love," in *Augustine Through the Ages*, ed. Allan D. Fitzgerald (Grand Rapids: Eerdmans, 1999), 509–10.

15. E.g., Aquinas, *Summa Theologica*, 1.2.65.

of God. This is who the triune God is, and accordingly we should not be surprised that this then frames how God acts.

AFFIRMATION 2
Creation is the overflow of God's love.

Since God *is* love, all his activity is the activity of love. Since he is complete in himself, any activity directed beyond himself is the outflow of his abundance of love to constitute other objects of his love (i.e., creation). In this way he can love purely because he doesn't need them and because love is who he is and what he does.

While it is common and right for Christian theology to speak of creation *ex nihilo* (out of nothing), we also confess that creation is *ex Deo* (out of God).[16] This is not a form of pan(en)theism, as if creation carried divine properties within it or as if God were somehow dependent upon creation. Rather, "creation *ex Deo*" affirms that something did not come from nothing, but from *God*: Once he brought into being that which did not previously exist, God became Creator.[17] This is why it can be true that while God is not his creation, and his creation is not God, "in him we live and move and have our being" (Acts 17:28).

This matters because understanding and relating to creation require that we understand and relate to God. One of the destructive aspects of modernity and the emergence of what Charles Taylor calls *A Secular Age* is that we imagine we don't need God or theology to make sense of human existence and experience.[18] This kind of secularity reduces the whole world to its material aspect, using only what Taylor calls the "immanent frame": "This frame constitutes a 'natural' order, to be contrasted with a 'supernatural' one, an 'immanent' world, over against a possible 'transcendent' one."[19] Such a view loses or ignores all sense

---

16. For a recent discussion raising some of the same kinds of concerns I am getting at here, see Daniel Soars, "Creation in Aquinas: Ex Nihilo or Ex Deo," *New Blackfriars* 102, no. 1102 (November 2021): 950–66.

17. To understand why and how creation ex nihilo emerged as an important distinctly Christian doctrine, start with Gerhard May, *Creation Ex Nihilo: The Doctrine of "Creation Out of Nothing" in Early Christian Thought*, trans. A. S. Worrall (Edinburgh: T&T Clark, 1994). Cf. the recent provocative push by Peter J. Leithart, who stresses that the God we discover in Scripture is always known as Creator, and we should be careful about trying to go before or beyond that claim in attempts to speak of God apart from that designation: *Creator: A Theological Interpretation of Genesis 1* (Downers Grove, IL: IVP Academic, 2023), esp. ch. 4.

18. Charles Taylor, *A Secular Age* (Cambridge: Harvard, 2007).

19. Taylor, *A Secular Age*, 542.

of the transcendent and therefore jeopardizes our relationship with the Creator and creation.

"The transcendent" is a brief way of referring to realities that can't be accounted for in terms of everyday, hands-on, this-worldly experience and thus point beyond it. Christian theology, for example, claims that our everyday world depends on God as its Creator and upholder. Those who omit God from their accounts of ethics, for example, often end up reducing ethics to a form of emotivism (something is declared wrong because we *feel* it is wrong) or utilitarianism (something is wrong because it doesn't bring the greatest amount of happiness to an individual or majority group), and in all their accounts they struggle to overcome the chasm between *description* and *prescription*, between the way things *are* and the way we think things *should* be.[20] David Hume commented that we can't easily produce an "ought" from an "is."[21] In this secular age we still feel compelled to put forward convictions about why things are wrong or right, but if we deny ourselves access to God, then we have to ground those ethical impulses within a closed, this-worldly system, and such foundations usually seem both arbitrary and flimsy: It becomes hard to refute the evolutionary pattern of survival of the fittest. But if human creatures were made from the start to relate to God, their neighbor, and the earth, then forgetting or ignoring God affects not just vertical relations but all relations. Knowing who this God is and how and why he created the world can provide a solid foundation for ethics and right relations. This takes us to the seventeenth century.

In 1676, former Oxford Vice Chancellor John Owen delivered one of his short but beautifully insightful discourses on the sacraments. In this sermon he takes us to the thesis for this chapter, which was the original inspiration for it. Based on Matthew 3:17, Owen reflects on the heavenly voice that declares over the Messiah: "This is my beloved Son, with whom I am well pleased." Since Owen gives this sermon before serving the Lord's Supper, he encourages his listeners to realize that the primary purpose of celebrating the Eucharist is to be mindful of "the love of Christ."[22]

---

20. See, e.g., the recent critique (esp. of the Positive Psychology method) in James Davison Hunter and Paul Nedelisky, *Science and the Good: The Tragic Quest for the Foundations of Morality* (New Haven, CT: Yale University Press, 2018).

21. E.g., David Hume, *A Treatise of Human Nature*, 3.1.1. Cf. Max Black, "The Gap Between 'Is' and 'Should,'" *The Philosophical Review* 73, no. 2 (1964): 165–81.

22. John Owen, "Discourse XXII," in *The Works of John Owen*, ed. William H. Goold (Edinburgh: Banner of Truth Trust, 1965), 9:612.

His body and blood, which are given "for us," take us straight into the mystery of God, for they bring us to the significance of the person and work of the Messiah. Owen proclaims, following in the Augustinian tradition, that our theology and ethics must be grounded in the triune God and focus on the incarnate Christ before we can examine our response to God.

Owen, like the apostle John and Augustine, affirms that God is love and acts accordingly. God's eternal *being* thus precedes his relation to creation, which by definition has a beginning. From all eternity "the essential blessedness of the holy Trinity consists in the mutual love of the Father and the Son, by the Holy Ghost; which is the love between them both."[23] This will become important because Owen doesn't believe that the Father starts loving the Son at the River Jordan. Although this heavenly declaration of the Father's love for the *incarnate* Son in that baptismal scene adds to our understanding of the incarnation, Owen also wants us to see that it points to an eternal reality: "The delight of the Father from all eternity was in the Son. The ineffable love and mutual delight of the Father and the Son by the Spirit is that which is the least notion we have of the blessedness of the eternal God."[24] The Father does not become loving at some point in time (thus implying that, before that point in time, he was not loving), but the eternal generation of the Son by the Father and the eternal procession of the Spirit in this eternal bond demonstrate that this love of God has no beginning or end. Put simply: The Father eternally, rightly, and perfectly loves the Son. This divine love is also an act in the freedom of God, but *not* in the sense that failing to love himself was some kind of possibility: On the contrary, such a statement is a contradiction in terms and even more radically so than saying that equal things are not equal at all. When you say "God," you say "love," and that must exclude "not love." But God is indeed free in his love by being free in *how* he loves. What he does is always love, but he is also creative beyond imagining.

In this sermon, Owen clarifies that the love of God in the immanent Trinity is not something started in time, but an eternal activity of the triune life of the one God: "The first love of God the Father to the Son is that which we call *ad intra*, where the divine persons are objects of one another's actings;—the Father knows the Son, and the Son knows

---

23. Owen, *Works*, 9:613.
24. Owen, *Works*, 9:613.

the Father; the Father loves the Son, and the Son loves the Father; and so, consequently, of the Holy Ghost, the medium of all of these actings."[25] This "first love" is not about a chronological beginning in which something changes in God, but rather here he is speaking of the difference between God's self-love (primary) and then what he will describe as God's love of creation (secondary).

This may sound speculative, but ordering matters. While we *epistemologically* move from our experience back to the truth of God, we also must recognize, in contrast, that theology *ontologically* moves the other direction: *from God to us*. Here is a difference between being and knowing, between God and creation. If we are to understand God's love for us, which is most clearly revealed in the incarnate Christ, then we must confess that love is first *in* God and not a later development. And this love constitutes the appropriate foundation for ethics in general and Christian life in particular. We are now ready to discuss creation.

Owen looks at the Trinity to make sense of creation's *telos*: "God never did any thing *without himself*, but the end of it was to manifest what is *in himself*."[26] That is, the triune God, who by his own nature loves himself, freely acts to make that which is not himself (i.e., creation), and then God freely loves what he makes. In other words, just as God *ad intra* is love, so God *ad extra* freely and happily expresses himself in love. Therefore, *all tastes and experiences of creaturely love point back*—even if through a darkened glass—*to the God who is love*. We tend to think of love as an emotion or thought that we produce, grounded in the observable world, needing no transcendence, no deity. And yet, if love is greater than the primal urge of survival of the fittest or the propagation of the species, then we must look beyond ourselves to find its nature and source. This does not belittle our meaningful experiences and expressions of the particularities of love; it seeks a foundation for them.

In the twentieth century, some have declared that love has no origin: It is nothing but a label used to describe a physiological response to evolutionary triggers, and it certainly doesn't point to anything that transcends our empirical knowledge. As Lauren Slater's article "True Love" attempted to explain in her 2006 contribution to *National Geographic*, one no longer needs religions or myths to understand love, since "for the first time, new research has begun to illuminate where love lies in

---

25. Owen, *Works*, 9:614.
26. Owen, *Works*, 9:613.

the brain, the particulars of its chemical components."[27] However, as philosopher Tim Pickavance rightly observes about her statements, she is not talking about "the chemical components of the physical correlates of love," but her claim is "the chemical components of *love itself*."[28] That is, she is making a category error, confusing the thing known (love itself) with our mode of experiencing it (the "physical correlates" of the experience). Maybe such neurological activity helps the propagation of the species, but I believe that our experience of love points to more (though not less) than mere chemical reactions. I think this is partly what Augustine is getting at when he argues that Paul, in Romans 1:20–28, is building his argument that all are without excuse in rejecting God because all creation points to God's love.[29]

At the end of the nineteenth century Friedrich Nietzsche expressed a similar concern in his famous story of the "madman" who proclaims, "God is dead."[30] While Nietzsche was no fan of Christian orthodoxy, in that powerful scene the madman is not attacking naive believers but the supposedly sophisticated Germans who had rejected Christianity's account of God and the universe and yet continued to live on the benefits of those beliefs. These nonbelievers were still living as if their lives had purpose, as if love transcended the material and was easily recognizable, as if they could live in a liberating forgiveness that cleansed the stains of cruelty and neglect in their lives. But Nietzsche called their bluff: to live on these principles was to assume a God-centered world, a world these same people had rejected. They wanted to enjoy the benefits of Christianity while denying its truth and demands. They supposed meaning without a source of meaning. Nietzsche's conclusion was not that they should turn to God but that they must become brave enough to enter into this new world where raw power—not a benevolent deity—was what shaped their lives and gave them purpose.[31] In this view, humans alone can give meaning, and therefore it is really up to us to

---

27. Lauren Slater, "True Love," *National Geographic*, referenced and then cited by Tim Pickavance, *Knowledge for the Love of God* (Grand Rapids: Eerdmans, 2022), 89–90.

28. Pickavance, *Knowledge for the Love of God*, 90.

29. Augustine, *The Confessions*, ed. John E. Rotelle, trans. Maria Boulding, 2nd ed. (Hyde Park, NY: New City, 1997), 242.

30. Friedrich Nietzsche, *The Gay Science*, trans. Walter Kaufmann (New York: Vintage, 1974), 181–82.

31. Cf. Friedrich Nietzsche, *Beyond Good and Evil: Prelude to a Philosophy of the Future* (New York: Vintage, 1989); Nietzsche, *The Will to Power*, ed. Walkter Kaufmann (New York: Vintage, 1968).

do so, and only those controlling the competing power structures can determine the ethical concerns of a good life. Such a vision, however, necessarily restricts itself to a this-worldly, material framework and has no transcendent source or goal. The system is self-enclosed and thus self-determining. Only a naive hope would look within these limits for an ethical foundation that transcends cultures, history, and all the various forms of constructed power.

But what if we don't reduce love and goodness to chemicals in the brain, nor to the whims of powerful people who get to set the rules; what if love and goodness flow from the transcendent God? Returning to Owen: "The sole reason why there is such a thing as love in the world among the creatures, angels or men,—that God ever implanted it in the nature of rational creatures,—was, that it might shadow and represent the ineffable, eternal love that the Father had unto the Son, and the Son unto the Father, by the Spirit."[32] Our experiences shadow something greater, deeper, fuller than themselves. And so while philosophers and poets, musicians and storytellers, can meditate on the wonder, strangeness, beauty, simplicity, and complexity of love, merely observing the phenomenon of love can never take them all the way to its source, to its origin. This leads us to ask, doesn't love point to more than a passing feeling, a primal urge, a sentimental impulse? How are we to recognize true love amid the endless, imperfect expressions of it? According to Owen, all of these expressions and experiences of love can be "traced" to the source from which they ultimately arise: the "God [who] necessarily loved himself."[33] All love, from the original creation and in the new creation, is really best understood to "resemble and shadow out this great prototype of divine love."[34]

Simply put, God creates not in order to fill some hole or need he has but freely in order to express the overflow of his eternal triune love. "Creation need not have been," as John Webster puts it.[35] And because creation is an expression of "gift-love" rather than "need-love," to quote C. S. Lewis, then we can recognize creation as the utterly gratuitous act of grace that it is.[36] Once we have clearly established

---

32. Owen, *Works*, 9:613.
33. Owen, *Works*, 9:613.
34. Owen, *Works*, 9:614.
35. John Webster, "'Love Is Also a Lover of Life': *Creatio Ex Nihilo* and Creaturely Goodness," *Modern Theology* 29, no. 2 (April 2013): 160.
36. C. S. Lewis, *The Four Loves* (New York: Harcourt, 1960), 1–9.

LOVE

this, we can see that creation—with humanity as its center—has as its goal our reflection of and participation in God's love. This grounds and guides human life.

AFFIRMATION 3

The purpose of creation, with humanity at the center, includes its reflection of and participation in God's love; when this is happening, we call it "shalom."

Creation is an overflow of the life and love of the Trinity, which is why, from the beginning, all that God created both *reflected* and *participated* in divine energy. The flourishing that thus characterized the world is called *shalom*, which is usually translated as "peace." However, the English word *peace* does not often convey its Hebrew counterpart's robust, positive content. Shalom is not merely psychological peace, which is how we have often interpreted it in our affluent Western church. Biblically, shalom is much bigger, earthier, fuller, and more dynamic than merely an absence of conflict, whether internal or external.[37] It represents wholeness, fullness, harmony, well-being, both spiritually and materially throughout God's good creation. Not only were the distinct parts of creation good in themselves (e.g., trees being trees), but creation was good as a whole and interactively (e.g., trees sheltering and providing food for cardinals and koalas). Genesis 1 builds that picture, concluding with God's Sabbath rest in the goodness of what he made. The created world didn't merely reflect his love but actively participated in it. It was good!

Human beings were created to be the centerpiece of this creation, both in developing it and in leading the praise directed back to the Creator. Their priestly and kingly roles would nurture love and delight. This was their worship, both in giving praise to God and in leading the rest of the world to do the same. Their commission to be fruitful and multiply (Gen 1:28) would express their faithfulness, all within the presence, power, and love of the God who walked with them in the garden (Gen 3:8). They would have not simply talked with the Lord but

---

37. See, e.g., Claus Westermann, "Peace (Shalom) in the Old Testament," in *The Meaning of Peace: Biblical Studies*, ed. Perry B. Yoder and Willard M. Swartley, trans. Walter W. Sawatsky, 2nd ed., Studies in Peace and Scripture, vol. 2 (Elkhart, IN: Institute of Mennonite Studies, 2001), 37–70.

done the good work the Creator put before them, from tilling the soil to building communities.

This doctrine of creation reminds us that God is not like a narcissistic celebrity who only feels good about himself when he receives the mindless praise of fans. As we have already discussed, God is full, happy, and complete because God is love in himself. The classic doctrine of divine aseity (self-existence) does not imply that God is distant, apathetic, or utterly unknowable, but reminds us that because God doesn't need us to complete himself, his love for us is free from distorting, self-interested entanglements. God is secure and comfortable being God: He *needs* no other. Furthermore, God is comfortable with creation *not* being God: Each creature needs God and the rest of creation. This is a sign not of sin but of the goodness of mutual dependence among creatures. None of God's creatures—even humans!—were made to be infinite or divine, but interdependent and good. Affirming the beauty and uniqueness of God's independence prepares us to affirm the beauty and life-giving connection of creaturely dependence. We do praise and worship God, but *not because he needs it*. We do so because he truly is worthy, because to refuse to do so is to deny reality and thus distort our relationship to the Creator *and* with ourselves and his creation. Our choice to worship God reflects the connection that ethics has with divine transcendence. Since God in his holy love is the center of reality, to ignore or rebel against him puts one at odds with all of reality.

Shalom is God's goal for creation, and the oxygen of shalom is love. Since we were the centerpiece of creation, living in shalom consists in large part in our exercise of love toward God, neighbor, the earth, and even ourselves. In this environment of health and harmony, the self is meant to be secure in its connection to God's life-giving presence and to the others with whom we share life.

Finally, since God's free act of creation occurred out of the overflow of his inner life of love, we should avoid imagining the created world as a fixed, static object. Shalom never described something like a family photo hanging on the wall, reminding us of a single static moment. Creation enjoying shalom was a vibrant, life-giving, harmonious existence. The "goodness" of creation mentioned in Genesis 1 included its development in time. Each part of it related to God and to the other parts, all in harmony and wholeness, growing and developing under God's love.

AFFIRMATION 4

Sin disrupts and disorders love, thus rupturing the communion of the creation with its Creator and distorting the nature of the created order.

Human relations were designed not merely for breeding and protection, but to be the means of communion. If love was the oxygen, and shalom the intended harmony and wholeness, sin was the poison introduced into that primal air of creation because of human unfaithfulness. As a part of the material world, we were uniquely called to participate in the Creator's care for the earth and its inhabitants, thus called to express our role as God's image bearers, reflecting his presence and love. Rather than reinforcing the goodness of God's design, however, humanity's rebellion altered the world, infecting everything with the corruption of our sin. The good creation remains but is now deeply disturbed as this poisonous gas of sin spreads across all aspects of the world. Our lives move from marital intimacy to murder within a family, from harmony with the earth and life-affirming work to dissonance and resentment of labor. Sin produces not merely a single distortion but a cascade of dysfunction and conflict.

Because our being is essentially communal and not merely individual, this disruption of shalom,[38] which disorders communion with God, neighbor, and the earth, also corrupts our internal world.[39] Even our "self" is now divided. The self was historically understood in terms of external relations with other people (family, tribe, vocation) rather than merely in terms of internal feelings or self-perception.[40] The kind of

---

38. E.g., Cornelius Plantinga Jr., *Not the Way It's Supposed to Be: A Breviary of Sin* (Grand Rapids: Eerdmans, 1995), esp. 7–38.

39. For some of the dogmatic issues related to the nature of sin, its consequences and how it relates to various aspects of the faith, see Keith L. Johnson and David Lauber, eds., *T&T Clark Companion to the Doctrine of Sin* (London: T&T Clark, 2016), esp. chapters 18–27. For more on the social and structural nature of sin, start with Derek R. Nelson, *Sin: A Guide for the Perplexed* (London: T&T Clark, 2011), esp. 78–115.

40. Robet A. Di Vito sums it up well: The person, according to the Old Testament, is "more radically decentered, 'dividual,' and undefined with respect to personal boundaries but also that, in sharp contrast to modernity, it is identified more closely with, and by, its social roles, that it is transparent rather than deep, heteronomous rather than autonomous and self-legislating. In all these ways the biblical construction of personal identity differs dramatically from the modern." Di Vito, "Old Testament Anthropology and the Construction of Personal Identity," *Catholic Biblical Quarterly* 61 (1999): 237. Cf. Carol A. Newsom, *The Spirit Within Me: Self and Agency in Ancient Israel and Second Temple Judaism* (New Haven, CT: Yale University Press, 2021), who recognizes a complex web for early options of self-understanding but argues for a slow development toward eventually a more introspective model in Second Temple literature. See also Richard Sorabji, *Self: Ancient and Modern Insights about Individuality, Life, and Death* (Chicago: University of Chicago Press, 2006).

identity we perceive by primarily "looking within," which is the chief method in much of the modern Western world, is a fairly new phenomenon.[41] Given that earlier conceptions of the self were drawn primarily from external relations, one could argue that internal harmony was produced or reflected by living in healthy and right relationship to God, neighbor, and earth. Western culture has produced a predominantly individualistic understanding of the self, and this often contributes to making us more unsettled, chaotic, and confused.[42] We need a correct account of creation and sin if we are to order ourselves rightly, and this requires that we not only look inside ourselves but also examine our relations with God, neighbors, and even the earth. It will require that we see ourselves as the product of God's love in the creation of a good world, and that we recognize the disordering effects of sin on our internal and external worlds.

Sin disorders everything, from our heads to our hearts, from the land to political systems, from our souls to the social structures we inhabit. A realist analysis of Christian life will include, in its proper place, an examination of this disorder. Everything is not terrible, but there is no part of God's good creation that hasn't been affected by sin. It hardens hearts, inserts hostility between humanity and the rest of creation, and produces the panic and blindness of self-absorption. We feel our lack of shalom, and we long for it.[43] Now, instead of enjoying the life-giving communion we were created for, we try to live as though we are autonomous and alone rather than belonging to God and each other. The result is an inhumane world, and we can feel it.[44]

All of creation groans (Rom 8:22). We groan. The disordering effects of sin can be felt everywhere, from nationalism run amuck to dysfunctional families. From our addictions to our apathy, from our

---

41. For extensive historical and philosophical background on this, see Charles Taylor, *Sources of the Self: The Making of Modern Identity* (Cambridge: Harvard University Press, 1989); Carl R. Trueman, *The Rise and Triumph of the Modern Self: Cultural Amnesia, Expressive Individualism, and the Road to Sexual Revolution* (Wheaton, IL: Crossway, 2020).

42. For a powerful historical and literary telling of how this movement toward self-generation led to making ourselves our own gods, see Tara Isabella Burton, *Self-Made: Creating Our Identities from Da Vinci to the Kardashians* (New York: PublicAffairs, 2023).

43. This grief and longing is the occasion and justification for our lament. See Kelly M. Kapic, *Embodied Hope: A Theological Meditation on Pain and Suffering* (Downers Grove, IL: IVP Academic, 2017), 27–41.

44. A good recent treatment of how this experience is pervasive in our day can be found in Alan Noble, *You Are Not Your Own: Belonging to God in an Inhuman World* (Downers Grove, IL: InterVarsity Press 2021).

self-absorption to our self-hatred, from racism to injustice, from sexual abuse to isolation, from my greedy heart to the cancer deteriorating the bodies of those I love. The poison of sin attacks and disorders, making shalom sound like an impossible fairy tale and nothing more. It makes believing that God is love almost impossible.

But Jesus. . . .

AFFIRMATION 5

The incarnate Son is both the embodiment and object of divine love.

Let us return to Owen for a fresh perspective on how the incarnation addresses this history of creation, fall, and restoration.

Having affirmed that the eternal love of God *ad intra* is full and complete, Owen ponders how God manifests his love *ad extra*. As we examine his comments on the matter, keep in mind some of the challenges we face when trying to talk about God's relationship with that which is *not* God (i.e., with creation) in light of the differing dynamics of time and eternity. In particular, how might the incarnation—first actualized in space and time two thousand years ago—connect God's eternal self-love (*ad intra*) to his love for creation (*ad extra*)?

Here is Owen's surprising claim: "The first act of the love of God the Father wherein there is any thing *ad extra*, or without the divine essence, is the person of Christ considered as invested with our nature."[45] In other words, the eternal God,[46] who himself is love, first expresses his outward love toward creation by his love of Jesus, the incarnate Christ, the eternal Son assuming a full and true human nature. Though Owen distinguishes between what he calls the "first" and "second" creation, it still sounds as if Adam and Eve are not the pinnacle of creation, because Jesus *is*. They anticipated him, and he is the focus. They were made *in* God's image (Gen 1:27), but Jesus *is* God's image and likeness (e.g., 2 Cor 4:4; Col 1:15–17; Heb 1:3), the prototype for all humanity and for all the goodness of creation. Owen's claim appears to give the

---

45. Owen, *Works*, 9:614.
46. Since all the works *ad extra* of God are the works of all three persons of the Trinity (*opera ad extra indivisia sunt*), one can both say that this is the first *ad extra* work of God and call it the first *ad extra* work of the Father.

incarnate Christ ontological priority not only over Adam and Eve but over *everything*, over all that is not God.[47]

It is difficult, however, to integrate that assertion with Owen's statements elsewhere—namely, that the incarnation does not occur as a *necessary* part of God's creation, but logically is understood as a decree that follows in light of the tragedy of human sin.[48] Owen's articulated viewpoint aligns with the dominant Western Christian tradition, with Thomas Aquinas most clearly articulating what became known as the majority position.[49] Since the early church fathers were not exactly asking *if the incarnation would have happened even if there were no sin*, it is now widely agreed that there is no clear patristic position on that particular question; however, it is generally recognized that the early Fathers usually spoke of the incarnation in connection to redemption, which lends itself to the later majority opinion, though one could gather select quotes to support the minority viewpoint.[50] Writing in the seventeenth century, Owen was well aware of the minority position, likely starting with Rupert of Deutz (d. 1135), claiming that even if there were no human fall into sin, the eternal Son still would have become incarnate. In this way, the incarnation was strongly linked to the decree of creation rather than original sin. As Owen knew, this position was generally expanded upon and supported by the likes of Alexander of Hales and Albertus Magnus, but most memorably, in the medieval period, it was Duns Scotus who so strongly upheld this view that linked the incarnation to God's original design of creation. Later, during the Reformation, Andreas Osiander followed Scotus's view. Owen shows his knowledge of this history and is even able to cite all the relevant sources for and against this view. Still, following John Calvin and others, Owen rejects Scotus's position.[51]

---

47. It should be noted that Owen generally holds an infralapsarian position, which does raise questions about how one avoids making the fall necessary while also holding that the "first [*ad extra*] act of love . . . is the person of Christ considered as invested with our nature." Cf. *Works*, 8:291–292; 10:321. But as Timothy R. Baylor carefully demonstrates regarding Owen's infralapsarian view on the order of decrees, with the incarnation linked to the removal of sin: "His methodological commitment to an exposition of the history of revelation sometimes inclines his thoughts in a more supralapsarian direction." Baylor, "A Great King Above All Gods: Dominion and Divine Government in the Theology of John Owen" (PhD diss., University of St. Andrews, 2016), 34.
48. See esp. Owen, *Works*, 1:23–24.
49. See esp. Aquinas, *Summa Theologica*, 3.1.3.
50. See Georges Florovsky, "*Cur Deus Homo?* The Motive of the Incarnation," in *Creation and Redemption*, vol. 3 of *The Collected Works of Georges Florovsky* (Belmont: Norland, 1976), 163–70.
51. Calvin, *Institutes*, 2.12.4–7; Owen, *Works*, 1:23–27. Owen believes he has most of the key players on his side, citing primary source material from the likes of Irenaeus, Cyril, Chrysostom, Augustine, Theodoret, John of Damascus, Anselm, and many others. But he also cites key

Having said that, we also must keep in mind Timothy Baylor's observant comment that Owen "expresses some hesitancy about the Scriptural warrant for this endeavor" to discern the logical order of divine decrees in the mind of God, "stating in one place that, 'there is more of curiosity than of edification in a scrupulous inquiry into the method or order of God's eternal decrees or counsels.'"[52] For all of Owen's logical rigor, at times he may be more comfortable with ambivalence than we might appreciate or regularly allow.

This takes us back to Owen's statement regarding "the first act of the love of God . . . wherein there is any thing *ad extra*." Given that the majority opinion in historic, orthodox theology (including Owen) is that if there had been *no* sin and fall, then the incarnation would not be required, how do we make sense of Owen's claim? This raises the question: What is Owen implying when he says that the *first* act of God's love *outside* of his eternal self-love is "the person of Christ considered as invested with our nature"? Does he mean (1) the first *ad extra* act is *loving* the person of Christ, or (2) the first *ad extra* act of God's love is *the very person of Christ*? He may mean that the person of Christ *in himself* (via the assumption of human nature) constitutes the first and ultimate act of love, that is, the act of uniting the divine and human natures. Another way of approaching it would be that one could read Owen's use of "first" (a) chronologically (which would seem to require incarnation whether there were sin or not), (b) fundamentally (i.e., all God's acts *ad extra* are rooted in the Father's love for the incarnate Son by the Spirit), or (c) teleologically (i.e., "first" equals ultimate end, like "first reason" or "first motivation"). Part of the challenge here is that, as Bernadinus De Moor (1709–80) explained, "the *Decree* is an Immanent Act, Internal, since it posits nothing outside of God; yet it is not an Internal Act *ad Intra*, because it tends *ad Extra* objectively and terminatively, that is, things to be placed outside of God are its object: hence it is called an Immanent Act *ad Extra*."[53] While we cannot work through all of the details here, nor will this turn into a historical investigation of Owen,

---

opponents (e.g., Rupertus, Petrus Galatinus, Scotus, etc.) and where in their works one can find their position laid out.

52. Baylor, "A Great King Above All Gods," 33, quoting from Owen, *Works*, 1:62.

53. Bernadinus De Moor, *Didactico-Elenctic Theology*, trans. Steven Dilday, in "De Moor VI: Divine Decrees as Internal Acts ad Extra," https://www.fromreformationtoreformation.com/post/de-moor-vi-divine-decrees-as-internal-acts-ad-extra.

a few words of theological background might help before we get to the more important implications for our study.

God, who is love, loves his created world; further, that world is rightly ordered and represented most clearly in the incarnate Christ. Owen's comments help set the stage for our later discussion of the importance of Jesus as the Mediator between God and humankind. In the singular incarnate Son, God extends his self-love as love for his creation. Owen holds that in the opening scenes of Genesis, God manifests his love for the original creation, and we can further state that his love includes his commitment to healing that creation from the depredations of sin. Owen comments, "From the first eternal love of God proceeds all love that was in the first creation; and from this second love of God, to the person of Christ as incarnate, proceeds all the love in the second creation."[54] Because Owen's connections in this Lord's Supper sermon are less than clear, it becomes hard to understand his ordering of God's *ad extra* love when speaking of the events in Genesis 1–2 and those of Matthew 1. How do we relate God's "first" *ad extra* love to the creation of our time-and-space world to the event of incarnation in Mary's womb? What does it mean to say that God's *first* act of love was actualized only after other aspects of creation came into being?

A brief comment on God's eternity may prove necessary here since the language of "first" can be extremely confusing when used in that context. While the Son does not assume a human nature in time until the Spirit hovers over the Virgin Mary and she conceives, this historical happening is not *new* to the eternal God, who is not subordinate to time in himself. While I do not want us to get bogged down in technical philosophical debates here, we need at least a brief word of background before we look at the most interesting reflection on why Owen's comment can help us with a theology of Christian life. But for those who are most interested in the main argument here and don't want to wade through a few particular and dense philosophical debates and details about Owen's work, feel free to jump ahead a few pages to the last two paragraphs of section five.

The triune God is eternal, having his attributes in their completeness, from his exhaustive knowledge to his full presence and life—there is nothing God does not know and no place from which God is absent.

---

54. Owen, *Works*, 9:614.

Boethius (480–525) writes the most influential definition of *eternity* that is, with minor modifications, employed throughout history not only by medieval theologians like Anselm and Aquinas but also by later Protestant scholastics and reputable contemporary philosophers like Eleonore Stump.[55] Something along these lines appears to have been Owen's working idea as well. Boethius writes that eternity "is the complete, simultaneous and perfect possession of everlasting life."[56] Boethius believes this becomes clear when you contrast the Creator (who alone *is* eternity) with the creation (which is finite and exists in time). The eternal God is not restricted by beginning or end, nor does he *in himself* have temporal sequence. God is not an evolving deity, but full and complete; his knowledge is not growing, but all-encompassing and exhaustive; and he does not simply know all but is also present to all, for he is *himself* eternal life. Owen is addressing the question of how God's eternal being—since he is complete in himself and not confined by time—relates to his actions outside himself (*ad extra*). Expressing the assumption of a human nature by the Son in terms of a simple linear development in time and history (as Jesus appears many centuries after Abraham or Moses) might be insufficient to express the truth of God's eternity. As Stump explains, "Each moment in time is simultaneous with the whole of God's atemporal life. The whole of God's life is thus simultaneous with the assumption of human nature," which occurs at a specific point in space-time history.[57] Within this model, therefore, "there never was a part of God's life when the second person of the Trinity had not assumed human nature," for God does not himself change.[58] Consequently, we must understand Owen's comment as built not simply on the immutability and eternity of God but also on the logical (not temporal) ordering of God's love as directed toward that which is not God, namely, creation itself. Thus we can posit a "first" in terms of the nontemporal ways that one thing relates to another. For Owen, this "first" is the unique beloved Incarnate One. Priority of place and love is not determined by time and therefore does not belong to a

---

55. For an extensive survey of the background of eternity in theology and philosophy, and some of the debates surrounding it, see Natalja Deng, "Eternity in Christian Thought," *The Stanford Encyclopedia of Philosophy* (Fall 2018 ed.), ed. Edward N. Zalta, https://plato.stanford.edu/archives/fall2018/entries/eternity/. For a sample of Eleonore Stump's excellent work in this area, see *Aquinas* (New York: Routledge, 2003), esp. 131–58.
56. Boethius, *The Consolation of Philosophy*, trans. V. E. Watts (1969), 5.6.
57. Stump, *Aquinas*, 408.
58. Stump, *Aquinas*, 408.

billion-year-old Big Bang or to prehistoric *Homo sapiens*, but to Jesus Christ, the Son incarnate. Owen's claim that "the first act of the love of God the Father wherein there is any thing *ad extra*, or without the divine essence, is the person of Christ considered as invested with our nature,"[59] therefore, does not chiefly concern chronology but priority and purity, telos and goodness. Owen's claim has great relevance for our construction of a theology of Christian life, so let's interpret him generously as we follow his basic argument.

Owen sees Christ as uniquely God's "elect," God's servant "in whom my soul delighteth" (Isa 42:1 KJV). The New Testament uses these words from the Old Testament to refer specifically to Jesus. Twice! In both Matthew 3:17 at Jesus's baptism and in Matthew 17:5 at his transfiguration, God speaks these words over the Messiah as the one "in whom I rest, in whom I am well pleased and delighted."[60] Owen, following a fairly common Puritan tradition and one employed throughout the history of the church, uses his sanctified imagination to put words into the Father's mouth. With "emphatical words," the Father declares, "Let the sons of men . . . take notice of this, that the infinite love of my whole soul is fixed on the person of Jesus Christ as incarnate."[61] The Messiah is the Son of the Father and has been given everything by the Father. Out of his love for the Son, the Father shows him everything (John 3:35; 5:20). The Father consequently identifies and invests the incarnate Son as *the great embodiment and expression of God's eternal love now made manifest in the flesh.* Thus "the person of Christ is the complete, adequate object of the love of the Father. The great satisfaction of the soul of God, wherein he rests and delights, consists in love to Christ as incarnate."[62] God who eternally rests in his own triune life and love, whose love overflowed through the act of creation, is now here portrayed as fully resting in his good creation; not generically, but in the particular connection between the Creator and his creation actualized in the Son, who assumes a specific human nature. Let's make sure we understand Owen's main point and why it is so significant for our purposes.

In the incarnation God manifests his own eternal life and love, uniting his deity with humanity in the person of Jesus Christ. Therefore,

---

59. Owen, *Works*, 9:614.
60. Owen, *Works*, 9:614.
61. Owen, *Works*, 9:614–15.
62. Owen, *Works*, 9:615.

to understand God or his creation, especially from our sin-stained perspective, we have to look to the Christ, who embodies and reveals God's love to us. This requires that we conform our methods and theology to him to understand and describe true shalom with God and the rest of creation. Moving away from that standard tends to distort our views of God, other people, the earth, and even ourselves. The Christian imagination can take proper form only by consistent conformity with the incarnation. This is why we trust Jesus, for he alone brings reconciliation between God, humanity, and creation.

AFFIRMATION 6

Loving the incarnate Christ necessarily means loving God and his creation.

How does it come about that we love God or his creation?

We learn to love by experiencing love. This is no generic spirituality or vague religion but a Christ-centered faith in which we are immersed in the love of the Father and empowered and comforted by the Spirit. We are able to love because God has caught us up in the action of the love that occurs between the Father and the Son in the Spirit. Our love for Christ, therefore, carries over into love for the Father and everything the Father loves, including his created world.

Loving Christ

Owen shows how specifically loving Christ must be at the forefront of our theology of Christian life.

> Proportional to the renovation of the image and likeness of God upon any of our souls, is our love to Jesus Christ. He that knows Jesus Christ most, is most like unto God; for there the soul of God rests,—there is the complacency of God: and if we would be like to God . . . it must be in the gracious exercise of our love to the person of Jesus Christ.[63]

As with creation, God re-creates out of his eternal triune love, which is most clearly and centrally expressed through the incarnate Christ.

---

63. Owen, *Works*, 9:615.

GOD TO US

Jesus Christ is the incarnation of God himself and is, therefore, the embodiment, object, and revelation of God's love, as well as the pattern, source, and goal of ours. This leads to the following affirmations:

- God is love, so Jesus, as God the Son incarnate, is literally the embodiment of God's love.
- Since the activity between the Father and the Son is always love, Jesus as the incarnate Son of God is always the object of God's love.
- Jesus Christ is God's revelation of himself to us, the place Scripture points us (as in Heb 1) to learn who God is. Who he is, what he does, and what he says reveal *God*. In this way, he is the criterion for our knowledge of God and for all methods of gaining such knowledge.
- Because he is fully human as well as fully God, Jesus Christ is the pattern for us to follow in knowing how to be human.
- Because he is the Logos from the beginning, he is also the source of our being and humanity and therefore the source of our loving.
- Because he is love incarnate, he is the proper object and goal of our love.
- Christian life recognizes in Christ the inbreaking of shalom, and as we experience his love and life, we are invited to participate in the inbreaking of shalom even in this fallen and hurting world.

The God who *is* love and creates out of the overflow of his love goes about the work of re-creation not by starting a new love but by operating out of that same eternal triune love, which is here centered on and expressed through the incarnate Christ. As both the embodiment and object of divine love, the incarnate Son reconciles us to God and sets us free by his Spirit to participate in the motions and movements of shalom even in this fallen world. True shalom, which is made manifest in the kingdom of God, always centers on the Son incarnate. Jesus, the incarnate Son, is uniquely the place where God's love and our love meet.

The Father loves his incarnate Son, and we respond to God's self-revelation and work by loving Jesus. Owen puts this slightly differently: We don't love God "immediately as God, but our love to God [is exercised] by and in Christ."⁶⁴ We believe in and through Christ, and we live and love through Christ by the Spirit. Owen introduces a test to frame his understanding of Christian life in light of this underlying theology: "Here is the trial . . . of our return to God, and of our renovation of his image in us,—namely, in our love to Jesus Christ. There God and man do meet,—there God and his church above and below centre."⁶⁵

God draws us to himself through Christ as both the embodiment and object of God's love. Owen believes that Christ's love for us, most clearly expressed and seen on the cross, has what he calls in another sermon—an "attractive power." Employing Jesus's words where he anticipates being "lifted up" and then drawing people to himself (John 12:32), Owen conceives of this drawing to include both an initial coming to believe in Christ and also "the *following efficacy* of the love of Christ to draw souls that do believe *nearer* unto him."⁶⁶ This love not only initiates but sustains the relationship. We are told that none come to the Father but through the Son, and all whom the Father has given him are drawn to the Son (John 14:6).

Simply put, the great expression of Christian life is loving Christ. This love from and to the incarnate Son is what constitutes and explains Christian life: Only by and through Christ can we live in the kingdom of shalom, in loving communion with God, neighbor, earth, and even within ourselves. And this leads us to one final step, which moves beyond Owen's reflections.

Loving Our Neighbors and the Creation

Because Christ has the nature of God and the nature of a creature (i.e., human), he puts us back into a right relationship not only with God but also with creation, including our neighbors.

Biblically, love for our neighbor and for God's created world is an immediate and obvious result of loving Christ. The apostle John often makes these connections: "Beloved, let us love one another, for love is from God, and whoever loves has been born of God and knows God. Anyone who does not love does not know God, because God is love" (1 John 4:7–8). "Beloved, if God so loved us, we also ought to love one

---

64. Owen, *Works*, 9:615.
65. Owen, *Works*, 9:615.
66. Owen, *Works*, 9:608, Goold's emphasis.

another" (1 John 4:11). And then, just in case we missed it, he brings his themes together in a way that captures the entirety of this chapter: "We love because he first loved us. If anyone says, 'I love God,' and hates his brother, he is a liar; for he who does not love his brother whom he has seen cannot love God whom he has not seen" (1 John 4:19–21). According to John, God's love made manifest in the person and work of Christ by its nature also produces our responsive love to God and neighbor.

This is not a model of debt repayment, in which God does something for us, so we try to pay him back by good deeds. Not at all. That misunderstands and perverts the whole thing. No, the reason the love of God has all of these relational consequences is that the God of creation is the same as the God of re-creation. He made us to live in communion not only with himself but with our neighbor, the earth, and even ourselves. Being reconciled to God, therefore, includes our being brought back into the stream of eternal divine love and the goodness of shalom. So, although the world is fallen and remains tainted by sin, the Spirit of Christ reshapes our lives and our loves. He remakes us to relate rightly not only to himself but to our neighbor, the earth, and even ourselves. But God's love is vast and consequential for our lives.

In the fourteenth century Julian of Norwich said, "He makes us to love all that he loves because of his love."[67] We can love even the unlovely "because God's love has been poured into our hearts through the Holy Spirit who has been given to us" (Rom 5:5). Let's return to the apostle John and Augustine again to tease out this love of creation.

Building upon the first epistle of John and his assertion that God is love, Augustine writes about the implications of this love for the rest of creation. God is the source of all love, the energy or force behind all true love, and the final object or destination of all love. To understand the relations of love for God and love for creation, Augustine distinguishes between what he calls *uti* (use) and *frui* (enjoyment): God alone is to be "enjoyed," while creation is meant to be "used." This language grates harshly on modern ears and seems contrary to the nature of love. It appears to belittle the goodness of creation, whether we are talking about people, things, or actions. But while this language may be awkward, I believe Augustine's theological point should not be casually dismissed.

---

67. Julian of Norwich, *The Complete Julian of Norwich*, ed. Father John-Julian (Brewster, MA: Paraclete, 2009), §61, p. 291.

Let me explain both why it's hard for us to hear him as he intended and why his observation deserves serious consideration.

Immanuel Kant's ethical imperative, warning against treating people as means rather than ends, has conditioned us to reject Augustine's wording.[68] Some theologians like Anders Nygren appear to believe Augustine is guilty of this or a closely related problem that somehow undermines genuine love of neighbor because only God is to be "enjoyed,"[69] although others have strongly defended the early Father against such accusations.[70] For instance, Mario Naldini comments on their respective ethical perspectives, writing that "Kant's is immanent ('the realm of ends'), Augustine's is transcendent and metaphysical."[71] If we confine our ethical analysis to an immanent (this-worldly) framework, then Kant is hard to refute, although one can still raise questions about the basis from which he arrives at his universally applied principle.[72] But our considerations here require us to look beyond that immanent framework because we speak of God, who transcends our universe, our being, and our love precisely because he is their source. Kant's maxim (i.e., that people are ends and not means to other ends) must be reconsidered in this expanded context. The ontological shift to this new context produces qualitative and not merely quantitative distinctions: The Creator-creature difference means that God's love for us and ours for him are different in kind (and not merely in size) from our love for each other—but in a way that establishes those immanent loves and does not undo or compete with them. Kant rightly warns us against using people, but what if the true and final end of love isn't a created person or object, but God himself, who *is* love? What if the vocabulary of *using* employed by Augustine doesn't mean loving a person less but elevates every person who is the

---

68. Immanuel Kant, *Grounding for the Metaphysics of Morals*, trans. James W. Ellington, 3rd ed. (Cambridge: Hacket, 1993), 36.

69. Anders Nygren, *Agape and Eros*, trans. Philip S. Watson (London: SPCK, 1953).

70. For an example of a strong defense of Augustine on this, see Tarcisius J. van Bavel, "The Double Face of Love in Augustine," *The Journal of the Augustinian: Institute at Villanova University* 17 (1986): 169–81, esp. 179–81.

71. Mario Naldini, introduction to *Teaching Christianity* (*De Doctrine Christiana*), ed. John E. Rotelle, trans. Edmund Hill, The Works of Saint Augustine: A Translation for the 21st Century, 1/11 (Hyde Park, NY: New City, 1996), 17.

72. I am aware that Kant's ethics actually appear to have space for the transcendent in that he ended up including the idea of a future judgment to help make sense of the problem of unjust people living their whole lives without consequences, while some just end up suffering a great deal in this life. But in practice, Kant's system is, as Naldini explains, driven purely by the immanent and not the transcendent.

object of our love beyond what that love could be if the person were indeed the ultimate end?

For Augustine, *enjoyment* "consists in clinging to something lovingly for its own sake," whereas *use* is meant to communicate properly loving what comes your way yet seeing that it points ultimately to the great object and source of love itself.[73] Loving our neighbors as a way of loving God increases (quantitatively) and deepens (qualitatively) our love for them. "The things therefore that are to be enjoyed are the Father and the Son and the Holy Spirit, in fact the Trinity, one supreme thing."[74] Why? Because God *is* love! And all experiences of love necessarily point beyond themselves to God and flow from him. The distinction Augustine is making between *uti* and *frui* is necessary, not antagonistic nor reductionistic, because the *uti* has its being and possibility only in the context of the *frui*.[75]

To illustrate this, let us follow the apostle Paul in his doxology, where he writes that all things are "from him and through him and to him," and thus "to him be glory forever" (Rom 11:36). Paul's point here is not that mountains are unimpressive, that puppies can't be celebrated, that sex is terrible, or that children shouldn't be loved. That would be offensive to the Creator. But Augustine reminds us that all of these wonderful things and experiences are gifts *from* God, meant to be enjoyed *with* God and to take us back *to* God. Understanding this gives us better ground to understand both Augustine's *uti* and *frui* as well as the apostle Paul's distinction between the problem of the "flesh" and the indispensability of the "spirit" (e.g., Rom 8:6; Gal 5:16–17). As commentators commonly observe, Paul isn't pitting the *spiritual* against the *material*. Not at all. For Paul, the flesh and the spirit represent two ways of living, two approaches to life. While we will consider this distinction more fully in a later chapter on the Holy Spirit, we must here not miss the relevant distinction.

"The flesh" is a life lived by reducing everything to the created order, to the material world, to our animal nature, and thus is a life in rebellion

---

73. Augustine, *Teaching Christianity*, 1.4, p. 107, emphasis mine.
74. Augustine, *Teaching Christianity*, 1.5, p. 108.
75. For more helpful work on this distinction in Augustine, see Rowan Williams, "Language, Reality and Desire: The Nature of Christian Formation," in *On Augustine* (London: Bloomsbury, 2016), 41–58; and for this development and variations in tradition, see Simeon Zahl, "Tradition and Its 'Use': The Ethics of Theological Retrieval," *Scottish Journal of Theology* 71, no. 3 (2018): 308–23, esp. 318–19.

against God, denying his presence, power, and goodness and therefore degrading our understanding of what is truly good and human.[76] "The spirit" is a life lived in touch with God by his own Spirit dwelling within us, not belittling the material world or our physical bodies, but informing us how to live in faith, hope, and love. Living *by the flesh* hardens our hearts, dims our vision, limits our imagination to this world, and so leads us to try to satisfy all of our desires there, when what we most desire is God. When we treat good gifts as ultimate ends, they can only disappoint us. Worse, doing so turns good gifts into bad masters.

Properly loving the created world acknowledges its finite ability to satisfy and sees beyond the gift to the Giver. Walk in the woods, giggle with your children, use your skills to build great technology, and do so knowing that all of this has its being and significance from the source and goal of love and life, God himself.

When we see God beyond creation, then all of creation will act as a vehicle carrying us to our home in God, not away from him. This pilgrimage imagery echoes Augustine's comment: "If we wish to return to our home country, where alone we can be truly happy, we have to use this world, not enjoy it."[77] As John E. Rotelle writes, it is not that Augustine didn't enjoy his own various journeys, but these tastes of joy were not his final goal.[78] Despite some of the stereotypes (which do occasionally have some grounding), Augustine at his best is not against enjoying a wonderful meal, the pleasures of friendship, or the awe of a stunning sunrise. These experiences are not tainted or bad, but they are all good signs that point to something beyond themselves, to the Signifier.

Sacraments will end up being the great concentration of this principle, but all God's gifts testify to the Creator-creature distinction and the original purpose that God had for us to enjoy him *in* and *through* the good use of what he made and sustains. Thus, for example, to love a neighbor—if truly from love—is nothing less than loving your neighbor from or "out of God."[79]

---

76. Augustine, though not commenting on Paul here, expresses a similar sentiment when talking about the problem of sin's disordering: "Human beings, greedy to enjoy the creature instead of the creator, had taken on the coloring of this world—and so were most aptly called by the name of 'the world.'" Augustine, *Teaching Christianity*, 1.12, p. 111.
77. Augustine, *Teaching Christianity*, 1.4, p. 108.
78. See John E. Rotelle, in Augustine, *Teaching Christianity*, 126n4.
79. Augustine, *On the Trinity*, 8.12, pp. 253–254.

You cannot, therefore, love your neighbor more than you love God, for true love flows out of God toward love of neighbor. Given that God is love, "the man who loves love certainly loves God; and the man who loves his brother must love love."[80] Why? Love is not like a pie that can be divided up, nor does it exist in a finite quantity that must be spent wisely lest we deplete it, like money from a bag. Since the eternal God *is* love, we *receive* and *participate* in this divine love, but we do not generate it nor diminish its reserves: True love, Augustine remarkably concludes, is nothing short of God. That is why Augustine exclaims that the one who "loves love certainly loves God."

There is no such thing as "too much love." When someone worries that they have made an idol out of their spouse or child because they are "loving them too much," they are speaking a falsehood: Their problem is not that they love their spouse too much but that they have somehow distorted true love. We cannot love a person or a dog or a job too much. What we call "love" is often a more complicated phenomenon, where mixed motives, self-gratification, and self-centeredness often masquerade as pure love. For example, what newlyweds sometimes call "love" can prove to be an unacknowledged and unhealthy expectation for each other, imagining they can give ultimate satisfaction, delight, and hope. This will obviously cause problems. Similarly, we don't run the risk of loving our children too much, but only too little or in a wrong way. When we try to make them everything in our lives, that is not because we are loving them too much but because we misunderstand their goodness and make them serve as instruments for our satisfaction.[81] We treat them either as ultimate goals, which they can never be, or as means to other ends. Children are to be honored, cherished, delighted in, and loved, but they cannot bear the weight of being our idols. When parents try to make their children into their ultimate purpose in life, it can only cause serious problems. Disordered loves don't allow the other to flourish, to be other, to be free to respond in love. God alone is able to perfectly love himself and everything that is not God because he never expects creatures to be divine, and

---

80. Augustine, *On the Trinity*, 8.12, p. 254.
81. C. S. Lewis eloquently captures this point about a mother consumed inappropriately with her son in *The Great Divorce: A Dream* (San Francisco: HarperCollins, 2001), 114: "Excess of love, did ye say? There was no excess, there was defect. She loved her son too little, not too much. If she had loved him more there'd be no difficulty."

thus he expects us to remain finite creatures whom he brings into the motion and movement of divine love. We don't generate the love; we just participate in it.

We must avoid thinking of love as a spiritual substance or a commodity we possess. Love is more like a living stream, a moving river of fresh water. God is love in the activity of the Father and the Son toward each other in the Spirit. Creation has its basis and source in this activity and thus reflects and participates in that love. Thus it contradicts the nature of a created entity to attempt to make it the end, or *telos*, of love: Loving sees all creatures as pointers to him who is Love and therefore loves them within their limited nature. The objects and actions of our love, as part of the created order, were designed not to be the final stop of our loves but rather to help cultivate, enrich, and elevate our love, all ultimately taking us back to God himself. This can sound to us as if it either belittles our love for objects or belittles the objects of our love. Instead, it establishes that love: They themselves remain true objects and recipients of love, but who is this "they" of whom we speak? They have their being and nature and distinction in a particular action of God, upholding them, making them to be the "them" that we see in front of us, so that to love them is to love not only this particular action of God that upholds them, but also to love the God who has blessed us by giving us this "them" to love. Paul presents this dynamic to us when he writes, "For from him and through him and to him are all things. To him be glory forever. Amen" (Rom 11:36).

We can look beyond the gifts to the Giver, from the experience of love to the one who is Love—not because the gifts are insignificant but because they have so much significance beyond even themselves. They are good gifts, and "every good gift and every perfect gift is from above, coming down from the Father of lights" (Jas 1:17).

Not only are we to love our neighbor as ourselves, but as "we love ourselves all the more, the more we love God."[82] All of this is true because genuine love, whether for neighbor, for other parts of creation, or for ourselves, is necessarily a love *from* God himself that also leads us back *to* God himself. This is Augustine's way of holding together the two great commandments of loving God and loving our neighbor.

---

82. Augustine, *On the Trinity*, 8.12, p. 254.

CONCLUSION: ON LOVING THE LOVING GOD

Now let's go back to the opening story, to young Jonathan, wondering what it would look like to love God and to be loved by God. Seven-year-old children don't need to work through deep theology to have their questions answered. So, given all the background work we have done, what might we say to this child?

As parents, we asked Jonathan to consider the times he has felt deep love. We talked about when we wrestle on the ground, when he laughs uncontrollably with his sister, when he delights in his mother's approval and snuggles with Ruby the labradoodle. Whether giggling over tickles or tasting a cold orange on a hot summer day, we would tell him, "This is God's love." In his own ways he started to realize all goodness around him points back to God's love.

God's love comes to us not only in moments of delight, not just when we are doing good and helpful things, but also in our great moments of need. It's often true of seven-year-olds that they have already experienced sadness and pain from the world, as well as having a sense that their own hearts can sometimes be cruel or negligent. Yet God's love can be found there too. And so we get to talk about Jesus. Our Creator didn't abandon us to our sin and misery, to our tantrums and greed, but came to be with us in Christ, to reconnect us to himself and to the good world he made. Jesus is the center of love, so we can love him as we delight in his gifts, whether the forgiveness of our sins or the enjoyment of playing with our Legos—for all love ultimately comes from God and leads us back to him.

Loving the Creator and loving his created world go together. When Paul says to "set your minds on things above, not on earthly things" (Col 3:2 CSB), he isn't disparaging God's creation but pointing us to Christ. He explains that this means putting to death evil actions and attitudes like slander, wrath, covetousness, sexual immorality, evil desire, and so on. Why? Because these things oppose the good God and his good creation. They oppose love. They oppose shalom! But by keeping your mind on Christ (i.e., things above) we connect ourselves to God *and* his world. What might that look like? Paul lists compassion, humility, meekness, patience. *Attitudes and actions that nurture shalom through divine love.* God draws us into his love and shows us how to participate in it.

Loving God, far from rejecting creation, involves recognizing God's presence and work throughout it. And loving Christ means we can love not just our friends but even our enemies. It means deeply breathing the oxygen of God's love so that we can, in a small but significant way, push back against sin and darkness in us and in the world. It means pointing others to Christ because we want them to encounter Love—God himself. For that to happen, we must show them that Jesus, the incarnate Son, is where God's love and our love meet. May it be so for us.

CHAPTER 3

GRACE
The Coming of God's Love

> *He might minister the things of God to us, and ours to God.*
> —ATHANASIUS[1]

> *Jesus Christ is Mediator in such a way that in his incarnate Person he embraces both sides of the mediating relationship. He is God of the nature of God, and man of the nature of man, in one and the same Person. He is not two realities, a divine and a human, joined or combined together, but one Reality who confronts us as he who is both God and man.*
> —THOMAS F. TORRANCE[2]

> *The love of the Father towards [the incarnate Son] is more than it can be towards any other, neither can any attain unto that perfection of love which he beareth towards his heavenly Father. Wherefore God is not so in any, nor any so in God as Christ, whether we consider him as the personal Word of God, or as the natural Son of man.*
> —RICHARD HOOKER[3]

---

1. Athanasius, *Against the Arians,* "Discourse IV," §6, in *Athanasius: Select Works and Letters,* Nicene and Post-Nicene Fathers 4 (1892; repr., Peabody: Hendrickson, 1994, orig), 4:435. Emphasis mine. Henceforth abbreviated as NPNF.
2. T. F. Torrance, *The Mediation of Christ,* new ed. (Edinburgh: T&T Clark, 1992), 56, original emphasis.
3. Richard Hooker, *Of the Laws of Ecclesiastical Polity,* 2 vols. (London: Dent, 1954), 55.4, p. 2:226.

BEING HUMAN: A HUMAN KNOWLEDGE OF GOD

Where to begin a discussion of Christian life? When presenting a *theology*, it makes sense to begin with God. But since this is about Christian life, we must at the same time talk about anthropology—about humans. In its opening lines, John Calvin's sixteenth-century *Institutes of the Christian Religion* famously states that knowledge of God and knowledge of self are two parts of all true wisdom. Although distinguishing which of these should have primacy is not immediately obvious because they are so intertwined, Calvin decides to begin with God rather than the self.[4] Yet even after this decision, we see he is always aware that this is *human* knowledge of God. A theology of Christian life cannot merely discuss God in himself (*ad intra*) but must necessarily ask about God as he relates to that which is outside of himself (*ad extra*), since that is the only way we know him—as he is *to his creation*. This does not deny or downplay the importance of God's eternal independence and beauty, but it recognizes, as we must, the nature of human knowing and living in reference to God.

God's eternal being takes priority over our knowledge of that being; our lives are always a *response* to God's being and work, and failure to acknowledge that fact risks treating God as if he were only a projection of human values. We do truly know and love God because he has revealed himself to us. Consequently, when we talk about *Christian* life, we do so in agreement with Philip Melanchthon's claim that "we know Christ by his benefits" and not chiefly through abstractions about him.[5] We know Christ as he comes to us clothed in the gospel, such that Christ is known in his saving action. Melanchthon expresses serious doubt that a person who doesn't understand "'The Power of Sin,' 'The Law,' and 'Grace'" can ever become a Christian.[6] He says this because he sees that every Christian's personal story occurs within a much larger story, the story of creation and redemption, and it can only be understood within that

---

4. Calvin, *Institutes*, 1.1.1, 3, pp. 35, 39.
5. Philip Melanchthon, *Loci Communes Theologici*, trans. Lowell J. Satre and Wilhelm Pauck, LCC (Philadelphia: Westminster, 1969), 21. We should admit (or warn) that Melanchthon's comment has too often been distorted and misapplied. For helpful reframing, see, e.g., T. F. Torrance, *Incarnation: The Person and Life of Christ*, ed. Robert T. Walker (Downers Grove, IL: IVP Academic, 2008), 33–35; R. Michael Allen, *Justification and the Gospel: Understanding the Contexts and Controversies* (Grand Rapids: Baker Academic, 2013), 113–14.
6. Melanchthon, *Loci Communes Theologici*, 21.

larger context. Theology is not just the story about God but the story of God's dealing with his creation, and that story shapes and reshapes our lives. Further, since God's people know him most clearly through Christ, looking at the benefits of Christ reveals who this God is.

A theology of Christian life must always emphasize that the Creator is also the Sustainer and Redeemer. Only within this threefold framework—united in the one God—can we see that human life was designed to be good, and then why repentance and lament become vital when that good has been distorted, and finally how the creator God is also the same God who is able to make human life whole again. We do not have three different deities, nor is the eternal God evolving to fit the times. No. Our God acts in our history to heal us. Specifically, the Son of God sent by the Father in the Spirit also becomes truly the son of Adam. Human life is thus framed by the first and the final Adam, connecting creation with re-creation and destroying our sin. Unless we appreciate the original goodness, design, and purposes of humanity (which we outlined in the previous chapter), we will not properly appreciate what God has done in Christ, and we will miss God's vision for our lives now as Christians. In the person and work of Jesus, we discover the great grace of our God, a grace that lights up not only God's glory but also the glory of human creatures.

Eastern Orthodox theologian John Anthony McGuckin is right to observe that "the real problem today is not that men and women who have become secularized (nonreligious, or whatever) have lost the sense of God. The problem is that they have lost the sense of what it is to be truly human."[7] What, then, is the sense of being truly human?

Building upon the foundation laid in the previous chapter, we can affirm that humans were designed to worship and commune with the God who loves us. That is God's original, continuing, and final intent for human life. While there is more to being a human creature than experiencing communion with God, there is not less: When worship is disrupted, ignored, or perverted, the fullness of human flourishing is compromised even as love is disordered. To love rightly means that we respond to God, others, ourselves, and the whole created order by serving them according to their respective natures and delighting in them because they are good. This activity is asymmetric in a complex

---

7. John Anthony McGuckin, *The Eastern Orthodox Church: A New History* (New Haven, CT: Yale University Press, 2020), 302.

way: The good of a tree is different from the good of a horse; the good of God is different from that of any creature. Service to God, therefore, will differ from service to my sisters and brothers, and all of it involves both creativity and profound love. The six days of creation reflect this complexity, and God calls it all good and very good (Gen 1). Living in this richness of mutual love, delight, and creativity is what we sometimes call "human flourishing"; the Hebrew Scriptures call it "shalom."

How do love and delight fit into our relationship with God? When we see God as who he is—loving and sovereign, present and transcendent, the giver of more goodness than we will ever be able to appreciate—then we will also notice that love and delight are part of the dynamic of knowing, and vocalizing it will be a natural outflow. The more compact words for that vocalizing are *praise* and *worship*, and we do this not because God needs an ego boost but because God alone is worthy, and he amazes us. This is why our communion with God has the essential character of worship. Again, while there is more to being a human creature than experiencing communion with God, there is not less. To ignore or forget such communion is to jeopardize human flourishing and integrity, and that also tends to distort our understanding of who Jesus is and why his life, death, resurrection, and ongoing intercession are so central not simply to Christian orthodoxy but to Christian life.

John Zizioulas points out that the biblical narrative, which puts humans at the "end of creation," did so because humans are "the highest of all creatures . . . who [are] to bring the entire material world into communion with God."[8] In other words, humankind—as the "crowning glory" of creation—has the function not merely of experiencing its own awareness of God but of being a conduit through whom the rest of creation experiences the fullness of shalom.[9] This was God's original design, not a revised plan based on sin. Appreciating the grace of God and the significance of Christ's person and work requires we keep both creation's original purposes and the eschatological vision in mind. When we do, we will be ready to bask in the wonder of the incarnation. But first, we must briefly revisit the problem of sin.

---

8. John Zizioulas, *Lectures in Christian Dogmatics*, ed. Douglas H. Knight (London: T&T Clark, 2008), 94.

9. Zizioulas, *Lectures*, 95. He adds, "Man is created to fulfill the destiny of the created world, and he does this both by giving his consent on behalf of creation and by the authority he has to make use of creation."

CREATED AND RE-CREATED TO WORSHIP

The four dimensions of relation (the relational ecosystem of God, neighbor, creation, and self) can serve as a helpful matrix for making sense of what it means to be human. They also help us see the consequences of sin more fully. Sin affects not merely a small part of our lives but all of creation, including our whole selves.

Our relation with God is at the foundation of our being, so our rebellion against him also affects everything else, distorting our humanity and all our other relations in countless ways. Sin breeds oppression and apathy, cruelty as well as indifference. To be truly human means to reflect God's love for others, the creation, ourselves—and most of all for him. That love seeks the nourishment and good of others, their development and glory. Putting love toward God into action is also worship. Sin frustrates all of those created ends. So sin affects not only our relationship with God but all relationships. That rebellion against God takes us to the heart of the problem.

Sin, in all of its variations and manifestations, always destroys and undermines the deep communion and worship God created us for. Prophets like Zechariah looked forward to a day when one from David's house would come to cleanse the people "from sin and uncleanness" (Zech 13:1). He points out the idolatry (vv. 2–3) that perverted worship and the people who participated in it. Because we become or imitate what we worship (Pss 115:8; 135:18; cf. Rom 1:23), idols have godlike power over us, and consequently, we need to be restored in the image of the Creator for our healing to take place (Gen 1:27; Col 3:10). Idolatry is overcome at its root, however, only when God comes in his Messiah to take to himself the wounds of his friends (Zech 13:6), cast out idols, and restore proper worship and harmony with his people—which is the righteousness we so need. Because the Shepherd is struck on behalf of his sheep (Zech 13:6, 7), the people will eventually call upon God, and God will call them "my people," and they will say, "The LORD is my God" (Zech 13:9). Jesus the Shepherd (John 10:1–18) thus comes as the protector and Savior of Israel, knowing his sheep and laying down his life for them, calling them to respond to his voice, thus reestablishing communion between the Shepherd and the sheep. And the Scriptures also call Jesus a sheep, or—as we will see in our treatment of Revelation 4–5 at the end of this chapter—*the Lamb of God*. Somehow he is both Shepherd and sheep? How can this be?

According to the biblical story, God heals and reconciles his creation to himself not by snapping his fingers or merely saying, "Let it be so," but by becoming incarnate as this man Jesus. While the incarnate Word of God does not cease to be God, with the assumption of a human nature he also becomes what he was not: fully human. Here we return to Augustine of Hippo for help in describing this mystery.

THE NEED FOR A MEDIATOR

In *The City of God*, Augustine writes that we cannot delight and abide in God's unchangeable light until our minds have been healed of the perverting power of sin. For this purpose "the Son of God, having assumed humanity without ceasing to be God [*Homine assumto, non Deo consumto*], established and founded this same faith, so that man might have a path to man's God through the man who was God."[10] For Augustine, only with his assumed human nature can the Son act as both "mediator" and "the way," securing for us the "one way that is fully proof against all errors."[11] Only through the incarnate Son of God can renewal and healing come to sinful humanity: "God being the goal and man the way" (*quo itur Deus, qua itur homo*),[12] echoing John 14:6, affirming that Jesus is the way, the truth, and the life. In this sense, we use the word *Mediator* to designate Jesus.

John of Damascus (675–749) also comments on our need for a Mediator (although he doesn't use the word) in his work *An Exact Exposition of the Orthodox Faith*,[13] in which he summarizes the teachings of the early church fathers, notably the Cappadocians. He writes that humanity was not made bad nor even neutral but positively and emphatically good, designed for fellowship with God. John lists the kinds of

---

10. Augustine, *The City of God*, 11–22, 1/7, in The Works of Saint Augustine: A Translation for the 21st Century, trans. William Babcock (New York: New City, 2013), 11.2, p. 3 (NPNF 2, p. 206).

11. Augustine, *City of God*, 11.2, p. 3.

12. The translation of this last phrase is borrowed from the Loeb edition rather than the NPNF. See Augustine, *The City of God*, trans. David S. Wiesen, LCL (Cambridge: Harvard University Press, 1968), 11.2, pp. 430–31.

13. John of Damascus, *The Orthodox Faith*, in *St. John of Damascus: Writings*, trans. Frederic H. Chase Jr., The Fathers of the Church (Washington, DC: Catholic University of America Press, 1958), 165–406.

virtues (e.g., wisdom, absence of vice, goodness) with which humanity was made to illustrate that goodness and the fact that *humanity was created to and for communion*, especially with God. He explains, "[God] put man in communion with Himself and through this communion with Himself raised him to incorruptibility, 'for He created man incorruptible.'"[14] Sadly, sin "obscured and canceled out the characteristics of the divine image," chiefly understood in terms of the communion with God for which we were designed.[15] We were "stripped of the divine communion." Then he describes how Christ rescues us: "Since He had shared with us what was better and we had not kept it, He now takes His share of what is worse, of our nature I mean to say, that through Himself and in Himself He may restore what was to His image and what to His likeness, while also teaching us the virtuous way of life."[16] Here is both representation and imitation. According to John and the tradition, God is redeeming us from the "tyranny of the devil," overcoming sin and death in the process, all in and through Christ, and all with the purpose of healing what had been lost or destroyed, namely our communion with the creator Lord. Even without the word itself, we have here another description of Christ's work as Mediator, restoring our communion with God and others through himself.

In other contexts, a mediator is a third party, often neutral, reconciling two other parties that are at odds with each other. Some modern presentations of the gospel imply that Jesus Christ is a third party between us and God, which could be misleading. Instead, Christ the Mediator is the union of the being of God and humanity. The person of the Mediator is the one incarnate Son of God (1 Tim 2:5). Jesus of Nazareth mediates for us because he is both fully God and fully man, reconciling us to God.

Affirming that the Savior is both uncreated Word and created man naturally takes us to some complicated areas of theology, but Augustine shows us why we affirm both his full divinity and his full humanity. Preaching from John's gospel, Augustine commented, "He knew how, at the same time, *to hate in each one of us what we made* [i.e., sin], and *to love what he made* [i.e., us in his image]."[17] Here the Father of Western

---

14. John of Damascus, *The Orthodox Faith*, 4.4, p. 337.
15. John of Damascus, *The Orthodox Faith*, 4.4, pp. 337–38.
16. John of Damascus, *The Orthodox Faith*, 4.4, p. 338.
17. Augustine, *John's Gospel*, 110.6 (NPNF 7, p. 411), trans. and quoted in Calvin's *Institutes*, 2.16.4, p. 507, emphasis mine.

orthodoxy is careful neither to belittle God's good creation nor to ignore or downplay sin. Loving us as his own, the triune Creator resolved to destroy the sin that had so distorted us.

We needed reconciliation and healing, but how were they to be achieved? In his *Confessions*, Augustine comments that others tried to "make their way back to you [God]" but didn't have the power, wisdom, or righteousness, thus making them vulnerable to temptation by false spirits and sinful distortions.[18] Because we are now "mortal and sinful" humanity, we need a "mediator to stand between God and men who should be in one respect like God, in another kin to human beings, for if he were manlike in both regards he would be far from God, but if Godlike in both, far from us; and then he would be no mediator."[19] Our theology of Christian life will be built on the dual affirmation that the Mediator is fully divine and fully human.

A Just, Faithful, and Loving Mediator

This Mediator "appeared to stand between mortal sinners and the God who is immortal and just: like us he was mortal, but like God he was just."[20] But why do Augustine and others talk of justice in relation to the Mediator? Does he view God as a divine accountant who frets about keeping lists of rights and wrongs and then seeing how the balance sheet ends up? That kind of imagery can appear in Augustine and others in the Western tradition, but we need to examine the deeper concerns that drove their attention to justice and righteousness, keeping in mind the connections between reconciliation and justice in the Scriptures.

To put it another way, if justice is not chiefly a matter of accountancy—a matter of balancing so much sin with so much punishment—what is it about? It is chiefly about setting things right, about restoring shalom, about fulfilling the covenant. Yes, it also involves chastisement, punishment, and the annihilation of anything that threatens God's people. But these, also, have the further goal of restoring shalom. Thus a just or right life has always been a matter of walking in the ways of the covenant. For example, in Genesis 15:6, when Abraham responds with faith to God's promises, God assesses this as "righteousness"—or perhaps "rightness"

---

18. Augustine, *The Confessions*, ed. John E. Rotelle, trans. Maria Boulding, 2nd ed. (Hyde Park, NY: New City, 1997), 10.67, p. 281.
19. Augustine, *Confessions*, 10.67, pp. 281–82.
20. Augustine, *Confessions*, 10.68, p. 282.

is the better translation—precisely because it is the response appropriate to God's covenant promises. Augustine goes further, writing that even before the fall, good human creatures were dependent upon the Creator "to retain the life of justice."[21] This reminds us that obedience to God and his commandments has always been fundamentally about *life*—human flourishing, in the context of loving communion with the good Creator. Sin destroys all of that. Augustine gives his view of the relational dynamics of righteousness when he declares, "Now the wage due to justice is life and peace," but since sinful humanity disobeyed God, life and peace were lost to violence and death. He calls this "slavery," saying that only God's grace and mercy embodied in Christ are able to liberate us and enable the Creator-creature communion to be restored.[22] As Augustine also says, "Through the justice whereby [Christ] was one with God he broke the power of death on behalf of malefactors rendered just" (cf. 2 Tim 1:10; Rom 4:5).[23]

What we needed was to be set right. This is biblical justice. This is God's act of grace in Christ. The issues are set within a relational structure of creation and covenant, which is the grounding of the laws. Human rightness—our reflection of the eternal divine glory—is a matter of responding rightly to God. But what is a reasonable, appropriate response to the one who combines abundant grace, the tenderest love of a parent, the astonishing beauty of the stars, and endlessly engaging creativity—all in someone who actually pays gentle attention to us? Such a response would combine thankfulness, affection, delight, praise, shouts of joy—in a word, *worship*! Disobedience is a failure of worship and a rejection of joy, and this, in turn, corrupts our horizontal relationship with the rest of creation, including our neighbors and ourselves.

A word about forgiveness and Christian life is needed here. "To forgive" in common English primarily has a subjective content (to cease blaming or feeling anger toward someone for an offense) and secondarily a more objective content (to cease requiring payment or punishment for an offense). Christian contexts, perhaps oddly, sometimes reverse that order and use "forgive" chiefly to mean "acquit, set free from a legal charge." We sinners clearly need both from God. But the gospel is too

---

21. Augustine, *The Enchiridion on Faith, Hope, and Charity*, ed. Boniface Ramsey, trans. Bruce Harbert (Hyde Park, NY: New City, 1999), §106, p. 335.
22. Augustine, *The Enchiridion on Faith, Hope, and Charity*, §106, p. 335.
23. Augustine, *Confessions*, 10.68, p. 282.

often reduced to a courtroom transaction of dismissing legal charges against us, ignoring not only the gospel's personal aspects but also the conquest of our spiritual enemies and the healing of our souls. God's aim is the restoration of communion, in which we love God and neighbor while living in right relation with the rest of his creation. The biblical imagery of marriage and adoption, for example, shows us this.

All of it has a legal and declarative aspect, but that does not constitute the heart of the matter. As Michael Horton comments, "In covenant theology, the legal and relational aspects are never set at odds, as they typically are in modern theology."[24] This brings us back to the problem of reductionist accounts that treat the forgiveness of sins as the beginning and end of the gospel. Horton rightly reminds us, "It is not simply forgiveness of sins that is required . . . for a right relationship with God, but obedience—conformity to God's righteous statutes, love of God and neighbor that is not abstract or generalized, but concrete and particular. God is looking for the holiness, righteousness, and justice that he created us to exhibit as image-bearers."[25] The Gospels refer to the Old Testament to exhibit the significance of not only Christ's death but his whole life of faith as well.[26] Again Horton: "That which he offered was not merely a sacrifice of atonement, but an obedient *life*. At the end of the day, it is not sacrifice but obedience (*ḥesed*, covenant love) in which God delights (Ps 51:16–17; Isa 1:11; Hos 6:6)."[27]

Caspar Olevianus (1536–1587) exemplifies early Protestant efforts to articulate the importance of Christ as Mediator to Christian life. In sum, "the main reason" that we needed a Savior who is fully God and fully human is "that God wanted to declare His infinite love."[28] Olevianus and the tradition highly value what is often lost or ignored in our day: The eternal Son did not take on a human nature merely for one dramatic moment in history but permanently—that is, *he would "never again" set aside his human nature*.[29] "Becoming human" was not a temporary necessity for accomplishing something else. No, the Father sent the Son to assume a human nature and to maintain his love and solidarity

---

24. Michael S. Horton, *Lord and Servant: A Covenant Christology* (Louisville: Westminster John Knox, 2005), 223.
25. Horton, *Lord and Servant*, 224.
26. Horton, *Lord and Servant*, 225.
27. Horton, *Lord and Servant*, 226, emphasis original.
28. Caspar Olevianus, *An Exposition of the Apostles' Creed*, trans. Lyle D. Bierma (Grand Rapids: Reformation Heritage, 2009), 70.
29. Olevianus, *An Exposition of the Apostles' Creed*, 68.

with his children in the rightness for which he made us. Thus did God "declare simultaneously His unchangeable justice and wrath against sin and His mercy toward us."[30] Here two distinct expressions appear to be in tension—wrath versus mercy, justice versus communion—but they are not. God's wrath against sin accomplishes his mercy toward us; his justice, which consists in setting us right, restores the communion we had lost. While we are tempted to pick between these terms, much of the Christian tradition viewed this as a false choice. Justice was not the manifestation of a disgruntled deity but the strong arm of a Father protecting and rescuing us. Like a virus that clings to and destroys healthy cells, sin attached to all humanity, and it kills us and all the good of God's creation. God's justice and wrath are not the unthinking outburst of a temperamental curmudgeon against an unruly bunch of people who have spoiled his plans, after the manner of the unneighborly neighbor who yells, "Get off the grass!" at passing children and turns the sprinklers on to punish them. Rather, like chemotherapy is needed in the fight against the plague of cancer, justice or wrath is needed to fight against the plague of sin. Wrath consists in the destruction of that which would destroy us; justice is the larger picture of our restoring us to the place where we belong and fitting us for it.

Our Elder Brother and Priest

We are often tempted to wonder why God doesn't just immediately dismiss the problem of sin with a spoken word. It seems so unnecessary or even overly dramatic to claim that the eternal Word of God must become "man." But here is an example where the tradition takes creation far more seriously than we tend to, which means it also takes the concreteness of sin more seriously than we do. As Olevianus explains, "he punished sin in human flesh, indeed in the flesh of His only begotten Son" because only in this way could he "show His mercy in such a way as not to deny His justice."[31] Then he draws on language that only rarely appears in the Scriptures (Titus 3:4; cf. Acts 27:3; 28:2) but is used by some key patristic authors, like Athanasius,[32] and later even by

---

30. Olevianus, *An Exposition of the Apostles' Creed*, 68–69.
31. Olevianus, *An Exposition of the Apostles' Creed*, 69.
32. For a treatment of Athanasius's use of this specific term, which T. F. Torrance calls "Athanasius' favourite word for God's active love toward us," see Torrance, *The Trinitarian Faith: The Evangelical Theology of the Ancient Catholic Church* (Edinburgh: T&T Clark, 1998), 74, 147–48.

Puritans like John Owen.³³ *Philanthropia* (φιλανθροπία) means "lover of humanity," and this impulse of the Creator informs our understanding of Christ and his purposes: "The justice and mercy, or φιλανθροπία, of God wonderfully and with perfect wisdom converge in Christ Jesus."³⁴ The patristic tradition all the way through the Reformers like Olevianus stresses that out of God's love for humanity the Son assumes a human nature, not just for a time, but rather he promises never to set it aside, for that is now "him." The Son is now eternally the *enfleshed* Son, the great embodiment of the philanthropic love of God: His people, as part of his body, are now secure in the eternal life and love of the triune God.

By becoming human, not only does Christ become a substitute and sacrifice, but he also takes on the role of being our "brother." As Calvin states, "We are often reminded that the biblical doctrine of adoption brings us into the warm embrace of our Heavenly Father, but we don't always remember that at the same time this act of God also makes Christ our brother. As Mediator, Christ deals with us "in a brotherly way" because he now is truly and will "eternally remain our Brother."³⁵ The author of Hebrews tells us that Christ our elder brother not only suffered on our behalf; he also now leads our singing and praise of God "in the midst of the congregation" (Heb 2:11–12). We trust him who "partook of the same" flesh and blood as ours so that he "might destroy the one who has the power of death, that is the devil." In the process Christ our elder brother delivers us from slavery (2:14–15). The chapter then concludes, "Therefore he had to be made like his brothers [and sisters] in every respect, so that he might become a merciful and faithful high priest in the service of God, to make propitiation for the sins of the people" (2:17). That is, having personally united us to himself and living in faithful worship of God, he now leads us in his continuing worship of God. Understanding his representative role and our participation in his life is vital to a theologically and pastorally robust vision of Christian life. Although we will circle back to this theme in chapter 6 on Messiah, we do well to spend more time laying the groundwork here.

---

33. E.g., Owen, *Works*, 2:29. For more background on this discussion, see Kelly M. Kapic, *Communion with God: The Divine and the Human in the Theology of John Owen* (2007; repr., Grand Rapids: Baker Academic, 2024), 173–74.

34. Olevianus, *An Exposition of the Apostles' Creed*, 69. Cf. Herman Witsius in *The Economy of the Covenants Between God and Man: Comprehending a Complete Body of Divinity* (Edinburgh: Turnbull, 1803), 2.1.4, p. 169.

35. Olevianus, *An Exposition of the Apostles' Creed*, 69.

Jesus, as the Son incarnate, is the *eschatos* ("final") Adam (1 Cor 15:45–47). Unlike the first Adam, he faithfully obeys the Father as he depends on life and provision from the Spirit. Christ's obedient life was what we might simply call a life of perpetual *worship and communion*! As Augustine argues in his *Enchiridion*, by living and dying "without sin," the incarnate Mediator fulfilled a life of perfect human dependence upon and love of the Father, and this is the life he presents in sacrifice to the Father as the life we should have lived. Only in this specific way could "human pride . . . be rebuked and healed by the humility of God." Jesus reveals "how far [humanity] had wandered from God" even as he calls us back, and in so doing he also provided "an example of obedience."[36] To see this as solving a mathematical problem of merits and demerits distorts the whole picture.[37] Augustine and the others who, in the long history of Christian theology, have examined the meaning of the life and death of Jesus had their eyes on the resulting restoration, forgiveness, healing, and hope for humanity. Thus not only does Jesus provide a model for how to live as those who are now filled with God's Spirit; he also continually supplies us life and strength and guidance by that same Spirit (John 14:16; 15:1–11), drawing us back into the life-giving worship that we abandoned but toward which we are headed (Heb 2). Let's pause to make sure we are understanding the key point.

Just as the Messiah represents God's philanthropic love for us (*philanthropia*), he also represents, embodies, and accomplishes human love for God (*philotheia* or *theophilia*). Jesus is the faithful worshiper, the head of Israel, restoring Israel from unfaithfulness by a life of unbreakable communion with God and sinless relations with his sinful neighbors. Jesus is the representative, the covenant keeper, the final Adam. He embodies Israel, with his church functioning as his body, of which he is the head (e.g., Eph 1:22; 5:23; Col 1:18; 2:10).[38] In all of these metaphors and other imagery, beyond being sinless, Jesus positively accomplishes

---

36. Augustine, *The Enchiridion on Faith, Hope, and Charity*, §108, p. 336.

37. Having said that, we should not too quickly dismiss this concern about "demerits" and "merits," since rightly understood it has a long history in the Christian tradition, especially regarding one's treatment of the poor. While this topic is particularly hard for those of us who are Protestant, I do wish we would listen carefully to Gary A. Anderson's provocative but deeply informed study, *Charity: The Place of the Poor in the Biblical Tradition* (New Haven, CT: Yale University Press, 2013).

38. For more on Jesus's identity and relationship to Israel, and then how the church relates, see e.g., David E. Holwerda, *Jesus and Israel: One Covenant or Two?* (Grand Rapids: Eerdmans, 1995), esp. 27–58.

a life of right human relations with the Father in the Spirit.[39] And so when Jesus dies, he does so as one who does not deserve death; he is an innocent Lamb offered for the sake of his people, giving his life for theirs. Augustine is worth quoting at length on this as it shapes his prayer:

> For our sake he stood to you [the Father] as both victor and victim, and victor because victim; for us he stood to you as priest and sacrifice, and priest because sacrifice, making us sons and daughters to you instead of servants by being born of you to serve us. With good reason is there solid hope for me in him, because you will heal all my infirmities through him who sits at your right hand and intercedes for us. Were it not so, I would despair. Many and grave are those infirmities, many and grave; but wider-reaching is your healing power. We might have despaired, thinking your Word remote from any conjunction with humankind, had he not become flesh and made his dwelling among us.[40]

To this Mediator the prophets pointed forward, and to this same Mediator's life, death, and resurrection we now continue to look. Believers are all joined to him by the faith in which he implants us, and which is always centered on him personally, not just on some indefinite divine power or presence—and it is by and through him that we exercise our faith and our worship.

John Calvin similarly emphasized the unique centrality of Jesus as our eternal and abiding Mediator against what he perceived was the temptation to treat other leaders as our mediators. His concern was that praying to historic saints or treating living priests as needed for our access to God risked undermining the uniqueness of Christ's mediatorial role and the grace it embodies and provides. Calvin insisted that when it comes to the mediation of Christ, less is more: Multiplying would-be mediators

---

39. Friedrich Schleiermacher makes some useful observations about Jesus having the most complete "God-consciousness" or "feeling of absolute dependence" possible for a human. Explaining Christ's sinlessness, for example, he writes that "in Christ every element of his behavior had to have been determined by God-consciousness." Schleiermacher, *Christian Faith: A New Translation and Critical Edition*, trans. Terrence N. Nice, Catherine L. Kelsey, and Edwina Lawler, vol. 3 (Louisville: Westminster John Knox, 2016), 98, p. 2:610. Whether or not one appreciates Schleiermacher's account, we should see the importance of Jesus's sinlessness like Schleiermacher, who avoided the more trivial interpretation of making it merely about not doing "bad" things and instead seeing it manifested in his life of ongoing dependence and unbroken communion (my word) with the Father.

40. Augustine, *Confessions*, 10.69, p. 283.

obscures the one true Mediator between God and humans. Failure to appreciate Christ's singularity as Mediator "obscures" both the "glory of his birth" (incarnation) and risks making "void the cross" (atonement).[41] Appealing to inferior mediators—who are no mediators at all—would introduce barriers to God rather than the personal access secured through Jesus's life, death, resurrection, and ongoing heavenly intercession on our behalf. Calvin had high regard for gospel ministers, but they could never function even as a lesser version of the one Mediator. As Calvin makes clear, Jesus alone is our advocate when we sin (1 John 2:1), and his ongoing incarnate existence at the right hand of God *is* our continued intercession (Rom 8:34). He alone is the "greatest and truest priest of the Church," and he alone is able to represent humanity to God.[42]

Some common misunderstandings of Christ's role as heavenly Mediator do persistently misrepresent the good news. We find this when Jesus is seen as the kindness of God and the Father as the wrath or anger of God, for example, seeing Christ as trying to persuade the angry Father to forgive us. Calvin rejects this false portrait, making it clear that Jesus is not just a human representative but the personal embodiment of God, revealing the love that God has for us. The incarnate Son is the self-revelation of the Father. Thus the ascended Christ should not be pictured as "kneeling before God" and "pleading" on our behalf, since that seems to misunderstand the significance of the incarnation and the cross in the first place. Instead, "the power of his death avails as an everlasting intercession in our behalf" as both the expression of God's holy love and the victory of that just love over the ongoing taunts of sin, death, and the devil.[43]

But why does Jesus, as our elder brother and Priest, matter so much? Why do these images have particular importance in a theology of Christian life? In a later chapter, when we explore Christ's leading role in our liturgy of communal worship, we will more fully discuss Christ's role as Prophet, Priest, and King. But here we need to appreciate how his role as Priest and human representative makes him not just the voice of God's grace but the agent of it. Ambrose lays it out for us beautifully when he states that the incarnate Son "is our mouth, through which we speak to the Father; he is our eye, through which we see the Father; he is

---

41. Calvin, *Institutes*, 3.21, p. 879.
42. Calvin, *Institutes*, 3.20, p. 878.
43. Calvin, *Institutes*, 3.20, p. 878.

our right hand, through which we offer ourselves to the Father. Unless he intercedes, there is no intercourse with God either for us or for all saints.'"[44] To move from seeing grace as merely an idea to seeing it instead as central to the gospel of King Jesus—because the Christ *is* the grace—we will need to see how he is both our head representative (Priest, Prophet, King, and elder brother) and the object of our worship (our God). That is why he, in his incarnate life, is the way of grace for fallen humanity.

CENTERING CHRISTIAN LIFE ON THE LIFE OF CHRIST

What does it mean to live a life shaped by Christ—that is, Christian life? And if, as I am arguing, the heartbeat of a theology of Christian life is worship and communion, then how do the life, death, and resurrection of Christ the Mediator shape that worship and thus form Christian life?

J.-J. von Allmen states that the New Testament frames the Christian response to God through the entire life of Jesus, seeing this reflected, for example, in how the Synoptic Gospels are structured.[45] Although other writers are far more hesitant to say that the authors of Matthew, Mark, and Luke purposely employed in their books a strong pattern taken from early liturgies, we can at least say that the basic pattern and framework of the Gospels anticipate and even strongly point to later liturgical patterns. Let me summarize the broad outline of the synoptic pattern as Allmen paints it (my paraphrase and italics):[46]

- First, they assert and confirm the *coming* of the Messiah.
- Second, they focus on the *preaching* of Christ and his calling—especially during his Galilean ministry—for the *people to respond* in faith and new life.
- Third, they turn their focus to Jerusalem in particular, concentrating on *Jesus's death*, but then also the eschatological "irruption" [sic] of *his resurrection*.

---

44. Ambrose, *On Isaac or the Soul*, 8.75 (CSEL 32.694; MPL 14.520). Cited here by Calvin, *Institutes*, 3.21, p. 879.

45. J.-J. von Allmen, *Worship: Its Theology and Practice* (New York: Oxford University Press, 1965). This book is both provocative and stimulating, peculiar yet brimming with insights. Although I only discovered this volume after I had begun my research, it became clear that Allman and I shared many intuitions and reading of the material, especially about the christological importance of rightly understanding Christian worship and, by implication, Christian life.

46. Von Allmen, *Worship*, 22–23.

- Fourth, Jesus *blesses* and leaves his disciples, *sending* them to bear witness to the world.

From this basic pattern and plenty of other biblical material, von Allmen gains a conviction that the New Testament presents the entire life and ministry of Jesus the Messiah as central to Christian existence: "His whole life [serves] as a liturgical process and in fact as *the* liturgy, *the* life of worship, accepted by God."[47] He adds that "the Christological basis of the Church's worship consists of the ministry of Jesus, the act of perfect worship which He made of His life. It is of this messianic cult that the Church is both a memorial and an effective echo."[48] While one could debate the details of von Allmen's structural reading of the Synoptics as purposely laying out a liturgical framework by their very design, his more important point is correct and helpful: He reminds us to connect Christ, worship, and the earliest church's instincts to respond in faith, praise, and devotion, all of which inevitably have liturgical significance. This then becomes how later Christians are formed in word and deed, faith and life, communally and personally. While later chapters will be needed to explore more fully the relationship between Christ and liturgical patterns, this chapter will lay the groundwork for how the incarnate Son is both the object and leader of our worship and thus also of our Christian life. Only by appreciating Christ as Mediator in this way can we fully appreciate the grace of God that is ours in Christ by his Spirit.

Josef Jungmann's seminal work *The Place of Christ in Liturgical Prayer* has provoked discussion since it was first published in 1925.[49] In this work, which is steeped in readings from the ancient church and early twentieth-century liturgical studies, Jungmann spots a concerning development in the history of the church's worship. Originally, he believes, the biblical and earliest church's practice was to offer prayers *to* God *through* the Son and *in* the Spirit. In this way, Jesus the Christ was the mediator (1 Tim 2:5) representing us to God; one did not pray

---

47. Von Allmen, *Worship*, 23, emphasis mine.
48. Von Allmen, *Worship*, 25.
49. Josef A. Jungmann, *The Place of Christ in Liturgical Prayer* (Cambridge: Cambridge University Press, 1989). The original German edition was published in 1925. Also of great importance is Josef A. Jungmann, "The Defeat of Teutonic Arianism and the Revolution in Religious Culture in the Early Middle Ages," in *Pastoral Liturgy* (New York: Herder and Herder, 1962), 1–101.

to Christ, but one prayed *through* the messianic representative. But later practice shifted toward offering prayers *to* the Son (*ad Christum*) and not simply *through* the Son (*per Christum*). Jungmann believes this may have occurred primarily as an overreaction to the rise of Arianism. But when the Orthodox made this change, offering prayers to the Son and the Spirit instead of using the earlier Trinitarian pattern of worshiping *in* the Spirit *through* the Son *to* the Father, Jungmann believes it may have had the unintended consequence of undermining the full humanity of Jesus the Savior. The challenge here is that of liturgically reflecting both the full divinity and full humanity of Christ.

While Jungmann rightly brings out the rich Trinitarian liturgical approach to God used by the early church, in my opinion his observation fails to appreciate the significance of our worship directed to the Son in his unique mediatorial role. Put differently, we ought to avoid picking between the *per Christum* and *ad Christum*, instead putting both at the center of Christian worship and, as I will argue, at the center of our theology of Christian life.

I am not alone in sharing this response to Jungmann's conclusions: Recent scholarship has demonstrated problems with his somewhat lopsided theory. There is significant early evidence—including biblical evidence—that worship was directed not just through Christ, but *to* him.[50] I think we can learn a great deal from Jungmann's emphasis on Christ as the one who represents us in our praises and prayers, but we must not undervalue or neglect an equally significant and vital aspect of Christ's ministry: Even as Jesus leads our prayers and praises, he is also the object of them.

How do we make sense of these two currents of worship? How is it that we offer our prayers and worship to the Father *through* the Son, and yet also *to* the Son?

A rightly constructed theology of Christian life is built upon the Spirit-led recognition of God in Christ, our Mediator, who represents God to us and us to God. This foundation leads us to affirm Jesus both as the lead worshiper (the faithful, pious, perfectly righteous, covenant-keeping Messiah) and as the one worthy of worship (as *God* incarnate). This strange and mysterious dynamic has never been easy for the church

---

50. See esp. the volume Bryan D. Spinks edited in response to Jungmann: Spinks, *The Place of Christ in Liturgical Prayer: Trinity, Christology, and Liturgical Theology* (Collegeville, MN: Liturgical, 2008).

to articulate, although, as the creedal efforts of Nicaea and Chalcedon maintain and as the church's prayers and praises echo, this understanding does animate the Christian faith.

For the rest of the chapter, I want us to see how Christ as Mediator—representing both God to us and us to God—grounds and animates Christian life. To that end, we will draw from Athanasius, who was so important to Nicaea, and then go back further to explore how Revelation chapters 4–5 demonstrate this dual dynamic of the one who is both the lead worshiper and the one worshiped, since this biblical material shaped the ancient Christian presentations on Christ as Mediator and the center of our Christian life.

HOW CAN JESUS REPRESENT BOTH GOD TO US AND US TO GOD?

As is well known, Athanasius tirelessly gave himself to defeat the deeply flawed teaching of Arius, who rejected belief that the Son was the eternal God of God, light of light, true God of true God. Arius[51] affirmed that the Son was an exalted and even praiseworthy creature, but always and inevitably still a creature and not the Creator. Striving to maintain biblical reverence and worship of the eternal Son of God, Athanasius insisted that the Son is none other than "God from God."[52] But he also affirmed that this eternal Word became truly and fully human and, in this unique and distinct way, serves as the one Mediator uniting us with God. A closer look at Athanasius's refutation of Arian Christology can bring greater clarity to Christ's role as both the one worshiped and the lead worshiper.

The Arians were bothered by an important question: How could Jesus be considered "God" since Scripture describes him in very human terms, not only because he was known for hungering, sleeping, and weeping, but also as receiving and getting, and then even being exalted to God's right hand (citing Matt 28:18; John 10:18; Phil 2:9; Eph 1:20).[53]

---

51. NB, it is true that the actual historical Arius is probably far less significant than we often imagined, but for our purposes, we will not be able to unpack those nuances. For more, see Steve Holmes, *The Quest for the Trinity: The Doctrine of God in Scripture, History, and Modernity* (Downers Grove, IL: IVP Academic, 2012), esp. 83–88; and Rowan Williams, *Arius: Heresy and Tradition*, 2nd ed. (London: SCM, 2001).

52. Athanasius, *Against the Arians*, "Discourse IV," §1, NPNF 4:433.

53. Athanasius, *Against the Arians*, "Discourse IV," §6, NPNF 4:435.

Don't these kinds of expressions show that Jesus is merely a creature dependent upon God and is not God himself?

While we may be tempted to respond by ignoring the very creaturely actions and attitudes of Jesus in the Gospels that the Arians draw attention to, Athanasius instead insists that we take on the full witness of the Scriptures. The answer is to deny neither his humanity nor his divinity but to see how they relate in his person and why it matters for us. If we undermine the humanity of Christ to secure his divinity—something Apollinaris does and some scholars believe Athanasius occasionally flirted with—we lose sight of the profound good news of the gospel. Our hope lies in the fact that the eternally begotten Son of God "became Son of Man," and in this incarnation became the sole "Mediator between God and men." Why is this so vital? So that "He might minister *the things of God to us, and ours to God*."[54] Here Athanasius captures the truth that the incarnate Christ is not only the great revelation of God but also our Savior.

As our Mediator, the incarnate Son stands in our place as our representative: He takes our weak, distorted, even sinfully sullied attempts at faithfulness and praising God, and he makes them beautiful and right. This is the embodiment of grace. He receives "our human affections [including our weeping and weariness] . . . from us and offers [them] to the Father, interceding for us, that in Him" this sense of feeling forsaken, this hunger and hurt will end.[55] As Athanasius makes clear earlier, these "affections" or sufferings refer to the fact that the God who does not sleep, eat, weep, or die now endures these experiences for our good and our salvation by taking on our flesh. "He bore a true body, and that it was His own," and by taking on a real and particular human nature, he became the new Adam, acting on behalf of fallen humanity, restoring what had been lost.[56] And what had been lost? True, free, loving communion with God. Therefore, what Christ receives as incarnate, he receives on our behalf, since "these are gifts given from God to us through Him,"[57] since the eternal Son has no needs (cf. Phil 2).

Athanasius explicitly states that "the reason of His becoming man" was that the gifts or grace of God would be given to us through Christ

---

54. Athanasius, *Against the Arians*, "Discourse IV," §6, NPNF 4:435, emphasis mine.
55. Athanasius, *Against the Arians*, "Discourse IV," §6, NPNF 4:435.
56. Athanasius, *Against the Arians*, "Discourse III," §41, NPNF 4:416.
57. Athanasius, *Against the Arians*, "Discourse IV," §6, NPNF 4:435.

as Mediator. "For of such gifts *mere* man had not become worthy; and again the *mere* Word had not needed them."[58] So we need God's gifts of grace, of life, of holiness, all of which the eternal Son already has in his communion within the Trinity. Through the union of the human and divine natures in the person of the Son we have the realized reconciliation of Creator and creature.

Part of the problem that Athanasius sees is not only that we need the gifts of God but that even when God's gifts have been given to us, as to Adam in the garden, we squander those gifts, and as God gives them to man "he is liable to lose them again."[59] Put differently, one cannot just entrust fallen humanity with healing in itself because humanity has shown itself unable to stay healed. And yet the healing is, of course, *human* healing (as Anselm emphasized[60]). So the incarnate Son "received humanly" what we need, and yet there is assurance that "the grant is lodged with Him, [that] the grace may remain sure." This is what makes the grace then "irrevocable," based not on our faithfulness in keeping God's gifts, but on Christ, since "He Himself appropriates the gift."[61]

Employing a fairly common patristic hermeneutic, Athanasius reads the Gospels as testifying to the divine and human natures of Christ in the way Jesus does what only humans do (e.g., sleeping and dying) and has power that only God has (e.g., raising the dead and forgiving sin).[62] Thus while God needs nothing, Jesus as a man needs and receives. While God has no body, the incarnate Son has a body. Again, Athanasius shows the tightly woven patristic hermeneutic in his third discourse against the Arians when he navigates the textual evidence for claiming that Christ is both God and human—as not two but one person: "When there was need to raise Peter's wife's mother, who was sick of a fever, He stretched forth His hand humanly, but He stopped the illness divinely. And in the case of the man blind from the birth,

---

58. Athanasius, *Against the Arians*, "Discourse IV," §6, NPNF 4:435.
59. Athanasius, *Against the Arians*, "Discourse III," §38, NPNF 4:415.
60. A vital part of Anselm's argument in *Cur Deus Homo* is that the problem is fundamentally a *human* problem, not a divine one. One might charitably convey Anslem's argument as communicating that *humanity* had a need it could not fix; God had the resources to handle the need, but he himself wasn't the one who needed fixing. Humans, not God, were in need of rescue, healing, and reconciliation. For the healing and restoration to take place, you needed a theanthropic person – one who was perfectly human and perfectly divine. See Anselm, *Why God Became Man*, in *Anselm of Canterbury: The Major Works*, ed. Brian Davies and G. R. Evans (Oxford: Oxford University Press, 1998), 260–356.
61. Athanasius, *Against the Arians*, "Discourse III," §38, NPNF 4:415.
62. Athanasius, *Against the Arians*, "Discourse III," §40, NPNF 4:416.

human was the spittle which He gave forth from the flesh, but divinely did He open the eyes through the clay. And in the case of Lazarus, He gave forth a human voice, as man; but divinely, as God, did He raise Lazarus from the dead."[63] While there is some significant debate about potential problems with this hermeneutic, which could very easily slip into a multiple-personality Christ rather than a unified person, it was a common way to make sense of Jesus's identity in the Gospels.[64] Jesus's identity at the same time is affirmed as the eternal Word and yet also as the son of Mary, a single person who hungered and thirsted, who prayed and worshiped. Ty Kieser helpfully summarizes: "It is not that either nature of agency 'accomplishes' actions, since it is the theandric agent who performs actions 'by means of' both capacities."[65]

Roman Catholic priest and theologian Thomas Weinandy knows how easily this kind of partitive exegesis can go wrong so that you end up with Jesus as two distinct people: one divine and one human. Reflecting the intention and hope of the tradition (including Athanasius and Augustine), Weinandy wants us to be captured by the wonder of the incarnation, where we have one person who uniquely has both a divine and human nature. Drawing from Cyril of Alexandria, Weinandy concludes, "Within the incarnation the Son of God never does anything as God. If he did, he would be acting as God *in a man*."[66] The concern is that once the eternal Son assumes human nature and becomes "man," you don't have two different people (a divine person and a human person, or Nestorianism); there is the *one* incarnate Son, Jesus of Nazareth. If union of the natures is not tightly maintained, we end up succumbing to a form of adoptionism in which God is acting *through a man* rather

---

63. Athanasius, *Against the Arians*, "Discourse III," §32, NPNF 4:411.

64. Augustine is also a classic example of this approach. See Augustine, *On the Trinity (De Trinitate)*, ed. John E. Rotelle, trans. Edmund Hill, The Works of Saint Augustine: A Translation for the 21st Century (New York: New City, 1991), 1.3, pp. 74–81. Cf. Adonis Vidu who argues, "It is fundamentally mistaken . . . to distinguish between discrete activities of Christ: This carried in virtue of his human nature; that carried in virtue of his divinity. By becoming flesh, by entering into time and space, all divine activities unfold in a finite dimension and therefore are necessarily manifested in this way. . . . Christ does everything in a theandric way, which is not to deny the distinction between the operations but only to refuse to distinguish different works by this." Vidu, *The Same God Who Works All Things: Inseparable Operations in Trinitarian Theology* (Grand Rapids: Eerdmans, 2021), 207.

65. Ty Kieser, *Theandric and Triune: John Owen and Christological Agency*, T&T Clark Studies in Systematic Theology (London: T&T Clark, 2024), 200.

66. Thomas Weinandy, *Does God Suffer?* (Notre Dame: University of Notre Dame Press, 2000), 205. Emphasis original. For an excellent edition of Cyril's work, see Cyril of Alexandria, *On the Unity of Christ*, trans. John Anthony McGuckin (Crestwood, NY: St. Vladimir's Seminary Press, 1995).

than Jesus being the incarnate Son of God. But there is no Jesus apart from the Son, for he is the Son incarnate. He is not alternatively moving between divine and human, since it is the theandric *Jesus* who acts. What Weinandy highlights is that you don't have two separate people: a divine person and a human person. Since the incarnate Son is fully human, he always acts humanly, which is why, for example, we can speak of Jesus worshiping the Father. Jesus, the Son of God, is a particular person, but he is unique in that he alone has two natures. Adoptionism, as Weinandy warns against, is the danger of having a full human being that the Son then takes on to accomplish something, which would mean that you have a full human *before* the assumption by the Son takes place. Whether that happens in the womb of Mary or at the scene of Jesus's baptism, it would be an instance of what is called "adoptionism," and we could not rightly consider Jesus *himself* to be God, but only a man used by God.

Orthodoxy teaches otherwise: The Son assumes a human nature, not a human person. The human named Jesus never was nor ever will be anyone other than the Son of God incarnate. Without getting bogged down in discussions about the *communication of attributes*, we must not miss the key point. He is not *in* a man; he *becomes* a man, assuming a real human nature and all that is entailed by it, sin excepted. As T. F. Torrance explains, "This one person means that his human nature had *no independent subsistence* or *hypostasis*, no independent centre of personal being."[67] There is only one person, and that is the incarnate Son of God, and so all that he does is done not by a separate or isolated nature but by the one person of Christ. This is why Jesus can do what only God can do (e.g., forgive sins) and what only a creature can do (e.g., sleep). The Son of God *as man* eats carrots, and the incarnate Son of God raises Lazarus. Again Weinandy: "All that Jesus did as the Son of God was done *as a man*—whether it was eating carrots or raising someone from the dead. He may have raised Lazarus from the dead by his divine power or, better, by the power of the Holy Spirit, but it was, nonetheless, as man that he

---

67. See T. F. Torrance, *The Incarnation: The Person and Life of Christ*, ed. Robert T. Walker (Downers Grove, IL: InterVarsity Press, 2008), 229. Torrance then draws on the crucial anhypostasis/en-hypostasia distinction and summarizes: "The *anhypostasia* stresses the *general* humanity of Jesus, the human nature assumed by the Son with its *hypostasis* in the Son, but *enhypostasia* stresses the *particular* humanity of the one man Jesus, whose person is not other than the person of the divine Son" (229–30, emphasis in original). See also the careful articulation by Fred Sanders, "Introduction to Christology: Chalcedonian Categories for the Gospel Narrative," in *Jesus in Trinitarian Perspective*, ed. Fred Sanders and Klaus Issler (Nashville: B&H, 2007), 31–32.

did so."⁶⁸ This singular person is acting. Weinandy does not deny that Jesus is truly divine, but he is highlighting that once the Son assumes human nature, all that he does he does as the theandric person: Jesus eats carrots and Jesus raises Lazarus. Jesus, the God-man, lives and acts, not with multiple personalities, but as one person with two natures.⁶⁹

And so we feel the tension. It appears wrong to speak of the eternal Son obeying or worshiping God (that looks like ontological subordinationism, which has been consistently rejected by the church) since he is none other than God; he is not in *any* sense less than God. And yet *as incarnate*—in his state of humiliation *as man*—the Son incarnate obeys his Father in the Spirit, doing his will (Luke 22:42; Gal 4:4) and, most centrally, offering him worship and living in uninterrupted communion with the Father through the Spirit. The Arians—and strangely some contemporary evangelicals trying to ground male-female relations in the Trinity—try to read the obedience of the incarnate Christ back into the eternal Godhead. But that was never the point, and in fact, it undermines the true unique significance of the incarnation.

So how does God elevate us to right communion? The wonder of the incarnation is that the Son, who is *homoousios* (of the same substance or being) with the Father, very God of very God, becomes human, and as incarnate (the Son taking on creatureliness) he freely and rightly obeys the Father as he depends on the Spirit. Thus the Son incarnate is also *homoousios* with us—truly and fully human. He can stand in our place as our representative not just symbolically but in the matter of his being because he has organically connected himself to us. He is incarnate not merely as an isolated individual but as the one man who is connected with us in such a way that when he died, we died (2 Cor 5:14–15); when he was seated at God's right hand, we were seated with him (Eph 2:5–7).

Christ rightly relates to God, neighbor, and even the earth, doing so "*for us and our salvation*" in the words of the Nicene Creed. In his faithfulness he approaches our frightening enemies—sin, death, and the devil—and overcomes them for God's glory and our good (cf. Isa 43:25). He can do this because the person of Christ is always and truly the God-man.

---

68. Weinandy, *Does God Suffer?*, 205.
69. Cf. Owen, *Works*, 2:415.

JESUS AS BOTH WORSHIPED AND HEAD WORSHIPER

We can see incorporated in all this that Jesus (who has restored our ability to worship by leading us back to the Father in and by his Spirit) is the proper object of our worship as well (Rev 4–5). Worthy is the Lamb of God who was slain to receive our worship.

> Worthy are you, our Lord and God,
>   to receive glory and honor and power,
> for you created all things,
>   and by your will they existed and were created. (Rev 4:11)

And they sang a new song, saying,

> "Worthy are you to take the scroll
>   and to open its seals,
> for you were slain, and by your blood you ransomed people for God
>   from every tribe and language and people and nation,
> and you have made them a kingdom and priests to our God,
>   and they shall reign on the earth." (Rev 5:9–10)

There has been a fair amount of scholarly debate about the extent to which the book of Revelation generally (and chapters 4–5 in particular) reflects existing first-century Christian liturgy. A fair number of specialists think a liturgical setting plays at least a part in the book's overall design since scenes of worship are clearly significant throughout, including in chapters 4–5.[70] The opening pages of Oscar Cullmann's volume *Early Christian Worship*, for example, memorably make the sweeping claim that "the whole Book of Revelation from the greeting of grace and peace in chapter 1:4 to the closing prayer: Come Lord Jesus, in chapter 22:20, and the benediction in the last verse, is full of allusions

---

70. E.g., David Aune, *Revelation 1–5*, Word Bible Commentary 52a (Dallas: Word, 1997), 28–29; Aune, *Revelation 17–22*, Word Bible Commentary 52c (Nashville: Nelson, 1998), 587–605. This was originally brought to my attention by Gergus King, "*Lex orandi, lex credendi*: Worship and Doctrine in Revelation 4–5," in *Scottish Journal of Theology* 67 (2014): 40.

to the liturgical usages of the early community."[71] Since the publication of that book, however, other scholars have been hesitant to affirm that large structures of liturgy guide the book, but they nevertheless agree that the Apocalypse is hard to read without seeing liturgical material throughout. The same scholars, however, fear that Cullmann's argument too often assumes that the seer is simply moving *from* early worshiping communities (which he has apparently experienced) *to* projecting them up into the heavens; the problem with this assumption is that it may claim too much about the earliest church practices.[72] Did the first Christians really have a sophisticated and uniform liturgy in corporate gatherings even before the close of the first century? I do think there is warrant for some concern about overstatement in Cullmann's claim.

But what if the author of Revelation wasn't simply projecting his earthly experiences onto heaven to create a heavenly vision out of them and instead was moving in the other direction? Did he, or God, intend the heavenly visions in the book to inform and shape the growth of liturgical practices in the young church, which had already begun by the end of the first century? G. K. Beale makes such an observation when he notes that "just as the heavenly pattern of the tabernacle shown to Moses on the mountain was to be copied by Israel in the construction of their own tabernacle," so here John employs the heavenly vision to shape future earthly church patterns.[73] Beale acknowledges that Revelation 4–5 may demonstrate some signs of (1) the structure of the synagogue's morning liturgy and (2) early Christian practices, but he traces its strongest connection to (3) the Hebrew Bible, especially drawing from imagery in Ezekiel 1–2 and Daniel 7.[74] These ancient Hebrew scenes are echoed by this witness to the heavenly liturgy, but I believe that, when seen in light of the coming of the Son of Man as Messiah, the descriptions in Revelation of heavenly worship create expectations that the church's earthly worship ought to reflect the ongoing heavenly activity.

Even with the significant variety among early churches that Paul

---

71. Oscar Cullmann, *Early Christian Worship*, trans A. Stewart Todd and James B. Torrance (London: SCM, 1953), 7.

72. See esp. Paul F. Bradshaw, *The Search for the Origins of Christian Worship: Sources and Methods for the Study of Early Liturgy* (New York: Oxford University Press, 1992); Bradshaw, *Early Christina Worship: A Basic Introduction to Ideas and Practice* (Collegeville, MN: Liturgical, 1996).

73. G. K. Beale, *The Book of Revelation: A Commentary on the Greek Text* (Grand Rapids: Eerdmans, 1999), 312.

74. Beale, *Book of Revelation*, 311–69, here summarized on p. 316. Isaiah 6 and other places also appear prominently in Beale's construction.

Bradshaw and others have noted, it is easy to see how texts like Revelation 4–5 would directly or indirectly shape developing liturgical expectations in the succeeding centuries. Larry Hurtado believes, as do I, that Revelation 5 "affirms the standard for the proper pattern of worship of the recipients of the book."[75] The "standard" does not necessarily refer to all the particular instruments of worship (e.g., incense, crowns, thrones, etc.) but to the object of worship: God and the Lamb. Vital for our current purposes, Hurtado elsewhere reminds us that the seer envisions the "heavenly reality behind the related worship by the elect upon earth," giving primacy to the heavens over the earthly liturgies. He concludes, "The gifts for which the earthly elect praise God, in anticipation of the full enjoyment of them, are secured in heaven."[76] Here is an eschatological tension between the "now" and the "not yet." Only by respecting this tension can a theology of Christian life sustain us amid the highs and lows of this life. We have hope because we are united to Christ, who has already secured our position and leads the worship of God, and in response we also recognize and praise him not merely as our representative but as nothing less than our God!

What Revelation 4–5 presents is not so much a chronological but a logical ordering, one vision with two scenes. In another carefully argued article, Larry Hurtado concludes:

> Rev. 4 gives the picture of the idealized heavenly sovereignty of God, shared by the representatives of the elect, the elders; and Rev. 5 gives the means by which this heavenly reality was secured and is to be made a historical reality upon the earth, the exaltation and triumph of the sacrificial Lamb, and shows that it is this exalted figure who is alone worthy to execute God's eschatological plan.[77]

The book of Revelation consistently presents us with this twofold vision of reality: what we see on earth and what we don't see happening in the heavens. God sovereignly reigns from his throne, yet that reign does

---

75. Larry W. Hurtado, *Lord Jesus Christ: Devotion to Jesus in Earliest Christianity* (Grand Rapids: Eerdmans, 2003), 593. See also Lucetta Mowry, whom I will engage more below, and Otto A. Coper, "The Apocalypse of John and the Liturgy of the Ancient Church," *Church History* 20 (1951): 10–22.

76. Hurtado, "Revelation 4–5 in the Light of Jewish Apocalyptic Analogies," *Journal for the Study of the New Testament* 25 (1985): 115.

77. Hurtado, "Revelation 4–5," 117–18.

not mean there is currently no rebellion, pain, anguish, or sin in this present world. On earth it often appears as if all is lost, as if Babylon is winning and God is absent or unable to do anything. We live in this tension even now. Central to finding hope in this story is the figure who emerges in Revelation, whose earthly actions have ultimate cosmic significance, providing promise and hope. Revelation 5, following closely from chapter 4, gives us a snapshot of how Jesus acts as Mediator, functioning on behalf of God's people, but also as the one to whom praise can and should be directed. We live in this now-and-not-yet tension where our confidence is based on Christ's mediation and experienced in our imperfect worship of him even as we deal with the continuing challenges of sin, grief, and hardship.

While the rest of the book of Revelation will offer a stark portrait of the pain and suffering God's people will endure in this life, the seer brings us hope by concentrating on the one who opened the seal. We will need to wait until the fullness of heaven eventually comes to earth and we can experience the final renewal of all things (e.g., Rev 21:2, 5, 10); still we can claim this security and confidence even now because Jesus, the Lamb of God, has acted as the pioneer and perfecter of our faith (Heb 12:2). He has already been inaugurated as our King and Priest now in the heavens, and his perfect reign and rule will soon be realized forever on earth.

This Mediator, both by his words and his presence, promises to make the things on earth correspond to the things in heaven (cf. Matt 6:10). Only by assuming flesh, only by becoming our great divine-human High Priest, only by his perfect worship and sacrifice on our behalf could this eschatological vision be fulfilled, a hope that this present world denies.

In this apocalyptic vision, Jesus rescues his people, taking them into the presence of God, opening what had been sealed and reestablishing healing and hope. Only because this human priest is also God can he accomplish this, which demonstrates that he is worthy of our worship.

Jesus the Messiah proclaims that he is "the first and the last" (Rev 1:17; 22:13) as a way not of minimizing his humanity but of framing it within the larger context of God's presence and action in the world. We must never forget, as this heavily Jewish book will not let us forget, that creatures are not permitted to worship other creatures, whether they are exalted angels (Rev 19:10; 22:8–9) or the beast and dragon (13:4–8,

11–15; 14:9–12; 16:2; 19:19–20), because only God is worthy of such worship (14:6–7; 15:4; 19:4).[78]

Revelation's depiction of praise and worship toward the Lamb reflects other early Christian practices and demonstrates the belief he is to be treated as one would treat only God. It also shows the lopsided nature of Jungmann's claims, which don't seem to give adequate weight to prayers offered not simply through Christ but to him. Thus this final biblical book puts Jesus within the "divine identity" (to borrow Richard Bauckham's helpful phrase),[79] since God alone is the Alpha and Omega, the beginning and the end, the first and the last (e.g., Rev 1:17–18; 21:6; 22:13). And yet this same Jesus is also the one who is identified with Israel, with God's people, as the one who acts on their behalf and in their place. Revelation presents Jesus as the unique divine-human agent who carries out God's purposes. This takes us back to the twofold dynamic of Jesus's representative status as Mediator, the embodiment of God's grace.

Revelation 5 will suffice to demonstrate this point. Opening the scene, the "seer of Patmos" notices a sealed scroll at the right hand of the enthroned one, and an angel asks, "Who is worthy to open the scroll and break its seals?" (5:2). Clearly the rhetorical question expects that no one from the heavens or anyone "under the earth" could be found, and so the seer begins to weep (5:3–4). An elder interrupts, giving words of hope: "Weep no more." Why? Because "the Lion of the tribe of Judah, the Root of David, has conquered, so that he can open the scroll and its seven seals" (5:5). He hears a word of power and expects to see a warrior, but what he sees is "a Lamb standing, as though it had been slain" (5:6). Two loaded symbolic images emerge, one kingly and the other priestly, and both are keys to understanding the passage. He *hears* (5:5) that none other than the one from the line of Judah who comes as a kingly Lion will be worthy to break the seal, but then the one he *sees* (5:6) is a sacrificial Lamb who takes on the priestly role by offering the full and final Passover offering (cf. 1 Cor 5:7; John 1:29; 1 Pet 1:19).

Revelation makes clear that this King and this Lamb are not two people, but one and the same. Jesus the Messiah is both the conquering King and the sacrificial Lamb. Building on Revelation 2–3, which

---

78. Cf. Richard Bauckham, *The Climax of Prophecy: Studies on the Book of Revelation* (Edinburgh: T&T Clark, 1993), 137–38.

79. For more on this dynamic, see, e.g., Richard Bauckham, *The Theology of the Book of Revelation* (Cambridge: Cambridge University Press, 1993), 23–30.

presented this same Messiah in his prophetic role as he revealed the true situation of the seven churches of Asia to their leaders, we are now in a position to see that *this Prophet is also the Lamb who acts as the King.* He alone can take the scroll on behalf of the people, and even as he does those around him fall prostrate before him. And he expresses his kingship not through tyranny but by bonding with his people and sacrificing himself for them. The people respond not just in gratitude but by *worshiping* the Lamb!

At this point, one might ask why God himself didn't just open the scroll. J. P. M. Sweet rightly answered: The scriptural vision from the opening of Genesis was for humans to have dominion over the earth, so "however deeply man had abused [God's] trust [God] would not bypass man in bringing his purposes to completion (cf. Rom 5:11ff, Heb 2:5–10)." Only a human could and should open the seal, and this man was "truly embodied only in Israel and in the Man who was to come, the Messiah."[80] Primasius (465–530), bishop of Hadrumetum in North Africa, added that none were worthy to open the scroll of salvation not because angels were ignorant but because they were not human, and not even the most faithful or just human "remains perfect in this life," so "in order to be re-created man requires the assistance of him who alone is Creator."[81] It requires a human who is free of sin, which disrupts and corrupts worship, so this one and only theanthropic person was the sole hope for restoring communion between God and fallen humanity: None other than Jesus the Lion and Lamb could accomplish this.[82] He is grace embodied. Consequently, in Revelation the one who speaks (Prophet) and then acts on behalf of his people (as their Priest and King) is, in a stunning revelation, the same one who both leads worship and is worshiped. Holding the "bowls full of incense, which are the prayers of the saints," this Mediator, who is "slain" and "ransomed" by his blood for God's people, also becomes their hope and healing, and so they praise

---

80. J. P. M. Sweet, *Revelation* (Philadelphia: Westminster, 1979), 124. It is also appropriate because the divine contents of the scroll are to be revealed to human beings, so the instrument of revelation, here as elsewhere, is both fully God and fully man.

81. Primasius, *Commentary on the Apocalypse*, 5.3, quoted in William C. Weinrich, *Ancient Christian Community on Scripture: New Testament*, vol. 12, *Revelation* (Downers Grove, IL: InterVarsity Press, 2005), 71.

82. Augustine (354–430) poetically expands on this twofold imagery: "Who is this, both lamb and lion? He endured death as a lamb; he devoured it as a lion. Who is this, both lamb and lion? Gentle and strong, lovable and terrifying, innocent and mighty, silent when he was being judged, roaring when he comes to judge." Augustine, *Sermon 375*, A.1, quoted in ACCS 12, 73.

him (Rev 5:8–9). He is the way through which the prayers rise to the heavens, and he is also the object of their praises.

This unique representative—the Messiah—acts on behalf of his diverse and scattered people and turns them into "a kingdom and priests to our God" (5:9–10) who are now led to serve and sacrifice on behalf of others in his world. Following their King and Priest, believers are directed to live in Christ's kingdom and serve as his priests (cf. 1 Pet 2:9–10). Recognizing all that is accomplished by this singular person, they turn to him again in praise, with sacrificial and kingly images merging: "Worthy is the Lamb who was slain, to receive power and wealth and wisdom and might and honor and glory and blessing!" (Rev 5:12). Not just some people, but climactically "every creature in heaven and on earth and under the earth and in the sea, and all that is in them," respond by praising the Lamb and worshiping him (5:13–14). Originally God created humanity to reign graciously and wisely over the earth, yet after the failure of Adam compromised that goal, God was still faithful to his promise and brought it about through a human (the *eschatos Adam*; 1 Cor 15:45–47).[83] Beale argues that Jesus functions as both "executor and heir of the promise" in this scene, since in his lamb-like innocence he was able to execute the final judgment, receive the promises, and include his people as participants in both his priesthood and his kingdom (cf. Rev 1:5–6).[84]

We should not miss that the opening of Revelation 4 is, as it were, in red letters with the words coming from Christ: The Messiah on the throne in heaven confronts John (4:1), who was taken there in the Spirit (4:2). Revelation 4 presents worship directed to God the Creator "who lives forever," while Revelation 5 presents worship to the Lamb (i.e., *re*-Creator): these are not two different gods, however, but the one God who rules from his throne, a throne with two seats (*bisellium*) shared by the Father with the Son (Rev 3:21). From this position God holds out the promise that those who endure in allegiance to him will reign with him (cf. Rev 1:6; 5:10; 20:4, 6; 22:5).[85] John purposely draws a parallel "between God as creator and as redeemer through his work in Christ."[86]

---

83. Beale, *The Book of Revelation*, 341. Beale goes on to note that this kind of twofold dynamic is found in "the book of Hebrews [which] portrays Christ as both priest and sacrifice, and Revelation itself presents him as both Lord and temple at the same time (cf. 21:22)" (341).
84. Craig R. Koester, *Revelation and the End of All Things* (Grand Rapids: Eerdmans, 2001), 79.
85. Aune, *Revelation 1–5*, 262.
86. Beale, *The Book of Revelation*, 369.

God did not abandon his good work of creation, and the book reveals this through the vision of the One who is both Lion and Lamb; it is he who has redeemed us. This messianic Lord gives us hope of a new creation in which obedience and praise are again directed to the triune Creator of heaven and earth.

CONCLUSION

Jesus is not just a wonderful example of a particular human being: He is also the God who is worthy of worship. Not only can prayers therefore be offered to God *through* the Messiah (cf. Jungmann), but they can also be offered *to* him (cf. Hurtado). As none other than our God, the Messiah rightly deserves our praise and worship. But this same Messiah is also our friend, our elder brother, our real human representative, who was not play-acting, but who genuinely united himself to us to represent us to God, offering the worship that God deserved, but which we constantly refused in deliberate rebellion. Christ alone was not just full of faith but perfectly faithful. He alone could open the seal; he alone could serve as the Prophet, Priest, and King. He has led us to triumph through his incarnation, sacrifice, resurrection, and ascension. This takes us to one final note about early Christian worship and why it matters for our concerns in this book.

When Lucetta Mowry long ago argued that Revelation 4–5 might "have the earliest known form of a Christian service of worship," she may have been stating too much, reading back into the biblical text what became formal features in later and more developed church services. But her point still has importance for our purposes. The heavenly scene of worship does in various ways correspond to the basic shape of postapostolic worship: We have here a *call* to worship, divine *revelation* received, *praise* in song to the Creator and Redeemer, *prayers* offered, the active congregational response of *doxology*, and all done as worship directed to the God who is worthy.[87] As Mowry also makes clear, these chapters

---

87. Lucetta Mowry, "Revelation 4–5 and Early Christian Liturgical Usage," *Journal of Biblical Literature* 71, no. 2 (June 1952): 75–84. She writes: "It begins with an invitation to partake of the blessings of the service (Rev. 4:1). It continues with the singing of a trisagion, followed by a brief ascription of praise to God as Creator sung by the choir. After the congregation prostrates itself before the altar the major portion of the service is taken up with the reading of the scripture, the prayers which include a psalm of praise to Christ the Slain Lamb. In this psalm the congregation responds with an appropriate versicle. Finally the service closes with the congregational singing of a doxology to God and Christ concluded with a choral Amen" (84).

from Revelation prescribe that worship now also be directed toward the Mediator. Only the Lamb could open the scroll, and thus the *Agnus Dei* properly receives our praises. Mowry concludes that early worship services, not just the preaching, had the story of Jesus's life, death, and resurrection as their focal point, bringing a new vision of God and his world, including a vision of how his people were to live in it.[88] While it will be several chapters before we can turn to this idea more fully, let us here remember that this Christocentric vision then shaped not only the corporate worship experience of the early church but also the theology of everyday Christian life. But before we further explore the centrality of the Messiah and corporate worship, we first must turn to the Holy Spirit since apart from the Spirit we cannot receive the grace of Christ and rest in the Father's love—by the Spirit, fellowship with God moves from the theoretical to the actual.

---

88. Mowry, "Revelation 4–5," 84.

CHAPTER 4

FELLOWSHIP
The Connection to God's Love

Peace I leave with you; my peace I give to you. Not as the world gives do I give to you. Let not your hearts be troubled, neither let them be afraid.
—JOHN 14:27

Through the incarnation and Pentecost the Holy Spirit comes to us from the inner communion of the Father, Son and Holy Spirit, creates union and communion between us and the Holy Trinity. In other words, the Spirit creates not only personal union but corporate communion between us and Christ and through Christ with the Holy Trinity, so that it is the Holy Spirit who creates and sustains the being and life of the Church, uniting the Church to Christ as his one Body.
—T. F. TORRANCE[1]

The Spirit is the inner dynamic of the life of faith, life which "is hid with Christ in God" (Col. 3:3), and at its inmost core is formed by participation in a movement of communication, recognition and response issuing from the heart of God himself.
—ALASDAIR I. C. HERON[2]

---

1. Thomas F. Torrance, *The Trinitarian Faith: The Evangelical Theology of the Ancient Catholic Church* (Edinburgh: T&T Clark, 1988), 9.
2. Alasdair I. C. Heron, *The Holy Spirit: The Holy Spirit in the Bible, the History of Christian Thought, and Recent Theology* (Philadelphia: Westminster, 1983), 49 (emphasis added).

WHAT CHANGES?

When a person becomes a Christian, a strange thing often happens—nothing changes! If they were struggling financially before their conversion, their financial woes are not instantly taken away. If they were previously divorced, the new believer does not awake to find themselves happily married. If they were living under an oppressive government, they are not ushered straightaway into a land of liberty. While there are stories of radical change (e.g., the elimination of addiction, dissipation of long-held anger, etc.), it is often the case that, on the surface, nothing changes for the person who becomes a Christian.

However, the great promise of Scripture is that while on the one hand nothing changes, on the other hand everything does. To understand these changes, we will examine the work of God's Spirit in us and how he transforms the way we live in the present, even as we face the pain, frustration, and struggle of this life. What is God doing with us, and how do his love and grace shape Christian life?

In this chapter, we will see that the Holy Spirit brings us into fellowship with God, where we live in his love. Both creation and re-creation are the works of God's love to bring us into his fellowship. Therefore, even in our present struggles, we have confidence because it is God who is working in us, his people.

GOD'S PRESENT ACTION

The love that animates God's triune life is also the motive and ground of his work in creation and re-creation. Created in this God's image, humans were designed to reflect and participate in God's love, which put us in the middle of a larger picture that we called "shalom" in a previous chapter: a whole cosmos meant for well-being, mutual service, love, delight, and worship of God. The rebellion of Adam and Eve distorted and disordered the world, substituting sin for shalom, so that we are now alienated from God, more like enemies than his friends (Gen 3; Rom 5:10; Col 1:21). The sin that disrupted our communion with God also disrupted and disordered our relationships with our neighbors, the rest of creation, and even ourselves. The whole of creation was thrown into disarray. So how then do we—who are sinners—reconnect to God's love and the life that flows from him? How are we restored to the movement of divine holy love?

We first addressed that question by pointing to God's grace manifested in Christ. The Mediator is the eternal Son of God, who—sent from the Father and empowered by the Spirit—became the son of Mary, assuming a full human nature. Truly God and truly human, one person with two natures. Through his life, death, resurrection, and ascension, Jesus is the single mediator between God and humanity, the God-man, serving as our Prophet, Priest, and King, overcoming sin, death, and the devil, and reconciling us with God. Not only is the incarnate Son worthy of our worship, but he is also the lead worshiper! He is not only the object of our praise and prayers, our sacrifices and laments, but also offers lament, prayer, and praise to the Father on our behalf in such a way that our lament, prayer, and praise are a participation in his perfect offerings. Only in and through Christ are we brought back from our rebellion and into the love of God.

Yet we have this further problem: How do *we* experience God's love and life *now* because of who Jesus is and what he did several thousand years ago? How are his perfect obedience and role as lead worshiper beneficial to us, to me? Is Jesus just a great example of God's love and a beautiful picture of human faithfulness that we are meant to be encouraged by? Or is Christianity primarily an act of memory, where we learn about the past, and especially about Jesus so that his life might inspire us today? Or does the connection have some other nature? Jesus certainly lived an exceptional life and was a revered model others could emulate. Orthodox Christianity, however, believes that something more than simple historical recollection and inspiration happens in believers.

While Jesus of Nazareth is certainly a historical figure, Christian faith never consists in mere intellectual affirmation of past events in the ancient Near Eastern world, nor in the simple belief that a historical challenge was completed by a model citizen, nor just believing that Jesus solved an accounting problem so that some of us can now be on the right side of the ledger. Christian faith has always centered on trust (*fiducia*) in a person, on being brought into a new personal relationship with this God-man. It involves receiving and responding, not simply recalling. How then do Christ's person and work benefit us today and animate our present Christian life? Short answer: the Holy Spirit. An objective union with Christ takes place by God's Spirit.

Our experience of being drawn into fellowship with God is the action of his Spirit working on our spirits, enabling us to recognize him as Father (Rom 8:15–16). The Holy Spirit is the Spirit of Christ and is the way that Jesus is with us (John 14). The Spirit makes Jesus present not only *to* and *with* us, but *in* us: The Spirit renders the Christ who is *pro nobis . . . in nobis*. The work of Jesus in the past changed who we are. We experience that reality by his work in us through his Spirit. Secured by the Spirit, we now enjoy all the benefits of being in God's family and participating in the fellowship of the Trinity.

Renewed fellowship with God, with all of the benefits of forgiveness, reconciliation, joy, and holiness—nothing less than new life—comes to us as the fruit of the Spirit's presence and renewing power. The Spirit draws us into communion with God as he applies the crucified and risen Christ to our lives and enables us to rest secure in the Father's benediction. Here our restless hearts are finally able to rest in God's love. As we are drenched afresh in the overflow of the triune God's life-giving love, the Spirit of creation is the same as the Spirit of re-creation. By renewing us "in knowledge, righteousness, and holiness, with dominion over the creatures,"[3] the animating and ordering Holy Spirit again enables us to enjoy and foster communion with God, neighbor, and the rest of creation. This is the path of love. This is the inbreaking of shalom.

By being brought into this fellowship of divine love, we are not only healed but also energized to participate now in God's movement of love as we bring his words and works of healing and grace to his compromised creation. The rest of the chapter explains this under the following affirmations:

1. As the bond of love between the Father and Son, the Holy Spirit is also the bond of love between God and us.
2. The benefits of the grace of Christ become ours by the Holy Spirit.
3. The Spirit connects us to the cross and the resurrection.
4. Our life is now animated by the Holy Spirit.
5. The Spirit convicts and comforts.

---

3. Westminster Shorter Catechism, 10.

AFFIRMATION 1

As the bond of love between the Father and Son, the person of the Holy Spirit is also the bond of love between God and us.

Since we are created in the image of God for fellowship with God, it should not surprise us that a Christian life will in some modest ways echo the life of the Trinity.[4] A *theology* of Christian life must be about *God* even as it is also about us. In an earlier chapter we did briefly review the Holy Spirit's place in the Father's love for the Son and in the Son's love for the Father. Many have followed Augustine's conclusion that the Spirit is the "Bond of Love" between the Father and Son, understanding that "Bond" to be a person himself, not merely an attribute of God, but truly God. This is Augustine's structure of Lover-Beloved-Love.[5] It will help us to revisit this idea briefly. This section will require some mental work, but I believe the payoff will be worth the effort.

Let us start with looking at an example of how God relates to us in a Trinitarian fashion. John 14:16–17 records Jesus's promise to the disciples that he will not leave them alone: "I will ask the Father, and He will give you another Helper, so that He may be with you forever; *the Helper is* the Spirit of truth, whom the world cannot receive, because it does not see Him or know *Him; but* you know Him because He remains with you and will be in you" (NASB). In this event, we can understand the Father as God in heaven, who has sent the incarnate Son and will send the Spirit at Pentecost; the Son as God in front of us, the Logos, who faithfully conforms his being and action and words to the nature of the Father; and the Spirit as God within us. All three are one God, each

---

4. There has been plenty of controversy and legitimate warning about trying to construct politics, gender, or even general anthropology on the Trinity, given the massive and important Creator-creature distinction. See the warnings, e.g., in Karen Kilby, "Perichoresis and Projection: Problems with Social Doctrines of the Trinity," *New Blackfriars* 81, no. 957 (November 2000): 432–45; Kathryn Tanner, *Christ the Key* (Cambridge: Cambridge University Press, 2010), esp. ch. 4; Matthew Barrett, *Simply Trinity: The Unmanipulated Father, Son, and Spirit* (Grand Rapids: Baker, 2021), esp. 17–93. For concerns regarding Barrett's critiques, see Andrew Hollingworth, "On Critiquing Social Trinitarianism: Problems with a Recent Attempt," in *JBTS* 7, no. 2 (2023): 195–213. I am aware of these warnings and generally am sympathetic with many of them, but I think we can also become so cautious that we cease to be truly Christian in our conception of God, and how a necessarily Trinitarian conception of God might speak into what it means to be humans made in this God's image.

5. Augustine, *On the Trinity (De Trinitate)*, ed. John E. Rotelle, trans. Edmund Hill, The Works of Saint Augustine: A Translation for the 21st Century (New York: New City, 1991), 9.2, p. 272. For a fuller treatment of Augustine on this point, showing not only appreciation but also potential shortcomings and an expansion on this approach, see David Coffey, "The Holy Spirit as the Mutual Love of the Father and Son," *Theological Studies* 51 (1990): 193–229.

is God in completeness yet in such a way that God's relationship to us reflects his being in himself.

Dorothy L. Sayers, in her play *The Zeal of Thy House*, gives us another description of the Trinity that might help our imaginations and prepare us for later reflections in this chapter. At the end of the play, the archangel Michael makes the following analogy between the Trinity and works of art:

> For every work of creation is threefold, an earthly trinity to match the heavenly.
>
> *First*: there is the Creative Idea; passionless, timeless, beholding the whole work complete at once, the end in the beginning; and this is the image of the Father.
>
> *Second*: there is the Creative Energy, begotten of that Idea, working in time from the beginning to the end, with sweat and passion, being incarnate in the bonds of matter; and this is the image of the Word.
>
> *Third*: there is the Creative Power, the meaning of the work and its response in the lively soul; and this is the image of the indwelling Spirit.
>
> And these three are one, each equally in itself the whole work, whereof none can exist without the other; and this is the image of the Trinity.[6]

We must immediately remind ourselves this is but an analogy, and all analogies fall short; but that doesn't mean they are unhelpful. Granted, both pictures describe how the Trinity relates to us—God is Father, Son, and Spirit in himself before he relates to us. But these descriptions give us a first step to see how the persons are one and yet also distinct even as they relate to each other.

There is one God, that one God is three persons, and each person is distinguished by specific relations to each of the others.[7] The respective

---

6. Dorothy L. Sayers, *The Zeal of Thy House* (New York: Harcourt, Brace, 1937), 115, emphasis added. See also her later book, where she more fully develops this theme: Sayers, *The Mind of the Maker* (1941; San Francisco: HarperCollins, 1987).

7. Thomas Aquinas captures the Western tradition's Trinitarian approach when he defines *persona* as "a subsisting relation." *Summa Theologica*, 1.29.4. What the tradition means by this is that the one God has three *eternal* subsisting relations: Father, Son, and Spirit. To reflect biblical language and patterns, these *relations* are captured and represented in the personal names that reflect relations: paternity, filiation, and procession.

names of the persons indicate the relations: The Father eternally begets the Son, and the Spirit eternally proceeds from the Father (in the West we tend to add "and from the Son," but the Eastern church disagrees with that wording and disapproves of this addition to the original Nicene Creed). The Father is unbegotten, the Son is begotten but not made, and the Spirit is eternally proceeding. Orthodoxy, in its various shades, always guards against the idea that there are three gods who have three self-derived wills (that is called "tritheism"). Instead, the living God is the one God who wills from the Father through the Son and by the Spirit. This is partly what Dorothy Sayers was trying to reflect in her analogy. All three persons will, but each expresses the one being of God, and therefore each wills the one will of God.[8] Each of the persons *is* God.[9]

Basil the Great (330–79), an example of an early church leader, shows how this Trinitarian understanding guards the faithful worship of the one God while honoring the distinction of persons. Establishing that "the Holy Spirit is *indivisibly* and *inseparably* joined to the Father and the Son," Basil affirms divine unity through the classic use of what is often called the "inseparable operations of the divine persons."[10] Too often this language is misunderstood as supposing a collapse of the persons, but the principle doesn't work that way. Instead, it guides the church's liturgy and praise, which is *to* the Father *through* the Son and *by* the Spirit. While the implications are there for the Spirit, Basil begins with recognizing that the "work of the Father is not separate or distinct from the work of the Son," not because the Father becomes incarnate just like the Son, but there is no incarnation apart from the Father and Spirit.[11] Just as the Son, and not the Spirit or the Father, is incarnate in Jesus of

---

8. God's will is spoken and actualized from the divine person's mode of subsistence (cf. *taxis* or order). Thus there is no problematic distance between the will of a divine person (e.g., the Spirit) and the will of God, for the Father is God, the Son is God, and the Spirit is God.

9. NB: When Jesus prays, "not my will, but . . ." and seems to distinguish his will from that of the Father, this takes us into christological discussions about one person with two natures; much of orthodox tradition, ably articulated by Maximus the Confessor, held that the incarnate Son has two wills (divine and human, in perfect harmony). A careful unpacking of this would be needed if we were to see why the tradition so often affirms the one will of God even as it affirms the incarnate Son's submitting his will to that of the Father (even as it rejects the idea of an eternal subordination—since this is an outworking of the incarnation).

10. Basil the Great, *On the Holy Spirit* (Crestwood, NY: St. Vladimir's Seminary Press, 2001), 16.37, p. 60, emphasis added. For a thorough recent treatment on this topic, see Adonis Vidu, *The Same God Who Works All Things: Inseparable Operations in Trinitarian Theology* (Grand Rapids: Eerdmans, 2021).

11. Basil the Great, *On the Holy Spirit*, 8.19, p. 60.

Nazareth, so the Spirit, and not the Son or the Father, is poured out at Pentecost. The Spirit is God himself working throughout creation, working in and on people in order to bring them into communion with the risen Christ, who reigns and rules at the Father's right hand. The useful expression *opera trinitatis ad extra sunt indivisa* (the external acts of the Trinity are undivided) does not undermine personal distinctions in God but grounds them in a unity of action and being. The "transmission of will" in the Godhead does not act as a movement from a greater to a "subordinate" or lesser, but rather "like the reflection of an object in a mirror, which reaches from Father to Son without passage of time."[12] Basil takes the example of the creation of angels to make his point about how God works.

> When you consider creation I advise you to first think of Him who is the first cause of everything that exists: namely, the Father, and then of the Son, who is the creator, and then the Holy Spirit, the perfector. So the ministering spirits exist by the will of the Father, are brought into being by the work of the Son, and are perfected by the presence of the Spirit. . . . And let no one accuse me of saying that there are three unoriginate persons, or that the work of the Son is imperfect. The Originator of all things is One: He creates through the Son and perfects through the Spirit.[13]

We do not have a fourth entity behind the three persons, but one Deity who lives in three relations. There can be no disunity or conflict within the Trinity, for this would compromise the *Shema* (Deut 6:4). The distinct divine persons do not constitute an ontological hierarchy but do reveal the one God who has relationality and otherness within himself. This is very different from tritheism because, as Giles Emery explains, "these relations are identical to the very being of God; they are identified with the essence of God, which is pure existence: these relations subsist."[14] This understanding of the being of God clarifies how, even before there was anything outside of God, *God* is love. Father, Son,

---

12. Basil the Great, *On the Holy Spirit*, 8.20, p. 40.
13. Basil the Great, *On the Holy Spirit*, 16.38, p. 62.
14. Gilles Emery, *The Trinity: An Introduction to Catholic Doctrine on the Triune God*, trans. Matthew Levering (Washington, DC: Catholic University of America Press, 2009), 107. Emery goes on: "The divine person is not the result of a composition of the divine being with another thing. God is simple. . . . These relations distinguish the divine persons" (107).

and Spirit live in love; thus God *is love*. God does not become love, because that is just who the triune God eternally is. Kathryn Tanner more recently put it together powerfully by concluding: "Reinforcing the unity of being between Father and Son by a unity of love and joyful affirmation, the Holy Spirit is the exuberant, ecstatic carrier of the love of Father and Son to us. Borne by the Holy Spirit, the love of the Father for the Son is returned to the Father by the Son within the Trinity."[15] All of this careful explanation was necessary in order that we might more fully appreciate the promise included in Paul's benediction that ends, "the fellowship of the Holy Spirit be with you all" (2 Cor 13:14).

How can we say both (1) that the triune God is love and (2) that the Holy Spirit is the love between the Father and Son? Peter Lombard (1100–1160) navigates this question by following Augustine's lead in affirming that "the Holy Spirit is the love or charity or affection of the Father and the Son."[16] But is this compatible with the apostle John's statement that *God* is love (1 John 4:16)? Can we speak of the Spirit in this way and still fairly represent the biblical revelation of the inner life of God? Yes, we can since there is no actual conflict between the two statements: We similarly speak of the wisdom of God generally, and we also recognize that the Scriptures speak of the Logos of God as Wisdom personified.[17] Like wisdom, "in the Trinity, love is sometimes ascribed to the substance, which is common to the three persons and is entire in each of them, and sometimes especially to the person of the Holy Spirit."[18]

While we are familiar with John's proclamation that God is love, the scriptural affirmations linking the Spirit with love may not be as obvious. But Augustine and Peter, still working within Johannine literature, derive both affirmations there.[19] "Beloved, let us love one another, for love is from God, and whoever loves has been born of God and knows God" (1 John 4:7). Peter observes a twofold dynamic here: "Love is God from God."[20] Not only is God love, but love comes from God, and the love from God is nothing short of God; God is love. Reasoning that the

---

15. Kathryn Tanner, *Jesus, Humanity, and the Trinity: A Brief Systematic Theology* (Minneapolis: Fortress, 2001), 14.
16. Peter Lombard, *The Sentences*, book 1, *The Mystery of the Trinity*, trans. Guilio Silano (Toronto: Pontifical Institute of Mediaeval Studies, 2007), disp. 10.1 (34), 1, p. 58.
17. Peter Lombard, *The Sentences*, disp. 10.1 (34), 4, p. 58–59; 10.2 (35), 2, p. 59.
18. Peter Lombard, *The Sentences*, disp. 10.1 (34), 4, p. 59.
19. Augustine, whom Peter is mostly borrowing directly from, provides his exegesis and theological deductions especially in *On the Trinity*, 15.5.31, pp. 420–21.
20. Peter Lombard, *The Sentences*, dist. 10.3 (35), 3, p. 60.

Father alone cannot be *from* God, the love that comes must point to the Son and/or Spirit, both of whom come to us in their own distinctive ways. John comments that because God is love, we ought to love in response to having first been loved (1 John 4:10–11). This love of God, which existed before the creation of the world, is manifest both in the sending of the Son "to be the propitiation for our sins" as well as in the indwelling Spirit whom "he has given us" (1 John 4:13). Just as the incarnate Son is both the embodiment and object of divine love, so the Scriptures also speak in other distinctive ways about the Spirit.

John asks and answers several vital questions that distinctly connect the Spirit, love, and us. First, how do we know that we abide in God, and God in us? By his Spirit (1 John 4:13). Second, what is the evidence of the Spirit's dwelling in us? Love (1 John 4:7–21). Out of love the Father sends the Son as the embodiment and object of divine love, and the Spirit proceeds from the Father and the Son as the presence and power of this divine love, thus enlivening, animating, and sustaining believers by bringing them into fellowship with God.

A basic principle in Trinitarian theology is that the *ad extra* (external work) relates to the *ad intra* (internal being) of God: God's self-revelation really tells us about Godself.[21] In this case, the strong claim that God's abiding in us and us in God is *love*, and the way this is actualized in us is by the presence of the Spirit. Peter Lombard makes a beautiful connection: "The Holy Spirit is the love of the Father and Son by which they love themselves mutually and us, but also the love by which we love God."[22] In other words, just as one can speak of the person of the Spirit as the bond of love between the Father and Son, so it is good and right to praise God the Spirit who is the bond of love between God and us. We also should note carefully how Peter Lombard even connects *our* love for God with the Holy Spirit who *is* love: While the primary emphasis is on God's own internal, Trinitarian love and God's love for us, he also hints that *our responsive love for God* is dependent on the Spirit as well. Building on John, Augustine similarly observes that "it is the Holy Spirit of which he has given us that makes us abide in God and him in us. And this is precisely what love does. He then is the gift of

---

21. For a careful unpacking of this idea and potential dangers engaged in often by contemporary theologians, see Fred Sanders, *The Triune God*, New Studies in Dogmatics (Grand Rapids: Zondervan, 2016).
22. Peter Lombard, *The Sentences*, dist. 10.3 (35), 3, p. 60.

God who is love."²³ This Gift is the Holy Spirit. What does that mean? Thankfully, Jesus helps by explaining this to his disciples and us during the final days of his earthly ministry.

AFFIRMATION 2
The benefits of the grace of Christ become ours by the Holy Spirit.

Before his arrest and crucifixion, we find Jesus in an expectation-setting scene in the upper room. There he explains to the disciples that God's own Spirit will come to them, linking God with his people. Following his logic requires us to listen carefully.

In this setting, Jesus declares to the disciples that he is glorified by the Father since "all that the Father has is mine" and "he will take what is mine and declare it to you" (John 16:14–15; cf. 10:30). This prompts us to ask how this is all conveyed to believers in such a way that it truly becomes theirs. How will the Son, who is about to "go to the Father" and thus will no longer be bodily with the disciples (John 16:10), extend his presence and grace to his followers? The answer: by the Spirit. The Spirit of truth will draw people to him who is the Truth not by bringing a new or different message but by both *being* God and *showing them* God (John 16:13). This is the Spirit's act of uniting.

New Testament scholar Herman Ridderbos argues that the Spirit here functions as a "mediator" in that he unites us to the incarnate Son and enables us to enjoy God's gifts. The Spirit "takes 'what is mine,' bringing forth the treasure entrusted to Jesus, in order to redistribute it in his own way," and in this way acts as "the permanent mediator between Jesus and those who belong to Jesus."²⁴ The phrase *permanent mediator* does not indicate a barrier that keeps us *from* Jesus but rather a living and active link *to* him. The Spirit is how God's gifts are distributed to us. While it is "through" Christ that we have "access . . . to the Father," that access is also "in one Spirit" (Eph 2:18). From the beginning of our new life as adopted children of God, all that we have comes to us through Christ from the Father by the Spirit. God our Father, Christ our elder brother, all true and kept by the Spirit, who draws us into this life and

---
23. Augustine, *On the Trinity*, 15.5.31, pp. 420–21.
24. Herman N. Ridderbos, *The Gospel According to John: A Theological Commentary* (Grand Rapids: Eerdmans, 1997), 536.

love of the triune God. All the riches of God's love made known and secured in the grace of Christ become ours by the fellowship (*koinonia*; 2 Cor 13:14) of the Spirit who takes all that is the Father's, all that is the Son's, and gives it to God's people. We receive God by his Spirit. This is how *God gives us himself* even now. It is the Spirit who brings us into fellowship with God and with his people.

The Spirit, who is the bond of love between the Father and Son, is also the bond of love between God and us. The Spirit moves in us, and through him we experience God's love and rest. He is the way Christ is present to us. Our life in and by the Spirit is the way we truly know God, since he is God himself moving in us, bringing life, enabling communion, and keeping us secure in God's love. We say that the Son—not the Father or the Spirit—has become incarnate in Jesus of Nazareth but that God is fully present to him in all three persons. Similarly, we say that the Spirit—not the Father or the Son—is the Paraclete who indwells us but that God is fully present to us through him because he is the Spirit of the Father and of the Son. Thus Jesus promises that he and the Father "will come to him [who loves God] and make our home with him" by the Holy Spirit (John 14:23–26). The triune God dwells in us by his Spirit. He is the one who brings us into the life of God.

The one God is the giver, the given, and the gift.[25] The Father is the giver who sends his Son, the Son is given as the external reality of God's self-revelation to us, and the Spirit is the internal reality of that revelation.[26] We respond to God by his gift as he is given in order that we might love the giver. Not three gods, but one God who gives us himself: Father, Son, and Spirit. All things *from* him, *to* him, and *through* him (Rom 11:36). While this dynamic deserves a book rather than a paragraph, it at least required mention here.[27] But for now, we are focusing on how this relates to love and Christian life.

---

25. Cf. Basil the Great, who concludes liturgically that "first we thank the messenger who brought the gift; next we remember him who sent it, and finally we raise our thoughts to the fountain and source of all gifts." *On the Holy Spirit*, 16.37, p. 61.

26. Karl Barth, for example, calls Jesus Christ the objective reality of God's self-revelation to us, and he calls the Spirit the subjective reality of God's revelation to us. Jesus Christ objectively changed our reality; the Spirit enables us to recognize, confess, and engage that reality. See esp. Karl Barth, *Church Dogmatics* 1.2, *The Doctrine of the Word of God*, ed. G. W. Bromiley and T. F. Torrance, trans. G. W. Bromiley, 2nd ed. (Edinburgh: T&T Clark, 1956), §13.1–2, §16.1; pp. 1–44, 203–42. Thanks to John Yates for reminding me of this dynamic in Barth.

27. For examples of my own thoughts on this threefold dynamic, see Kelly M. Kapic, *The God Who Gives: How the Trinity Shapes the Christian Story* (Grand Rapids: Zondervan, 2018); Kapic, "The Spirit as Gift: Explorations in John Owen's Pneumatology," in *Ashgate Research Companion*

God as God is love, so all three persons of God are love. Therefore, we cannot say that *only* the Spirit is love, since that would deny the love of the Father and the Son, but we can say that "God's love has been poured into our hearts through the Holy Spirit who has been given to us" (Rom 5:5) because it emphasizes one particular action without denying others. The Spirit proceeding from the Father and through the Son comes to us as the bond of love who draws us back into the life and love of God.[28] We know and love God by the action of the Spirit within us, engrafting us into the love of the Son for the Father, causing us to grow in grace and truth. To this dynamic we now turn.

AFFIRMATION 3

The Spirit connects us to the cross and the resurrection.

We experience the love of God through the grace of Christ by the fellowship of the Spirit. This is not because the Father alone is loving, the Son alone is gracious, and the Spirit alone is relational. Rather, God is love in all three ways of his being—Father, Son, and Holy Spirit. God shows us his grace most clearly in the incarnation, taking our flesh upon himself. And God's communion, which is love in its activity of loving, is also God himself, the Holy Spirit, reaching into our hearts to join us to his.

Too often, however, we confuse the fruit for the root. Incarnation and Pentecost are not events that make God love us but the fruit of God's love for us. Jesus's life, death, resurrection, and ascension are *not* what convinces the Father to care about us; rather, he embodies the Father's love for us (John 3:16), and these events come about because of that love. Similarly, the Spirit's work in us is *not* what makes God pay attention to us—the Spirit is God himself in us, taking care of us *because* he loves us. When we confuse the root and the fruit, it distorts our image of the Father and harms our Christian life—after all, how can a distorted image of our Father *not* hurt our fellowship with him? Therefore, we must never forget that it is God who saves us, rescuing us for himself because he loves us already. There is no friction or tension among Father,

---

to *John Owen*, ed. Kelly M. Kapic and Mark Jones (Aldershot: Ashgate, 2012), 113–40. Others trying to unpack this dynamic include Stephen H. Webb, *The Gifting God: A Trinitarian Ethics of Excess* (New York: Oxford University Press, 1996), but also the creative ways John Barclay sees resonances in Paul's approach to grace in *Paul and the Gift* (Grand Rapids: Eerdmans, 2015).

28. Augustine, *On the Trinity*, 15.19, n37.

Son, and Spirit because he is one God worthy of worship, the Father saving us through the Son and by the Spirit. In joy and thankfulness, we praise God. Knowing that his will for us is loving and wise, we seek to live according to it. Our love and willingness are possible only because we are empowered by the Spirit who unites us to Christ and draws us continuously into divine love.

We belong to Christ, and he to us. The apostle John compares this belonging, this union, to a branch connected to a vine and bearing fruit (John 15); the apostle Paul compares it to a body with its various members, each supporting the others (Rom 12:4–8; 1 Cor 12:12–31). And when Jesus promises the disciples, "If anyone loves Me, he will follow My word; and My Father will love him, and We will come to him and make Our dwelling with him" (John 14:23 NASB), it is in the middle of his talk about the Holy Spirit's coming presence to be with them. The Spirit doesn't just connect us with *all that Jesus did*; he also is the way that Christ *continues to be with us*. The phrase *union with Christ* refers to both of these conditions. While the theme of union with Christ is taught throughout the New Testament,[29] it is especially pronounced in Paul's writings. In particular, the Pauline expression "in Christ"—in its various forms (e.g., "in him")—appears over 150 times; however, probably because they are so brief and fairly common, we too easily miss their importance. Yet "in Christ" is a packed phrase that has much to teach us about salvation and the life of faith. We will return to more fully unpack the theme of union in chapter 7 on the ego, but a few points can be made here in this context.

First, thanks to the Spirit, Christians are not mere antiquarians. Although history and remembrance are hugely important to Christianity, the Spirit connects us not simply to the past, but to the eternal God in our own place and time. In other words, the Spirit is not simply taking credit deposited into an account millennia ago by Christ and spending it on our behalf: The Spirit actually connects us to the crucified and risen Lord. We as the church—and I as an individual who is part of that body—are even now united to Christ, our head. His life, death, resurrection, and ongoing reign are determinative for our death, resurrection, and ongoing life.

---

29. For a treatment of union with Christ that highlights distinct contributions to this theme from most New Testament books, see Robert A. Peterson, *Salvation Applied by the Spirit: Union with Christ* (Wheaton, IL: Crossway, 2015).

Second, the Spirit connects Christians to Christ and all of his work, including his cross *and* his empty tomb. Too often our sermons, prayers, and lives concentrate only on the death of Jesus, forgetting the central place his ongoing life has for our present existence. Preaching the cross without proper attention to the resurrection encourages poor theology both about Jesus and about Christian spirituality. Problems surface here from misunderstanding not just Christology but also pneumatology.

The cross of Christ is obviously central to Christian proclamation: "The cross" is shorthand for God's defeat of the great enemies—sin, death, and the devil. Apart from Christ's death our sin condemns us, the devil accuses us, and death would still hold us. In our place, Jesus faced these enemies, absorbing and then silencing the judgment, the darkness, and the accusations, defeating death itself. Through the ages Christians have spoken of their sins nailed to the cross. Or as Paul tells us, you have been "crucified with Christ" (1 Cor 2:2; Gal 2:20; 5:24), and "you have died, and your life is hidden with Christ in God" (Col 3:3). Consequently, those who by the Spirit are united to Christ rightly contemplate the cross as the place where he takes away our sin, shame, and condemnation.

But Paul also tells us how God "raised us up with him [Christ]" (Eph 2:6; cf. Col 2:12; 3:1). Further, he writes, "For I handed down to you as of first importance what I also received, that Christ died for our sins according to the Scriptures, and that He was buried, and that He was raised on the third day according to the Scriptures, and that He appeared to Cephas, then to the twelve. . . . But if there is no resurrection of the dead, then not even Christ has been raised; and if Christ has not been raised, then our preaching is in vain, your faith also is in vain" (1 Cor 15:3–5, 13–14 NASB). In other words, the work of Jesus did not stop with his obedient earthly life and sacrificial death: He also includes us in his resurrection from the grave and his ongoing life at the Father's right hand.

A sign that we miss this in our preaching and discipleship is revealed when we find ourselves speaking only about forgiveness and rarely expecting signs of the Spirit's fruit in our lives. When this happens, we may be missing part of the good news of life in Christ. While we will say more about this in chapter 5 on the law-gospel dynamic, a bit more must be said here. For if we speak of the gospel only in terms of an event that happened long ago with no expectation of God's present power or action, then we probably have an underdeveloped appreciation for the presence and work of the Spirit in our lives. God's work in us, however, does not stop with forgiveness: He daily brings us afresh into communion with him. God the Holy Spirit works in us, enabling us to love God and neighbor and to exercise faithful care of the rest of creation. Jesus did not merely die to rescue us *from* sin; he also rose to rescue us *to* new life. The Spirit connects us not simply to a past death but to a present life! To a new creation, lived by our connection to the firstborn from the dead (Col 1:15–19).

AFFIRMATION 4
Our life is now animated by the Holy Spirit.

In Romans, Paul makes these connections between us and Christ's death and resurrection, with one pointing to the death of sin and the other to our new life in God (Rom 6:1–11). But we should never forget that life, not death, is the goal. Affirming that the Spirit of creation is the same as the Spirit of re-creation, we benefit from the Spirit of Christ's ongoing work in our lives, renewing us in the image of the Son.

To get a clearer sense of what the apostle does with this idea, we will concentrate on Romans 8, which applies these themes to the Spirit for Christian life.

The Flesh and the Spirit

In Romans 8, the apostle Paul contrasts the life of the flesh with the life of the Spirit. The first way looks backward, while the second way looks forward. To appreciate Paul's perspective, we must begin by identifying what he means by *flesh* and *spirit*.

When Paul calls Christians to "walk not according to the flesh but according to the Spirit" (8:4), he is not primarily making a distinction between the physical and nonphysical. In chapter 7, the flesh represented living under the power of "sinful passions" and death, containing nothing good (Rom 7:5, 14, 18). Flesh in this context is not physicality as such but signifies human rebellion and enmity toward God, a mind dominated by unrestrained impulses, not in harmony with God or his intended shalom. "For the mind that is set on the flesh is hostile to God, for it does not submit to God's law" (8:7). Life in the flesh is focused on self, rebellion, and idolatry. Life in the Spirit is characterized by freedom before God—freedom *from* the enslavement of sin, the law, and self-absorption, and freedom *to* love God and serve others.[30] Such an understanding of freedom guides the life of the believer.

We should bear in mind this contrast between life in the flesh and life in the Spirit when we read that "by sending his own Son in the likeness of sinful flesh and for sin, [God] condemned sin in the flesh" (8:3). Of course, *likeness* here cannot mean only similarity, as if Jesus were not fully human; Jesus certainly did have a real physical body, a human mind, and emotions.[31] Yet by the power of the Spirit, from conception through ascension, Jesus was without sin. Nevertheless, he lived in a fallen world, meaning that real suffering, sadness, and even death were not outside his experience. Jesus, however, remained free from the power of indwelling sin, and thus he embodied life in the Spirit as opposed to life in the flesh. Sin was all around him in the world, but it found no residence within him—no evil spirit could reside in the one who was filled with the Spirit beyond measure (John 3:34). He genuinely felt the pain and anguish of a broken world, wept and expressed anger over death and sin, and was tempted in all ways as we are—yet by the Spirit he remained without sin. This same Spirit who preserved Jesus in purity is given to God's people.

What fundamentally distinguishes the Christian from the rest of humankind is not a change of external circumstances nor a new physical body but the indwelling of God's Spirit. "You, however, are not in the flesh but in the Spirit, if in fact the Spirit of God dwells in you" (Rom 8:9). Why is that so important? This Spirit is our link to the life of God. Notice Paul's fluidity of language in verses 9–11, where he speaks of him who dwells in us as the "Spirit of God," the "Spirit of Christ," "Christ is in you," "the Spirit [who] is life." The Spirit is God himself with us here and now. He changes our orientation to the present and the future. The Spirit, rather than human faithfulness, is the sign that God's promises will come to fruition for the saint (Eph 1:14; cf. 2 Cor 5:5). He is the Spirit "by whom you were sealed for the day of redemption"

---

30. Although the language of *Spirit/spirit* (*pneuma*) appears throughout Romans (thirteen times in chapters 1–7 and 9–16), in chapter 8 *Spirit* (*pneuma*) appears twenty-one times, far more than in any other chapter in the New Testament, and almost all of them seem to refer specifically to the Holy Spirit. See C. E. B. Cranfield, *Romans: A Shorter Commentary*, American ed. (Grand Rapids: Eerdmans, 1985), 172.

31. For historical context of this debate, see Kelly M. Kapic, "The Son's Assumption of a Human Nature: A Call for Clarity," *International Journal of Systematic Theology* 3, no. 2 (2001): 154–66.

(Rom 8:11; Eph 4:30). Thus the Spirit, who raised Jesus from the dead and who now lives in us, enables us to live not only in the present but in hope for the future.

Dying to Live: The Spirit's Ongoing Work in God's Children

John Calvin, drawing from the imagery of Romans 8, used the language of *vivification* and *mortification* to explain the dynamics of Christian life.[32] Philip Melanchthon, the great Lutheran Reformer, employed this same terminology when he discussed the life of repentance in the first systematic theology of the Reformation, which he produced in 1521.[33] As we look at these ideas, we must remember that Christian life is a matter of following God's Spirit and living by his power, as outlined in Romans 8. It is far too easy for the believer to fall into an impossible program of "self-help" moralism rather than trusting in God's renewing work in his children.

Vivification (from *vivificátio*) conveys the idea of giving life—to vivify or quicken. Simply put, the Christian is the person who is made alive by the Spirit of God. According to Calvin, that means not simply being born again at one moment in time but also being refashioned by the Spirit through time to reflect the image of God more and more. It is, as Calvin says, the "desire to live in a holy and devoted manner" that arises from "rebirth" in the power of the Spirit.[34]

Mortification (from *mortificátio*) conveys the idea of putting something to death. This language was used to convey the Christian's call to "put to death the deeds of the body" (Rom 8:13). Theologians have often explained this in terms of warfare, war against sin and Satan. Elsewhere Paul employs similar imagery, like "put off your old self [think *mortification*], which belongs to your former manner of life and is corrupt through deceitful desires, and to be renewed [think *vivification*] in the spirit of your minds, and to put on the new self, created after the likeness of God in true righteousness and holiness" (Eph 4:22–24).

---

32. E.g., John Calvin, *Institutes of the Christian Religion*, ed. John T. McNeill, trans. Ford Lewis Battles, 2 vols., Library of Christian Classics (Philadelphia: Westminster, 1960), 1.3.3, pp. 1:3–16. For more background, see Randall C. Gleason, *John Calvin and John Owen on Mortification: A Comparative Study in Reformed Spirituality*, Studies in Church History (New York: Peter Lang, 1995), esp. 45–77.

33. See Melanchthon's chapter on repentance in *Loci Communes* (1521), found in Wilhelm Pauck, ed., *Melanchthon and Bucer*, Library of Christian Classics 19 (Philadelphia: Westminster, 1969), 140–41.

34. Calvin, *Institutes*, 3.3.3, p. 1:595.

In his letter to the Colossians, Paul similarly calls the congregation to put to death the "earthly" in them (Col 3:5–11): "sexual immortality, impurity, passion, evil desire, and covetousness, which is idolatry." Paul adds to this list other sins that formerly characterized those whose "life is hid with Christ," who have "put on the new self" in Christ. Thus believers are called to put away destructive ways of life such as "anger, wrath, malice, slander, and obscene talk from your mouth." Lying to one another displays the former life (i.e., life in the flesh), which is to be abandoned since believers have put on the new self (i.e., life in the Spirit). Again, Paul is not generally attacking physicality when he says to get rid of the "earthly," but rather he is warning against sins that characterized believers' former life in the flesh. Because the renewing presence of God works in them, believers can now seek to live lives of "compassionate hearts, kindness, humility, meekness, and patience, bearing with one another and, if one has a complaint against another, forgiving each other. . . . And above all these put on love, which binds everything together in perfect harmony" (Col 3:12–14).

We cannot help but think of the fruit of the Spirit that characterizes the saint. As Paul wrote to the Galatians, Christians walk by the Spirit, which means they attempt not to "gratify the desires of the flesh" (Gal 5:16–26). Why? The Spirit and flesh are two different manners of life: One imitates God, the other imitates those at enmity with God; one is *constructive*, while the other is *destructive*. Signs of the Spirit in a person are love, joy, peace, patience, kindness, goodness, faithfulness, gentleness, and self-control, while the marks of the person without God's Spirit include impurity, enmity, strife, jealousy, fits of anger, rivalries, dissensions, envy, drunkenness, and orgies. To live according to the Spirit does *not* require you to hate your body or God's good creation; rather, it recognizes that bodies are not all that we are, that letting physical impulses set our goals leads to destruction, and that God's Spirit shows us how to follow after him who is "the way, and the truth, and the life" (John 14:6).

But when a believer reads the various traits of the flesh as opposed to the Spirit, very often they sense they have more in common with the former than the latter. Believers are sometimes far more aware of the sin that so easily entangles them (Heb 12:1) than they are of renewal. Just as new believers do not awake after their conversion to find themselves free from previous financial problems, neither do they, under normal circumstances, instantly find themselves free from longstanding struggles with anger, jealousy, and lust. If anything, new saints sense their failing in these areas more than before coming to faith. They now have eyes to see their sin with painful clarity.

Here we find the importance of gaining what might be called an "eschatological perspective." *Eschatology* simply refers to a discussion of the "last things" (*eschatos*). Commonly when we talk about eschatology, we focus our attention on what is yet to come, such as the last judgment, and label those events as "not yet" here. According to Paul, however, those events of the future already touch us. By God's Spirit we taste the future in the present—we enjoy true fellowship with God *now*, even though in the future such experiences will be far richer. The eternal Spirit who now dwells in us links us to the eternal Christ and therefore to his actions that we do not yet see. Inaugurated and realized eschatology is a major theme in John's gospel as well; especially relevant for our purposes here would be the Johannine emphasis on the "now-ness" of eternal life.[35]

Let us try to bring the significance of these things together in terms of Romans 8. Christians are those whom the Spirit of life has set free from the bondage and dominion of sin's reign. The Spirit has awakened them to life with God, to whom they cry out, "Abba" (8:15). Only those who have the Spirit of Christ see God that way or come to him as his children (Gal 4:6–7). God's perfect love has cast out our fear of condemnation and punishment, setting us free to enter God's presence in confidence, knowing that we come as sons and daughters of the King. God's Spirit not only gives us life and access to him but also empowers us to mortify sinful desires and actions. Believers live in the tension between the promise of unhindered communion with God in heaven and wrestling daily with sin in the present. Unchecked sin inevitably obstructs a Christian's experience of fellowship with God, although it does not place our union with him in question.[36]

Therefore, we must consistently rise against sin in the power of the Spirit, for this enemy does not grow tired of attacking God's people. According to Calvin, "This warfare will end only at death."[37] Similarly,

---

35. Marianne Meye Thompson, "John, Gospel of," in *Dictionary of Jesus and the Gospels*, ed. Joel B. Green, Scot McKnight, and I. Howard Marshall (Downers Grove, IL: InterVarsity Press, 1992), 368–83, esp. 380–81.

36. See Westminster Confession chapter 17 on perseverance.

37. Calvin, *Institutes*, 3.3.8.

John Owen, who wrote a whole treatise based on Romans 8:13, exhorted Christians, "Be killing sin or it will be killing you."[38] Indeed, our union with Christ assures us that even at the end of our earthly lives, our own deaths are not wasted or meaningless; rather, death itself becomes an inevitable and final opportunity for mortification and the taking up of one's own cross. Even as we make war against our sins, the ongoing struggle of life and brokenness—and ultimately death—can usher us into a further realization of union with Christ, both in his suffering and in his glorification (Rom 8:17). Victory has been secured, but we presently await the full realization of that victory.

New Testament scholar Oscar Cullmann memorably compared the Christian experience to living between D-Day (June 6, 1944) and VE-Day (May 7–8, 1945).[39] Once the Allies successfully invaded Normandy on D-Day, there was little doubt that the final victory over the German army would eventually be realized. Men and women who remained in the towns and prisons still occupied by the Nazis tell of being able to hear the approaching American troops—they waited expectantly for their final deliverance, but they could not fully enjoy their freedom until the victory was complete on VE-Day. Similarly, believers live between a D-Day (the cross and resurrection) and VE-Day (the triumphant return of Christ). Our lives are shaped by God's climactic work on the cross, where we hear the earth-shattering words, "It is finished" (John 19:30). In the shadow of the cross, we are confident of God's faithful ongoing renewal in the present, and the yet-to-be experienced but certain completion of his work in the future. Seeing how the work of Christ is not constrained by time is what forms a true eschatological perspective.

Hope: Confidence That God Is with Us

An eschatological perspective reminds us that we toil and struggle not in our own strength, but "with all *his* energy that *he powerfully works within*" us (Col 1:29, emphasis added). God's Spirit in us changes us. Our lives are not free from suffering and pain, but we live in the confidence that "he who began a good work in you will bring it to completion" (Phil 1:6).

---

38. John Owen, *The Works of John Owen*, ed. William H. Goold, 24 vols. (Edinburgh: Johnstone & Hunter, 1850–55; repr., London: Banner of Truth Trust, 1965, 1991), 6:9.

39. Oscar Cullmann, *Christ and Time: The Primitive Christian Conception of Time and History* (Philadelphia: Westminster, 1950), 84. VE-Day stands for "Victory in Europe" day.

Paul gives us a remarkable example of promise and fulfillment in Romans 8. Early in the chapter he claims that we received the "Spirit of adoption" who enables us to cry out to God as our Father (8:15). Later in the same chapter he also highlights the yet-to-be-realized nature of our adoption when he writes that "we ourselves, who have the firstfruits of the Spirit, groan inwardly as *we wait eagerly for adoption* as sons, the redemption of our bodies" (8:23, emphasis added). We are God's children now, and yet we still long for the time when we will be fully present with the Father without the presence of sin, free from decay and transience (1 Cor 15). The Spirit, whom Christ sent, points us to our Lord reigning in heaven, whose love is immeasurable and heavenly intercession unceasing. That love is the basis for our divine predestination, calling, justification, and ultimate glorification (Rom 8:30). That love, as shown in Christ, is the foundation of our hope in the present.

The apostle Paul puts our current struggles into a larger context when he writes, "For I consider that the sufferings of this present time are not worth comparing with the glory that is to be revealed to us" (8:18). Just as Jesus suffered and died, so we inevitably face grief, often for his name's sake. In fact, Paul and the apostle Peter agree that Christian suffering for the gospel is the normal and expected experience of believers (Rom 8:17; Phil 1:29; 3:10; 2 Tim 2:3; 1 Peter 4:12–19).

Christian hope is not based on the absence of pain but instead comes from the presence of God's Spirit even as it looks toward what we patiently expect (Rom 8:24–25; Heb 11:1). We cannot fully see the future, but we have seen him who is the future—the risen Christ. His Spirit in us even now enables us to pray in the midst of confusion, fear, and grief. While we may not be able to find the right words in our prayers, God's Spirit takes our groans and intercedes for us (8:27). He connects our vision of the future to Christ, and he enables us to see the present in light of God's completed and promised work: "If then you have been raised with Christ, seek the things that are above, where Christ is, seated at the right hand of God. Set your minds on things that are above, not on things that are on earth. For you have died, and your life is hidden with Christ in God. *When Christ who is your life appears, then you also will appear with him in glory*" (Col 3:1–4, emphasis added). Consequently, even in our tears we can claim—not naively, but with proper confidence—that "in all things God works for the good of those who love him" (Rom 8:28 NIV).

What is the evidence that God can be trusted with our hopes? The only way to cling to hope is to look on him in whom we hope, God in Christ. "If God is for us, who can be against us?" (8:31). How do we know God is for us? If God was willing to give his own Son *for us* and then raise him from the dead, how could we not trust him with our own lives? The risen and reigning Lord has united himself to us by his Spirit. Our Intercessor stands in the authoritative position at the right hand of the Father. God's people, therefore, stand justified and free from condemnation because we are sheltered in the finished work of Christ. This is the most secure position a person could ever ask for, and it provides the basis for Paul's beautiful doxology. We conclude this observation with Paul's own words:

> Who shall separate us from the love of Christ? Shall tribulation, or distress, or persecution, or famine, or nakedness, or danger, or sword? . . . No, in all these things we are more than conquerors through him who loved us. For I am sure that neither death nor life, nor angels nor rulers, nor things present nor things to come, nor powers, nor height nor depth, nor anything else in all creation, will be able to separate us from the love of God in Christ Jesus our Lord. (8:35–39)

We are safe in God's love because Christ has rescued us and has given us his Spirit; secure in the fellowship of the Spirit of Christ, we are confident God will not let us go.

AFFIRMATION 5

The Spirit convicts and comforts.

The Holy Spirit, who comforts God's people, always draws us back to Christ and will not let us go (John 14:16; 15:26; 16:7). Part of that comforting may not seem comfortable at the time because he also confronts us with the sins that distract us from Christ (Heb 12:1). Since sin damages our lives and our neighbors, the Spirit exposes what the problems are (John 16:8; cf. 1 Thess 1:5). Sometimes a fully engaged love for both God and neighbor is only possible through repentance from sin. We especially recognize the Spirit's convicting and comforting work (e.g., Acts 9:31) as we hear the proclamation of the Word.

For example, after Pentecost, when "all were filled with the Holy Spirit" (Acts 2:4) and the followers of Christ prophesied and spoke in foreign languages that they didn't even know beforehand. This was so all those present could hear and understand; Peter explained that this event resulted from a "pouring out" of the Spirit (2:17; cf. Joel 2:28–32). He was able to use this event to bring a word of salvation and hope for those who called upon the Lord (Acts 2:21). But Peter did not merely cite past events nor the filling of biblical predictions; instead, he told his listeners that this Jesus was not dead but risen and now "exalted at the right hand of God, and having received from the Father the promise of the Holy Spirit" (2:33). As the Spirit worked in and by the Word, Peter's hearers "were cut to the heart" and wondered how they should respond (2:37). They were told to repent and be baptized, all with the promise of receiving the gift of the Spirit (2:38). When the Holy Spirit brings this kind of conviction, the purpose is not just to make people feel guilty or bad about themselves but to free people from their sins so that they might follow Jesus, whom "God has made . . . both Lord and Christ" (Acts 2:36; cf. 4:8–12, 31). This is repentance unto life.

The Holy Spirit doesn't convict people only of their sins; he also convicts us of the presence and power of Jesus, drawing us to the incarnate Son, and this conviction is our comfort. The Spirit shows us a historic Messiah who was crucified in a particular place and time and shows us that this same Jesus is the risen and reigning Lord who loves and cares for us right now (Heb 4:14–16). This revelation is meant to bring us great joy (Acts 13:52) and a strong sense of security in our connection with Jesus, as well as enable us to confess that "Jesus is Lord" (1 Cor 12:3). We will discuss this theme more fully in chapter 6. The risen King is fully present with us by his Spirit, and this same Spirit brings great comfort and guidance even in the hardships and threats of this life.

Those indwelt by the Spirit receive not just information for their minds but new affections and a freshly empowered will that opens us up to a new quality of life characterized by love for God and for our neighbor. Paul writes that the most important gift of the Spirit is not speaking in tongues, offering prophecy, healing, or other miracles, but *love* (1 Cor 13:1–13). The Spirit's power in Acts shows up in a variety of ways, and Paul tells the Corinthian church that these are all gifts from the living Spirit dwelling in them. He also makes clear that *the gifts understood and exercised apart from love cause problems.*

In a masterful way, the apostle shows how the Spirit unites us not only to God but also to one another: Working out of this twofold union is meant to be the unity and upbuilding of love. First, he affirms that all good gifts come from God by his Spirit: "Now there are varieties of gifts, but the same Spirit; and there are varieties of service, but the same Lord; and there are varieties of activities, but it is the same God who empowers them all in everyone" (1 Cor 12:4–6). Notice that the Spirit doesn't make us all the same but actually empowers us to be different! The Spirit enables some to give an "utterance of wisdom" and others a word of "knowledge," while still others are empowered to help with healing, the working of miracles, prophecy, discernment, tongues, interpretation, and so on (12:8–10). What unites these people is not their similarity of gifting or interest but the one Spirit. Second, all the Spirit's work, with all its great variety, is always meant "for the common good" (12:7). "All these are empowered by one and the same Spirit, who apportions to each one individually as he wills" (12:11). In this way the Spirit is answering the very prayer of Jesus from the garden of Gethsemane as he asked that his disciples "may all be one, just as you, Father, are in me, and I in you, that they also may be in us, so that the world may believe that you have sent me" (John 17:21). The unity of the Father and Son is the model for the unity among the disciples.

Distinction does not erase unity—they are two dynamics of the one love in the Spirit! Paul honors our differences. Because of who the Spirit is and how he works, our distinctions and differences compose this "one body," and in that body "there may be no division" (1 Cor 12:25). He isn't saying, "Let's agree to disagree"—although he might support that decision on all manner of issues. Beyond any mere spirit of toleration, Paul proclaims the unity we have—apart from and prior to our agreements—through the Holy Spirit. These are not natural familial relations but a union of people from various tribes and tongues, female and male, young and old, strong and weak, poor and rich. His claims were revolutionary in the first century and remain revolutionary in our day. His pneumatology, accordingly, leads him to claims that "if one member suffers, all suffer together; if one member is honored, all rejoice together" (12:26). Why? Because the one Spirit unites us together beyond our doing or understanding and leads us into the one confession that Jesus is Lord and Christ.

CONCLUSION

God the Holy Spirit brings us into communion with God by the embodiment of grace whose name is Jesus Christ so that we may enjoy the Father's love. The Spirit is God, the very Love shared between the Father and Son and yet distinguished from them. And by this Spirit we are brought into the life and love of God.[40]

Let us conclude this section by listening to Jonathan Edwards, who echoes Augustine when he builds on this triune reality as a framework for Christian life in his *Treatise on Grace*. Edwards maintains that God's "infinite delight is in himself, in the Father and the Son loving and delighting in each other," and this love between the two divine persons is no mere feeling or notion, but is a third divine person who is the Love of God.[41] And the person and work of the Spirit draw us into fellowship with the triune God. Synthesizing images and language from Revelation 22, John 7, Ezekiel 47, and Psalm 36, Edwards describes how the water of life that comes from the throne of God is the living water that is none other than the Holy Spirit, who is God's own pleasure and "infinite delight"; thus God's Spirit is poured into us, drawing us by this same Spirit back into the life and love of the eternal triune God.[42]

The circle is completed: All things are from him, through him, and to him. In other words, love begins in and with God himself, but then it returns back to God through human creatures who are empowered by the Spirit. Thus the Spirit is God's love abiding in our hearts not simply so we might resist temptation but so that we might again actively love God and neighbor. By Christ's very human life, death, and resurrection and the Spirit's peculiar enlivening power, heaven and earth are reconciled. As living participants, we are embedded by the Spirit in the movements of God's love, and in this way we bear witness to shalom breaking into this present world. Accordingly, we worship and adore the Holy Spirit, who is the "Lord and Giver of Life," including our Christian life!

---

40. Parts of this chapter first appeared in an earlier form in Kelly M. Kapic, "Are We There Yet? An Exploration of Romans 8," *Modern Reformation* 15, no. 4 (July/August 2006): 22–27.

41. NB, Jonathan Edwards observes how in Scripture, while one reads of the love of the Father for the Son and of the Son for the Father, "yet we never once read either of the Father or the son loving the Holy Spirit, and the Spirit loving either of them." Edwards, "Treatise on Grace," in *Writings on the Trinity, Grace, and Faith*, ed. Sang Hyun Lee, Works of Jonathan Edwards 21 (New Haven, CT: Yale University Press, 2003), 186.

42. Edwards, "Treatise on Grace," 21:186.

PART 3

INTERLUDE

No one gives himself freely and willingly to God's service unless, having tasted his fatherly love, he is drawn to love and worship him in return.
—JOHN CALVIN[1]

---

1. Calvin, *Institutes*, 1.5.3, p. 55.

CHAPTER 5

THE LAW-GOSPEL DISTINCTION
Framing the Human Response to God

> *By winning favor through faith with the one who justifies, they attain righteousness, observe it, and live in it.*
> —AUGUSTINE[1]

> *Law, so prominent in Scripture, is not to be understood as creating relationship. Rather, law nourishes relationship.*
> —ESTHER LIGHTCAP MEEK[2]

> *All through the incarnate life and activity of the Lord Jesus we are shown that "all of grace" does not mean "nothing of man," but precisely the opposite: all of grace means all of man, for the fullness of grace creatively includes the fullness and completeness of our human response in the equation.*
> —T. F. TORRANCE[3]

---

1. Augustine, *The Spirit and the Letter*, 51, in Works of Saint Augustine, ed. John E. Rotelle, trans. Roland J. Teske (Hyde Park, New York: New City, 1997), 1.23, p. 184. The next sentence reads: "For a work that brings life to the one who does it is only done by a person who has been justified."

2. Esther Lightcap Meek, *Loving to Know: Introducing Covenant Epistemology* (Eugene: Cascade, 2011), 197.

3. T. F. Torrance, *The Mediation of Christ*, new ed. (Edinburgh: T&T Clark, 1992), xii, original emphasis.

INTERLUDE

We now move our emphasis from divine to human agency. The book's first half stresses *God's* movement toward us; the second half stresses *human* movement toward God. This chapter on how to navigate the law-gospel distinction will serve as a necessary interlude between the two.

How does divine agency not undermine the reality of human agency? The short answer is Christ, who uniquely is the theanthropic one—truly God and truly human. He alone is able to embody both divine and human agency. While we spent time on this key point in chapter 3 on grace—Christ is the embodied gift of God—we will return to the Messiah as the key at various points in this second half of the book as well. For only Christ can perfectly represent and reveal both God and humanity. However, without a good understanding of how the biblical story portrays God and his vision for humanity, discussions of Jesus and his central role in Christian life too easily go sideways. At the extremes, Jesus becomes either merely a great moral example or a replacement who makes our agency irrelevant. While there is always some truth in extremes, danger comes when other truths are lost in declaring only one aspect of various biblical affirmations. How can we avoid this?

We must ensure that we (1) do not create tension in our understanding of the Trinity by pitting the divine persons against one another, even as we also (2) maintain a healthy understanding of continuity and discontinuity in the history of redemption.

We are called to speak of and worship the one triune God. We do not have a divided deity, but *this* God is the God of creation and the same as the God of re-creation. Central to this God's work in both creation and re-creation is humanity. Consequently, when we speak of a theology of Christian life, we need to connect the Torah with the Gospels, the Hebrew Prophets with the book of Revelation: This includes understanding human agency not in the absence of divine presence and power but against that backdrop. And as we learned earlier in our discussion of Christ the unique Mediator, the point of the incarnation was not to undermine humanity but to save us by rescuing and freeing his people so that we might again love God and neighbor and even rightly relate to the rest of creation. The point was never to undermine creation in general or human agency in particular but rather for us to see the Mediator, the Christ, not as just a truly human one but as the Savior of the world. His redemptive purposes were to bring forgiveness and new birth, as well as to reconcile, heal, and set free. Simply put, to love! Jesus came to rescue us from judgment so that we might have life. And that life abundantly. A properly conceived theology of Christian life never compromises the radical nature of God's grace, nor does it undermine the clear dignity and beauty of human response to God. To better understand how to navigate this dynamic, we will begin by revisiting the serious debates about how to relate law and gospel. Here we see crucial aspects of how the human response to God properly fits into a theology of Christian life.

DOES GOOD NEWS MEAN NO HUMAN AGENCY?

"*Gospel* is now a dead word for you! Please stop using it."[4] Finally reaching a point of exasperation, I let these words fly one day in a college course I was teaching in the early 2000s. While it felt odd to say that, I was serious. I told students they couldn't use the word *gospel* for a season of time. Doesn't that sound outrageous? Is that offensive to Christian faith and practice? Why would I ever do that? The short answer is that the word *gospel* was being thrown around carelessly left and right, and it wasn't clear that people knew what they were talking about. Divorced from any biblical and theological setting, the word was starting to sound hollow, and that hollowness was damaging the minds and hearts of the students.

Anecdotally, it appears to me that over the past twenty or thirty years, the term *gospel* has regained a special prominence, especially in the spheres where American evangelicals and conservative Reformed believers overlap. Gospel hermeneutics, gospel sermons, gospel churches, gospel conferences, and even a Gospel Coalition were popping up all over. Out came *gospel* study Bibles and *gospel*-centered manuals to help you discover your latent legalism. A new simple litmus test developed: "Is it gospel?" You prayed? Good. But was it a *gospel* prayer? You exegeted a passage of Holy Scripture? Good, but was it *gospel* exegesis? Simply say the word *gospel* and you instantly have a trump card. Conversations cease and you win. Furthermore, *gospel* was almost always reduced to a mere equation with the idea of "justification by faith alone." Not surprisingly, when students would actually read their Bibles, especially the Gospels,

---

4. While there are numerous changes, much of this chapter first appeared in an earlier version in my essay "The Law-Gospel Distinction in Reformed Theology and Ministry," in *God's Two Words: Law and Gospel in the Lutheran and Reformed Traditions*, ed. Jonathan A. Linebaugh (Grand Rapids: Eerdmans, 2018), 129–51.

they soon discovered you cannot simply substitute the phrase *justification by faith alone* every time you run across the word *gospel*: It creates confusion, not clarity. Let me be clear: I believe justification by faith alone is central to what the gospel tells us about, but it isn't directly what the New Testament authors refer to when they use the word *gospel*, nor does that word exhaust the gospel. More on this point later.

In many ways, this resurgence of a "gospel focus" is a genuine gift to the church. Some who were previously suffocating in various forms of moralism were finally receiving words of grace and hope. In that way, I don't believe you can ever have too much gospel. Having written and participated in many of these gospel-branded activities and publications, I have found much of it personally helpful, and I do hope many have been encouraged and strengthened by these various efforts.

As is often the case, however, excitement about (re)discovering any idea can unexpectedly create new misunderstandings and challenges. And as we found in the Reformation itself, handing down the content of the gospel from one generation or leader to the next is not always easy. Assumptions once intuitively obvious—such as the legitimate place for Christian obedience to divine commands—were sometimes tossed aside in the name of radical grace.[5] Yes, antinomianism is always a genuine danger (cf. Rom 6:1–2), but presenting God's law in a way that subtly or not so subtly makes divine grace contingent upon repentance and law keeping is as bad a mistake in the opposite direction.[6] Legalism is not simply a danger Protestants once needed to be aware of, but it remains an ever-present enticement that must be resisted.

At their best, Christian theologians have helpfully parsed out the distinction between law and gospel not merely because they enjoy scholastic theology but because our understanding of this relationship has

---

5. Cf. Synodical Declaration of Berne, 1532. Jan Rohls believes Berne represents an antinomian propensity; Rohls, *Reformed Confessions: Theology from Zurich to Barmen*, trans. John F. Hoffmeyer, Columbia Series in Reformed Theology (Louisville: Westminster John Knox, 1997), 197. To determine why this accusation is made, see "The Bern Synod (1532)," in *Reformed Confessions of the Sixteenth and Seventeenth Centuries in English Translation*, vol. 1, *1523–1552*, ed. James T. Dennison Jr. (Grand Rapids: Reformation Heritage, 2008), esp. chs. 6–17 (pp. 237–45).

6. A powerful example of the subtle but deadening effects of creeping legalism comes in the Scottish Marrow controversy. For a brief history of the debate as well as relevant theological and pastoral reflections upon it, see Sinclair B. Ferguson, *The Whole Christ: Legalism, Antinomianism, and Gospel Assurance—Why the Marrow Controversy Still Matters* (Wheaton, IL: Crossway, 2016). A nicely edited version of the book behind the controversy (originally published in 1645), including Thomas Boston's early eighteenth-century editorial notations and extended reflections, is also now available: Edward Fisher, *The Marrow of Modern Divinity* (Fearn, UK: Christian Focus, 2009).

THE LAW-GOSPEL DISTINCTION

massive pastoral consequences. I hope that the version of the law-gospel distinction presented here both reflects the fullness of Scripture and can help all believers make more sense of Christian life.

Returning to my students: When I asked them to stop saying the word *gospel* for a season, it was because I wanted them to rediscover what the word actually means—not just academically but personally. Simply repeating the word is no guarantee that you understand the good news of the gift of Christ, nor that your life is being lived in and out of that gospel reality! Much recent confusion on these matters reflects historical challenges that can arise from within the Reformed tradition itself. Hopefully we can all learn together here. Let us therefore consider the law-gospel distinction and then conclude this chapter with specific reflections on pastoral care and preaching, since our vision of Christian life is often shaped in such work.

CONFUSION ABOUT THE LAW?

It may surprise some readers, but there is often real confusion and even debate about what one means by *law* in Christian theology and proclamation. This puzzlement is especially strong among the laity. Does *law* simply refer to the Levitical code? Does it refer only to the Ten Commandments, or to all five books of Moses, or perhaps to the Scriptures in their entirety? Oddly enough, this ambiguity can be useful. The Hebrew word commonly translated as "law" (*Torah*) sometimes signifies God's will (e.g., Jer 18:18) or priestly decisions (e.g., Hos 8:12); sometimes it points to specific laws within the Pentateuch, and at other times it represents the whole of the first five books of the Hebrew Scriptures.[7] Similarly, the New Testament also uses the Greek equivalent *nomos* in different ways, "ranging from law as a principle revealed in nature or reason, to the Old Testament Scriptures as a body, the first five books of the Scriptures, or any single command of the Scriptures."[8] Early Protestant use of the word reflects this broad biblical usage,[9] which we

---

7. See "Torah," in *New International Dictionary of New Testament Theology*, ed. Colin Brown, 4 vols. (Grand Rapids: Zondervan, 1975–1978), 1:70.

8. "νόμος," in *Greek to English Dictionary and Index to the NIV New Testament: Derived from the Zondervan NIV Exhaustive Concordance*, entry 3795. Cf. "νόμος," in *Greek-English Lexicon of the New Testament: Based on Semantic Domains* (New York: United Bible Societies, 1996), entry 3551.

9. For more on how law was particularly understood in the Reformed tradition, especially after Westminster, see Michael Allen, "The Law in the Reformed Tradition," in *God's Two Words: Law and Gospel in the Lutheran and Reformed Traditions* (Grand Rapids: Eerdmans, 2018), 45–62. For

INTERLUDE

can see, for example, in the Leiden Synopsis (first published in 1625): It summarizes what they believed were six different meanings or uses of law found in sacred Scripture.[10] Yet all these variations still, in some way, point to the revelation of God.

Part of what makes our reading of the New Testament texts difficult is that when the apostle Paul refers to the law, he sometimes appears to have in mind what Herman Ridderbos calls "Jewish-synagogical nomism," a Pharisaical misuse of Israel's ordinances that Paul himself had once embraced.[11] More recently, scholars like James Dunn have argued that Paul's warnings against "works of the law" are not about earning salvation through law keeping but rather about making salvation depend upon one's link to national Israel, with law keeping (especially circumcision, Sabbath laws, and food laws) serving as an identity marker.[12] Thus Paul is denouncing not what Moses said or originally intended but rather a perverse reading and application of the law in some Second Temple Jewish circles. The whole New Testament, including Paul, takes a Christocentric view of law: Jesus fulfilled the law by serving as Priest, King, and Prophet, liberating his people from its condemning power and giving them his Spirit so that they can now freely follow the commandments to love God and neighbor. Later we will return to contemporary Pauline scholarship when I discuss how to ground our ethical framework as Christians.

John Calvin long ago observed that the key to understanding Paul was to differentiate not so much among moral, civil, and ceremonial laws (although that could fruitfully be done), but between a narrow and broad use of the law. One functions destructively while the other serves a more positive purpose. Calvin exhibits this distinction in his exegesis of Romans 3:21–4:25, where Paul highlights the righteousness of God "apart from the law." The *narrow* view of the law seeks, in whatever

---

a similar treatment focused on the Luther tradition in the same volume, see Piotr J. Malysz, "The Law in the Lutheran Tradition," 15–44.

10. William Den Boer and Riemer A. Faber, eds., *Synopsis of a Purer Theology*, vol 1, *Disputations 1–31* (Landrum: Davenant, 2023): 181–82 (i.e., disputation 18:1–12). In sum, these six are: (1) anything instituted by God, (2) a particular moral, ceremonial, or forensic law, (3) as a metonym for the Torah, (4) used by synecdoche for all the books in Old Testament, (5) as a "metonym of the adjunct" it can be used of the Levitical ministry, and (6) "figuratively for the natural directive of human reason."

11. Herman Ridderbos, *Paul: An Outline of His Theology*, trans. John Richard De Witt (Grand Rapids: Eerdmans, 1975), 156–57.

12. See J. D. G. Dunn, *Jesus, Paul, and the Law: Studies in Mark and Galatians* (Louisville: Westminster John Knox, 1990), 191–203.

form, whether ceremonial or civil, to give law or works a power to make one righteous, and Calvin emphatically rejects this (as he believes he is merely echoing Paul here). The *broader* view of the whole law, however, still serves as a positive "expression of the will of God," which means it contains "the promises" that are established in Christ.[13] God's will and promises found in the law thus can speak to its continuing helpful place for the Christian. We see God's moral law here; it raises our awareness of our sin and guilt, thus leading us to Christ. But Calvin adds, "Faith then confirms and establishes the law." He explains: Justification is not based on the law, but "in justification the exact righteousness of the law is imputed to human beings." But that is not all, since as Barbara Pitkin observes in Calvin, "in the process of sanctification human hearts are formed to the law."[14] In other words, when sinners attempt to use the law as a means of justification, they have misunderstood their relationship to the law. When saints, filled with the Spirit, listen to God's revelation in his law, they are able to glean from the law God's good promises as well as wisdom for how to live now as children of God.

We look back at Christ and see the law in terms of the fulfillment of the messianic promises, and this changes our orientation to the law without annihilating the law's value. For example, Calvin elsewhere observed that David praises God's law in Psalm 19, but in the broad rather than narrow way. By *faith* David saw the law in his redemptive-historical context in terms of the free promises of salvation that were to come. But when Paul in Romans 1:18–23 draws on texts like Psalm 19, he is opposing those who employ the law in the narrow sense—that is, attempting to use law as the basis of their right standing with the God of Israel. They divorced law and gospel, and the result undermined both. Writing in a different context from David's, Paul therefore warns against misusing the law.[15] It was meant to point to Christ, not to serve as a substitute for him. But those who trust in Christ also seek to live in obedience as described by God's revelation, including the law. This takes us back to a question about how we speak of the law, whether in our pulpits or personal conversations.

---

13. Here I am drawing from Barbara Pitkin, *What Pure Eyes Could See: Calvin's Doctrine of Faith in Its Exegetical Context*, Oxford Studies in Historical Theology (New York: Oxford University Press, 1999), 44–45.
14. Pitkin, *What Pure Eyes Could See*, 45.
15. Pitkin, *What Pure Eyes Could See*, 100–103.

INTERLUDE

IS THE LAW PURELY NEGATIVE?

Imagine that every time a person hears the law or commandments of God mentioned from the pulpit, it is in a mostly negative context. Repeatedly one only hears that the law condemns, it crushes, it judges; or that Christians are supposed to be people of the gospel and not of the law; or that looking to the law only shows a person what a miserable sinner they are. The law, it is said, is like an unforgiving mirror that shows you every blemish, every wrinkle, every imperfection. Again and again, the listener hears versions of this, but never any positive word about God's commandments. Is that a problem?

We must be very careful here, but I have come to believe this one-sided reference to the law adds to our confusion about the law and—maybe more significantly—stunts the experience of grace for the saints of God. For example, if we only hear how the law judges us, at some point we are apt to ask if the giver of the law is himself unkind or even cruel. And if the law has no place for the Christian, then is God now unconcerned with righteousness and obedience? Does he not care about injustice or cruelty? Or was all of that just a game in the past? How does one even define righteousness and obedience without reference to God's revealed will? Does such one-sided emphasis also undermine any appropriate place of human agency for the Christian? If we only speak of the condemning voice of the law and God's commandments, then we are undermining the hearer's ability to understand not only the law, but also what a life shaped by the gospel looks like.

As is well known, the early Reformers, including Luther and Calvin, and their confessional statements basically agreed that the law (in its various meanings) served at least a pedagogical role. It exposed the fallen human as a sinner who now stands exposed before a holy God. The law of God certainly has functioned well to show sinful humanity its place under divine judgment. But is it right to speak of the law *only* in terms of judgment? Throughout the Old Testament, God's law is something to be delighted in (Ps 1:2), stored in one's heart (Pss 37:31; 40:8; cf. Josh 1:7–8), and considered praiseworthy (e.g., Neh 9:13–14). It is perfect and sure (Ps 19:7). The longest psalm in Scripture endlessly glories in the gift of God's law (Ps 119).

If we speak only negatively of the law, I fear we will lose sight of the full power of God's grace. Paul declares, "Do we then overthrow the law by this faith? By no means! On the contrary, we uphold the law" (Rom 3:31). "The law is holy, and the commandment is holy and righteous and good" (Rom 7:12; cf. 1 Tim 1:8). Obedience was a struggle for Paul and our relationship with the law is complex, but he nevertheless declares, "For I delight in the law of God, in my inner being" (Rom 7:22). He was not always successful in following it, but he knows that it presents God's character to us and that, properly understood, it can protect and promote love (cf. Jas 2:8–12). Jesus clearly stated that he came not to abolish the law but to fulfill it (Matt 5:17). John puts it this way: "The law was given through Moses; grace and truth came through Jesus Christ" (John 1:17). This grace and truth—this person—is where the believer is liberated from the law's curse. In that liberation, God enables his saints to hear wisdom and purpose in the law rather than merely judgment and death. We no longer live in the Mosaic dispensation of approaching God through the law, but that doesn't mean the law is now merely negative or irrelevant. Why? We now see the law in light of Christ by the indwelling presence of his Spirit.

WHAT GROUNDS CHRISTIAN LIFE?

We must stop imagining that Paul advocated God's grace whereas his fellow Jews rejected grace. John M. G. Barclay makes this abundantly clear in his recent magisterial study entitled *Paul and the Gift*. But Paul's opponents did differ from him in how they understood and used the idea of grace, and this had profound implications.[16] One theological strand appearing among the Second Temple Jews has been called "covenantal nomism," which held that grace was extended specifically to Israel by God's establishment of his covenant and that law keeping was essential not for *entering* the covenant but for *staying in it*. Paul, in contrast to that tradition, recognizes the essential *incongruity* of grace: It has nothing to do with the inherent worthiness of the recipients. There is nothing one can do to prepare oneself to be worthy of receiving God's great gift (*charis*), nor to stay in God's grace. It is grace upon grace, from first to last. Grace puts one in, and grace keeps one in. God even freely gives

---

16. John M. G. Barclay, *Paul and the Gift* (Grand Rapids: Eerdmans, 2015). Paul was especially provocative in how he highlighted the *incongruity* and *superabundance* of God's grace, whereas others were drawing on different "perfections of grace," thus creating a chasm between the two perspectives. On various "perfections" of grace, begin with Barclay, *Paul and the Gift*, 66–78; cf. 562–74.

grace to the unworthy gentiles, who were normally deemed unfit to receive such divine favor. Having received the gift of Christ, Paul called the saints to respond to God joyfully in the new relationship believers have with God in Christ.

Barclay's research into the discipline of anthropology proves illuminating. It is arguably a very modern notion that for something to be a "pure" gift rather than merely a transaction, there can be no sense of expectation of return (e.g., Jacques Derrida[17]). That is to misunderstand gift giving and social relations. Put simply, historically gifts are often given with the purpose of establishing or strengthening a relationship, and that can be a good thing for families, communities, and others. Obviously, this dynamic can be and has been abused. Gifts have been employed to manipulate, put people in debt, and so on. The gospel is radical because a person does not need to be "fit" to receive this gift, nor is the relationship based upon reciprocation.

The gospel is grace down to its roots. It "bypasses and thus subverts pre-constituted systems of worth,"[18] so that no one needs to be "fitting" to receive this gift. Although the divine-human relationship does not require crass gift giving as repayment, it does institute a new kind of reciprocity of grace flowing from grace. Barclay and Peter J. Leithart recognize this aspect of divine gift giving in the biblical and Christian traditions.[19] God freely gives and we freely receive his gifts by faith, but the core of the gift is to put us in his continuing fellowship of love and trust, a fellowship that works because he establishes and maintains it: All things are from him, through him, and to him (Rom 11:36).[20] This gift is active, enabling, reciprocal, and relational. And because it is new life, it includes responses and actions of obedience and service. This is not a transactional response (contract) but an effected response (covenant).[21]

According to Paul, personal obedience to God's law does not function

---

17. Jacques Derrida, "The Time of the King," in *Given Time: I. Counterfeit Money*, trans. Peggy Kamuf, Carpenter Lectures (Chicago: University of Chicago, 1992), 1–33, esp. 27.
18. Barclay, *Paul and the Gift*, 6.
19. Peter J. Leithart, *Gratitude: An Intellectual History* (Waco: Baylor University Press, 2014).
20. Cf. Kelly M. Kapic, *The God Who Gives: How the Trinity Shapes the Christian Story* (Grand Rapids: Zondervan, 2018).
21. Cf. the hard-fought distinction the best Puritans made between *covenant* and *contract*: "It is the difference between 'therefore' and 'if.' The former [i.e., covenant] introduces *implications* of a relationship that has been established; the latter [i.e., contract] introduces the *conditions* under which a relationship will be established." Ferguson, *Whole Christ*, 115.

THE LAW-GOSPEL DISTINCTION

as the means of either getting into or staying in God's favor—but that doesn't mean it has no value for those living under the blessings of divine favor. C. E. B. Cranfield long ago warned us not to forget that Paul was not working in the later developed doctrinal environment that used the language of *antinomianism* and *legalism*, and so instead the apostle used the language of *law* in a variety of ways to communicate such concerns. The careful reader must honor that diversity by paying attention to how, in each context, Paul is speaking about the law.[22] Navigating through this complexity, Paul, following Jesus, does not advocate a hatred of the law but rather believes the only way to understand the law rightly now is through the lens of the Messiah's advent, death, and resurrection. With the coming of the Messiah (i.e., the gospel), it makes sense that subtle distinctions within the law (e.g., civil, ceremonial, and moral) could become useful and justifiable.[23] How, then, does the coming of the Gift of God (the Christ!) fulfill, inform, and transform the law's place and purpose?

Concerning the relation between gospel and law, Karl Barth asked a useful question: What grounds Christian ethics? This question helps advance the conversation. Drawing on Zwingli and then Calvin, Barth believed these Reformers recognized that we need to ground our ethics not simply on the law but upon grace.[24] This distinction is subtle but crucial. Whether it is historically accurate, Barth saw early Protestants as having two main options on which to ground their ethics: faith or grace. Obviously both views speak of the vital importance of faith and the unquestionable dependence we have on God's grace, so neither choice ultimately rejects the other. But what Barth suspected he would find—and I leave the historical accuracy of this assertion to historians for now—was that each tradition actually did put more weight on a different

---

22. See C. E. B. Cranfield, "St. Paul and the Law," in *New Testament Issues*, ed. R. Batey (London: SCM, 1970), 148–72.

23. There are legitimate reasons to recognize that God's law is a unified whole and that trying to divide it up according to civil, ceremonial, and moral can start to feel like a foreign imposition on the Hebrew Bible. On this, most biblical scholars currently agree. Thus this threefold division of civil, ceremonial, and moral has fallen on hard times. However, for its prevalence and remaining relevance, see, for example, John Witte Jr., "Law and Theology in the Western Legal Tradition," *St Andrews Encyclopaedia of Theology*, ed. Brendan W. Wolfe et al. (2022), www.saet.ac.uk/Christianity/LawandTheologyintheWesternLegalTradition. Also, for a recent robust defense of this threefold distinction, see Philip S. Ross, *From the Finger of God: The Biblical and Theological Division of the Law* (Glasgow, UK: Mentor, 2010).

24. Karl Barth, *The Theology of the Reformed Confessions*, trans. Darrell L. Guder and Judith J. Guder, Columbia Series in Reformed Theology (Louisville: Westminster John Knox, 2002), 87.

INTERLUDE

piece of the puzzle: Whereas *faith* was the key in Luther's conception of Christian life and therefore the foundation for his understanding of Christian ethics, those in the Reformed tradition explicitly chose to use grace as their foundation for constructing a Christian ethic,[25] allowing that ethic to employ the law in positive ways without becoming a slave to the law, as happens to those outside the grace of our Lord.

Grace enables us to delight in God's gift of the law without being condemned by it. Drawing on Calvin, Barth comments, "He who gave the gospel also gave the law; as seriously as the gospel is to be taken in faith, so seriously is the law to be taken for the will."[26] In this context he says that, for Calvin, "to be sure, ethics is established not directly upon faith, as Luther attempted to do, but upon grace." From this subtle but critical distinction, Barth continues: "The law does not establish obedience, as little as the gospel itself establishes faith. Rather, both obedience and faith are established through the grace of the Holy Spirit, and as the gospel sets the direction there, now the law does so here."[27]

Obviously, this also relates to one's concept of the will. Early writers in the Reformed tradition strongly emphasized not merely the catastrophic effects of sin on humans born into sin but also the life-giving power of the Spirit. Sin remains a real problem for believers, but the Spirit calls us also to find joy in the resurrection life we can now participate in. Echoing Bullinger, Barth agrees that indwelling sin remains a problem, but by the Spirit, "the human person should know that through grace he has really been put on his feet in order to *walk*."[28] Put differently, the redeemed sinner—brought to life by the Spirit and secure in Christ's atoning work—was not made alive to become a passive rock, but to live, to love, and to serve. Guidance for this new life comes from God's revealed will, including his law.

---

25. A detectable shift from faith to grace as that foundation appears in the early Reformed leaders. Although my reading of Luther and Melanchthon has been hugely helpful for me through the years, I am not qualified to comment on the accuracy of Barth's assessment.

26. Barth, *Theology of the Reformed Confessions*, 101.

27. Barth, *Theology of the Reformed Confessions*, 101. Barth's concern is partly that faith can reduce the importance of this question to the "specifically religious sphere," seeing the "problem of human life in its totality," and thus the need to better see what it means to love God in all of life, following him in a "universal way" (101). See also Michael Allen, "'The Visible Renewal of Human Life': Barth's Ethical Assessment of the Reformed Confessions," *Scottish Journal of Theology* 77, no. 3 (2024): 224–31.

28. Barth, *Theology of the Reformed Confessions*, 92.

ZWINGLI AND THE POSITIVE ROLE OF THE LAW

As early as the 1520s, Zwingli was already noticing biblical, theological, and pastoral problems with people's understanding of the place and function of the law. He observed that those who spoke of the abolition of the law did so in a "wholly clumsy fashion."[29] I will draw on Zwingli here to show that even at their beginnings, Reformed writers did not ignore or reject the law once the Messiah had come but recognized that the gospel revolutionizes a person's relationship to the law. It still has value for the Christian, so we can still praise God for his holy ordinances.

Zwingli recognized that we are not allowed to view the law in a simply negative manner. It is, after all, a gift from God. In 1523, Zwingli described it this way: "The law is nothing but a manifestation of the will of God."[30] That is, the law reflects the eternal will of God, and so we must treat the law thankfully as "*conducive* to the godliness of the inner person."[31] Zwingli's pastoral concern for the heart of the believer, beyond all mere ritual or external obligation, sees the law as positive rather than negative. His word *conducive* reveals and establishes a Reformed approach to law: "Laws do not have the power to make a person godly or righteous; rather, they point out only how a person should be if he wants to live according to the will of God, become godly and come to God."[32] Others after him further developed and clarified this intuition, and properly understood, that development can resonate widely across Christian traditions.

Thus we find that the law serves more like a map than like an engine. It was *never* made to empower, only to guide (cf. Acts 13:39; Rom 2:13). Treating the law as a source of power, which we do when we try to obey the law to justify ourselves before God, fails us and distorts our understanding of the law's purpose and function. We look to the law for guidance but to God's Spirit for power. This is where wisdom and life come together.

Like a map—think here of a GPS system that provides direction

---

29. Huldrych Zwingli, "A Short Christian Instruction . . . ," in *Huldrych Zwingli Writings: In Search of True Religion; Reformation, Pastoral, and Eucharistic Writings*, trans. H. Wayne Pipkin, vol. 2 (Allison Park, PA: Pickwick, 1984), 63.
30. Zwingli, "A Short Christian Instruction," 53.
31. Zwingli, "A Short Christian Instruction," 53 (emphasis added).
32. Zwingli, "A Short Christian Instruction," 53.

INTERLUDE

while you drive—the law rightly judges you when you are lost and going the wrong way, but it can also point you in the right direction. On its own the law doesn't take you anywhere, but it does show you the path. One might think here of the Old Testament language of the law's role as announcing blessing and cursing (e.g., Josh 8:34). The law does not make one blessed or cursed, but it lets one know where one stands in relationship to God's will. Here is where the "third use of the law" often comes in, as it does not merely show one's sinfulness before a holy God but also can helpfully guide Christian life. What the law cannot do, nor was ever meant to do, is give you the power to get where you need to go. And the presence of sin deprives us of all such power within us. We are absolutely dependent on God's grace and provision. Apart from his grace we are dead in sin (Eph 2:1). The map shows how far off the target we are, and we realize we have no energy or ability to correct the ship's course. The map alone will not save us. What we need is wind; what we need is the life-giving breath of the Spirit of God.

The law shows us how far short we fall of God's will: We do not love God and neighbor with our whole heart, soul, and strength. Jesus tells us that this intention was always at the heart of the law.[33] All sinners who stand before the law apart from Christ stand judged. But God's gift of himself to us in Christ has become our life: Christ confronts us and brings us into the communion announced in the gospel. In his brief work "Divine and Human Righteousness," Zwingli wrote, "You learn through the word of the divine will what a great treasure God is. For the goodness which he prescribes for us, he is in himself and he conducts himself as he bids us to do; for he is not at all like the tyrants who devise superb laws which they themselves never keep."[34] Thus we must view all of life as a free gift from God in Christ. Receive this gift, stand in awe of the treasure, and follow your new King. His gift does not make obedience insignificant; it just means that obedience is not the basis of the new relationship. But the laws are his laws, telling us the shape

---

33. Zwingli draws on Luke 16:16 and following, noting that the law and prophets served Israel until John the Baptist, but now Messiah has come. The law lasted until John, but even after John it did not become void. Fully aware how contradictory this sounded, Zwingli argued that since the law comes from God himself, so we must follow carefully the implications. Accordingly, he first observes that all the ceremonial laws of the Old Testament served as a shadow of Christ, and when the light itself comes, the shadow disappears (cf. Heb 10:1). These ceremonies, unfortunately, were often treated merely at the external level rather than dealing with the inner man.

34. Huldrych Zwingli, "Divine and Human Righteousness," in *Huldrych Zwingli Writings*, 2:8.

THE LAW-GOSPEL DISTINCTION

of our communion and our place in it, and so they remain good. The moral law is a good thing in Christ because it "shows the will of God."[35]

Zwingli uses the law against theft as an example to help us understand the point. The law clearly calls us not to steal. When we look beyond the surface, this law points both to actual physical robbery and to greedy hearts. It judges our thoughts, motives, and actions, showing us our need for our sinless Savior, who not only avoided theft, but also gave us himself. We who are now united to Christ by the Spirit are set free from the law's condemning power. We have been crucified with Christ: Through the law we have died to the law (Gal 2:19–20). In this way, the law has lost its power over us. There is therefore now no condemnation for those who are in Christ Jesus (Rom 8:1). Nevertheless, as Zwingli comments, to imagine that it is irrelevant whether a *Christian* steals or not—whether a Christian is greedy or not—is to misunderstand both the law and the gospel. Of course Christians should not steal, and we learn this from God's law. And Christ displays the flip side of that coin: Fully obeying this command means extending generosity, not just avoiding robbery. Christ gave us everything he had, including his own life! The Westminster Larger Catechism uses this hermeneutic to apply the Decalogue to us: "Where a duty is commanded, the contrary sin is forbidden; and where a sin is forbidden, the contrary duty is commanded."[36] Jesus embodies faithfulness to God's commandments, and now he dwells in his people by his Spirit. It makes sense, therefore, that as he spreads his love into our own hearts we now seek to imitate our Lord's sacrificial love.

FREE TO OBEY

Paul announces that "the law of the Spirit of life has set you free in Christ Jesus from the law of sin and death" (Rom 8:2). "Free in Christ"—because Christ became a curse for us, we are free from the curse of the law (Gal 3:13), but this doesn't mean that the Torah is no longer of value to us. This line of thinking may be what causes some to believe that the Old Testament is no longer relevant to us. But does the Decalogue, which is applied throughout the Old and New Testaments,

---

35. Zwingli, "A Short Christian Instruction," 62.
36. Westminster Larger Catechism, 99.4.

not have abiding value for Christians even as we are also set free from the law's damning power?

It is *loving* to teach saints the will of God as found in his moral law so that we can learn how to live freely as his kingdom people. "Free in Christ"—while sin enslaves and perverts, the gospel not only frees us *from* sin's corruption and the law's judgment, but also frees us *to* live in fellowship with God in accordance with our true nature. Breaking God's commandments entangles us in sin (Heb 12:1); we have been set free from that prison of sin's domination, so why act like we are still in jail? We praise God for his law not merely because it shows us our sin but because it guides us in our Christian freedom. Such freedom is the liberty to follow Christ out of gratitude and love for our Lord, not because we dread punishment. We are free to love God and neighbor.

Zwingli's long 1523 *Exposition* . . . tells us that the law no longer condemns the believer, and then he comments, "Not that that which God bids and wills should no longer be done."[37] Those who were swindlers have ceased their swindling not only out of fear but because their obedience "is kindled increasingly more by the love of God" as they discover divine grace and "friendliness" in increasing measure. "The greater this love, the more one does what God wills."[38] *Love*, not guilt, compels us to follow God's revealed law, a moral law that promotes "doing good." Zwingli rejects legalism because the law, which has been satisfied by Christ, no longer condemns the believer. No one can secure God's favor through law keeping; it is already ours in Christ. But he also rejects antinomianism because we who have experienced God's love and grace, and in whom God now dwells by his Spirit, respond in love toward God and follow his commandments. Yet our love and obedience do not arise from our own strength. "Rather, God effects in him love, counsel and works," so that "where God is," as he noted earlier, "you need not have to worry how to do good."

Calvin demonstrated similar assumptions when he described the "pious mind" of the believer: It is a mind persuaded that God is "good and merciful," not doubting God's loving-kindness.[39] A godly person

---

37. Huldrych Zwingli, *Exposition* . . . , in *Huldrych Zwingli Writings: In Defense of the Reformed Faith*, trans. E. J. Furcha, vol. 1 (Allison Park, PA: Pickwick, 1984), art. 22, p. 189.

38. Zwingli, *Exposition*, art. 22, p. 189. The following quotes in this paragraph also come from this article.

39. John Calvin, *Institutes of the Christian Religion*, ed. John T. McNeill, trans. F. L. Battles, Library of Christian Classics 20 (Louisville: Westminster John Knox, 1960), 1.2.2, p. 42.

"deems it meet and right to observe [God's] authority in all things, reverence his majesty, take care to advance his glory, and obey his commandments."[40] We do not seek to earn God's favor—we already have it and stand secure in our Father's delight. In contrast with the impious mind that only fears God for his potential punishments and has not learned to obey God out of love, "this [pious] mind restrains itself from sinning . . . because it loves and reveres God as Father, it worships and adores him as Lord. Even if there were no hell, it would still shudder at offending him alone."[41] Notice how this follows the distinction made by Thomas Aquinas (building on Augustine) between servile and filial fear: God's children do not fear the punishment of a heartless master whom we are forced to serve, but we do have a healthy and even loving fear of our heavenly Father who is ours through the incarnate Son.[42] Similarly, the 1559 French Confession of Faith states that we "must seek aid from the law and the prophets for the ruling of our lives, as well as for our confirmation in the promises of the gospel."[43] The law shows us not only our sin but also the glory of all that Christ has fulfilled on our behalf. In the context of our union with Christ, the law gives instruction for living in God's grace and wisdom. To borrow Matthew W. Bates's provocative language, this might be described as the pathway and life of "gospel allegiance."[44]

For the Christian, the law is still not power, but when rightly employed it serves as a trustworthy map for following God and lovingly relating to our neighbors and the rest of creation. The power for walking that path, however, is supplied by the triune God himself: We are known and called by the Father, cleansed in the atoning blood of the Son, and enlivened and kept in the sanctifying fellowship of the Spirit (cf. 1 Pet 1:2; Jude 1; 2 Cor 13:14; Heb 9:14). This is what it means to live in the grace of God.

---

40. Calvin, *Institutes* 1.2.2, p. 42.
41. Calvin, *Institutes* 1.2.2, p. 43.
42. Aquinas, *Summa Theologica*, 2.19 (esp. art. 1–10).
43. "French Confession of Faith" 23, in *The Evangelical Protestant Creeds*, vol. 3 of *The Creeds of Christendom*, ed. Philip Schaff (Grand Rapids: Baker, 1983), 372–73. Rohls, who also quotes this memorable portion from the French Confession, nicely summarizes the Reformed conclusion: "The law thus also applies to the justified, serving as a standard of orientation for sanctification," Rohls, *Reformed Confessions*, 201.
44. Matthew W. Bates, *Salvation by Allegiance Alone: Rethinking Faith, Works, and the Gospel of Jesus the King* (Grand Rapids: Baker Academic, 2017); Bates, *Gospel Allegiance: What Faith in Jesus Misses for Salvation in Christ* (Grand Rapids: Brazos, 2019).

INTERLUDE

PUTTING THE PIECES TOGETHER: ADVICE FOR MINISTERS

It is now time to put some of the puzzle pieces back together. Given that many readers of this volume will be theologians, pastors, and Christian counselors, I will conclude this chapter by providing some reflections more explicitly aimed at helping those who minister to God's people. These discussions about the relationship between the law and the gospel are not presented merely as academic discussions but to reflect abiding pastoral concerns. Whether in the counseling office or from a pulpit, pastors and leaders must employ wisdom, joy, and hope as they bring the good news of the gospel to their listeners. With this particular audience in mind, I would like to close the chapter with three final reflections:

- First, don't pit love against the law.
- Second, do differentiate between union and communion.
- Third, finish the sermon!

Love and Law

Scottish-born theologian John Murray, writing in 1935, confronted expressions of sentimentality in the church that seemed to distort the more classic Christian concepts of law and gospel. Some Christian voices were pitting God's moral law against love. Since Christians were under grace and gospel, these voices claimed the law had no place in our lives: To value the law was to devalue love. Murray, following his Reformed tradition, reframed the situation: "We are not saved by obedience to the law, but we are saved unto it."[45] This observation is based on his view that the law of God is not arbitrary but derives ultimately from God's own nature, primarily his purity and holiness.[46] If God's character does not change, then the law must have abiding relevance for the believer. Obviously, we must take into consideration progressive revelation, redemptive historical developments, and so on, always with Christ as the focal point. But failure to see any abiding significance for the law is a failure to see the connectedness of revelation and the unity of God. Ministers who fail to preach from the Old Testament deprive their

---

45. John Murray, "The Sanctity of the Moral Law," in *Collected Writings of John Murray*, vol. 1 (Edinburgh: Banner of Truth, 1976), 199.
46. Murray, "Sanctity," 196.

congregations of understanding the New Testament's context. Rather than showing God's love to be the fulfillment of the law, Murray's opponents were at risk of making love and law enemies. Murray, using the word *love* here to refer to the sentimental impulses that people feel, assesses the problem thus:

> What our modern apostles of love really mean is the very opposite of this: they mean that love fulfills its own dictates, that love not only fulfills, but that it is also the law fulfilled, that *love is as it were an autonomous, self-instructing and self-directing principle*, that not only impels to the doing of the right but also tells us what the right is. This is certainly not what Paul meant when he said, "love is the fulfilling of the law [Rom 13:10]." He tells us not only that love fulfills, but also what the law is which it fulfills.[47]

According to Murray, this law was most markedly and simply laid out in the Decalogue. But as in the time of the judges, when the Israelites did what was right in their own eyes (Judg 17:6; 21:25), people today also keep looking inside themselves rather than to external resources to know the good, the true, and the beautiful. We determine love now solely by our intuitions rather than by using any external guidance from a transcendent God. Recent volumes by Charles Taylor, David Brooks, Carl Trueman, and Tara Isabella Burton have ably demonstrated this modern turn toward the inward and have observed the social and personal consequences this shift creates.[48]

Although God certainly works in our consciences, sin still exerts its destructive inward corruption there, making the conscience alone simply not reliable as a moral guide. It needs both cleaning and education.[49] Despite stereotypes, the positive use of the law is not a uniquely Reformed invention but has been valued throughout the Christian

---

47. Murray, "Sanctity," 199 (emphasis added). He later adds, "The directing principle of love is objectively revealed statutory commandments, not at all the dictates which it might itself be presumed to excogitate."

48. Charles Taylor, *Sources of the Self: The Making of the Modern Identity* (Cambridge: Harvard University Press, 1989); David Brooks, *The Road to Character* (New York: Random House, 2015), esp. 3–15, 240–70; Carl R. Trueman, *The Rise and Triumph of the Modern Self* (Wheaton, IL: Crossway, 2020); Tara Isabella Burton, *Self-Made: Creating Our Identities from Da Vinci to the Kardashians* (New York: PublicAffairs, 2023).

49. J. W. Gladwin, "Conscience," in *New Dictionary of Christian Ethics and Pastoral Theology*, ed. David J. Atkinson et al. (Leicester, UK: Inter-Varsity, 1995), 251–52.

tradition. According to Lutheran theologian Philip Melanchthon's mature thought, for example, "a third use of the law is necessary," as it serves "to inform the good conscience and encourage it to obedience."[50] It should not surprise us, then, that the young French theologian John Calvin picked up this idea and described it in his first edition of the *Institutes*.[51] Jan Rohls describes how this idea informs the Reformed view of freedom: "The conscience is free only when God is the sole Lord of the conscience, and this means that the law as God's unsuperseded goodwill is also valid for Christians who have been redeemed and set free from the law's curse."[52] This is why many, even Melanchthon, speak favorably of a "third use" of the law.

Jesus, too, connects love to law: "If you love me, you will keep my commandments" (John 14:15). "Whoever has my commandments and keeps them, he it is who loves me. And he who loves me will be loved by my Father, and I will love him and manifest myself to him" (John 14:21). He also links our commandment keeping to his own obedience to his Father: "If you keep my commandments, you will abide in my love, *just as I have kept my Father's commandments and abide in his love*" (John 15:10, emphasis added). The incarnation did not eliminate God's moral concerns but answered them through the coming of his Son, who generates love in us by his love for us. Murray was, of course, right to reject the sentimentalizing of love when it was put into opposition against the moral commandments of God. Christians live by faith in Christ, but this is *life*—that is, we still move and act and love, and thus we are still concerned to live *well*. But how shall we know what it means to live well, especially when our knowing is so very faulty? We must look to God's revealed will as described in the Scriptures and look to his Spirit for guidance in understanding and applying what he says there. We have been liberated into a life of communion with the triune God, who tells us the shape of that life.

Union and Communion

Those outside of the Reformed tradition are sometimes baffled by our insistent valuing of both the law and the gospel. To understand this dynamic we must look at the distinction between *union* and *communion*.

---

50. Timothy J. Wengert, *Law and Gospel: Philip Melanchthon's Debate with John Agricola of Eisleben over* Poenitentia (Grand Rapids: Baker, 1997), 205.
51. Wengert, *Law and Gospel*, 206.
52. Rohls, *Reformed Confessions*, 200.

THE LAW-GOSPEL DISTINCTION

This distinction takes us right into important pastoral challenges and possibilities. On the one hand, union is both a status and condition into which God puts us: Those who are made alive by the Spirit of Christ are made children of God, a position of security, comfort, and rest. On the other hand, communion is an activity that we carry on within the given status and condition of union: Our life is life with God, a fellowship that he treasures and in which he leads us as Lord. His love for us guides us toward constructive and away from destructive actions so that we can accurately summarize God's law as loving God and loving our neighbor. Our response to God's law, then, has genuine consequences for our *experience* of communion. Let us look at the pastoral importance of union, communion, and their connections.

Our obedience never was and never could be the foundation of Christian life. Christ and Christ alone is that foundation. He always was and always remains our security and salvation. We expound and celebrate this fact in the doctrine of union with Christ. The Reformed tradition holds that the Holy Spirit unites us to Christ and thus liberates us to enjoy fellowship with God. Union is not the goal of Christian life, as it can appear in some Christian traditions, but is its starting point. There is no Christian life, no fellowship with God, apart from this union with our Mediator. Nor does this union ebb and flow like the tides of the ocean, but it remains always full. In other words, a believer's behavior cannot affect this union because the union was established objectively by God's grace alone; it was not based on our obedience to the law. Our union with Christ is thus a great comfort to struggling believers as they realize that their lapses have not compromised God's love and commitment to them. God does not love them less or more today because of their obedience or lack thereof. They are secure in his Fatherly love.

As Karl Barth notes, "This same God [of gracious regeneration] also makes man obedient for his service."[53] Because believers are God's

---

53. Barth, *Theology of the Reformed Confessions*, 148. Under the covenant of grace, the law "materially" remains in force, but its function has now been changed: "It is no longer a means of justification, but rather a standard of sanctification." As Rohls concludes, "The third use of the law (*tertius usus legis*) consists of justified sinners showing gratitude in the form of obedience to the law for the justification that has occurred" (Rohls, *Reformed Confessions*, 202). In his well-crafted book, Wengert argued that Melanchthon "wanted desperately both to defend the Reformers from the charge that they denied the necessity of good works and at the same time to avoid robbing the conscience of the gospel's consolation. So he devised a way to speak of the necessity of works for the believer by excluding their necessity for justification" (Wengert, *Law and Gospel*, 188).

newborn children, their new life in Christ leads them to want to know their Father's wishes, to learn from him what is good and best. In this context, God's law is a gift that helps guide the children's desire to follow their wise Father.

The love of our holy and good heavenly Father for his children never grows nor diminishes based on their obedience. Still, the Christian's experience of intimacy with God is often helped by acts of repentance and obedience or hindered by acts of neglect and disobedience. God's chief concern is not with our law keeping or ritual keeping for their own sakes but with the quality of our communion with him. If one spouse neglects another, a husband and wife may still be united in marriage, but their communion suffers. Similarly, our union with Christ is secure, and the nature of that union gives our actions consequence within that communion. Does it matter if we pray or not? It doesn't change the union, but it clearly affects our communion. Does it matter if we commit adultery or not? It does not destroy our union, but it certainly affects our communion. As James declares, we are to be "doers of the word, and not hearers only, deceiving [ourselves]" (Jas 1:22). Today's actions shape today's communion and tomorrow's needs. And in all of that, Jesus does not let us go. He comes to the persons that we are, with all our obedience and faithlessness, our love and our despair, and he ministers to the needs and possibilities and impossibilities of the day. Our works do demonstrate who we are and the condition of our faith (Jas 2:14–26), yet good works are not done to earn God's favor but are entirely a consequence of God's favor. When our works demonstrate our sinfulness as well as our faith, they do not put us out of our union with Christ at all. Jesus uses even these sins and shabby works to draw us into communion with himself.

John Owen unabashedly points out that *communion* requires what he calls "mutual communication."[54] Communion is based on union but is distinct from it. Owen explains, "Our communion, then, with God consisteth in his communication of himself unto us, with our returnal unto him of that which he requireth and accepteth, flowing from that

---

54. John Owen, *Of Communion with God the Father, the Son and the Holy Ghost*, in *The Works of John Owen*, vol. 2 (Edinburgh: Banner of Truth Trust, 1965), 8. For a full treatment of Owen's distinctive Trinitarian approach to union and communion, see Kelly M. Kapic, *Communion with God: The Divine and the Human in the Theology of John Owen* (2007; repr., Grand Rapids: Baker Academic, 2024), esp. 147–205.

union which in Jesus Christ we have with him."[55] Living with one foot in the imperfect "now" and the other in our eventual "not yet," we experience this communion as "initial and incomplete" while also breathing the air of the "perfect and complete" communion that it will eventually become.[56]

The preaching of the full gospel requires that ministers proclaim the security of our union with Christ,[57] to reassure our congregations that their sin and shortcomings before the law no longer condemn them. We need to silence those voices of condemnation in the hearts of our people. We rest in the robe of Christ's righteousness. As those who are secure in Christ, we can discover and proclaim to each other more of who this Christ is, learning and teaching about his goodness, his kindness, his compassion. Further, to understand both our Lord and our life with him, we also must look at Christ in light of the law that he fulfilled. As we rest in the kindness of our Father, we also seek to grow in our knowledge and love of him by loving what he loves and eschewing what he eschews. The law is one way that God gives us continued guidance into that discipleship.

Finish the Sermon

Let me now return to where I began this chapter, looking at the occasional overuse and misuse of the word *gospel*. The gospel is news, good news about who Jesus is, what he has accomplished, and what he continues to accomplish: "The kingdom of the world has become the kingdom of our Lord and of his Christ, and he shall reign forever and ever" (Rev 11:15)—quite the banner headline. Those liberated by the gospel live under our new King and great High Priest and eagerly listen to his prophetic voice, a voice that the entire Old Testament, including the law, anticipated and promised. We long to know what it means to live in God's kingdom. Such a life and the knowledge of it can never arise from trying to add something to grace, but it does require that we preach the full counsel of God, both Old and New Testaments. It requires preaching in a Jesus-centered way from the Law and the Prophets. It requires that we meditate on God's law by looking, again

---

55. Owen, *Of Communion*, 8–9.
56. Owen, *Of Communion*, 9.
57. For a recent wonderful unpacking of the place of union—from a Reformed perspective—for theology and ministry, see J. Todd Billings, *Union with Christ: Reframing Theology and Ministry for the Church* (Grand Rapids: Baker Academic, 2011).

and always, through the lens of who Jesus is and what he has done. And to the question of whether those texts have relevance for Christians besides simply saying Jesus has fulfilled them, we have to answer yes.

Some sermons or "gospel presentations" involving the law amount to no more than adding more impossible requirements to our already heavy hearts. Moralist preachers simply use Scripture to tell stories of virtue and being good, crafting their sermons as a means of behavioral conditioning, trying to persuade or maneuver (or sometimes scare) their listeners into becoming good citizens, good family members, and faithful worshipers of God. That method and goal rest on a misunderstanding of the Scriptures and the gospel to which they point.

One kind of reaction to such moralistic preaching, however, completely fails to demonstrate any continuing relevance of the law to the believer today. It acknowledges our inability to keep the law and preaches salvation in Christ, but it treats the law as having no further hold on us and fails to show any further use of it. However, the good news of Jesus Christ does not make our actions irrelevant. Anyone who preaches that exertion of any sort is somehow inherently anti-gospel is simply not listening to Jesus. Dallas Willard put it starkly: "Grace is not opposed to effort, it is opposed to earning. Earning is an attitude. Effort is an action. Grace, you know, does not just have to do with forgiveness of sins alone."[58] I have become suspicious, on the basis of various factors, that something psychological often happens when people hear sermon after sermon that always boils down to this:

1. You are a sinner and nothing you do can merit God's favor (true).
2. Jesus was faithful and in him we are forgiven (true).
3. The end (incomplete).

At first, such a structure can be wonderfully liberating. Praise God, my standing before a holy God is not based on my meager efforts and mixed motives. Praise him for the wideness and depth of his mercy. But extended exposure to such preaching begins to persuade its listeners that any attempt to follow God's commandments, and any pattern of exerting effort, can only be taken as a sign of "works righteousness" and that such attempts must inevitably be from mixed motives and incomplete

---

58. Dallas Willard, *The Great Omission: Reclaiming Jesus's Essential Teachings on Discipleship* (New York: HarperCollins, 2006), 61.

faithfulness. Therefore, *why try*? If you do, you must be a legalist. Further, it commonly produces a combination of self-loathing and apathy in those who consistently sit under this pattern of preaching.

Some might respond: "How can there be self-loathing? Look what God has done for you in Christ!" But look again. The message says, "God demands. In our corruption and sin we fail. God cannot really stand to look upon us in our sin. But hurrah! God doesn't have to because the Father now sees the Son and not us in our sin, and therefore we are loved." After a series of such sermons, the listeners haven't been listening very hard if they don't wonder, "Does God actually love *me*? Does he even know *me*? Or does the Father merely love the Son? How am I supposed to have any sort of personal relationship with someone who can't stand to look at me?" Preaching that says, "God the Father can't stand you, but he loves you when you look to Christ," is not the gospel, and as a gospel substitute, it puts people into theologically and spiritually unstable positions. It is a distortion of union with Christ. I have explored this troubling phenomenon and the theology underlying it elsewhere, but a few things can and should be said here.[59]

God loves *you*. He knows *you*. And not only does he forgive you, but he also wants *you* to live. He wants *you* to receive and extend love. He wants you to be the true you that you sometimes get a glimpse of and are often striving to be. What does that look like? The true you acts and knows and loves out of the core of your being, a being that isn't isolated but has its life in communion with the triune God, with your neighbors, and with all of creation. And who is this God? He is the one who designed and made you, who redeemed you and upholds your being, who reveals to you who he is and who you are. Each of us is really a mystery, filled with complexity and deserving great care. And if *we* are a mystery, consider what a mystery the created cosmos and the creator God are! Of course, we need help navigating all of this mystery. That's what the law is for, to tell us who we are and what our place is in connection with God, our neighbors, and the rest of the world. Jesus the Christ has followed that path, and our renewal in the image of Christ includes liberty to imitate Christ, to enter into the movement of divine generosity, to participate in God's grace as he extends himself to and through us. We are not mere observers of that grace, but participants.

---

59. Kelly M. Kapic, *You're Only Human: How Your Limits Reflect God's Design and Why That's Good News* (Grand Rapids: Brazos, 2022), esp. ch. 2.

INTERLUDE

Entering into God's love causes us to love. And loving God and neighbor has always been the summary of the law.

Sermons that proclaim Christ crucified also must proclaim, "Christ is risen, and in him, we have been raised to life. So *live* in him!" Too often our sermons speak in terms of the cross but neglect the promise of resurrection,[60] a promise that applies not only to a future life but also to our present. We have been raised in him, and we live in that new life *now*. Our life is thus necessarily a life informed and transformed by the renewing of the mind (Rom 12:1–2), a renewal that happens by Word and Spirit. They give guidance on how to live as God's people. The Reformed tradition from which I come affirms the use of the law, never as a means to become justified, never as a means to make oneself secure before God, but as a means of understanding God and ourselves better. And this perspective can be found roughly throughout all Christian traditions and certainly isn't just in Reformed communities. Thus used, God's law shapes us, guides us, challenges us, and encourages us. Yes, we should flee from abuses of the law. But when it is rightly preached, meditated on, and understood through the person and work of Christ, God's law is a law of liberty. Faithfully done, a sermon promotes love of God and neighbor, not self-loathing or apathy.

THE GOSPEL OF THE CRUCIFIED AND RISEN CHRIST

The gospel, the good news that Jesus is Lord and cares for his people, proclaims both Christ crucified and Christ risen. Our union with Christ gives us a secure life in fellowship with God, who loves us and teaches us how to live that life. Therefore, we look to God's law not for power but for profitable instruction. Christ teaches us how to use the law as a map, and the law teaches us more about Christ. The gospel proclaims to us both that we are liberated from the law's condemnation and that we are free to obey our Lord and Savior. Christ has died. Christ is risen. In him we now live as his people until he comes again. With this connection, we are ready to more fully unpack our theology of Christian life, which at its most basic level is a response to the love of God.

---

60. To grasp how central the resurrection is to a Christian conception of ethics, see Oliver O'Donovan, *Resurrection and Moral Order: An Outline for Evangelical Ethics*, 2nd ed. (Grand Rapids: Eerdmans, 1994).

PART 4

US TO GOD

Human Agency—Responding to God's Love

CHRISTIAN LIFE IS A RESPONSE TO THE LOVE OF GOD.

> And I will walk among you and will be your God, and you shall be my people. . . . I have broken the bars of your yoke and made you walk erect.
> —LEVITICUS 26:12–13

> Steadfast love and faithfulness meet;
>   righteousness and peace kiss each other.
> Faithfulness springs up from the ground,
>   and righteousness looks down from the sky.
> —PSALM 85:10–11

> Christ is both the covenant-making God (along with the Father and Son as the holy Trinity) and the covenant-keeping man.
> —GRAHAM A. COLE[1]

---

1. Graham A. Cole, *God the Peacemaker: How Atonement Brings Shalom*, New Studies in Biblical Theology (Downers Grove, IL: InterVarsity Press, 2009), 106.

CHAPTER 6

MESSIAH
The Foundation of Christian Life

> *He was the same who anointed and who was anointed, as God anointing Himself as man.*
> —JOHN OF DAMASCUS[1]

> *In Jesus, the human vocation is accomplished.*
> —ALBERT VANHOYE[2]

> *Jesus loved God with his entire being and his neighbor as himself.*
> —DANIEL TREIER[3]

Turning now to the last section of the book, we will consider a few ways to anchor a theology of human response to God in Christ by the Spirit. We will look at how a biblical account of human response to the love of God is centered on Christ, unfolded in the corporate body, and particularized in the individual. This movement from Christology to personal and ecclesial observations is necessary to avoid either reducing the gospel to some Pelagian account of human effort, on the one hand, or, on the other hand, undermining the unique centrality of Christology in order to try to secure human dignity or worth. We will seek to avoid picking between the uniqueness of Christ and the significance of personal responsibility, between valuing the corporate nature of our

---

1. John of Damascus, *The Orthodox Faith*, in *St. John of Damascus: Writings*, trans. Frederic H. Chase Jr. (Washington, DC: Catholic University of America Press, 1958), 4.14, p. 365.
2. Albert Vanhoye, *A Perfect Priest: Studies in the Letter to the Hebrews*, ed. and trans. Nicholas J. Moore and Richard J. Ounsworth, WUNT 2:477 (Tubingen: Mohr Siebeck, 2018), 218.
3. Daniel J. Treier, *Lord Jesus Christ* (Grand Rapids: Zondervan Academic, 2023), 232.

identity and the value of our particularity. The hope is that we can then move forward in a way that is christologically faithful, ecclesiologically sound, and existentially satisfying.

Considering corporate worship in particular, the last two chapters of this book will argue that key ecclesial practices are meant to shape our lives deeply, even when we don't realize it. In particular, the basic liturgy contained in the weekly gathering of God's people reflects the arc of Christian life. In other words, Christian life reflects and is shaped by the basic contours in the arc of corporate worship, which moves in the rhythm of call and response: calling invites coming; proclamation provokes faith, prayer, and praise; Eucharist grounds and enables our gratitude made manifest in offerings; the peace of Christ enables us to live in peace with our neighbor; and benediction frees and sends us out in love to sacrificially serve a broken and hurting world. This arc of corporate worship should be understood in a threefold manner: in terms of Christ, the community of faith, and the individual. Accordingly, we turn to the threefold cords of human response to God's love: Messiah, ego, and ecclesia.

A THREE-CORDED ROPE: CHRIST, ME, AND ECCLESIA

Let us begin by stating what has been and will be a guiding principle in this book: *God loved us, and through the incarnate Christ, he also loved himself for us.* Put differently, in Christ we find both God's ultimate expression of love for humanity and humanity's ultimate expression of love for God.

As is well known, there is never simply one danger to be aware of in Christian life. We reviewed several common false dichotomies in the opening chapter of this book: objective and subjective; catholic and particular; transcendence and immanence; Trinitarian and Christ-centered; representation and imitation. Having briefly laid these out, we then reflected on the love, grace, and fellowship that are ours by God's revelation, his self-giving, and his drawing us into participation in his life and love. We emphasized God and God's work.

That is all wonderful. But as Simeon Zahl has recently commented, theologians too often remain at the level of abstraction and ignore or downplay real human experience—that is, discerning how the life-events of Christians influence their theologies and how theology affects their lives. This happens for all manner of good reasons. It is, of course, a complicated matter. Zahl rightly traces the lineage for many of these issues back to the Reformation.[4] The excesses of early sixteenth-century "enthusiasts" and leaders like Andreas Bodenstein Karlstadt[5] raised concerns for Luther and his followers about allowing one's personal experience to be a foundation for shaping theology, as contrasted with using the Scriptures as the final arbiter of theology. But in the process of trying to avoid the dangers of subjectivity, they so strongly emphasized Scripture as the objective standard of theology that, at least at the level of rhetoric, they seem to have produced some false dichotomies (e.g., Scripture *or* experience, revelation *or* emotion). Early leading Protestants like Luther rejected the Roman Catholic corporate view of authority (i.e., church tradition at the same level as Scripture) as well as the spiritualists' or enthusiasts' privatized view of spiritual experiences.[6] They viewed both corporate and individual experience with great suspicion.

From then on, much of Protestant theology has struggled with this tension regarding the place of personal experience in theology: Do knowing and loving God shape how we view him? Friedrich Schleiermacher (1768–1834) felt this question keenly and leaned hard on the personal-experiential side, defining doctrines as "accounts of the Christian religious affections set forth in speech."[7] In response to a later challenge by Emil Bruner's views on natural theology, Karl Barth (1886–1968) jumped to the other side of the balance when he cleared his throat with a loud, unmistakable declaration: "Nein!"[8] Don't trust or build upon something as unreliable or subjective as experience in building a theology, whether that is cultural or privatized; look only to the objective, to God himself as "Revealer, Revelation, and Revealedness" to construct doctrine.[9]

---

4. See esp. Simeon Zahl, *The Holy Spirit and Christian Experience* (Oxford: Oxford University Press, 2023), 18–26.

5. Zahl, *The Holy Spirit*, esp. 20–22.

6. For a vivid portrait of Luther's evolving concerns about emerging enthusiasts, see James Reston Jr., *Luther's Fortress: Martin Luther and His Reformation Under Siege* (New York: Basic, 2015), esp. chs. 7 and 14.

7. Friedrich D. E. Schleiermacher, *The Christian Faith*, trans. H. R. Macintosh and J. S. Steward [of the 2nd German ed. of 1830–31] (Edinburgh: T&T Clark, 1928), 76.

8. For both Emil Brunner's work and Barth's response, see *Natural Theology: Comprising Nature and Grace by Dr. Emil Brunner and the Reply No! by Dr. Karl Barth* (Eugene, OR: Wipf & Stock, 2002).

9. Karl Barth, *Church Dogmatics* 1.1, *The Doctrine of the Word of God*, ed. G. W. Bromiley and T. F. Torrance, trans. G. W. Bromiley, 2nd ed. (Edinburgh: T&T Clark, 1975), 295.

Clearly, each side of this debate brings up legitimate concerns and contributions. Besides the most radical examples (and even these are debatable), Christians do not typically fall into two cleanly divided groups, those who *only* value experience and those who *only* value revelation. Good theologians throughout the ages are always more nuanced than that. As Zahl ably shows, from Paul to Augustine, from Luther to Barth, each of these leaders may have emphasized one side of the continuum at times, but at their best they avoided simplistic dichotomies and sought to discern and articulate the theological foundations and functions of Christian experience in the work of God. This is especially true since experience was often a way of speaking about the Spirit's work—something to which all orthodox theologians give due attention.

As an heir of this ongoing challenge, I am interested in putting forth a proposal that appreciates rather than ignores the tensions. I'm not interested in putting forward a vague or generic *via media*; instead, in this and the following chapters, I seek to lay out a concrete proposal that hopefully honors the beautiful and needed tensions I already noted in chapter 1.

How might we discern the steady ground of the objective realities in a way that establishes (rather than undermines) the value and clear necessity of the subjective side of our lives? How might we respect divine transcendence while also affirming divine presence and transformative action? How might we put forward a vision that genuinely retains the catholicity of Jesus's prayer (John 17) and the historic and global nature of the Christian faith while also highlighting the local and particular? How shall we respect the glorious awe provoked by the triune revelation of the love of God to us while also centering the faith on the one mediator between God and humanity, the Lord Jesus Christ? And how might we honor the significance of Christ's unrepeatable life, death, resurrection, ascension, and ongoing session while also not undermining the personal call to follow this risen Lord? Sometimes our problem is that we pick one biblical truth to the neglect of others, a false choice that distorts not just our *theology* of Christian life but our actual lives!

A biblical account of human agency requires a threefold amen; we must say yes to three factors that are all essential but not interchangeable. First, we must say amen to the fact that the human response to God's love is led by the unique theanthropic figure: Jesus of Nazareth, God incarnate. As our forerunner, the Messiah alone leads and grounds the human response of faith to God's love. This is something done outside of me (objectively) and yet done by one of us—a true human. Second, we also must give attention to particular Christians: me and you! As well as doing his work *outside* of me, as stated above, Christ does his work *in* me (subjectively) by his Spirit. A biblical account of Christian life must avoid radical individualism while also affirming personal involvement and dignity. *I* am called to believe, be baptized, trust, and follow the Savior. Third, we broaden our focus to explore how the ecclesia constitutes the context of Christian life. Since the body of Christ corporately follows its head, to speak of Christian life apart from this larger communal framework is to assert a condition foreign to the biblical descriptions. One's Christian life is connected not only to Christ but also to his people.

Christ, ego, and ecclesia—each of these three cords is necessary for the rope of Christian life to be strong, faithfully representing the biblical picture. These three cords together allow us to be christologically centered, personally engaged, and ecclesiologically anchored. This structure enables us to affirm the importance of both objective truth and our subjective experience of it. Each is necessary for the usefulness of the other, so trying to pick one from among them is a false and destructive choice.

We can now devote the rest of this chapter to examining how Jesus, as our Lord and God, grounds and leads our Christian life and therefore our theology about it. Here we will expand the conversation we started in chapter 3 by looking at how the Messiah is the leader of human response to the love of God, giving particular attention to his ongoing heavenly role as depicted in the book of Hebrews.

MESSIAH: REPRESENTING AND LEADING GOD'S PEOPLE

Why did Jesus live? Many people will immediately answer, "So that he could die." There is certainly a great deal of truth to that, but its incompleteness is revealed by questions like: Why did he have to live decades before he died? Why couldn't he just die as an infant? Why couldn't the Son just drop down out of heaven, take on the body of a thirty-year-old person, then jump on a cross to be crucified? Why does the incarnation—in its fullness—matter? Many involved in the "quest for the historical Jesus" movements have asked these questions, seeking (with varying degrees of success) to understand Jesus in the context of his time and place.[10] Apart from historians, many believers sometimes wonder if the resurrection and ascension matter to Christian life as much as the cross. What, if anything, does the ongoing humanity and intercession of the Son mean for us? As we will see, the biblical accounts treat the whole movement of his incarnation—from the womb to the ongoing session at the right hand of God—as no less important than any particular events in it. But why?

We discover in Scripture that *Jesus's life* is the foundation for Christian life. It is the *theological* foundation, for it is a word about God, and it is the *anthropological* foundation, for it is also a word about humanity.

As we saw in an earlier chapter, Jesus is the mediator between God and humanity because he is both fully God and fully human without compromising the integrity of either nature. Eastern Orthodox theologian John Behr states it thus:

> The heart of the definition of the Council of Chalcedon is that what it is to be human and what it is to be God—death and life—are seen in one concrete being (*hypostasis*) with one "face" (*prosopon*). That is, we do not look at one being to see God and another to see man. No! Both are revealed together,—"without confusion, change, division, separation." What it is to be God and what it is to be human remain the same, but the miracle is that each is now revealed together in one and, therefore, also through each other.[11]

What may not be appreciated, however, is that this classic creedal point makes clear that Jesus's full life and not merely his death matters for our Christian *life*. The Messiah didn't just secure future glory for us; his full life—both before and after his cross—is meant to shape our lives now. Not simply because his earthly life was a moral or religious example for us: It was that, but also so much more. Only by his perfect and complete life does he act as our mediator in a way that both secures our redemption and shapes our new life in the Spirit. Jesus Christ, the God-man, connects us with God in all the facets of our life and being.

---

10. For an exhaustive treatment of the "quest" that stresses attempts at historicizing Jesus, see Colin Brown with Craig A. Evans, *A History of the Quests for the Historical Jesus* (Grand Rapids: Zondervan Academic, 2022).

11. John Behr, *Becoming Human: Meditations on Christian Anthropology in Word and Image* (New York: SVS, 2013), 24–25.

Consequently, Jesus, the Son of God, is not only the object of our worship: He also acts as chief worshiper as he leads us in worshiping the Father. *He* is the human agent leading the human response to God's love. He uniquely serves as the head of his body, the church. He leads his people as our Priest, King, and Prophet. The glory of the gospel is not simply that God has come to us, but that in and through the incarnate Christ, *the Son of Man leads our return to God.* He didn't just make a bridge to God; he also leads us back across that bridge himself. We simply follow him. Old Testament scholar Patrick Miller, when reflecting on the Ten Commandments and Christ, captures this action when he muses, "Following Jesus is not to replace the object of our worship but is a commitment to follow no other gods, however tempting that may be, and to worship the Lord your God and the Lord alone." Miller later adds, "The incarnate one embodies a faithfulness to the First Commandment that shows the way for all who follow him. This is the beginning of his ministry; it is the way he will go to the end."[12] Jesus secures our standing before God, drawing us back into communion with the Living One, enabling us to participate in the life and love of the Trinity. We follow Jesus.

Christian life centers on worship. Jesus, "the founder and perfecter of our faith," both leads and receives our worship, since "for the joy that was set before him endured the cross, despising the shame, and is [now] seated at the right hand of the throne of God" (Heb 12:2). Not only did his life serve as preparation for his death and resurrection, but he also continues to live as the obedient and faithful Messiah, bringing us before God. He lived, he died, he rose, and he lives evermore as our Lord and our God (John 20:28). His life is the source and trajectory of our life.

The Messiah came not simply to help a particular region in the ancient Middle East but to reconcile heaven and earth (Col 1:20), to bring about a new creation (2 Cor 5:17; Gal 6:15), to see shalom again planted and spread on the earth with the promise that one day peace will reign, with no more evil, hatred, sin, or death (e.g., Isa 25:8; Hos 13:14; 2 Tim 1:10; Rev 1:18; 21:4). Put differently, the Messiah came not merely to cancel debts and offer forgiveness of sins (though these are unquestionably crucial!) but for communion and shalom. Evil is not merely wiped away, it is replaced by the good, namely, by the kingdom

---

12. Patrick D. Miller, *The Ten Commandments* (Louisville: Westminster John Knox, 2009), 44.

of God in which Jesus has (re)established our fellowship with God. As Irenaeus (130–c. 200) puts it, "While God needs nothing, man needs communion with God. This is the glory of man, to continue and remain in the service of God."[13] We can boil this down to one word: *worship*. Forgiveness and reconciliation have always had the further *telos* of love and communion.

This unique person is our faithful priest, reigning king, and trustworthy prophet. His being shapes our being as he now lives in us, so we follow him in faith, hope, and love. Remember the thesis of this book: *Christian life is a response to the love of God*. Jesus is the one who leads that response. Jesus is not just the embodiment and object of God's love (see ch. 3); he also is the Faithful One who perfectly loves God and neighbor (2 Cor 5:21; Heb 4:15; 1 Pet 2:22), who is doing the work of renewing creation and leading us as we respond to God. Believers are not generating our love for God; we are receiving, drinking, and enjoying this living water of grace that becomes ours through the Son and by his Spirit.[14]

Divine agency does not conflict with or undermine human agency but rather establishes it.[15] The surprise—especially for many of us in the modern Western world—is that human agency begins not with each individual believer but with Jesus of Nazareth. His life shapes my experience. Only by taking account of him and his continuing action can we see the community of faith accurately; and in turn, this community, the church, shapes our own responses as particular persons.

Thus Jesus's life matters not just to save us from something but to produce Christian life in us. His life is the foundation for our life—our future life and this present one.[16] To better understand this dynamic christological orientation and how it relates to a theology of Christian life, we turn to Irenaeus, an early apologist for the faith who powerfully made such connections.

---

13. Irenaeus, *Against Heresies*, 4.14.1. Here trans. from Robert M. Grant, *Irenaeus of Lyons* (New York: Routledge, 1997), 147.

14. This seems to be part of what C. H. Spurgeon was trying to get at when he declared, "Grace is the first and last moving cause of salvation; and faith, essential as it is, is only an important part of the machinery which grace employs. We are saved 'through faith,' but salvation is 'by grace.'" Spurgeon, *All of Grace* (1886; repr., Musaicum, 2019), ch. 7.

15. Cf. Kathryn Tanner, *Jesus, Humanity, and the Trinity: A Brief Systematic Theology* (Minneapolis: Fortress, 2001), where she argues for "a non-competitive relation between creatures and God," 2, *passim*.

16. Oscar Cullmann, *Christ and Time: The Primitive Christian Conception of Time and History*, trans. Floyd V. Filson (Philadelphia: Westminster, 1950), 88, 93, 137, etc.

IRENAEUS: PROTOLOGY AND ESCHATOLOGY

Doctrines cannot be neatly separated from one another. They necessarily interweave in mutual connection and strengthening. If these interconnections are not acknowledged, doctrine becomes vulnerable to misrepresentation and misapplication. Consequently, one always needs anthropology and Christology, creation and eschatology, soteriology and ecclesiology—all of these go together. We can distinguish in order to investigate, but this is more a matter of shifting our point of view from which to see the whole rather than picking out separable parts. To treat them as separable strands within a rope weakens each strand as well as the whole rope. Consequently, a theology of Christian life must consistently draw on Christology, anthropology, ecclesiology, soteriology, and so on. This takes us to Irenaeus's insight, which deeply shapes my own theology of Christian life: He requires that we detect and appreciate theological connections.

Whatever one's account of human origins may be, the Bible presents humankind as having a distinct and definite character. To be human has a specific content and structure. Gorillas and angels are not bad, but they are not human. While we have a solid connection to what is below (animals and land) and above (angels and heaven), we were made uniquely in God's image and likeness (Gen 1:26–27). This reflective character informs us about what constitutes Adam and Eve's humanity (and ours); this character grounds the human species, and it can serve as a guide to behavior and goals. Ignoring, distorting, or trying to escape that divine image and likeness, therefore, doesn't empower anyone to become more human because it amounts to a fruitless attempt to destroy what lies at the root of our being.

So what does "being human" mean? Discussions of Christian life too often pass right by this fundamental question. In the process, we risk offering a vision of Christian life that devalues creation, distorts sanctification, and trivializes glory. Why? Because we have failed to grasp that God's goal for humanity was never other than that we might be fully and truly human. When we forget that truth, we often overspiritualize our counsel and underappreciate this present life, even amid the brokenness. A faithful theology of Christian life is not trying to get behind or beyond being human but focuses on what it means to be fully human: participating in the righteousness and love in which we humans were made to grow and flourish. Chapter 2 discussed how our vision of human flourishing must be shaped by love for God, neighbor, and the rest of creation. A right love of self emerges out of this threefold movement of love. What we must emphasize now is that this image and likeness—framed in terms of love and flourishing—is a dynamic, not static, condition.

Second-century church father Irenaeus of Lyons brilliantly described God's intention of process and growth for humanity. He understood that if we want to know what it means to be human, we must always keep in mind both protology (beginning) and eschatology (end).[17] One feature of the Bible's instruction about human life is that it always looks both backward and forward, to our origins and to God's goals for us.

Throughout the four books that make up *Against Heresies*, Irenaeus moves between destruction (stating and then attacking heretical views) and construction (stating and supporting a biblical vision for orthodox Christianity). Within this back-and-forth there is a growing sense in which two agents must be highlighted: God and humanity. This is not to neglect the rest of creation, whether animals, angels, or other aspects of creation, but it is to place everything else in relation to divine and human persons. Even the devil, whom Irenaeus acknowledges as having some influence and power, must be understood as a creature whose agency is secondary to that of God and humanity.[18] In other words, the Accuser is never stronger than God, and he only gains power over humanity because humans first exercised their agency in a way that surrendered it to the Serpent.[19] And in this rebellion and folly, human freedom was *lost*, not found: Now, following Adam's misused agency, humanity finds itself enslaved to sin, death, and the devil. God is life; our disobedience brings bondage and death. That basic dichotomy describes much of our theology of Christian life: Our goal is freedom in Christ, exercised in love of God and neighbor, since we have been freed from our enslavement to sin. The Christian vision of life has a positive content, not simply forgiveness of sin, but a life filled with love, bounty, and faithfulness.

---

17. For more on my own thinking and development of this dual emphasis on protology and eschatology, see Kelly M. Kapic, "Anthropology," in *Christian Dogmatics: Reformed Theology for the Church Catholic*, ed. Michael Allen and Scott R. Swain (Grand Rapids: Baker Academic, 2016), 165–93.

18. Irenaeus, *Against Heresies*, 5.22.2, p. 551 ANF.

19. Irenaeus, *Against Heresies*, 5.23.1–2, p. 551 ANF. Cf. fragment 16, which seems to be wary of making God in any way the "author of sin." Irenaeus, *Fragments from the Lost Writings of Irenaeus*, 570 ANF.

God, of course, is the Creator and Lord of the universe, thus also our Creator and Lord. Part of the problem with so many of the heresies (Valentinians, Marcosians, etc.) that Irenaeus reviews in his books is that their vision of the gods is weak and ultimately unworthy of full worship and devotion. They cause disorder and harm to the world and the people in it. Further, these heresies led to evil and the manipulation of people, not righteousness and love.[20] In contrast to these destructive accounts of the world, the true God, by his two "hands" (Word and Spirit), makes what is and puts his human creatures at the center of his action.[21] While all of creation was distinctly from God, humankind in particular plays a unique and central role as the very image (*imago*) and likeness (*similitudo*) of God on earth.[22]

Irenaeus muses, "God is the glory of humanity, but humanity is the vessel of God's working, of all His wisdom and power."[23] Humanity's position and calling were always vital for creation. But this does not contradict the distinction between God and his creatures. God was happy; he did not require self-healing, nor did he need any other entity for his fullness. However, even though made in God's image and likeness, humanity was initially not full or complete. Humans were created as developing creatures, designed to grow from immaturity to maturity. Created good, free, and "like" (*homoios*) God, humans were to "rule over everything upon earth" with increasing ability, since God had fashioned both humanity and the earth for this relationship.[24] This was the *telos* for humans.

Our place and function in the world were not problems for God originally but a joyful expression of divine life and love. Therefore, Irenaeus presses us not to collapse creation and eschatology into each other: Humans were not created as finished products but as growing creatures. Even as God made humans "lords" over the earth in the

---

20. E.g., Irenaeus points out how these heresies sometimes advocate a strong dichotomy between the "carnal" and the "spiritual" in a way that allows their followers to sexually abuse women. Irenaeus, *Against the Heresies*, trans. Dominic J. Unger (New York: Newman, 1992), 1.6.3–4, pp. 39–40. Breeding such unrighteousness is part of what makes it clear that they are indeed heretical.

21. Irenaeus, *Against Heresies*, 5.60.1.

22. Earlier theologians often took a few passing references in which Irenaeus appears to distinguish image and likeness and made far too much of them, whereas overall, it is clear in his work that these were not so much to be separated as to be treated as a unit.

23. Irenaeus, *Against Heresies*, 3.20.2, p. 96.

24. Irenaeus, *On the Apostolic Preaching* (Crestwood, NY: St. Vladimir's Seminary Press, 1997), 1.11, p. 47.

beginning, he also made them childlike and developing.[25] In "Paradise," before any sin or fall, God "would walk and talk with the man prefiguring (*protypoō*) their future condition, that He would dwell with him and speak with him, and would be with mankind, teaching them righteousness."[26] This expectation of growth in Adam and Eve wasn't a flaw in the Creator's original design or a sign of sin but the starting point of a beautiful aspect of the Creator's plan in his relationship to creation. A child who is too young to solve math equations or ride a bicycle is not evil or bad; instead, they still have growth and delights ahead of them. That is a positive, not negative, trait. Their childlikeness isn't the occasion for bemoaning their innocence or naïveté but for celebrating them and their approaching development. Goodness gives birth to more goodness in this unfolding plotline. This is why, technically, one might declare that God didn't make a "perfect" (i.e., complete or finished) world, but he made a "good" one.

God made everything good, but *not consummated*. In Adam and Eve's original "guileless and childlike mind" there was no knowledge of sin nor practice of unrighteousness.[27] This does not entail that they were made neutral or as blank slates; they were good and had a life-giving trajectory. Their path included growing in maturity of communion with God, in love of neighbor, and as divinely gifted representatives to the rest of the unfolding creation. For Irenaeus, this growth always presupposed an increasing openness to and dependence on the God from whom all goodness and life are received.[28] Modern popular psychological assumptions often portray "growth" as happening only from "within" us—the "growing self." But this view is foreign to Irenaeus and the biblical tradition.[29] In his more ancient model, growth often comes first from the outside, pointing back not only to creation but to the ongoing work of the Creator and Sustainer. God plants. God waters. God brings growth. Life always has been and always will be that way—and it is a pattern of Christian life.

Sin is a rejection of this Giver and his gifts. Sin created a problem

---

25. Irenaeus, *On the Apostolic Preaching*, 1.12, p. 47.
26. Irenaeus, *On the Apostolic Preaching*, 1.12, p. 47.
27. Irenaeus, *Against Heresies*, 3.23.5 This translation from St. Irenaeus of Lyons, *Against the Heresies*, book 3, trans. Dominic J. Unger (New York: Newman, 2012), 108.
28. And that receiving begins with life, both what might be called natural life and eternal life. Cf. *Against Heresies*, 5.3.3.
29. Gustaf Wingren, *Man and the Incarnation: A Study in the Biblical Theology of Irenaeus*, trans. Ross Mackenzie (1959; Eugene: Wipf & Stock, 2004), 33.

because it not only constitutes a rebellion against God but also gave the devil a foothold, introducing human death and consequently changing the shape of human life. Faithfulness to God in our theology of Christian life requires that we form ideas about the nature of our humanity in terms of its original design as well as its *telos*.

To do this, we must connect our biblical anthropology with Christology, as Irenaeus does. The great Irenaeus scholar Gustaf Wingren commented, "It is no limitation of Christ's humanity that He has no sin, but on the contrary His very freedom from sin qualifies Him for achieving the thing which is truly human, but which no other human being is capable of doing, for the whole of humanity is bound, captive, and unnatural."[30] Simply put, Jesus's rejection of sin (Heb 4:15; 1 Pet 2:22) makes him *more*, not less, human. The only hope for us to become fully and truly human again is the new life that we have in Christ, the incarnate Lord who uniquely combines protology and eschatology in his humanity.

Some of Irenaeus's contemporaries reasoned that the Messiah must have had a beginning because he was born to Mary. In contrast, Irenaeus reasoned from the full biblical account and affirmed both the human birth and eternal generation of this one Son.[31] Assuming a human nature did not compromise or undermine the Son's divinity, but it did display God's original intentions for humanity. That is, "the historical Christ who lived on earth was the pattern which God had in His mind when he fashioned the first man. Christ was the man about to be, *homo futurus*, and the Creator, as it were, foresaw Christ. While the earth was being formed, Christ was in the mind of God, and matter took shape in the hands of God in accordance with this future pattern."[32] Again, here we bring together protology and eschatology. The incarnate Son "recapitulated in Himself the long unfolding of humankind," Irenaeus wrote, "granting salvation by way of compendium, that in Christ Jesus we might receive what was lost in Adam, namely, to be according to the image and likeness of God."[33] So now let us bring together how I

---

30. Wingren, *Man and the Incarnation*, 87.
31. Against those who deny that Irenaeus affirms the eternity of the Son, see Behr, *The Way to Nicaea*, Formation of Christian Theology (Crestwood, NY: St. Vladimir's Seminary Press, 2001), 127–28.
32. Wingren, *Man and the Incarnation*, 18.
33. Irenaeus, *Against Heresies*, 3.18.1. This translation from St. Irenaeus of Lyons, *Against the Heresies*, book 3, trans. Dominic J. Unger (New York: Newman, 2012), 87–88.

think Irenaeus can and should guide this christological orientation for our vision of Christian life.

According to Irenaeus's biblical theology, *life* and *seeing God* go together. "It is not possible to live apart from life," Irenaeus explains, "and the means of life is found in fellowship with God; but fellowship with God is to know God, and to enjoy His goodness."[34] In other words, human life was never merely a matter of material biology but also essentially a communal matter. We were designed to love God, neighbor, and the rest of creation, and this love and these relationships were designed to grow, not remain static. Sin has always been a problem because it shattered these relationships, distorted our loves, and undermined the fullness of human life. Of course non-Christians can live and breathe, laugh and love. But without "seeing God," we are not reflecting his image and likeness faithfully and therefore cannot live the life that is truly life (1 Tim 6:19). This is what Irenaeus was trying to help us see when he memorably concluded, "For the glory of God is a living man; and the life of man consists in beholding God."[35]

We were made for communion with God, a communion that would grow and develop. Yet sin made a right vision of God impossible, thus not just stunting the fullness of growing fellowship but producing outright ignorance, rebellion, and darkness. In God's revelation of himself, however, the invisible becomes visible: In the Lord Jesus Christ we behold both the glory of God *and* the glory of humanity. This glory or radiance is seen in this one person (Heb 1:3). We discover this glory not just in the face of Mary's baby, but in the bleeding and dying man on the cross and in the smiling face of our ascended Lord. So to him we look for life, true life, a life shaped by the love of the Father, enabled by the grace of the Son, and made ours by our fellowship in the Spirit. Jesus's full life is the foundation and source of Christian life—and not just his thirty years and crucifixion in the first century. Because he is the firstborn from the dead, his risen and continuing life is our life, and only as we are connected to him can we grow in grace and truth. Knowing that his life in Christ was bigger than merely biological life strengthened Ignatius of Antioch on his way to martyrdom (d. 110). In anticipation of finally moving from the shadows to the full reality of beholding Jesus's face, he declared, "When I shall have arrived there,

---

34. Irenaeus, *Against Heresies*, 4.4.5, p. 489 ANF.
35. Irenaeus, *Against Heresies*, 4.4.7, p. 490 ANF.

I shall become a human being (*anthropos*)."[36] To be fully human happens within the context of communion with God, and this communion with God is centered on Christ, who "alone" will be the church's "bishop."[37]

This is the hope of the biblical covenants, looking both backward and forward and ultimately placing Christ at the center. Accordingly, this is an appropriate place to look briefly at the biblical idea of covenant and how it fits the uniqueness of Christ and the structure of Christian life.

CHRIST, THE COVENANT, AND CHRISTIAN LIFE

Although covenant theology is especially associated with the Reformed tradition, this tradition is most certainly not the only one that sees the importance of biblical covenants for making sense of the canonical narrative and Christian life.

There is general agreement that we can't make sense of the New Testament (covenant) without the Old. While debate lingers about whether it is appropriate to speak of a prefall covenant with Adam (some see a covenant of creation or "works"; others describe it as the Adamic administration), few disagree that later covenants (Noahic, Abrahamic, Mosaic/Israel, and Davidic) help us in various ways to make sense of the significance of the person and work of the Messiah, the center of the new covenant. At its best, the Reformed tradition attempts to make sense of this connection. As Sinclair Ferguson fairly observed, "During the sixteenth century covenant theology came to be regarded as a key to the interpretation of *Scripture* and, during the seventeenth century, a key to the interpretation of *Christian experience*."[38] This tradition deeply influences my own thinking.[39] While I'll make no attempt here to

---

36. St. Ignatius of Antioch, *Letter to the Romans*, quoted in Behr, *Becoming Human*, 6.

37. St. Ignatius of Antioch, *Letter to the Romans* 9.1, in *The Apostolic Fathers: Greek Texts and English Translations*, 3rd ed., ed. and trans. Michael W. Holmes (Grand Rapids: Baker Academic, 2007), 235.

38. Sinclair B. Ferguson, *John Owen on the Christian Life* (Edinburgh: Banner of Truth Trust, 1987), 20. For more relevant material on Owen's covenantal theology, see Willem J. van Asselt, "Covenant Theology as Relational Theology: The Contributions of Johannes Cocceius (1603–1669) and John Owen (1616–1683) to a Living Reformed Theology," in *The Ashgate Research Companion to John Owen's Theology*, ed. Kelly M. Kapic and Mark Jones (Surrey: Ashgate, 2012), 65–84; John W. Tweeddale, *John Owen and Hebrews: The Foundation of Biblical Interpretation* (London: T&T Clark, 2019), esp. 53–82.

39. For a more detailed treatment of biblical covenants and their role, currently the most exhaustive treatment is found in *Covenant Theology: Biblical, Theological, and Historical Perspectives*, ed. Guy Prentiss Waters, J. Nicholas Reid, and John R. Muether (Wheaton, IL: Crossway, 2020). For

defend—much less fully unpack—a highly worked-out covenant theology, a quick review at this point is vital. Employing a big-picture view rather than a detailed analysis will serve our purposes here. My hope is that giving attention to the covenant patterns will help us relate Christ to our everyday life.

In short, the various biblical covenants contain not only God's promises and provisions but also a call for human response and responsibilities. Even if one does not speak of an Adamic covenant (cf. Hos 6:7), Paul nonetheless makes strong parallels between Adam and Christ (e.g., Rom 5:12–21). Each of them represents a people, either humanity in general or a new humanity in Messiah: "For if, because of one man's trespass, death reigned through that one man [Adam], much more will those who receive the abundance of grace and the free gift of righteousness reign in life through the one man Jesus Christ" (Rom 5:17). Thus Paul asks his readers this: Are you identified with the first Adam or the final Adam? Undoing the sin and death of our first parents, the promise in Christ is life, not death. Allegiance to the Messiah rather than fallen Adam is the way to enter that life.[40]

After Adam, God promised Noah (Gen 6:18; 9:8–17) that he would never again wipe out humanity (whether by flood or in another way). This didn't mean that unrighteousness no longer mattered to the Creator, but that God's long-suffering and mercy would hold out until the end. The rainbow was a sign of God's faithfulness, a reminder to encourage the development of trust and obedience to Yahweh.

In the Abrahamic covenant, God linked his blessing of a particular family (Abraham/Israel) to a blessing for the whole world: Abraham and his children have been blessed in order to be a blessing (Gen 12:1–9; 15:1–21; 17:1–14; 22:15–18; cf. Acts 3:25). God would be faithful to his

---

other studies to help fill in some biblical and historical background, consider beginning with Petrus J. Gräbe, *New Covenant, New Community: The Significance of Biblical and Patristic Covenant Theology for Contemporary Understanding* (Milton Keynes: Paternoster, 2006); Scott W. Hahn, *Kinship by Covenant: A Canonical Approach to the Fulfillment of God's Saving Promises* (New Haven, CT: Yale University Press, 2009); Michael S. Horton's four volumes deeply shaped and driven by covenant theology: *Covenant and Eschatology*; *Lord and Servant*; *Covenant and Salvation*; *People and Place* (Louisville: Westminster John Knox, 2002, 2005, 2007, 2008); Stephen Strehle, *Calvinism, Federalism, and Scholasticism: A Study of the Reformed Doctrine of Covenant*, Basler und Berner Studien zur historischen und systematischen Theologie 58 (Bern: Peter Lang, 1988); D. A. Weir, *The Origins of the Federal Theology in Sixteenth-Century Reformation Thought* (Oxford: Clarendon, 1990).

40. Cf. Matthew W. Bates, *Salvation by Allegiance Alone: Rethinking Faith, Works, and the Gospel of Jesus the King* (Grand Rapids: Baker Academic, 2017), who helps by pushing against many contemporary misunderstandings of "faith alone" that can end up communicating something very different from what the early Reformers intended, let alone the New Testament.

covenant, as implied in God's act of walking, in Abraham's stead (Gen 15:9–10, 17–18), between the cut pieces of the animals, thus "invoking the curse on himself, if he fails to fulfill the promise."[41] While Abraham's devotion is far from perfect, the narrative stresses his faith and the actions that flowed from that faith, all based on the faithful God who would "provide for himself the lamb" (Gen 22:8; cf. Heb 11:17) and not require the sacrifice of Isaac or any other child. The new covenant later presented Abraham as someone to emulate in our Christian life. It calls us to faith (Luke 19:9; John 8:39; Rom 4:1–16; Gal 3:6–18) and to a life imitating his obedience that flows from that faith (Luke 3:8, Heb 11:8; Jas 2:21–23). This faith is a confidence that God is the God of the living rather than the dead (Matt 22:32; Mark 12:26–27), who can be trusted to make all things right for his people (Heb 6:15). God achieves this not in spite of divine holiness and concern but because of it. God's covenant with Abraham informs us about not only God's own faithfulness but also Abraham's response of faith, which is also our appropriate response.

In the Mosaic covenant (Exod 19–24; cf. the whole book of Deuteronomy), Israel receives the law from the same God who first delivered his people from their bondage. This covenant is thoroughly a covenant of grace, even in its giving of the law (Deut 4:1–8; 6:20–25).[42] Deliverance preceded law. Whether or not one can make a tight case regarding the extent to which the Mosaic covenant follows the pattern of the Hittite covenants, at a minimum it seems clear that here God lays out both privileges and duties, summoning the people to live according to it. This has been called the "principle of reciprocity," wherein "*both partners in the relationship 'keep the covenant'* (see Deut. 5:10//Exod. 20:6 and Deut. 10:12–13; 11:1; Exod. 19:4–5 and Deut. 7:9)."[43] Moses serves as a kind of mediator of this covenant (Exod 19:3) in laying out the covenant stipulations to God's people (19:5), to which the people answer that they will indeed do "all that the LORD has spoken" (19:8). In this covenant, "the assumption is clear that the people can count on the Lord's preserving the covenant relationship with them, that the *obedience* of the people, their faithfulness, is reciprocated in the *faithfulness*

---

41. Gordon J. Wenham, *Genesis 1–15*, Word Biblical Commentary (Waco: Word, 1987), 332.
42. E.g., Daniel I. Block, "The Grace of Torah: The Mosaic Prescription for Life (Deut. 4:1–8; 6:20–25)" *Bibliotheca Sacra* 162, no. 255 (January–March 2005): 3–22.
43. Patrick D. Miller, *The Ten Commandments* (Louisville: Westminster John Knox, 2009), 420, emphasis original.

of God."[44] It sadly becomes clear, however, that in this "old" covenant, God's people are not faithful and often develop hard hearts, negligence, and ultimately rebellion against Yahweh. It will therefore take a "new" covenant to accomplish complete restoration, healing, and new life. This is the restoration that Jeremiah and Ezekiel anticipate (Jer 31:31–37; Ezek 36:25–28) and that New Testament authors see accomplished in Christ (Luke 22:20; 1 Cor 11:25; Heb 9:15; 12:24). But notice, God does not abandon his requirement of obedience (i.e., love of God and neighbor) with the coming of Messiah, even though the Messiah fulfills that requirement, both in his own life and in us.

To David, God gives the covenant promise of a faithful king (2 Chron 13:5; 21:7; 23:3; 2 Sam 23:5), echoing the promise at creation that a human ruler would reign over all of creation (Gen 1:28–31). When reigning well, King David reflects the ultimate Creator-King, not the greedy or cruel corrupt kings of the nations (cf. 1 Sam 8:4–7, 19–22; 2 Sam 7:8–16; Pss 89:3–4; 132:1–18). This shows God's concern not merely for his people's psychological longings or shortcomings but also for their particular communities, for their material needs, and for the land. God's goal has always been to establish and defend a people and place that would embody justice, righteousness, and love: in a word, shalom! Divine discipline came when God's people dishonored his name and misrepresented his character and purpose (e.g., 2 Sam 7:14; Ps 89:30–37). This discipline was the necessary and loving response of a wise and gracious Father, reshaping his children for their good (cf. Heb 12:6), not the rage of a tyrannical, irritable, power-hungry king.

This survey of the covenants prompts the question: How do we reconcile the conditional (*if . . . then*) and unconditional aspects of God's covenant with his people? This question is too often couched in the dangerous "either-or" form that we discussed earlier: Either we rely only on divine agency (God provides and human obedience is irrelevant), *or* we rely only on human agency (God will not act favorably unless humans are first obedient). Both sides of this false choice use biblical texts to support their case. On the one hand, some highlight the Divine Warrior setting down his bow (Gen 9:12–17; cf. 2 Sam 22:15; Hab 3:9) after the flood—or maybe even aiming the arrows now at himself, should he

---

44. Miller, *The Ten Commandments*, 420, original emphasis.

break the covenant,⁴⁵ and they highlight the dramatic vision given to Abraham where the Lord walks through the divided animal offering, thus seeming to make himself responsible for both sides of the covenant. Others highlight the consistent "blessings and curses" texts that clearly link divine provision to human acts of righteousness and goodness in response to the good Creator (e.g., Lev 26:1–46; Deut 11:26–28; 28:1–68; Jer 17:5–8). These conditions make the language of *unconditional* sound strange to many observers. This tension has everything to do with how one envisions a theology of Christian life. Since we touched on related topics in chapter 5 on law and gospel, I will try to be brief here.

Even while Israel was unfaithful, there remained hope and the necessity that a faithful king would come to keep the covenant. As Hebrew scholar Gary A. Anderson provocatively argues in an Anselmic fashion, only God himself could deal with the "debt" created by Israel's sin, but only humans needed to offer such payment.⁴⁶ One can argue that built into the covenant expectations was the need for the *theanthropic* one, the unique God-human, the incarnate Savior Jesus Christ, who would display God's unconditional commitment and love while also faithfully keeping the human responsibilities that the good God had designed for humanity and the world. This Savior would conform to God's character, to shalom, and to the dignity and place of humanity. The good Creator, the Lord of Abraham, and the God of David were not different deities but the same God who created the world and was also the Father of Israel. God kept the covenant in and through the Messiah, not only from the divine side but also from the human side!

The scriptural account of God's work in the world moves from *broad* (creation) to *narrow* (Abraham and Israel) to the *singular* (Jesus) and then returns to the *broad* (church) and then all the way back to care for the *universal* (the whole world). Individuals matter, but faith and practice are not isolated in individual packages. Our communion with God always has this larger covenantal background and expectation that includes

---

45. E.g., Laurence A. Turner, "The Rainbow as the Sign of the Covenant in Genesis IX 11–13," *Vetus Testamentum* 43, no. 1 (1993): 119–24; Ellen van Wolde, "One Bow or Another? A Study of the Bow in Genesis 9:8–17," *Vetus Testamentum* 63, no. 1 (2013): 124–49.

46. For a provocative reading of Old Testament material and how Anselm's own imaginative use of "debt" might reflect rather than distort relevant ancient Near Eastern emphases, with special attention given to "almsgiving," see Gary A. Anderson, *Sin: A History* (New Haven, CT: Yale University Press, 2009).

US TO GOD

a personal relationship with God and a reconnection with the rest of creation, starting with sisters and brothers in Christ.[47]

Christ, who embodies the "climax of the covenant," is the covenant keeper.[48] He is not only the *eschatos Adam* (1 Cor 15:45) but also the new Israel reconstituted in himself.[49] Greater than Moses, David, and Elijah, he is the great King, Priest, and Prophet. As we will unpack more fully below, especially in our treatment of the book of Hebrews, Jesus is the faithful one who in the Spirit perfectly loves and obeys the Father, and who, as "the Beloved" (Eph 1:6), lived a life of righteousness and compassion that perfectly satisfied all the covenantal requirements. He was the faithful Adam, so Paul describes our life as derived from our union to his life: we are now "in Christ," and Christ is now "in us," so that we who have faith in the Faithful One find ourselves secure within the Trinitarian life of God (Eph 1:3–23).

Accordingly, not just the life but the death of Christ is crucial to apostolic preaching and Christian life. While significant debates about atonement will continue, what should not be ignored is that Christ's death fundamentally shapes our life. Because Christ died, we no longer are held hostage to the terror of death, to the ugliness of sin, and to the taunts of the devil (e.g., Rom 6; 8:32–39; Heb 2:14–15; 1 Pet 2:24; 3:18; 1 John 3:8; Rev 12:10), however intimidating they may be. To continue the covenantal talk, Christ absorbed the covenantal curses we deserved in our rebellion and unbelief, but also by his Spirit he made us heirs of his own covenantal blessings (Gal 3:13–14). By faith we really are the children of Abraham—or better, sisters and brothers in faith who trust the one who is greater than Abraham (John 8:48–58; Rom 4:1–5; Gal 3:5–8; Jas 2:21–23).

---

47. Take just one example. In Acts, when the gospel was believed in Samaria, we are told that the Samaritans believed but "had only been baptized in the name of the Lord Jesus" and had not yet "received the Holy Spirit" (Acts 8:4–25). They had to wait for Peter and John to come down and pray for them to receive the Spirit (Acts 8:15). Why? Why this divide here when elsewhere Jesus and the Holy Spirit go together? Thomas Schreiner ably argues that the new covenant creates not different churches but rather *one* faith, the same faith for Jews from Jerusalem and Samaria. All are united under the apostolic witness to the Father, Son, and Holy Spirit. So these new Samaritan believers had to wait for Peter and John to come to lay hands on them, and then the Holy Spirit was given. This appears to reflect the unity of the church under the triune God—Jerusalem and Samaria, Jew and gentile, male and female, rich and poor. The covenanting God was faithful to bring reconciliation between God and humans and between humans. See Thomas R. Schreiner, *Covenant and God's Purpose for the World* (Wheaton, IL: Crossway, 2017), ch. 6.

48. N. T. Wright: *Christ and the Law in Pauline Theology* (Minneapolis: Fortress, 1993).

49. Cf. Bernardin Schneider, "The Corporate Meaning and Background of 1 Cor 15,45b— 'O Eschatos Adam eis Pneuma Zōiopoioun," *The Catholic Biblical Quarterly* 29, no. 3 (1967): 450–67.

Finally, we have the satisfying answer to the lingering question of how to reconcile what appear to be unconditional and conditional aspects of the covenant(s). God's love, compassion, and provision are unconditional. The conditional aspects, namely, our faithful responses to his holy goodness in keeping shalom, describe what life in the covenant is like, and so are essential to it. The surprise in the solution is that *God fulfills these conditions for us by meeting them himself in Christ, and he includes us in his work by uniting us to Christ by his Spirit.* This shows us why Jesus as our human leader and Lord is central to our understanding of the covenant.

Our theology of Christian life completely depends upon recognizing that the Father sends the Son in the Spirit, so that God not only acts *toward* us, but in his incarnation—in and as the Messiah—he also acts *for* us as our human representative—not simply *instead of* us but *including* us in his action. By his divine agency God establishes and upholds human agency in an unexpected way.

Our King, our Priest, our Prophet: Christ incarnate is the covenant keeper, embodying the unconditional promises of God and faithfully fulfilling the righteous conditions himself. In order to understand the nature of God and his covenant, we have to understand these conditions not as arbitrary rules or a barrier to the covenant but as the essence of the shalom that characterizes the covenant (e.g., Deut 26:12–19; Jer 7:5–7). Humankind was given the task of developing the created world into a fullness of enjoying God, neighbor, and the world around us. Instead of developing as intended, our trajectory was stopped and undercut by sin, so we need a new creation. Adam was good, but Jesus is even better. Moses and David were honored by God and of great significance, but they ultimately pointed beyond themselves to great David's greater son (2 Sam 7:12–14). Jesus alone is the climax of the covenant, the great King, Priest, and prophetic teller of good news. Praise be to God!

This set of events and relations shapes Christian life. First, our life is in Christ. Second, life in Christ is also intrinsically a communal life—to be reconciled to God is to be reconciled to his people (see chs. 8–9 on ecclesia). And third, our life is personal and interpersonal: God loves not just his created world as a system and not just his people as a body. God loves me in particular and gave me the very Spirit of Christ that I might echo the Messiah's praises, follow his ways, and enjoy renewed communion with God and neighbor and even renewed relations with creation and my own "self" (see ch. 7).

PRIEST, KING, AND PROPHET: SHARING IN CHRIST'S ANOINTING

A product of the Protestant Reformation movements, the Heidelberg Catechism was published in 1563. The authors used it to express a biblical mode of thought that would encourage, strengthen, and shape believers. After the memorable initial statement that "our only comfort in life and death" comes from the promise that "I belong—in body and soul . . . not to myself, but to my faithful Savior Jesus Christ," the catechism slowly starts to unpack the human situation.[50] First, it addresses the problem of sin (Q. 3–11) as a disruption of human good and flourishing. Then it addresses the hope of redemption and the grace secured only in Christ (Q. 12–85) and briefly describes the Trinity. Its description of the centrality of the Son includes a summary of Christian life, a summary that has great relevance for this book.

Question 31 of the Heidelberg Catechism asked why Jesus is called "Christ." The answer is that Jesus is "both ordained by God the Father and anointed with the Holy Spirit" to be our head. In this covenant role, he acts as *"our chief Prophet* and *Teacher . . . our only High Priest . . . our eternal King."*[51] The doctrine of the threefold anointing of Christ shapes question 32 in its discussion of the identity of individual believers.

Q. 32: "But why are you called a Christian?"

A. "Because through faith I share in Christ and thus in his anointing, so that I may confess his name, offer myself a living sacrifice of gratitude to him, and fight against sin and the devil with a free and good conscience throughout this life and hereafter rule with him in eternity over all creatures."[52]

The assertion that "I share in Christ and thus in his anointing" connects answers 31 and 32, and the verbs *confess*, *offer*, and *fight* are

---

50. I am using the translation from Mark A. Noll, ed., *Confessions and Catechisms of the Reformation* (Grand Rapids: Baker, 1991), 137.
51. The full wording of answer 31 is: "Because he is ordained by God the Father and anointed with the Holy Spirit to be our chief Prophet and Teacher, fully revealing to us the secret purpose and will of God concerning our redemption; to be our only High Priest, having redeemed us by the one sacrifice of his body and ever interceding for us with the Father; and to be our eternal King, governing us by his Word and Spirit, and defending and sustaining us in the redemption he has won for us." Noll, *Confessions and Catechisms*, 142–43, Noll's emphasis.
52. Noll, *Confessions and Catechisms*, 143.

our threefold response to his threefold office of Prophet, Priest, and King. This compact statement is brimming with theological and pastoral importance. But our challenge is this: Did we catch it? Driven by the organizing themes of grace and gratitude, the Heidelberg Catechism repeatedly reminds its readers that God continues to work in grace, so that we do not earn divine favor by our response but are animated by joyful gratitude for Jesus: He is the expression and security of divine favor. The catechism describes our union with Christ and encourages our participation in that union with this unique Messiah.

Centuries before Heidelberg, the Eastern Orthodox theologian John of Damascus similarly contemplated this mystery and declared, "He was the same who anointed and who was anointed, as God anointing Himself as a man."[53] Jesus as the perfect Priest, King, and Prophet has reconciled us with the Creator, and by his Spirit he is the personal liberator who enables us to love our neighbors.

In other words, *who Jesus is* and *what he does* establish the basis, context, and power of our security, comfort, and participation in Christian life. To echo the currently unpopular but still relevant Anselm: God in Christ does what only God could do, but what only humanity needed to do.

In and through the Messiah, the eternal Lord is known (prophet), communed with (priest), and followed (king). This anointed theanthropic mediator cleanses us from sin, restores us to worship, gives us a foretaste of shalom, and enables us to love our neighbors.[54] By his three offices, Jesus accomplishes the ancient promise repeated throughout Scripture, "I will be your God and you will be my people" (see Gen 17:7; Jer 30:22; Ezek 11:20; 14:11; Zech 8:8). God had promised to deliver his people from their enemies and to dwell among them as he did in the garden (Exod 29:45; Lev 26:45). Those who trust in Yahweh were told not to be anxious or to fear, for he delivers and strengthens his people; rather than rejecting us, he is consistently filled with compassion and is quick to welcome (Exod 20:2; Isa 41:10, 13; Zech 10:6). God's action, however, does not make our obedience, praise, and love an empty or

---

53. John of Damascus, *The Orthodox Faith*, 4.14, p. 365.
54. I am here assuming the Christology articulated in the classical and Reformed tradition, which views "'Christ' not merely as the Logos *simpliciter* but as the God-man who exists as a single subsistence in two natures and acts as a single theandric agent." Ty Kieser, *Theandric and Triune: John Owen and Christological Agency*, T&T Clark Studies in Systematic Theology (London: T&T Clark, 2024), 174.

mechanistic response, nor does it depend on that response—rather, God's grace in Christ establishes and makes a place for our obedience, praise, and love, which are at the heart of our truly human life and flourishing.

Adam, the original leader of humanity, had the task of shepherding the creation in praise, harmony, goodness, and shalom. Christian life is not a new idea that replaces or belittles God's original design: Instead, it moves us toward the Creator's original good purposes and goals for us—the *telos* where it was all meant to go in the first place. God does not forget or abandon his people, but his people themselves were unable to achieve their own redemption. Again, God's grace in Christ does not replace or ignore our obedience but rather establishes it. When the Old Testament tells us that God's people needed to "obey his voice" (Jer 7:23), turning from idols and sin to the living God (Ezek 37:23), faithfully serving and praising God as their King (Ps 47:6–7), it is describing core aspects of an abundant and joyful human life. The *Shema Israel* begins with this key idea of loving God (Deut 6:4–5) not to secure his favor but in response to this favor (Deut 4:31, 40; 5:2–6). As Lord and King, he gave his law to be a faithful and trustworthy guide for living in love, to instruct in flourishing and in resistance to evil (Deut 6:1–25). The promise of Immanuel, as seen in Matthew 1:23 (see Isa 7:14; 8:8), is fulfilled more intimately than we might have expected: We who receive the Messiah's Spirit are made temples of the living God, who "dwells" among and within us, who promises to "be [our] God" (2 Cor 6:16 // Lev 26:12). Christ as the head of the new covenant is our "minister in the holy places" (Heb 8:2) who not only represents us but also includes us as he leads the activity of worship (more on this below when we concentrate on the book of Hebrews). In this new covenant under Christ, he puts his laws not simply on stone tablets but on our minds and hearts (Jer 31:33; Rom 2:15), again with the promise that "I will be their God, and they shall be my people" (Heb 8:10), for he is "not ashamed to be called their God" (Heb 11:16).

Before we turn to Hebrews to close out this chapter, it is worth noting that this emphasis on Christ's *munus triplex* (threefold office) should keep us from falling into the trap of reducing the gospel to mere moralism, largely by transforming our understanding of human agency. Let me explain.

We often unthinkingly treat the offices of Christ in flat and uninspired ways. Just as we sometimes misunderstand the law by reducing it to a checklist of to-dos, so we sometimes imagine God as a distant taskmaster who is more interested in an orderly system than the well-being of his people. Similarly, we sometimes reduce the threefold offices of Christ to predictive answers that fulfill Old Testament prophetic texts, thus missing the heart of the biblical message. Just as the law was a guide to living a truly human life and not a set of arbitrary rules, so these three offices do not merely solve a biblical jigsaw puzzle but rather put God's creation back on a trajectory of holy love and communion.

The life, death, resurrection, ascension, and ongoing session of Christ are fundamentally a restoration of creation, pointing back to the originally intended shalom and forward to the renewal of all things. Here we have "new creation" breaking out. As noted earlier, the early church father Irenaeus used the language of *recapitulation* to capture this dynamic: The Son has entered into the desert of his fallen creation in order to bring about the bloom of new life, and starting with that seed, he would renew the whole world. Eventually, heaven would come down to earth!

Sanctifying each season of life, from his conception through his heavenly intercession, Jesus restores shalom where it had been violated and where it continues to be distorted. But this idea of recapitulation can also help us see how Christ embodies this renewal movement as Priest, King, and Prophet, restoring to us a true vision of who God is, serving as our representative and a sacrifice on our behalf, and then leading us by his holy and gracious rule of his church and world. These titles are best understood in terms of how Jesus is the faithful and pious servant of the Lord, who worships without ceasing and communes with the Father in the Spirit, drawing humanity back into the love and communion of God.

HEBREWS AND WORSHIPING GOD: OUR CHALLENGE, GOD'S ANSWER

As Christians, we sometimes wonder if we are passionate enough about God. At times our faith is strong, our hearts are grateful, and we feel close to God. But then occasionally—maybe even much of the time—whether because of sin, the busyness of life, or psychological challenges, we struggle to believe, to praise God, to trust him. What about loving God? For most believers, that love ebbs and flows. Why can't our love of God and neighbor always be full?

How can we find a solid foundation to withstand the fluctuations of our faith, love, and obedience? How do we navigate our inconsistent ability to worship? As we have shown previously, this is where Jesus is not only the foundation but the source and living guide of Christian life in a way that may surprise us, providing the stability we desperately need. To close out this chapter, we will briefly explore two key christologically shaped themes from the book of Hebrews: *worship* and *compassion*. God's people can here find the comfort and encouragement needed to keep the faith.

Worship: Jesus Is Loving God for Us

The cross is clearly central to Christianity, but we can easily mistake a key emphasis for a totality. What I mean is this: We can't make sense of the gospel apart from the cross, but the cross itself only makes sense in terms of the whole human life of Jesus. When I refer to the "human life" of Jesus, I mean not only the years from his birth to his death in the ancient Near Eastern world over two thousand years ago but also his resurrected and ongoing human life now. As we remind ourselves every Easter, Christ Jesus lives *today*! And he *doesn't* just live in our hearts.

We must give attention to Jesus's whole human life, pre- and post-cross. Ignoring that larger context detracts from the significance of the cross. From the womb of Mary through the darkness of death, from his rising out of the tomb to his ongoing physical presence in heaven, Jesus's entire human life is the foundation of our hope, our life, our very being. But why?

The short answer is that *worship matters*. Worship is the activity of our connection with God. We have already declared that we were made for love and communion with God. We call that communion "worship." Worship animates our love for our neighbor and enables us as humans to cultivate shalom throughout the rest of creation. Worship, therefore, is not peripheral to being fully human but rather is the core, the fuel, the guiding power. We're most fully and authentically human in true worship of God, and God's purposes in creation and redemption are fulfilled in this way. Worship is the heartbeat and vocation of humanity. Even unbelievers, when they love their neighbors, fight for justice, or enjoy the beauty of the world, give recognition, although unintentional and indirect, to the loving, righteous Maker of that beauty.

We were made to worship the Creator. This includes praise, gratitude, delight, and honor. Because humans are built—designed—for worship, it's never a matter of whether we'll worship, but *what* or *who* we'll worship, and to what end. Sin is the distortion and disordering of worship: it accordingly dehumanizes us. When sin entered this world, it started to erode the fullness of our humanity by making us turn *from* God rather than *to* him. All humans can now sense something is wrong, even if we can't always articulate it. And even for Christians, this lingering presence of sin in our lives and in the world is what makes our faith, our love, and our trust in God so uneven. Not even Christians worship God consistently.

This is partly why we must pay close attention not just to the cross but also to the resurrection and to Christ's current activity in heaven. Yes, of course we proclaim that Jesus died for our sins, that he has wiped away our sins, and that we live by faith in him. What a glorious gift and proclamation! But the gospel doesn't simply announce the forgiveness of sins. It certainly does not say *less* than that, but it says *more*. His goal for us is not death, nor merely the eradication of sin, but *life in Christ*. And this life in the resurrected Christ does not start in the future after we die. We live it right now.

The author of Hebrews tells us that *Jesus is not just the one we worship; even now he is the lead worshiper. He* is our life. Let me briefly explain.

Hebrews says that Jesus is the faithful "apostle and High Priest of our confession" (3:1). Not only does he bring God to us (as apostle), but as the "founder of [our] salvation" (2:10), he brings us to God (as High Priest).[55] Jesus speaks of God the Father as "his God" (cf. Heb 1:9; John 20:17).[56] The Gospels remind us again and again that Jesus prays. Just looking through Luke's gospel as an example, we see that prayer is central to Jesus's vocation and identity (e.g., Luke 3:21–22; 5:16; 6:12–13; 9:18, 28–29; 10:21; 11:1; 22:31–32; 23:34, 46; 24:30, 50–53). His life was a life of prayer, of deep communion with his Father, expressing real human trust, obedience, need, and love. This reminds us of the repeated

---

55. Jesus is the one who is both worshiped by angels and recognized as none other than God (Heb 1:6), and at the same time also somehow "anointed" by God to lead his "companions" (1:9).

56. Philip Edgecumbe Hughes, *A Commentary on the Epistle to the Hebrews* (Grand Rapids: Eerdmans, 1977): "The expression *thy God* [from Heb 1:9, quoting Ps 45:6–7] in v. 9 seems to comport ill with the preceding verse in which the Son is addressed as God; but the apparent anomaly is resolved by the consideration that as the eternal Son, the Second Person of the Blessed Trinity, the Son is indeed God (cf. John 1:1), while as the incarnate Son, and specifically in relation to his human nature, it is natural for him to speak of God as *his God* (cf. John 20:17). This is the explanation of the prayer-life of Jesus and of his cry of dereliction on the cross (cf. John 17; Mark 6:46; Luke 9:28; Mark 14:35ff.; 15:34)" (66–67).

Pauline refrain, "the God and Father of our Lord Jesus Christ" (Rom 15:6; 2 Cor 1:3; 11:31; Eph 1:3; cf. Gal 1:4; Eph 4:6; Phil 4:20; 1 Thess 1:3; 3:11, 13; see also Rev 1:6). This is a glorious mystery and paradox. On the one hand, we can and must speak of Jesus *as our God* (and thus worthy of our worship), and on the other, this Messiah also is *the one who himself perfectly trusts his God* (i.e., expresses worship). He who was made a little lower than the angels in his incarnation (Heb 2:7–9 // Ps 8:4–5; Zech 6:13) has kept the faith all the way to the grave and has been raised into the heavens: In his humanity the incarnate Son has mysteriously and salvifically taken us with him on this journey.[57] Now, at the "right hand of God," Jesus, the *eschatos Adam*, is there as the complete human—and we are there in him, just as he is in us. We easily miss this.

When Jesus ascended into heaven, he didn't shed his humanity as a snake sheds its skin; his humanity was not vaporized or destroyed, it was *glorified*. Having taken on "the form of a servant, being born in the likeness of men" (Phil 2:7), the enfleshed Son ascended to the Father's right hand. He is there in his resurrected body as our representative and our head—and we are there with and in him (Eph 2:6). As John Murray once rightly concluded, "Any conception that robs our [ascended] Lord of the reality and continuity of his human nature and experience is but a form of docetism which deprives the Saviour and our faith of what is indispensable to both."[58] The resurrected Christ remains the eternal Son of God, and he continues as our *human* Lord. As such, he is our security, our confidence, our hope. This point was pastorally emphasized much earlier by Tertullian (160–220) in his treatise *On the Resurrection of the Flesh*. Having emphasized the ongoing physicality of our Savior in heaven, Tertullian offers his listeners courage: "Be not disquieted, O flesh and blood, with any care; in Christ, you have acquired both heaven and the kingdom of God."[59] Why? Because the Mediator even now reigns and rules. He is Priest and Savior, head and

---

57. "But God, being rich in mercy, because of the great love with which he loved us . . . made us alive together with Christ . . . and raised us up with him and seated us with him in the heavenly places in Christ Jesus, so that in the coming ages he might show the immeasurable riches of his grace in kindness toward us in Christ Jesus. For by grace you have been saved through faith. And this is not your own doing; it is the gift of God" (Eph 2:4–8).

58. John Murray, "The Heavenly, Priestly Activity of Christ," *The Collected Writings of John Murray*, vol. 1, *The Claims of Truth* (Edinburgh: Banner of Truth, 1976), 51.

59. Tertullian, *On the Resurrection of the Flesh*, ANF 3 (1885; repr., Peabody: Hendrickson, 1994), 51, p. 584.

human representative of his people. His ongoing life shapes our present and future life, since *by faith* our life is defined and animated by our union to Christ.

Carefully drawing from Psalm 22 and Isaiah 8, Hebrews attributes particular phrases from these ancient words to the Messiah: "I will tell of your name to my [sisters and] brothers; in the midst of the congregation I will sing your praise" (Heb 2:12). Jesus, speaking to God, says "your name" and "your praise." In both his proclamation and praise, Jesus is referring to the Father.[60] Some believe Jesus's singing here is solely a reference to his earthly ministry, while others see it as referring only to the future time of glory; still, others see this as primarily a reference to his singing among his church now.[61] So what is this reference to Jesus's singing doing here? Why choose just one reference and not all? It appears best to recognize the larger framework of the incarnate life of Jesus, which means one can speak of him singing before the cross, over us now, and even in the future. Examples of the Messiah singing include:

- Jesus sings during his earthly ministry (e.g., he sings the Passover songs in the upper room; Matt 26:30; Mark 14:26).
- Exalted, he sings among us now (amid the current ecclesia, where two or more are gathered; Rom 15:9; Matt 18:20).
- In glory, not only does the Lamb receive praise (Rev 5:8–13; 7:9–10), but he will continue leading the praise into eternity (probably least clear, but see Heb 2:12; Rev 14:1–5).[62]

Through the incarnation, the eternal Son became genuinely human: As he was born, developed, died, and now ever lives to make intercession for us, his truly human life is of its nature a worshiping life. He was, is, and will be our leader of love and worship. As Zephaniah 3:17 describes God, we now see this made wonderfully clear in Christ:

---

60. Hebrews then puts additional words into Jesus's mouth: "I [Jesus] will put my trust in him [God]." Jesus says "I" not just about himself. He also says, "Behold, I and the children God has given me" (Heb 2:13). In other words, Jesus represents not simply himself but also those who are in his family.

61. For more on this dynamic, see Ron Man, *Proclamation and Praise: Hebrews 2:12 and the Christology of Worship* (Eugene: Wipf & Stock, 2007), esp. 7–16.

62. E.g., William L. Lane memorably draws from Hebrews 2:12 and links it to the consummation, concluding: "The exalted Lord who finds in the gathering of the people of God at the parousia an occasion for the proclamation of God's name and who as the singing priest leads the redeemed community (ἐν μέσῳ ἐκκλησίας) in songs of praise (cf. Rom 15:7–12)." Lane, *Hebrews 1–8*, WBC 47A (1991; repr., Grand Rapids: Zondervan, 2015), 59.

> The L<small>ORD</small> your God is in your midst,
>   a mighty one who will save;
> he will rejoice over you with gladness;
>   he will quiet you by his love;
> he will exult over you with loud singing.

God is a singing God, and in Christ we have a singing Savior. Jesus both leads the singing in our praise of God, and also his singing over us is a great comfort and grace. Our ascended Christ is not singing about how wonderful we are but how great God is. God, not his creatures, is always the final and appropriate object of true worship and adoration. God is the ultimate *telos* of human singing, the infinite beauty behind his beautiful creation.[63] And because that song about God is so beautiful, so true, so powerful, it calms and comforts us even in our brokenness and sin. Singing God's praise brings courage and hope. By being about God and his faithfulness, the singing indirectly becomes about us who are loved by God in Christ. This is not self-centeredness because it reflects this biblical pattern: Humans are never freer than when we are loving God (cf. John 8:31–47). We can sing because Jesus sang and continues to sing God's praises.[64] As we join this song, we are liberated to worship God, a worship centered on and deriving from the Lamb of God. God and the Lamb are one in Christ, and here we are back to the great paradox of the incarnation and Christian life.

John Calvin similarly applies Hebrews 2:12 to Christ, who directs his song not toward us but toward the Father. When we "hear that Christ leads our songs, and is the chief composer of our hymns," that is a "most powerful stimulant" to our own singing and praise.[65] Calvin recognizes how strange this is for us. The eternal Son of God, who himself is God, doesn't need to "trust" God since he is none other than God. But when this same Son, who is *homoousios* with the Father, takes a human nature and is thus "exposed to human necessities and wants,"[66] his life is thoroughly characterized by trust in his Father. So as we struggle

---

63. See ch. 2 where we earlier discussed Augustine's distinction between *frui* (enjoyment) and *uti* (use).

64. Edmund P. Clowney, "The Singing Savior," *Moody Monthly*, July/August, 1979, 40–42; Reggie Kidd, *With One Voice: Discovering Christ's Song in Our Worship* (Grand Rapids: Baker, 2005).

65. John Calvin, *Commentaries on the Epistle of Paul the Apostle to the Hebrews*, trans. John Owen (1853; repr., Grand Rapids: Baker, 1996), 66–67.

66. Calvin, *Hebrews*, 68.

to trust God, we can find great encouragement that "we have Christ as our leader and instructor," for indeed "we have it in common with Christ" to trust the Father: Since Christ has such trust, we can as well, for he is never wrong.[67] And this commonality is not reduced to a shared point of view or agreement but runs so much deeper because of our union with Christ by the Spirit: In this union "he presents himself and us together to God the Father."[68] This wording displays two factors to note here. First, Calvin asserts that we are not absent from Christ when he represents us, because "he presents himself and us together." Second, contrary to the false impression that the Father is driven more by wrath than hospitality, Calvin reminds his readers that "Christ brings none to the Father, but those given him by the Father" (cf. John 6:37), and this leading is "by the hand of Christ."[69] We do not have a division or debate within the Trinity; we have a single, inseparable operation, where the compassion and love of the Father flow through the Son and Spirit so that God brings us back to himself by uniting us in his Spirit to his incarnate Son, who takes us by the hand into the welcoming presence of the Father.[70] Brought into the divine fellowship by divine grace in Christ, we now experience divine love.

Still, we well may ask what happens when we try to sing or pray while our minds wander, daydreaming about our to-do lists, distracted by the little kid in front of us, or wondering what we will eat for lunch: What happens when we try to obey but do so with mixed motives? We are trying to believe, pray, sing, and love God, but it is all so far from perfect for us believers. How do we explain this situation both theologically and pastorally?

Imagine a little child trying to pick up something that is way too heavy for them. There is no way they can do it, not even a chance to get it off the ground. But then, before the child even realizes it, a parent is behind them and secretly starts helping them lift it. As the child starts to be able to raise the object, their face lights up. They are participating in something bigger than them even without fully realizing it. Their effort is not irrelevant, but it most certainly isn't the basis for this lift.

---

67. Calvin, *Hebrews*, 68.
68. Calvin, *Hebrews*, 69–70.
69. Calvin, *Hebrews*, 70.
70. See much later in his commentary when he likewise argues that "it is in vain for men to seek God in his own majesty, for it is too far removed from them; but Christ stretches forth his hand to us, that he may lead us to heaven" (Calvin, *Hebrews*, 154).

They think they are doing it on their own. But the truth is, on their own they could never even get it off the ground. That, in some general ways, corresponds to believers' experience of worshiping and loving God. Jesus leads us in worship, not instead of us but upholding us as we worship in him. Not only are we justified by him, but our ongoing life completely derives from Christ, just as the life and nature and fruitfulness of a grape branch completely derives from the vine from which it grows (see John 15). By the Spirit, we are joined to the incarnate Son who continues to lift the weight, inviting us to participate in his love and praise of God despite our shortcomings and sins. So even when our singing is a bit out of tune, out of rhythm, or otherwise out of order (as even our best work is), it still participates in and is redeemed by Jesus's singing. Our mistakes matter less than we are prone to fear, because here, as in all other aspects of life, he does what we can't and carries us in his action.

Let's return to an earlier question: Why is it so hard for us to worship God consistently? Why do our love, passion, and delight so often ebb and flow with respect to God? Short answer: because our sin makes it so *hard to see God*. His beauty, holiness, purity, and glory are overwhelming (Exod 33:17–23). At most we could handle seeing God's "back parts" (Exod 33:23 KJV). We typically feel more aware of our sin and failing than of God's presence, holiness, and grace. The hurt and brokenness in this world and our hearts often overwhelm us and make it difficult to behold God's goodness, his love, his wisdom and might. Simply put, our sin makes seeing God so difficult that our worship is often uneven and can feel forced. And yet our great longing is that we will behold God, that we will see his face and freely enjoy his presence (Pss 17:15; 27:4; Isa 6:1; Ezek 43:5; Acts 7:56; cf. Gen 16:13; Job 19:26; Matt 5:8; John 3:3; 14:8–9; Heb 11:26–27).

Now consider the resurrected and ascended Jesus. What does the risen Messiah behold? He perfectly beholds God! As our great divine-human High Priest, not only does Jesus offer the once-for-all sacrifice of his death, but his "indestructible" life allows him to be the eternal leader of our worship (Heb 7:16, 27; 9:12, 26; 10:10). As David M. Moffitt has convincingly argued, Hebrews emphasizes the cross as well as the value of Jesus's resurrection.[71] Moffitt makes clear that the "sacrifice" is

---

71. David M. Moffitt, *Rethinking the Atonement: New Perspectives on Jesus' Death, Resurrection, and Ascension* (Grand Rapids: Baker Academic, 2022); David M. Moffitt, *Atonement and the Logic of Resurrection in the Epistle to the Hebrews*, NovTSup 141 (Leiden: Brill, 2011).

normally killed first (in this case, on the cross) and then later brought to the altar as an offering (in the heavenly temple). This sacrificial imagery describes a *trajectory*, not just a single moment. We need the cross, but the sacrifice is completed and accepted as our High Priest in the heavens offers it (i.e., himself) to God. And Jesus remains in this heavenly temple as our eternal intercessor.

We, as a result, behold God in the face of the risen Christ. On this point I follow John Owen (1616–83), who asserts a christological center for the beatific vision. As Suzanne McDonald ably summarizes in her treatment of Owen:

> All our knowledge of and union and communion with God now, and everything about our salvation, comes to us through the Son incarnate. So it will be eternally. God will not change the way in which he reveals himself at the consummation of all things, as if making himself known in the person of the incarnate Son were merely a temporary emergency measure to be discarded. It will be part of God's glory, and our glory too, that the one who has glorified human nature by assuming it to himself will be the mediator of our knowledge, love, and adoration of the Trinity, and the salvation that comes from the Trinity, in heaven, just as he is the mediator of all of those things while we are still pilgrims *in via*.[72]

Jesus himself constitutes the communion between God and humanity in his being and action, not just now, but eternally. He is the embodiment of divine love, righteousness, and faithfulness, and he is also the embodiment of human obedience, faith, and divinely directed praise. As our High Priest, Jesus is not trying to convince the Father to love us. Christ lives and acts in heaven as the great manifestation of the Father's love for us.

God didn't just want to repair us; *he wanted us*. He *wants us*! In fact, God doesn't want to be who he is apart from us. And he wants love—given and returned. So here is what God did and does. *God came to us*: Love flows from the Father as he sends the Son in the power of the Spirit to become one with us. God's love is thus manifest in Christ—in

---

72. Suzanne McDonald, "Beholding the Glory of God in the Face of Jesus Christ: John Owen and the 'Reforming' of the Beatific Vision," in *The Ashgate Research Companion to John Owen's Theology*, ed. Kelly M. Kapic and Mark Jones (Surrey: Ashgate, 2012), 149–50.

the Messiah, we see the depth of God's love. But it doesn't stop there. Not only does God come to us, but he also *leads us by the hand back to himself.* The Spirit pours out God's love into our hearts as he connects us to the risen and ascended Christ (Rom 5:5), who even now lives and acts in heaven as the human response to God. Our Messiah and Priest is loving God for us and in our place, not instead of us but including us even now. This point is too easily missed, so let's highlight it.

God doesn't just love us. *Jesus loves God for us.* Consequently, we who are in Christ love God by his action. In and through the incarnate Christ, we have a steady foundation and fountain for our love, worship, and obedience, even though our experience is so uneven. This affirmation is essential for a theology of Christian life. God knows how weak, inconsistent, misguided, and sinfully tainted even our worship and love can be. So he solves that problem by being not simply the God we worship but also, through the incarnation of the eternal Son, the leader of our worship who includes us so that we also may worship. Mystery of mysteries indeed.

Our fragmented prayers are now woven into his powerful petitions. Our weak songs of praise are amplified by the Singer of Redemption. Our inadequate and incomplete offerings are made whole and beautiful as they are brought to God by our ascended Messiah. Worship does not begin with our songs and prayers because our songs and prayers are a participation in the worship of our High Priest, who never ceases to worship in heaven and never ceases to include us in his activity, even when we are not conscious of it, even when our worship is distracted and incomplete. God doesn't just love us. As the incarnate Son, Jesus loves and worships God for us. Therefore, we can love, worship, praise, and follow this Messiah who uniquely is both receiver and giver of love since he is both God and human in one person, our Mediator.

Compassion: In Jesus, God Knows Us from the Inside

One of my pet peeves is when people with limited information sometimes make strong judgments about me or a situation. At some point, we have all learned one or two bits of data and made a mostly uninformed judgment about someone else. But we have also received that kind of judgment, so we know it isn't totally fair. A person may be judged as lazy by someone who knows nothing about the health problems that devour the person's energy. Or people may claim that someone with eating challenges should be able to solve them simply by greater willpower, not realizing how abuse from the past has produced the perpetual anxiety that calls for comfort food. Explanations are not the same as excuses; empathetic people understand this distinction. Without ignoring problems, we can still seek to appreciate the complexities that produced the thorny situation. People who are quick to judge aren't always 100 percent wrong, but in their ignorance they often suggest unkind and inadequate solutions. They simply don't know enough. We experience this ourselves. Praise God, Jesus is so different.

Jesus is full of empathy for his people. Hebrews tells us that "we do not have a high priest who is unable to sympathize with our weaknesses, but one who in every respect has been tempted as we are, yet without sin" (Heb 4:15). Our sympathetic Savior, who has "fellow feeling" with us, has gone through the fullness of human experience.

But this brings up another theological question: How much does God know? Everything. The picture generally presented in Scripture is that divine knowledge is exhaustive (e.g., Pss 139:1–18; 147:5; Prov 15:3; Isa 40:13–14; 46:10; Matt 10:30; John 21:17; Heb 4:12–13; 1 John 3:20). Indeed. But if God already knows everything, then he must know what it means for humans to be tempted. It means God knows all the details surrounding the suffering of his human creatures. He must, at some level, "know" what it means for humans to have longings, to have questions, and to face the difficulty of doing really hard things. The God who knows all things must have always known this, right? Yes and no.

Why does Hebrews make such a big deal about Jesus being our sympathetic High Priest who has been tempted as we are, who has experienced suffering, who has dealt with disappointment and faced rejection? Why? Because God, who has always known everything, has always known it *as God!* Knowledge in the Scriptures is not merely cognitive but also experiential. Jesus is fully God; being fully man includes his sharing of our experiences, his taking on our burdens as his own, and therefore suffering our suffering himself. Jesus has personally experienced all of these things as a human, as a creature, not simply by observation as our Creator.[73] God himself has made our burdens his in Christ.

---

73. I have elsewhere explained this in terms of Bertrand Russell's distinction between "knowledge by acquaintance" and "knowledge by description." In a very real way, God has always known everything by way of "description," but in and through the incarnate Son he knows these things from the inside, from personal acquaintance. See Kelly M. Kapic, *Embodied Hope: A Theological Meditation on Pain and Suffering* (Downers Grove, IL: IVP Academic, 2017), 92–93.

In other words, while God always knew everything as God, now in Christ he knows these things from the human perspective. From the human side! Going through his experience of our humanity, according to Hebrews, made Jesus perfect. We too often confuse *perfect* with *sinless*, but they are not exactly the same.[74] Indeed, Jesus is certainly "without sin" (Heb 4:15; cf. 2 Cor 5:21; 1 Pet 2:22; 1 John 3:5) and thus in that sense perfect. But biblically, *perfect* often means full or complete, and so Jesus is made perfect not by denying our humanity but by ushering us "into heavenly intimacy with God."[75] As Irenaeus reminded us, this is about protology and eschatology, so when Hebrews says that through his sufferings and identifying with us Jesus became "perfect" (Heb 2:10), the point is that he experienced the fullness of being human. He completed the task. And now he knows us at an even deeper level than before.

This is why the author of Hebrews explains that Jesus "shared in our flesh and blood" and "partook of the same things" that we did (Heb 2:14). The book encourages us to find comfort and power in the fact that the Son became incarnate to be a "merciful and faithful high priest": "Because he himself has suffered when tempted, he is able to help those who are being tempted" (Heb 2:18). This contains great help for Christians, especially when we wonder if God appreciates our loneliness, our hurt, our struggle. Hebrews reminds us that no one in the entire world is more empathetic to us and our particular situation than the ascended Jesus. As he addresses our pain and sin and destructive behaviors, he always does so from a position of grace, understanding, wisdom, and power. He comes in love!

Listen to what Hebrews says about our ascended King and Priest: Jesus "is not ashamed to call" us *adelphoi* (sisters and brothers, his siblings; Heb 2:11). We are in God's family now: God is our Father, and by the Spirit of adoption we are brothers and sisters of the eternal Son who became one with us. And all this came to pass because of God's love.

Jesus doesn't need to convince the Father to be compassionate toward us; he *is* the greatest expression of the Father's compassion toward us.[76] God knows our problems, not simply our sin but our inconsistency,

---

74. For a fuller treatment of "perfect" in Hebrews, it is worth spending time in Albert Vanhoye, *A Perfect Priest: Studies in the Letter to the Hebrews*, ed. and trans. Nicholas J. Moore and Richard J. Ounsworth, WUNT 2/477 (Tubingen: Mohr Siebeck, 2018). Special attention should be given to ch. 3, "The *teleiōsis* of Christ: Chief Point of Hebrews' Priestly Christology," 59–75.
75. Vanhoye, *A Perfect Priest*, 69.
76. Murray, "The Heavenly, Priestly Activity of Christ," 53.

our weakness, our failings. So Jesus didn't just deal with our sin on the cross. He rose and ascended to the heavens to make intercession for us. And there he remains even now.

Don't miss this. Jesus *is* the intercession. His flesh, his body, his very presence at the right hand of God—his being as well as his activity—*is the intercession*. He is the sacrifice, the temple, the prayer, the praise. Representing and including us, he is our Priest and King.[77] And he lives and acts from a posture of sympathetic understanding, securing us in our being and standing with God, leading and encouraging us to worship God and to love both God and others.[78]

CONCLUSION: DRAW NEAR TO GOD

Jesus sits at the Father's right hand, as we are told in the Scriptures (e.g., Mark 16:19; Acts 2:33–34 // Ps 110:1; Eph 1:20–21; Col 3:1; 1 Pet 3:22; Heb 1:3; 8:1). But sometimes the Scriptures also portray him as standing up (Acts 7:55–56), most often when his people are in distress. When they are hurting, in danger, in need, the resurrected and reigning Messiah rises and pays close attention. And he will, in the end, make all things right for his people. We know this because he lives!

A consistent refrain throughout the book of Hebrews is its admonition to "draw near." Come, approach God with confidence. As James encourages us, "Draw near to God, and he will draw near to you" (Jas 4:8). Sometimes drawing near to God can be more difficult than people first appreciate. Maybe it is because we fear that God is distant, angry, or distracted. Underlying the challenge for us to draw near to God is this question: How does God view us? Yes, we are encumbered by our sin, by our disrupted worship and obedience. And yet the imagery of Hebrews can help us draw near with confidence.

Thomas Goodwin (1600–1680) was a leading Puritan involved with the Westminster Confession of Faith and a teacher at Oxford. Goodwin wrote a wonderful book called *The Heart of Christ in Heaven unto Sinners*

---

77. Jesus is both the "radiance of the glory of God and the exact imprint of his nature" (Heb 1:3) and "a minister in the holy places" representing his people at the right hand of the Majesty in heaven (Heb 8:1–2). Furthermore, "Christ has entered, not into holy places made with hands, which are copies of the true things, but into heaven itself, now to appear in the presence of God on our behalf" (Heb 9:24). He is not there to keep offering sacrifices since the cross was the once-for-all sacrifice (cf. Heb 9:25–28).

78. See Budianto Lim, "The Significance of the Ascension of Christ and Its Implications for Worship," *Theological Journal Kerugma* 6, no. 1 (April 2023): 11–20.

on Earth. Building on Hebrews 4:15 and the great promise that we have a sympathetic High Priest, Goodwin encourages his readers to "take our hands, and lay them upon Christ's breast, and *let us feel how his heart beats and his bowels yearn towards us*, even now he is in glory" (i.e., he has ascended).[79] Goodwin appreciated how easy it is for us to think ill of God, to question his motives or disposition toward us. Amid our hesitations about drawing near to God, Goodwin calls us to have the courage to look to Christ, to put our hand on his breast, and to discover the pounding of his heart in love as he thinks of us. It seems strange to even imagine. It is like the 2001 French film *Amélie*: When she was a little girl, her father, who was a doctor, believed she had a heart defect. Out of concern, he never touched her except to give her a monthly medical checkup. But because he never showed her affection, every time he would come near with the stethoscope to check her heart, her heart would beat much faster out of excitement. He misunderstood the speed of her beating heart for a defect, when actually it was a sign of hope and delight.

This takes us back to Goodwin's point. When we wonder what God thinks of us, or question if God cares or understands us and our situation, Goodwin encourages us to have the bravery to take our hand and lay it on Christ's breast. For our God is most clearly known in Christ, and our God is driven by love, sympathy, and mercy. As our great High Priest, Jesus doesn't simply love us; he also loves God for us so that even our weak efforts, our sin-laced struggles, and our inadequate prayers and praises all rise to the heavens as a glorious incense. This is a foundation for a properly framed theology of Christian life. When we get a taste of it, I think the only way we can respond is the way God made us to respond: *worship*!

---

79. Thomas Goodwin, *The Heart of Christ in Heaven, Towards Sinners on Earth* . . . , in *The Works of Thomas Goodwin*, ed. John C. Miller, vol. 4 (1651; repr., Edinburgh: James Nichol, 1861–66), 100.

CHAPTER 7

EGO

The Drama of Christian Life

> "The new man" is not simply the converted individual, but an eschatological entity, personal, corporate, and pneumatic, nearly identical with Christ himself.
> —N. A. DAHL[1]

> The fundamental issue [for a Christian moral imagination] turns on the question of how we construe personal identity. . . . The most interesting turn in moral philosophy of the past several decades is the growing persuasion, from a variety of quarters, that the modern individualist self is an illusion. . . . We do not become moral agents except in the relationships, the transactions, the habits and reinforcements, the special uses of language and gesture that together constitute life in community.
> —WAYNE MEEKS[2]

> Life in Christ is responsive obedience to what Christ has done, rather than an imitation of what he did.[3]
> —ANGUS PADDISON

---

1. N. A. Dahl, "Christ, Creation, and the Church," in *The Background of the New Testament and Its Eschatology: Studies in Honour of C. H. Dodd*, ed. W. D. Davies and David Daube (Cambridge: Cambridge University Press, 1956), 436. This was brought to my attention in Herman Ridderbos, *Paul: An Outline of His Theology*, trans. John Richard De Witt (Grand Rapids: Eerdmans, 1975), 63n65.

2. Wayne Meeks, "The Problem of Christian Living," in *Beyond Bultmann: Reckoning a New Testament Theology*, ed. B. W. Longnecker and M. C. Parsons (Waco: Baylor University Press, 2014), 222.

3. Angus Paddison, "P. T. Forsyth and the Christian Life," in *Paul, Grace, and Freedom: Essays in Honour of John K. Riches*, ed. Paul Middleton, Angus Paddison, and Karen Wenell (London: T&T Clark, 1990), 168.

US TO GOD

Three strands of doctrine (Messiah, ego, and ecclesia) must be woven together to form a scriptural doctrine of the human response to God's love. Jesus the Anointed One leads that response. His corporate body manifests this new life, and particular believers concretely receive life from the Messiah and participate in the larger christological movement that we call "the church." This dynamic animates and shapes Christian life in faith, hope, and love.

To change metaphors, these can serve as three different lenses through which to view Christian life. The first lens is that of the Messiah, whose life, death, resurrection, and ongoing ascended presence are the source and foundation of all Christian life. A second lens looks from the viewpoint of particular people. This emphasizes that the gospel is personal and penetrates all the way from the world through the community into individual lives, whereby each person is called to faith and to respond in love and obedience. Finally, the third lens is communal, showing that although Christian life is personal, it is not autonomous or isolated in orientation. Persons of faith, biblically speaking, exist within a larger communal structure (i.e., God's people). The *I* is always part of a larger *we*, although we frequently fail to recognize or appreciate that fact. Accordingly, this chapter will focus on the *I* and the following two chapters on the corporate *we*, giving special attention to ecclesial practices, ultimately concentrating on the significance of key elements in the liturgy during weekly corporate worship gatherings. I will therefore speak of the parts within this larger whole.

We begin with the contemporary and ancient challenge of locating the ego.

THE EGO: CONFUSION ABOUNDS

Ego is a transliteration of the Greek ἐγώ, which is normally translated as "I." That may appear clear, but both in our day and in the ancient world the word *ego* carries many complex shades of meaning. In contemporary usage it often refers to the self or one's sense of self, but sometimes we use it to speak of a person's self-centeredness. We might say that such people have a large or inflated ego, meaning that they have a distorted view of themselves. This false self-perception affects not merely their self-image but also their ability to relate well to others.

The modern Western world works with very individualistic

assumptions about what it means to be a person, often drawing a tight boundary around each one and defining the person as whatever is inside that boundary before the contents relate to what is outside that boundary. "Who I am" is discovered in purely self-referential terms. Similarly, we use the word *ego* to refer to the isolated, internal stream of consciousness and self-awareness of this unattached entity. "To know the *I* simply look *inside* yourself," we say. This foundational concept has affected all of us, not only non-Christians.

Our current moment celebrates the myth of self-creation, where the ego is understood as self-originating, self-sustaining, and self-directing.[4] Consequently, we treat the ego or self as all-important.[5] We are subtly and not-so-subtly warned, accordingly, about letting other people, institutions, or even religions shape us; instead, we are told to look within ourselves and discover—or even create—who we are. This is the *ego*. Tara Isabella Burton, for example, has described this dynamic well in her riveting work *Self-Made: Creating Our Identities from Da Vinci to the Kardashians*.[6] Pulling from history, literature, and cultural observation, Burton argues persuasively that our age has not marked the end of deities or religion but rather has replaced them with the ego—the ego has been divinized. While appreciating Charles Taylor's *Secular Age*, Burton contends that rather than entering a religionless period, worship has, for many, simply turned from the transcendent to the immanent, no longer looking outside ourselves but instead turning within to seek ultimate reality and wisdom.[7] Maybe this turn inward points to its own kind of transcendence. One must look to the self to understand how humans flourish and even what they worship.

One example of just how internalized and privatized our contemporary conceptions of the ego have become is that we sometimes view even our physicality—our own material body—as an unreliable source of *self*-understanding. This occurs in charged debates about sexuality (e.g., transgender discussions), as well as when we look at ourselves in the mirror and see someone twenty pounds heavier than we imagined

---

4. I treat this historical and theological development more fully in *You're Only Human* (Grand Rapids: Brazos, 2022), 72–94.

5. It should be noted that this dynamic can easily create both self-absorption and self-doubt, often serving as two sides of the same coin.

6. Tara Isabella Burton, *Self-Made: Creating Our Identities from Da Vinci to the Kardashians* (New York: PublicWorks, 2023). Also see her earlier relevant work, *Strange Rites: New Religions for a Godless Age* (New York: PublicAffairs, 2020).

7. Burton, *Self-Made*, 5–6, *passim*.

and declare: "That is *not* who I am." Really? There may be an element of truth in this idiomatic expression, but it also has serious problems. When we try to dislodge or disassociate the self from the body (and from social relations, as we will soon see), we can only understand the ego as a detached entity without context or ground. When we try to imagine who *I* really am without relating ourselves to our religious, social, institutional, and relational contexts, or even to our own bodies, this ego becomes hard to pin down and sustain. Trying to understand ourselves only in terms of our internal senses and activities produces a great deal of anxiety among people who think within those presuppositions.

Following upon the life and work of Sigmund Freud (1856–1939), the language of ego in the popular imagination has also acquired all manner of innuendoes, often deeply sexual, usually dark, and regularly troublesome.[8] Not just Christian theologians but many psychologists, neuroscientists, and philosophers have long left behind most of the details of Freud's original proposals, including his particular construction of the id, ego, and superego. Freud was wrong in many ways and on many levels, but where he was right—and partly why his name still lingers—was his intuitive recognition that even the internal world of a human person is deeply complex and multilayered.[9] A person cannot be reduced to a "brain in a vat." Fields such as psychology, neuroscience, sociology, and medicine—despite real disagreements and no unified theory—have abundantly demonstrated that human persons are complex organisms that mysteriously and wondrously emerge from biological, relational, and environmental realities.[10] This is partly why understanding the ego is so difficult. While the popular imagination currently tends to understand the ego by looking within, we are discovering more and more just how social the ego is: Self-understanding seems always to require others, for better or worse.

Recognizing and naming cultural dynamics like those noted above helps us develop a scripturally informed imagination for examining Christian life. The narratives and teachings of the Bible show that God's

---

8. Sigmund Freud, *The Ego and the Id*, The Standard Edition of the Complete Psychological Works of Sigmund Freud (New York: Norton, 1990).

9. Freud, for example, developed a three-layer approach to the mind or awareness: preconscious, conscious, and unconscious. See, e.g., Sigmund Freud, *The Unconscious* (London: Penguin Classic, 2005), for his definition and defense of the unconscious.

10. E.g., Shaun Gallagher, *How the Body Shapes the Mind* (Oxford: Oxford University Press, 2005); Elizabeth Lewis Hall, "What Are Bodies For? An Integrative Examination of Embodiment," *Christian Scholar's Review* 39, no. 2 (Winter 2010), 156–76.

people experience Christian life as he calls us—the particular within the collective—enlivening and sustaining us *by* the Spirit *through* the Son *before* the Father; this is the life of response to God's love as one enters his fellowship by the gift of divine grace. This Christian life is embodied and embedded in the church; it takes the shape of a multidimensional dialectic we will review in our last chapter: discussing our calling and baptism, word and confession, Eucharist and generosity, prayer and benediction. It is a life framed by faith and repentance, marked by justification even as it is expressed in sanctification; it is a life animated by faith, guided by hope, and kept by love (both received *and* given). This construct requires a different view of the ego from that of our culture, one that necessarily has both vertical (divine) and horizontal (human and creational) connections, not just internal or psychological ones. But before we can develop that construct, we must increase our awareness of contemporary presuppositions about the ego that shape our concepts and make the biblical story of Christian life feel especially foreign, even for believers.

EGO: EMBODIED AND EMBEDDED

We have begun with the brief digression above because a failure to appreciate the complexity of the ego limits our ability to examine our experience of Christian life and form a faithful theology about it. We do ourselves no favors by pretending that our culture's individualism does not profoundly shape both our lives and our exegesis. Evangelical spirituality, for instance, is often portrayed as working almost exclusively within a privatized and individualistic framework, as tending to reduce spirituality to matters of one's psychological state. While our interiority is of great importance, we will need our theological proposal to account for more than our interior states.

Biblical Christianity has long confessed and marveled at human complexity, both as it fosters the good and enables the problematic. Further, it not only clearly asserts that we do *not* simply "create" ourselves; it also understands who we are in terms of external relations. To illustrate with the obvious, we all have belly buttons. We come from someone (actually, from a pair of someones), from somewhere, and we live, breathe, and exist in a web of relationships. As Susan Eastman argues at length, human persons are "relationally constituted agents who are both embodied and embedded in their world."[11] And these relations are both human and divine.

Earlier generations of Western Christians, especially those in the Protestant tradition, have been—sometimes fairly—accused of presenting an extremely privatized and individualist version of faith and Christian life.[12] It isn't only Protestants, however, who shaped this aspect of modernity: René Descartes, Benjamin Franklin, and Freud, to name just a few, helped produce this individualistic soil from which the contemporary Western world has emerged. This same cultural mind-set has shaped how we read Scripture, often producing a reading that promotes autonomy and isolation rather than community.[13] This reflects modern rather than ancient instincts.[14] Recent decades, however, have seen a shift, including in biblical studies, where there is a strong scholarly reaction against this atomistic account of the human person as solitary or disconnected, partly as a reaction against the early twentieth-century academic existentialism of Rudolph Bultmann and partly against such early twenty-first-century self-help preaching as that coming from Joel Osteen. The pendulum of scholarship has now swung hard toward showing how communal, corporate, and connected the Bible's view of the ego is: This renewed social emphasis shapes current presentations of faith and Christian life.[15] Many scholars now argue that this more communal approach is both presupposed and presented by the biblical authors. However, some have suggested that this recent reaction against perceived modern individualistic readings runs its own risks. The hope is to avoid a false dichotomy.[16] How do we make sure we don't overcorrect?

---

11. Susan Eastman, *Paul and the Person: Reframing Paul's Anthropology* (Grand Rapids: Eerdmans, 2017), 2.

12. E.g., see the critiques by Brad S. Gregory in *The Unintended Reformation: How A Religious Revolution Secularized Society* (Cambridge, MA: Harvard University Press, 2012); *Rebel in the Ranks: Martin Luther, the Reformation, and the Conflicts That Continue to Shape Our World* (New York: HarperOne, 2017).

13. For more on the historical and sociological dynamics of forming this inherited social imaginary, see Charles Taylor, *Modern Social Imaginary* (Durham: Duke University Press, 2004).

14. E.g., E. Randolph Richards and Richard James, *Misreading Scripture with Individualistic Eyes: Patronage, Honor, and Shame in the Biblical World* (Downers Grove, IL: IVP Academic, 2020).

15. It affects not just anthropology but all doctrines. For example, the British Council of Churches memorably responded to concern about this individualistic turn by producing a three-volume study called *The Forgotten Trinity* (London: Inter-Church, 1989–91). While focused on the Trinity, one of the main driving concerns of that study committee was to present a theological response to the increasingly distorted view of human autonomy and isolation exhibited in Western culture.

16. E.g., Simeon Zahl, "Beyond the Critique of Soteriological Individualism: Relationality and Social Cognition," *Modern Theology* 37, no. 2 (2021): 336–61.

We can best avoid yet another false dichotomy not by following a vague *via media* but by situating our discussion within biblical categories that don't allow (much less force) a choice between the singular and the collective, between the personal and the corporate. In the middle of this complication stands the biblical ego. While the human is a psychosomatic unity, we also must appreciate how *relationality* necessarily shapes and reshapes that unity. Susan Eastman's assertion that humans are "embodied and embedded" helps us resist isolating the mental, physical, and social realities from each other, or picking which of them "really matters."[17] From a Christian perspective, we must happily confess that the embodied and embedded ego is formed not just by such horizontal factors as neighbor relations, our physicality, and our culture, among others, but also by vertical ones, especially our relations with God. The transcendent and sovereign Lord speaks and interacts not simply with humanity in general or only with select groups (e.g., Israel, the church); he also creates, sustains, and addresses *individual* persons (e.g., Abraham, Hagar, Anna, and Ananias). This is a matter of both-and, not either-or. It will be of fundamental importance to see and express accurately how the two relate, especially since we inhabit a fallen cosmos that affects both our internal and external worlds. Accordingly, to understand the issues at hand, the reader must understand the unity and interconnections of this chapter with the following two on ecclesia and liturgy.

EGO AND SIN: COMPROMISED AND THREATENED

Who *I* am and how *I* respond and relate to God (in rebellion or in faith) can only be understood within the much larger story of creation, fall, Israel, redemption, church, and consummation, as contrasted with trying to understand it only within the much more limited story of one's particular life.

God created all things, and initially all "was good." According to the Scriptures, the material composition of human persons matters deeply, since Adam was fashioned out of the soil by the very hands of God (Gen 2:7), indicating both our horizontal connections with the rest

---

17. Eastman, *Paul and the Person*, 2.

of the created world and our vertical connections with God.[18] This beginning means that we should never think of flesh or our created bodies and the world as intrinsically evil or bad. On the other hand, this materiality does not imply that we can be understood entirely in terms of chemistry, since the creation account also describes us as social beings, involving life-giving relations with God, neighbor, and the rest of creation. These various relations and interdependencies are part of the goodness of being a human creature. Sin invades that arrangement, distorting and twisting the good relationships and healthy dependencies of our spiritual-physical-social being. Sin, by denying our nature and its goodness, thus compromises and threatens human flourishing for everyone, not just those who outright deny or reject Yahweh.

The account from Genesis through Revelation asserts that we are affected by larger (and often mysterious) forces beyond our own internal sinful thoughts. I will use the "S/sin" designation at times to remind us that biblically, sin is not just occasional shortcomings we have or particular acts of disobedience, but it can be personified, viewed as a personal force or power: Sin is coming after us, crouching at the door (Gen 4:7). Hostile forces (e.g., S/sin) seem to come from both the inside and outside. For example, we see times when people were led astray both by unfaithful ancient leaders (external forces like an idolatrous king; e.g., 1 Kgs 12:28–33; 2 Kgs 21:1–18; 2 Chron 21:3-20; or compromised communities; e.g., Exod 32:1–35; Num 14:1–10; Ezek 20:6–8; Hos 7:14) and by disordered desires and rebellion against God (internal passions like greed or arrogance; e.g., Mark 7:20–23; Rom 1:21–32; Jas 1:13–15; 1 John 2:16). There are internal *and* structural distortions that seem to be used by Sin and promote sin. This reveals a tension that we too often try to ease by downplaying one side of a biblical dialectic. We must not ignore either the internal or external factors, for in this tension the ego emerges and navigates life in our broken world.

Early in the biblical account, something went terribly wrong, starting with the story of the deceptive serpent invading and upending human communion with God, right relations with other people, and even how humans interact with the earth and carry out their vocations (Gen 3). Since then, visible and invisible factors have emerged that oppose God

---

18. Cf. Dietrich Bonhoeffer, *Creation and Fall: A Theological Exposition of Genesis 1–3*, ed. Martin Rüter and Ilse Tödt, trans. Douglas Stephen Bax, Dietrich Bonhoeffer Works 3 (Minneapolis: Fortress, 1996), first 76–77, then back to 60–67.

and the things of God. A darkness hovers over the earth, "for our struggle is not against blood and flesh but against the rulers, against the authorities, against the cosmic powers of this present darkness, against the spiritual forces of evil in the heavenly places" (Eph 6:12 NRSVue). Several forces are pushing against God's creation and his shalom. In contrast with modernity's hard distinction between the supernatural and the natural, the biblical account stresses other categories, such as the Creator-creature distinction and the contrast between the visible and the invisible elements of the world (some of which are creatures; cf. Col 1:16). While humans do indeed sin and often wrestle with internal disordered desires, this larger threat and darkness is at times associated with special titles or descriptions that indicate agency, such as "the Satan" or "Accuser" (e.g., 1 Chron 21:1; Job 1:6–2:7; Zech 3:1–2; Matt 4:10), "the devil" or "deceiver" (e.g., Matt 4:1–11; 13:39; 25:41; John 8:44, Rev 20:10, etc.), "the ruler (*archon*) of this world" (e.g., John 12:31; 14:30; 16:11), or more generally the demonic (e.g., 1 Cor 10:20; 1 Tim 4:1; Rev 16:14).[19] The biblical account occasionally treats Sin as an active moral agent and not simply as a label for our own actions (see below). Thus, if we ignore or downplay the parts played by these external forces of darkness, we are, in the context of the Scriptures, naive and ill-prepared to make sense of our chaotic and damaged world.

S/sin and corrupting forces pursue humans (both particular and corporate), bringing accusations, temptation, and disorder. Sin represents a personified darkness and threat that hides and prepares to attack once the door is opened, hoping to overcome a person or people (Gen 4:7). When we are called by the author of Hebrews to "struggle against sin" (Heb 12:4), this is not merely "against evil impulses within your own hearts," as we often suppose, but at times, as Paul Ellingworth and Eugene Nida explain, it refers to a struggle against a personified moral agent, the larger forces of evil or sin.[20]

The apostle Paul occasionally treats S/sin as a semipersonified moral agent in his letter to the Romans:[21] It "seizes the opportunity,"

---

19. Cf. Gottfried Quell et al., "Ἁμαρτάνω, Ἁμάρτημα, Ἁμαρτία," in *Theological Dictionary of the New Testament*, ed. Gerhard Kittel, Geoffrey W. Bromiley, and Gerhard Friedrich (Grand Rapids: Eerdmans, 1964–), 267–316, esp. 308–13 as treated in Paul.

20. Paul Ellingworth and Eugene Albert Nida, *A Handbook on the Letter to the Hebrews*, UBS Handbook Series (New York: United Bible Societies, 1994), 292.

21. Cf. James D. G. Dunn, *The Theology of Paul the Apostle* (New York: T&T Clark, 2003), 96, 104; Craig S. Keener, *Romans*, New Covenant Commentary Series (Eugene, OR: Cascade, 2009), 76.

"deceives," "kills" (Rom 7:11), and can be described as an enslaving force that captures and oppresses humans (cf. Rom 7:14; John 8:34).[22] James Dunn notes that of the forty-one references to sin in Romans 5:12–8:3, only a few seem to have in view a concrete sinful action, whereas the rest treat S/sin as a "personified power."[23] Beverly Roberts Gaventa comments that Paul in Romans so effectively treats Sin as a personified entity that the "achievements of Sin's résumé create the portrait of a cosmic terrorist. Sin not only entered the cosmos with Adam; it also enslaved, it unleashed Death itself, it even managed to take the law of God captive to its power."[24] We needed not only a cosmic rescue achieved in Christ but the continuing presence and power of the Spirit of God to push back against these powers, whether arising from within us or from outside us.

Centuries ago, the Puritan John Owen wrote of Sin's threatening presence in the Christian life, although he—like many in the history of the church—stressed far more the problem of "indwelling sin."[25] Owen treated S/sin as a threatening, stalking, menacing hunter who seeks to devour its prey. You cannot make a truce with S/sin; you cannot ignore the taunts and temptations brought about by sin; instead, you must face it head-on, leaning on the power of the Holy Spirit and the perfect atonement of Christ, which enable the believer to push back against this present darkness and to enjoy more and more the light of the triune God. Only when believers appreciate this dynamic can they navigate the challenges of temptation and the opportunities for faithfulness. As this same Oxford don memorably urged his young university listeners, "Be killing sin, or it be killing you. . . . If this were the work and business of Paul, who was so incomparably exalted in grace, revelations, privileges, consolations, above the ordinary measure of believers, where may we possibly bottom [sic] an exemption from this work and duty whilst we

---

22. Johannes P. Louw and Eugene Albert Nida, *Greek-English Lexicon of the New Testament: Based on Semantic Domains* (New York: United Bible Societies, 1996), 578. Cf. Joseph A. Fitzmyer, SJ, *Romans: A New Translation with Introduction and Commentary*, Anchor Yale Bible 33 (New Haven, CT: Yale University Press, 2008), 446, 465.
23. Dunn, *The Theology of Paul the Apostle*, 111–12.
24. Beverly Roberts Gaventa, *Our Mother Saint Paul* (Louisville: Westminster John Knox, 2007), 130–31.
25. See his classic treatments in his works *On Mortification of Sin* (1656), *On Temptation* (1658), and *On Indwelling Sin in Believers* (1668), among others. For a compendium of Owen's four classic works treating this topic, see the recent collection in John Owen, *Sin and Temptation*, in *The Complete Works of John Owen*, vol. 15, ed. Kelly M. Kapic, Justin Taylor, Shawn D. Wright, and Lee Gatis (Wheaton, IL: Crossway, 2024).

are in this world?"[26] This threat of S/sin is cosmic, personal, and ruthless, and unless we resist it in the name of Christ and the power of the Spirit, it will continue its destructive work in us.

Since Sin's tentacles touch all people, even Christians will continue, throughout this life, to wrestle with its ongoing threat and effects. However, believers are no longer under its rule or dominion. Therefore, all humans face a stark question about their current position: Am I (ego) in the darkness or in the light? Those appear to be the only two existing possibilities in relation to sin. Notice that identifying one's condition depends not simply on looking within but primarily on seeing one's relation to what is beyond ourselves (*extra nos*), to Christ, and then to his body. Are we living in the realm and under the reign of sin and death (darkness), or in the realm and under the reign of Christ (light), whose death and resurrection have brought illumination and new life? One kingdom enslaves, while the other sets us free because this new Master liberates us from the oppressor (Rom 6:16–18; cf. John 8:36; 2 Pet 2:19).[27]

The juxtaposition is striking: Christ is the light of the world (John 3:19; 8:12; 9:5), and yet "everyone who does wicked things hates the light and does not come to the light lest his works should be exposed" (John 3:20). Paul employs this kind of imagery when he declares that either we are obedient slaves to sin (which leads to death) or we are obedient to Christ from a new heart, freed from sin's enslavement and now bound (even freely enslaved) to God in Christ (Rom 6:16–19). Slavery to Christ is not oppressive or troublesome because following this Master's rule and living in his kingdom produces shalom, love, and freedom; however, in this fallen world, that trifecta often looks like a cross and is experienced as self-denial and service. But that is *not* because the ego is inherently bad.

The Creator did not create a faulty ego; rather, *sin* has distorted and warped it so that we need a new birth, a (re)new(ed) life. So when we speak of killing the self or the ego, we do not speak about self-mutilation or self-hatred—a sentiment too often found in some Christian traditions. As I laid out in chapter 2 on God's love, God doesn't hate you—his child whom he made and redeemed in Christ—but he hates the S/sin that has

---

26. John Owen, *The Works of John Owen*, ed. William H. Goold, vol. 6 (Edinburgh: T&T Clark, n.d.), 9–10.
27. We should note that Paul does sometimes speak of slaves to righteousness or slaves to Christ (e.g., Rom 6:18; 1 Cor 7:22–23).

distorted you, that continuously seeks your downfall. God will put sin to death in you not because he despises you but because he wants you liberated from it, enabled to experience more fully his life and love. Unless believers appreciate the nuances here, they will be tempted to suppose that Christian life should be animated by the soul-destroying voice of self-hatred rather than the compassionate and kind Lord's liberating call to repentance, faith, and new life.

Now we have fully entered the drama of Christian life. One must leave the darkness, not by creating light, but by entering the light of God seen most clearly in the face of Christ. Thus some of the *"egō eimi"* statements from Jesus take on a personal sound, starting with his declaration that "I am [*egō eimi*] the light of the world. Whoever follows me will not walk in darkness, but will have the light of life" (John 8:12).[28] These statements address us, not merely making abstract claims about a distant Jesus, but asking implicitly, "And what about you? What will you do about this?" Thus when he later adds, "I am [*egō eimi*] the way, and the truth, and the life. No one comes to the Father except through me" (John 14:6),[29] the text makes an unspoken but definite claim, a claim that either sits in judgment on your life or liberates you into the freedom that I give. For God is "the Father of lights, with whom there is no variation or shadow due to change. Of his own will he brought us forth by the word of truth, that we should be a kind of firstfruits of his creatures" (Jas 1:17–18). Light or darkness, new life or the way of death? This should sober us and force us to ask where we stand. Here we face an undeniable tension: Experientially, we navigate a world of gray instead of pure light or utter darkness, and yet theologically, these realities are opposed, representing two different worlds or two different ways to exist. As the opening words of the *Didache*—one of the oldest noncanonical documents from the ancient church—clearly state, "There are two ways, one of life and one of death, and there is a great difference between these two ways."[30] One is the path of light, governed by a vertical "love of

---

28. Cf. John 6:19–20, which tells us that amid the frightening storm, Jesus declares, "It is I" (*egō eimi*) who walks on water, so don't be afraid. Before this Anointed One we stand exposed and vulnerable yet known and loved.

29. Against a more generic reading of this verse, F. C. Fensham defends a specifically religious reading of this *"egō eimi"* text that treats *way*, *truth*, and *life* as related particularly to God, thus highlighting the singularity of Messiah and his vital importance. Fensham, "I Am the Way, the Truth, and the Life," *Neotestamentica* 2 (1968): 81–88.

30. *Didache*, in *The Apostolic Fathers: Greek Texts and English Translations*, ed. and trans. Michael W. Holmes, 3rd ed. (Grand Rapids: Baker Academic, 2007), 1:1–2, p. 345.

God, who made you," as well as a horizontal "love [of] your neighbor as yourself," a twofold love on the one path of the light and life of God. The other path, which is of death, is "evil and cursed," poisoned with sin that breeds self-absorption, the abuse of others, and an unhealthy view of self, demonstrated in behaviors that erode loving community and reject a life of creation-honoring and God-glorifying shalom.[31]

Light and darkness may seem simple enough, but life is very messy. Christians are all too familiar with the ongoing struggle with S/sin. We live in a drama that raises questions about our assurance of salvation and what God realistically expects of his children.[32] Consequently, our theology of Christian life must treat believers as people of the light who still wrestle with temptation and sin (cf. 1 John 1:8–10). But we no longer *belong* to Sin; it no longer reigns and rules over us; only Christ the King does. Again, Susan Eastman, commenting on Romans 7:14–25, writes, "Despite Paul's cosmic claims regarding the distinctions between the self-in-relation-to-sin and the self-in-relation-to-Christ, in *felt experience* and daily life the sequence from the first to the second is not so clear-cut."[33] While something may be true ontologically (we *are* free from sin in Christ), our experience may reflect that reality imperfectly (we *continue* to wrestle with temptation and sin). As those who are *now* found in Christ, we hope to live more and more into what is eschatologically secure and true: *We are saints*!

Our objectively true new situation is that the Christian is a (re)new(ed) ego: a person who is "born again" (John 3:3, 7; 1 Pet 1:23) by the Spirit of God (John 3:5–6). Believers have a new reality in the incarnate *ego eimi*. Christ is their light and life, their way and truth, their promise and fulfillment. While not yet receiving a new physical body, each believer has been made part of this "new creation" in Christ (2 Cor 5:17; Gal 6:15). Yet this very personal new birth and new creation do not affect only the Christian in isolation, because this new being is not a being-in-isolation at all, but a being-in-community. The reborn Christian is part of a new, reborn community, connected to Jesus, and is

---

31. Didache 5:1–2, p. 353.
32. For a nuanced historical and theological treatment of related questions growing out of the Protestant Reformation, begin with Joel R. Beeke, *Assurance of Faith: Calvin, English Puritanism, and the Dutch Second Reformation*, American University Studies, series 7, Theology and Religion, vol. 89 (New York: Peter Lang, 1991).
33. Susan Eastman, *Paul and the Person: Reframing Paul's Anthropology* (Grand Rapids: Eerdmans, 2017), 116, emphasis original.

therefore a member of his body, the church (Col 1:18; Rev 1:5). His life is now our life. And this new life has consequences. This takes us to a brief review of the vital significance of union with Christ.

THE EGO UNITED TO CHRIST

If we are to locate the ego properly, we first must review a few aspects of why union with Christ is central to a theology of Christian life.

The doctrine of union with Christ comes not from a study of the word *union* in the New Testament but from gathering related concepts (e.g., belonging to Christ or "the Lord"), images (e.g., wedding, vine and branches), and especially the *in* phrases (e.g., "in Christ," "in him," "Christ in us"). These are the ideas behind Paul's description of Christian life, although they occur throughout the New Testament. The Johannine literature, for example, uses "in-one-another" language and imagery of Christ or God in us, and us in God or Christ: John weaves together oneness, participation, and life as he describes how believers are united to Christ.[34] It's important to absorb all these images as we form a theology of Christian life.

Taking a more synthetic approach that draws heavily from the entire New Testament and its use of the Hebrew Bible, G. K. Beale outlines how the resurrected Christ serves as a "corporate representative for the believer," marking an eschatological beginning to a "New-Creational Kingdom."[35] Although we cannot here repeat what other books on union with Christ have more ably unpacked, we can take a quick look at how this union undergirds the entire arch of Christian life.[36] We will then see how union combines this new life's vertical and horizontal aspects and look at the relationship between personal and corporate aspects.

Drawing primarily from the writings of the apostle Paul, Anthony

---

34. Clive Bowsher, *Life in the Son: Exploring Participation and Union with Christ in John's Gospel and Letters*, New Studies in Biblical Theology (Downers Grove, IL: InterVarsity Press, 2023).

35. G. K. Beale, *Union with the Resurrected Christ: Eschatological New Creation and New Testament Biblical Theology* (Grand Rapids: Baker Academic, 2023).

36. Some of the other recent works on union with Christ that I have found most helpful include J. Todd Billings, *Union with Christ: Reframing Theology and Ministry for the Church* (Grand Rapids: Baker Academic, 2011); Constantine R. Campbell, *Paul and Union with Christ: An Exegetical and Theological Study* (Grand Rapids: Zondervan, 2012); Grant Macaskill, *Union with Christ in the New Testament* (Oxford: Oxford University Press, 2013); Michael J. Thate, Kevin J. Vanhoozer, and Constantine R. Campbell, eds., *"In Christ" in Paul: Explorations in Paul's Theology of Union and Participation*, Wissenschaftliche Untersuchungen zum Neuen Testament 2, Reihe 384 (Tübingen: Mohr Siebeck, 2014).

A. Hoekema nicely captures the significance of union with Christ in the following eight observations:[37]

1. We are initially united with Christ in regeneration, making us alive with Christ (e.g., Eph 2:4–5, 10).
2. We appropriate and continue to live in this union through faith (e.g., Gal 2:20; Eph 3:16–17).
3. We are justified in union with Christ (e.g., 1 Cor 1:30; 2 Cor 5:21; Phil 3:8–9).
4. We are sanctified through union with Christ (e.g., 1 Cor 1:30; cf. John 15:4–5).
5. We persevere in the life of faith in union with Christ (e.g., Rom 8:38–39; cf. John 10:27–28).
6. We are even said to die in Christ (e.g., Rom 14:8; 1 Thess 4:16; cf. Rev 14:13; see also 2 Cor 5:14–15).
7. We shall be raised with Christ (e.g., 1 Cor 15:22–23; Col 3:1).
8. We shall be eternally glorified with Christ (e.g., Col 3:4; 1 Thess 4:16–17).

We could add other items to the list, such as our adoption; we now cry out, "Abba," to *our* Father—the Father of the Lord Jesus Christ (e.g., Gal 3:29; 4:5).[38]

From new creation to glorification, this union frames Christian life. It is not a step along the way but the reality that unifies the whole, even amid the different "steps" or ordering of salvation and new life.[39] This union allows us to assert the *inseparability* of God's various actions in salvation while also *distinguishing* them (e.g., justification, sanctification, glorification). Christian life grows from, is sustained by, and is fostered in our union with Jesus. Further, this union does not treat us as autonomous or isolated individuals (i.e., me alone).

The particular phrase *in Christ Jesus* (*en Christō Iēsou*) appears almost fifty times in the writings of the apostle Paul but not in the New Testament outside of his work (cf. 1 Pet 5:10, minority text), although the

---

37. I am drawing from Anthony A. Hoekema, *Saved by Grace* (Grand Rapids: Eerdmans, 1989), esp. 59–64.
38. Cf. John Murray, *Redemption Accomplished and Applied* (Grand Rapids: Eerdmans, 1955), 132–40; Julie Canlis, "The Fatherhood of God and Union with Christ in Calvin," in Thate, Vanhoozer, and Campbell, *"In Christ" in Paul*, 399–426.
39. Cf. John Murray, *Redemption Accomplished and Applied*, 161–73.

concept is there (see John 15). What we probably don't always remember is that the phrase most often communicates connection with Christ's church.[40] When we try to separate the personal from the corporate in this context, we are immediately moving in a direction that is foreign to the Old Testament with its conception of corporate identity or corporate personality and how, to use the language of Robert A. Di Vito, "the embedding of the individual" is always presupposed as key to understanding a person.[41] Both the Old Testament and then the apostle Paul, whose imagination moves in a similar manner, appear to believe the individual is understood only from within the communal or corporate. Take, for example, Paul's description of the church as Christ's body in Romans 12 and 1 Corinthians 12. Each Christian is a member of the body just as an ear or a foot is a member of a human body: The ear is not a foot, and the eye is not a hand, so each member retains its own character and identity while at the same time having that character and identity as part of a larger character and identity. You can't separate the eye from the body without both killing the eye and (at least partially) blinding the body. Thus the eye's identity and character are irretrievably intertwined with its function in the body, both serving and being served by the body. Unfortunately, in the overly individualistic West, we tend to think of ourselves less like members of a body and more like plates in a set of dinnerware: If you break one plate it diminishes the size of the set, but breaking a plate has no effect on the teapot. They are not organically connected, and the plate is replaceable. By contrast, members of the body are organically connected with one another. "If one member suffers, all suffer together; if one member is honored, all rejoice together" (1 Cor 12:26).[42]

Albrecht Oepke comments that Paul's language and imagery of being *in Christ* connects with his image of the two Adams, who are each "progenitors initiating two races of [people]. Each implies a whole world,

---

40. Albrecht Oepke, "ἐν," in *Theological Dictionary of the New Testament*, vol. 2 (Grand Rapids: Eerdmans, 1964), 541.

41. The classic text, although now helpfully critiqued and sharpened by others (e.g., Rogerson below), is H. Wheeler Robinson, *Corporate Personality in Ancient Israel* (repr., Philadelphia: Fortress, 1980); cf. J. W. Rogerson, "The Hebrew Conception of Corporate Personality: A Re-Examination," *Journal of Theological Studies* 2, no. 1 (1970): 1–16; I find Robert A. Di Vito's article especially helpful: "Old Testament Anthropology and the Construction of Personal Identity," *Catholic Biblical Quarterly* 61 (1999): 217–38, quote from 221.

42. Thanks to John Yates for helping me think through these images, including the plate analogy.

an order of life or death. Each includes his adherents in and under him."[43] That is, Paul's contrast of the first Adam with the final Adam (e.g., Rom 5) also contrasts two ways to exist in this world. Rather than remaining in the death associated with the first Adam, believers are new creatures who have eternal life in Christ. The content and character of this union, brought about by the Spirit, derive from the incarnate Son and what he did for his people, most clearly exemplified on the cross. "Christ redeemed us from the curse of the Law, having become a curse for us—for it is written, 'Cursed is everyone who hangs on a tree'—in order that in Christ Jesus the blessing of Abraham would come to the Gentiles, so that we would receive the promise of the Spirit through faith" (Gal 3:13–14 NASB). Even a gentile can be a child of Abraham because by faith we enter into the new covenant through Christ. Paul declares that for "our sake" God "made him to be sin who knew no sin, so that in him we might become the righteousness of God" (2 Cor 5:21). *He* "became sin" not just so that we might be forgiven, but so that "*we* might be the righteousness of God." Forgiven, yes, but as new creatures in Christ, we discover that his faith and faithfulness shape and determine our own, for we are found in him.

As those now in Christ, we are part of a new world, and that has changed not only the vertical realities but also the horizontal ones, starting with the church and then moving out to the world. But this change derives from who Jesus himself was and is, only becoming true of us because we are now found *in* Christ. For example, we are justified by faith in Christ (*extra nos*: referring to God's forensic declaration about us based on Christ's work as applied to us in our union with him) even as we are also sanctified by union with Christ (*intra nos*: in sanctification God's Spirit "*infuseth* grace" into us to transform us more and more into the image of Christ).[44] Theologians debate the relationship between these, but we find both in the New Testament, and union with Christ allows us to make distinctions between them without eliminating their fullness. We don't pick between (1) the legal or judicial aspects of our

---

43. Oepke, "ἐν," 2:542.
44. Westminster Larger Catechism, 77: "A. Although sanctification be inseparably joined with justification, yet they differ, in that God in justification imputeth the righteousness of Christ; in sanctification his Spirit infuseth grace, and enableth to the exercise thereof; in the former, sin is pardoned; in the other, it is subdued; the one doth equally free all believers from the revenging wrath of God, and that perfectly in this life, that they never fall into condemnation; the other is neither equal in all, nor in this life perfect in any, but growing up to perfection."

salvation (justification) and (2) the eschatologically definitive yet also progressive aspects (sanctification). The problems arise when we either crudely combine these or pick between them rather than hold them as inseparable yet distinct.

One quick example may help. Turning momentarily to a Reformation debate between Andreas Osiander (1498–1552) and John Calvin will highlight a key distinctive way that union became affirmed in the Reformed tradition and then in much of the Protestant world. With regard to justification, as mentioned in Romans 8:33, Calvin comments, "There it is plain that the question is simply one of guilt and acquittal, and the meaning of the apostle depends on this antithesis [between righteousness and sanctification]."[45] One is not becoming justified but either is or is not justified. Further, Calvin comments that "justified by faith is he who, excluded from the righteousness of works, grasps the righteousness of Christ through faith, and clothed in it, appears in God's sight not as a sinner but as a righteous man."[46] Later Calvin explains that "'to justify' means nothing else than to acquit of guilt him who was accused, as if his innocence were confirmed. Therefore, since God justifies us by the intercession of Christ, he absolves us not by the confirmation of our own innocence but by the imputation of righteousness, so that we who are not righteous in ourselves may be reckoned as such in Christ."[47] Calvin worried that Osiander, however, confused justification and regeneration, which then would undermine one's ability to enjoy the assurance of salvation, which is not based on internal transformation but instead gained through faith in Christ.[48]

Whereas Osiander linked righteousness with the divine and thus believed that someone *becomes* righteous as God enters them, Calvin never wavered from the Pauline idea that a person is *declared* righteous because they are united to the Mediator, who is himself righteous. Calvin worried that approaches like Osiander's make the believer vulnerable to our inconsistencies, and whether intentionally or not,

---

45. John Calvin, *Institutes of the Christian Religion*, ed. John T. McNeill, trans. Ford Lewis Battles, vol. 1, Library of Christian Classics (Louisville: Westminster John Knox, 2011), 3.11.6, p. 732.
46. Calvin, *Institutes*, 3.11.2, pp. 726–27. The next sentence adds: "Therefore, we explain justification simply as the acceptance with which God receives us into his favor as righteous men. And we say that it consists in the remission of sins and the imputation of Christ's righteousness."
47. Calvin, *Institutes*, 3.11.3, p. 728.
48. David C. Steinmetz, "Andreas Osiander (1498–1552)," in *Reformers in the Wings: From Geiler Von Kaysersberg to Theodore Beza*, 2nd ed. (Oxford: Oxford University Press, 2001), 69.

they place the burden of salvation and assurance upon the effort and inner transformation of the individual. Instead, look to Christ, not to yourself. This is the point of faith. Christ's righteousness does not ebb and flow; thus our standing before God is unrelated to our successes or failures in resisting sin at any given time. Our justification, therefore, is based solely on the gift of the incarnate Christ himself, who is counted as worthy. Our status is changed because this new Adam is our new head through union by the Spirit.

For Calvin, one's union to Christ frames how a believer navigates life, both amid challenges and to locate true comfort. Against what he believed was Osiander's misunderstanding, Calvin emphasizes this "incomparable good" that is *not* ours

> until Christ is made ours. Therefore, that joining together of Head and members, that indwelling of Christ in our hearts—in short, that mystical union—are accorded by us the highest degree of importance, so that Christ, having been made ours, makes us sharers with him in the gifts with which he has been endowed. We do not, therefore, contemplate him outside ourselves from afar in order that his righteousness may be imputed to us but because we put on Christ and are engrafted into his body—in short, because he deigns to make us one with him.[49]

This is the basic working assumption in my argument that *Christian life is a response to the love of God* and that the incarnate Son not only embodies God's love but also leads the human response of love back to God. We benefit from this human response of Jesus as we are incorporated into Christ by the Spirit; thus in flowing from this union we receive the benefits of Christ's obedience, life, death, resurrection, and ongoing heavenly intercession. In other words, when we turn from Christ to the ego, if we are speaking of Christian life, we are not, in fact, turning from Christ at all. But instead, this ego is now placed *within* Christ rather than outside of him. And that is fundamentally what separates Christian life from non-Christian life.

Justification is by faith, and those who believe are in Christ and

---

49. John Calvin, *Institutes of the Christian Religion*, ed. John T. McNeill, trans. Ford Lewis Battles, vol. 1, Library of Christian Classics (Louisville: Westminster John Knox, 2011), 3.11.10, p. 737.

thus declared righteous, based not on their own résumé or faithfulness, not on their own motivations or present success in fighting against sin, but solely upon the faithfulness of Christ himself (e.g., Rom 3:25–26; 4:25; 5:1; 10:6–8). Jesus's righteousness is credited to us not because we ourselves generated some new internal goodness but because we are united to the One who was perfectly full of faith and perfectly faithful.[50] Jesus was and is the Righteous One who loved Father and neighbor without failure or compromise, thus without sin, yet this same Jesus also willingly entered into our forsakenness—our very sin—serving as a propitiation for us in our stead (Rom 3:25; 1 John 2:2; 4:10; cf. Heb 2:17). Our hope is grounded in benefiting from Jesus's person and work, which becomes ours only by faith, and faith alone, thus following the example of Abraham, who "believed the LORD, and [God] counted it to him as righteousness" (Gen 15:6; cf. Rom 4:1–9, 22; Gal 3:6–9; cf. Jas 2:23). Accordingly, this righteousness is "outside" or "alien" to us, rather than native or self-generated.

While no "infused" righteousness becomes the basis of our secure standing before God, we can be declared or counted as righteous because out of the love of the Father the Spirit truly unites us to the incarnate Son; therefore, all that Jesus is and has done is treated as if it were true of us (e.g., Rom 3:28; 4:3, 5, 9–11, 22–24; Gal 3:6). In this way justification is objective rather than subjective, even as one can observe that because of union God goes on to transform us, not only changing our identity (definitive sanctification) but also slowly conforming us more and more into the image of Christ (progressive sanctification). But since I have addressed some of these themes already in chapters 4 ("Fellowship") and 5 ("The Law-Gospel Distinction"), I want to turn now to a deeper exploration of the somewhat downplayed aspects of this union to Christ.

UNITED TO (THE BODY OF) CHRIST

What may surprise many contemporary readers, especially evangelical ones, is that Paul's picture of union with Christ is directed first toward the body of Christ as a whole and secondarily to the individual as a member of

---

50. Michael Allen nicely navigates the various current discussions here, appreciating historical readings of the Reformed Protestant tradition while also trying to show the genuine insights of those who emphasize the faithfulness of Christ. See Allen, *The Christ's Faith: A Dogmatic Account* (London: T&T Clark, 2011); and Allen, *Justification and the Gospel: Understanding the Contexts and Controversies* (Grand Rapids: Baker Academic, 2013).

it. Take, for example, Paul's use of the phrases *the old self/man* (Gk. *palaion anthrōpon*) and *the new* (Gk. *kainon*) *self/man* (see Eph 4:22–24). The *old* "belongs to your former manner of life and is corrupt through deceitful desires," whereas the *new* is "created after the likeness of God in true righteousness and holiness" (Eph 4:22–24). This contrast of old and new parallels his contrast of life in the fallen Adam with life in the crucified and risen Adam. In Colossians, he similarly encourages his readers to put away vices like anger, wrath, malice, slander, and lying, "seeing that you have put off the old self with its practices and have put on the new self, which is being renewed in knowledge after the image of its creator" (Col 3:8–10). But in both of these locations Paul addresses his *you* not to a single person but to the group plural, the collective or ecclesial *you*—or, as they say in the South, *y'all*. Nor is this plural just the collection of many separate individuals. But before we look at the corporate nature of this *you*, we need to examine more closely our connection with Christ and then return to our connections with each other.

The New Testament scholar Herman Ridderbos is particularly insightful in how he navigates Paul's treatment of the old and new *anthrōpon*, highlighting both the christological and ecclesiological connections that I have been anticipating throughout. Though writing almost sixty years ago, Ridderbos could see the chasm between what Paul was speaking about and the interpretations of many readers today. Accordingly, he observed that often we wrongly assume that the old man should be read only "in an individual sense" and that the language of "crucifying and putting off of the old man" is really about "the personal breaking with and fighting against the power of sin."[51] When taken in this way, the contrast of old versus new seems to address the individual Christian's preconversion versus postconversion experience. In other words, the contrast addresses something about us, namely, are we regenerate or not? It then focuses on the conduct or lifestyle of an individual Christian. Ridderbos argues that this reading misunderstands and thus misapplies Paul here. Rather than understanding the old versus new as first and foremost about the *ordo salutis*, Ridderbos pushes us to see it chiefly in terms of the larger story of redemptive history! He connects Messiah and ecclesia here, so that we must understand ourselves within this matrix rather than as separate or disconnected Christians who are

---

51. Herman Ridderbos, *Paul: An Outline of His Theology*, trans. John Richard De Witt (Grand Rapids: Eerdmans, 1975), 63. Published originally in Dutch in 1966.

all addressed at once. For Paul, this old-versus-new contrast "is a matter here not of a change that comes about in the way of faith and conversion in the life of the individual Christian, but of that which once took place in Christ and in which his people had part in him in the corporate sense."[52] Consider Romans 6:6, which describes when our "old self was crucified." This points us to Golgotha, to Christ's own death. His death becomes the defining death for those united to him in faith by the Spirit. Union with Christ means that "we who died to sin" (Rom 6:2) can't live in it, not because we did something, but because of our union with Christ! The cross was a historical once-for-all event (Heb 10:10), but its ongoing significance defines those found in Christ. As Paul elsewhere clearly states, "For you have died, and your life is hidden with Christ in God" (Col 3:3). One man (fallen Adam) stands under the curse and under death, while the other Adam (*eschatos Adam*) stands right with God in love, obedience, and holiness. Jesus didn't sin, but because of his willingness to be linked with us, both in his incarnation (truly human) and by the cross (under the curse), he absorbed the consequences of sin and death for his people to whom he was united. It is "not first of all in a personal and ethical sense" that Paul speaks of old versus new but instead "in a redemptive-historical, eschatological sense."[53]

Of course, this old-versus-new distinction describes particular believers and not just a group. But we would do well to let the patterns of Scripture shape our imaginations rather than let more contemporary, overly individualistic assumptions rule our theology. Biblically, union with Christ immediately implies union with his body; the same Spirit who puts us into this union also thoroughly reshapes the ego in newness of life, from our faith to our ethics, from our vocational understanding to our use of resources. Particular believers are made new in Christ and belong to him (Rom 14:7–8), and as new creations in Christ, God's children put off sin, the old self, and the flesh (again, Eph 4:22–24; Col 3:8–10).[54] Ridderbos argues that this both reflects the postbaptismal reality of the Christian and retains "a supra-individual significance." We are in Christ, secured by the Spirit, and stamped by our baptism. Because we are connected to the crucified and risen One, *together* believers now have new life so that we not only are declared justified before God but

---

52. Ridderbos, *Paul*, 63.
53. Ridderbos, *Paul*, 63.
54. Note the frequency of the second-person plural pronoun in these examples.

also, through this union, experience the new creation as "a continuing process (Col 2:9), just as mortification of the old man is a continuing process (Eph 4:22)." Yet let us not miss the root of these comments in Ridderbos: "It is the redemptive-historical transition, effected in Christ's death and resurrection, that is working itself out in this process."[55]

And now we complete the loop through Christ, me, and ecclesia. Adam and Christ are not just solitary people but also corporate entities. Paul's language and imagery are so shaped by the "corporate unity with Christ" that at times when he speaks of the "one new man" (Eph 2:15; cf. Gal 3:28), he speaks of believers as united, as Christ's body. The phrase *union with Christ* does not refer primarily to a mystical dehumanizing experience but rather to the objective, personal connection we have with Christ himself, to his redemptive-historical accomplishment as our new and final Adam, and to our corporate identity in him. Thus defined, our *union*—as noted in chapter 5 where I distinguished it from *communion*—does not ebb and flow, and our subjective experience of it (i.e., communion) depends completely on the objective reality of that union. Again Ridderbos: Union with Christ, rather than consisting in moments of ecstasy, is instead "an abiding reality determinative for the whole of Christian life, to which appeal can be made at all times, in all sorts of connections, and with respect to the whole church without distinction (cf., for example, Col. 2:20ff; 3:1ff). Rather than with certain experiences, we have to do here with the church's 'objective' state of salvation, for which reason an appeal is repeatedly made to baptism (Rom. 6:4; Col. 2:12)."[56] This is really the same kind of idea Luther was getting at when encouraging the Christian facing the deceptive devil: "The only way to drive away the Devil is through faith in Christ, by saying, 'I have been baptized, I am a Christian.'"[57] In faith, Luther reaffirmed his union with Christ and his body; in and from this union the individual believer can find comfort and courage.

The ego must be understood in terms of its relations with others, and from a Christian perspective, that means in terms of its relationship to Christ and his body. Let us now turn to this distinction between two bodies as highlighted by Paul.

---

55. Ridderbos, *Paul*, 64.
56. Ridderbos, *Paul*, 59.
57. Quoted by Heiko A. Oberman, *Luther: Man Between God and the Devil* (New Haven, CT: Yale University Press, 2006), 105.

TO WHOM DO YOU BELONG? TWO BODIES, ONE EGO

Christian life takes place because of our *union* with Christ by the Spirit, which not only allows us to enjoy the triune life and love of God but also joins us to the life and love of Christ's body, the church. This doesn't mean that a believer becomes a fourth person of the Trinity; rather, because we are united to the risen Messiah, God "raised us up with [Christ] and seated us with him in the heavenly places" (Eph 2:6). We are secure in *his* place and power, and through *him* we can enjoy the fullness of the life and love of God. As already noted, the New Testament describes this in communal terms. As is often bemoaned, English readers tend to read every *you* in Paul's letters as a singular rather than plural (*you all*) pronoun, making this communal context much more challenging to recognize and honor. Exegetes and preachers do well to consistently remind ourselves and others of the consequent relational dynamic. But far more than the linguistic challenge is the cultural one, which obscures the fact that our personal encounters with God happen within corporate connections.

Christ's people collectively are his one body. I (ego) do not lose my particularity by entering the church, but this new life is not a solitary one: It is necessarily communal, meant to be filled with family and neighbor love. This doesn't mean God cannot save an isolated individual, just as he can save a thief on the cross, but even in those cases the individual is saved into a community. We do well to avoid allowing exceptions, rather than the overarching emphasis on the communal in both testaments, to govern our interpretations. Notice, for example, how the language of *the elect* and *election* or *chosen* by God most often refers chiefly to a community and only subordinately to individual members of it (e.g., Deut 7:6–8; 10:14–15; Pss 33:12; 65:4; 106:5; Hag 2:23; Acts 13:17; Rom 9:11; 11:28), or how the language assumes the church, thus foregrounding the corporate as the appropriate context for the particular (e.g., Rom 8:33; Eph 1:4; Col 3:12; 1 Thess 1:4; 2 Tim 2:10; Titus 1:1; 1 Pet 1:1–2; 2:8–9; 5:13; Rev 17:14). This matters because our relations with fellow followers of Yahweh are not just a pleasant side effect but a constructive and constructing force. This connectivity is also why the *warnings* from God in Scripture are often directed not just to individuals but to the collective of God's people (e.g., the seven churches in Revelation 2–3).

Who Christ is, who I am, and who God's people are—all of these are woven tightly together. The Christian ego lives in this matrix, liberated from Sin's dominion and now experiencing God's life in us through Christ and by his Spirit. This makes Christian life both personal and relational, always directed toward God and neighbor, both internally relevant and externally applicable. We do not choose between the vertical and horizontal, between the divine and human, between heaven and earth, between the mind and heart. No, our theology of Christian life must incorporate all of these aspects. Otherwise our theology of Christian life is too narrow and confined. Because of union with Christ, a believer is justified before God (vertical; e.g., Rom 4:3, 6, 9, 11, 22; Gal 3:6) and *also* now situated in his family as a child of God (horizontal; e.g., John 1:12; Rom 8:15–17; 1 John 3:1–2), thus requiring that we not imagine the Christian ego apart from such indispensable relations grounded in Spirit-driven unity (cf. John 11:51–53).

As noted above, arising out of the soil of the Protestant Reformation and growing under the sun of the Enlightenment and modernity, the default reading of Pauline texts (and the entirety of Scripture) has commonly been individualistic in orientation, especially by the nineteenth and early twentieth centuries. One can see this reach a kind of crescendo in Rudolf Bultmann's existentialist account of Paul.[58] Bultmann's goal of demythologization was not unbelief but rather a deeply personal and immediate experience that could liberate and transform an individual. *My* decision, *my* belief, and *my* engagement were what mattered most for Bultmannian existentialist interpretation.[59] The individual was front and center for interpretations of this kind. But reactions to this extreme subsequently began to surface, for example, in Bultmann's own student, Ernst Käsemann.

Eventually, the pendulum gained momentum as it started to swing, seeking to place the emphasis not so much on the singularity of the believer but more on the believer's identity within a larger network. Dale B. Martin, for example, pushes hard against what he saw as a skewed modernist reading of Paul and the New Testament, and his treatment of the body in Paul exemplifies this. While in our day readers might

---

58. See esp. part 2 of Rudolf Bultmann, *Theology of the New Testament*, trans. Kendrick Grobel, 2 vols. (Waco: Baylor University Press, 2007), 187–350.

59. This extreme is partly what Bultmann's student Ernst Käsemann so strongly reacted against when he put forth his own account of the New Testament in general and Paul in particular.

speak of a "social body," Martin contends we commonly take this as meaning "simply the aggregate of many individual bodies. And it is the individual aspect that, in the end, counts."[60] Rather than imagining an "individual" as we do, Martin argues that the ancient world that Paul inhabited had a much stronger social framework shaping their concepts.[61]

For the apostle Paul, people are not isolated individuals but persons connected to larger networks and realities that can be called bodies. While Christians often are familiar with the language of the "body of Christ" (*tou sōmatos tou Christou*; Rom 7:4), they are commonly less familiar with Paul's other designation, "body of sin" (*to sōma tēs hamartais*; Rom 6:6). This reminds us that our problem is not just particular sins, but S/sin. Going back to Romans 5 with the Adam-Christ typology, Beverly Roberts Gaventa vividly captures the tension between

> the powers of Sin and Death and the power of God and Jesus Christ. Sin and Death entered the world, Death extended itself throughout humanity (5:12), Death ruled as a king (5:14, 17, 21), Sin increased (5:20), Sin was an enslaver of humanity (6:6, 17, 20). All of this reign is overturned by Jesus Christ through whom grace superabounded, so that it is now grace itself (i.e., the gospel itself) that rules (5:21). The controlling question in [Romans] 5 . . . is this: 'Who is in charge? Who is in control of the world and humanity?'[62]

The apostle Paul appears to take for granted that one's identity or moral life is not confined to one's individual choices but is an activity in relation to the body of Christ and/or the body of Sin: The first grants new life, while the second remains a looming and threatening force that seeks to devour, destroy, and ultimately bring death. Such "bodies" are more porous than might be assumed by modern readers, since we tend to define a *body* by means of distinction and separation.

Matthew Croasmun is one of the most interesting scholars pushing for a greater recognition of this social dynamic in Paul and in our lives. "One was always a member of a social body," Croasmun contends, and so when someone joined the churches Paul was working with, "this was

---

60. Dale B. Martin, *The Corinthian Body* (New Haven, CT: Yale University Press, 1995), 15.
61. Martin, *The Corinthian Body*, 20–21.
62. Beverly Roberts Gaventa, *Our Mother Saint Paul* (Louisville: Westminster John Knox, 2007), 140.

not opting out of independence and for the first time into communal life. Rather, they were transferring from membership in one social body to membership in another."[63] Croasmun's major contribution—which we cannot here fully outline, appreciate, or critique—is that we would do well to think more in terms of organic connection and "emergence," especially when trying to make sense of Paul's description of the problem of sin.[64] We often reduce the problem of S/sin to particular actions or thoughts (e.g., I coveted my neighbor's car or yelled at my child). Yet humanity's problem is not simply sin (although it is *not* less than particular sins); our problem is *Sin* as a powerful force—sin in us, outside of us, throughout the world. Here Croasmun is especially helpful in avoiding reductionistic accounts, instead suggesting a perspective that incorporates the fullness of the biblical portrait and our ongoing human experience. Note how he affirms human agency and responsibility, but he does not reduce the problem to solitary individuals:

> The dominion of Sin is established through the rebellion of human beings, the natural consequences of which are permitted by God. This is a picture of the power, Sin, emerging from the sinful rebellion of human beings. This rebellion provides the base on which the cosmic power, Sin, supervenes. Human beings then ironically experience the real dominion of this creation of their own hands. . . . We are the authors of our own tragedy, demiurges of a slave master that holds us in bondage. The turn to idolatry is, in a certain sense, ironically successful. The story of the advent of idolatry is the story

---

63. Matthew Croasmun, "'Real Participation': The Body of Christ and the Body of Sin in Evolutionary Perspective," in Thate, Vanhoozer, and Campbell, *"In Christ" in Paul*, 129.

64. Croasmun contends for an "emergent" understanding of bodies. For example, he draws from sociologist Dave Elder-Vass, who has observed how we often assume that social structures don't have "causal power" since really they can be explained simply in terms of individuals and their relations. Yet those individuals, at the bodily level, could be explained "in terms of the causal contributions of their cells and the relations between them, the effects of cells in terms of the causal contributions of the molecules that are their parts between them, and so on. They would not be individualists but would have to successively become cell-ists (!), molecule-ists, atom-ists, and so on." Dave Elder-Vass, "Top-Down Causation and Social Structures," *Interface Focus* 2, no. 1 (2012): 89, quoted by Matthew Croasmun, *The Emergence of Sin*: The Cosmic Tyrant in Romans (New York: Oxford University Press, 2017), 96. In other words, even at the level of our physicality, the truth is the individual is still a composition of larger forces (cellular, molecular, etc.), and the person who emerges is likewise necessarily part of a larger social structure or network. This has a bearing on our discussion of the ego and the drama of Christian life since we commonly default to separation and forms of agency that may sometimes be more mythical or at least more deceptively clean than we realize.

of the creation of a real, superhuman power that truly does exercise dominion over its human subjects.[65]

Even in contemporary language and imagery we can speak of something that cannot be reduced to particular persons and is greater than the sum total of the individuals involved (e.g., "the market," "the network," "the Man," etc.). Yet it is not less than those individuals. This is true whether one speaks of being part of the body of Sin or the body of Christ.

Greater recognition of the social and emergent nature of human persons and S/sin means we must pay attention to personal choices *and* structural factors: They both contribute to one's identity and the exercise of one's agency. Paul calls us to ask if we are members of Christ's body or of the body of Sin. If we are incorporated into Christ's body by the Spirit, then he urges us, "Do not present your members to sin as instruments for unrighteousness, but present yourselves to God as those who have been brought from death to life, and your members to God as instruments for righteousness" (Rom 6:13). A theology of Christian life is built on this corporate image of Christ's body and our organic connections within it. In Christ we are liberated from S/sin's dominion and this then shapes our pilgrimage. Let's briefly look at Romans 12 as an example of how this works out.

BOTH PARTICULAR AND CORPORATE

The body of Christ is one, but that one body is composed of sisters and brothers who collectively present their particular bodies (plural) to God as a living sacrifice (singular): Together as one, we are transformed by the renewing of our minds (Rom 12:1–2), seeing ourselves now within this new arrangement. Although Paul is addressing a collection of particular people in Rome, he does so in light of their organic union—their shared membership as the body of Christ, where each may have different gifts, but all are part of this one body and share their gifts in genuine love (Rom 12:3–9). Whether we speak in the classic imagery of hands and eyes or the more contemporary scientific language of cells and molecules, neither picture loses particularity for the sake of community but rather establishes it within the larger social

---

65. Croasmun, *The Emergence of Sin*, 108.

and theological complex that is the body of Christ. A body doesn't work because it contains isolated individual cells but because of the relations or interactivity in which they live. A hand cut off from the body—while still looking like a hand—is not able to function and will quickly die. In other words, that biblical imagery doesn't show only that we are different from each other (although it certainly does illustrate that) but also that we function *only* because we are connected to each other in Christ. In other words, thinking of eyeballs or molecules only as isolated entities actually obscures their nature and function; understanding their nature and function requires that we appreciate their vital relationship to the whole body. In this way we recognize their distinctions within that unbreakable union.

Back to Romans 12:1–2. Rather than *arguing* for a social conception of the body of Christ, Paul simply *presents* it and works out the implications of this organic union. Located in Christ by the Spirit, the believer's identity and relational network have changed; thus the believer's mind, behavior, and whole manner of being in the world are changed. And yet we are still part of this fallen world (Gk. *kosmos*) that participates in the body of Sin, so we inhabit this uncomfortable time when the *now* and the *not yet* overlap. In Romans 8:23, Paul reflects on this tension: "Not only the creation, but we ourselves, who have the firstfruits of the Spirit, groan inwardly as we wait eagerly for adoption as sons, the redemption of our [plural] body [singular]" (ESV). As Croasum unpacks this relation of the plural with the singular, he notes that believers "were constituted as the Body of Christ in baptism (invoked explicitly in Rom 7:4), when they entered *into* Christ (6:3), such that they now live *in* Him (6:11, 8:1–2, 39, 12:5). Because of the social body that they are, they ought to behave in a particular way."[66] Before this entrance into a new body, they were part of the old corrupt and corrupting body—the dominion of Sin. But now they are part of something new.

To be in Christ means to have been incorporated into his body. Christian life cannot be reduced to therapeutic outcomes or a solitary moral regimen. This is instead a participatory life: a life lived by the believer among and connected to God's people—Christ's body. As part of this new body, the believer is no longer dominated by the power of S/sin but leaves it behind, entering the shared life of faith, hope,

---

66. Croasmun, *The Emergence of Sin*, 117. Croasmun also first drew my attention to the relevant plural/singular dynamic in Romans 8:23.

and love, the life of gospel obedience, the life of goodness and mercy. Here I am reminded of J. Louis Martyn's memorable observation in his commentary on Galatians, that "when Paul speaks about placing one's trust in Christ, he is pointing to a deed that reflects not the freedom of the will, but rather God's freeing of the will."[67] Entering Christ's body is new life, a life of God's love and God's freedom, a life in which we may find shalom. Nevertheless, in this fallen world, seeking that shalom often means being willing to elevate others at one's own expense, dying to sin because one is now alive in Christ. But from beginning to end, the New Testament presents this life as operating within extended communal dynamics, always as a life in the company of brothers and sisters.

IN CHRIST, THE EGO ENTERS NEW AND TRANSFORMATIVE RELATIONSHIPS

Paul's construct places the ego within the larger family of the body of Christ. His description uses the imagery and advocacy of friendship, as John T. Fitzgerald shows in comparing Paul to ancient backgrounds, especially Aristotle.[68] This body transforms isolated individuals into those who share a "oneness of mind" (see 1 Cor 1:10), in contrast with the friction that can arise between believers and those who are hostile to apostolic teaching and the gospel (1 Cor 15:33). True friends speak with "frankness of speech" (2 Cor 3:12), not lording over others (which undermines friendship) but serving as coworkers (2 Cor 1:24; 6:1). The gospel brings people together in a unity that runs deeper than their own decisions and understanding so that, although fallouts between God's people (i.e., family or friends) are deeply painful (cf. 2 Cor 2:1–4; 7:12), God's people always have the hope of reconciliation and restoration (2 Cor 5–11; Rom 16:23; relationship with Gaius is healed in hospitality) because their unity rests on Christ and not on themselves.

Recognizing these bonds of unity and friendship in Christ is necessary for making sense of Paul's letter to Philemon. There appears to be a mutual delight and gratitude between Paul and Philemon, and yet because Paul brought the gospel to Philemon, there was also a legitimate

---

67. J. Louis Martyn, *Galatians*, Anchor Bible 33A (New York: Doubleday, 1997), 276.
68. The following two paragraphs are deeply indebted to John T. Fitzgerald, "Paul and Friendship," in *Paul in the Greco-Roman World*, ed. J. Paul Sampley, 2nd ed., vol. 1 (London: Bloomsbury, 2016), esp. 359–60.

sense in which Paul could say that Philemon "owed" him his "own self" (Phlm 19). Nevertheless, Paul has also received great comfort and joy from Philemon's faithfulness, since "the hearts of the saints have been refreshed through you" (Phlm 7). Now to our point: Paul's letter to Philemon assumes a shared union both with Christ (Phlm 3, 8, 23) and with one another (Phlm 8–11, 16–17). Out of this connection Paul calls for a changed situation for Philemon's slave Onesimus: This is a theological observation (he is now in the family of God, Phlm 10) that Paul works out in terms of current experience (he is no longer a slave but now a brother or friend; Phlm 15–16).

As bondage to the slavery of sin is broken by Christ, so now those united to Christ and one another can use their imaginations and power to find creative ways to treat one another. No longer arranged by the unjust hierarchies of the world, believers are the family of God in the kingdom of God, which operates by the values of love and righteousness, compassion and service. Along these lines, Fitzgerald clarifies that Paul is here "invoking the idea of the friend as one's *alter ego*."[69] Remember that for Paul the ego does refer to the self, but that self has its being within a larger communion (e.g., body of Christ or body of Sin). His new identity in Christ has implications not simply for Paul's life but for the community and for his role in encouraging the community to reflect God's family. God's church gathers to worship Christ, whose kingdom now reigns in their hearts and lives.

Yet again, Christian life and spirituality are not merely internal or private matters: They consist of particular persons in a unifying communion. Christian life and spirituality cannot be correctly understood apart from that basic observation. Both the vertical and horizontal dimensions of our union with Christ are consistently asserted, promoted, and emphasized in Paul's writings and life. As Michael Wolter similarly concludes regarding Philemon, through faith in Christ, one enters a new world, a new reality: "In the symbolic universe of the everyday world, Paul certainly has no 'authority to command respect,' but 'in Christ' he does, because in this symbolic universe the social roles between Paul and Philemon are allotted quite differently from those in the everyday world."[70] While in the eyes of the world Philemon would be the one with

---

69. Fitzgerald, "Paul and Friendship," 360.
70. Michael Wolter, *Paul: An Outline of His Theology* (Waco: Baylor University Press, 2015), 231–32.

power, our union with Christ asserted in the apostolic preaching has put us into a new world where not just Paul and Philemon come together but also Onesimus (whose name means "beneficial"). Onesimus is no longer viewed as a slave but as a friend and member of the family, and his entrance into this communion has benefited the whole community, including Philemon. This was a revolutionary concept in the ancient world, and it remains so in our world. Unfortunately, we sometimes try to separate this union's vertical and horizontal dimensions, which distorts the expectations for and experience of Christian life.

LIVING IN THE NOW AND NOT YET: 1 JOHN AS MODEL

We live in confusing conditions, with factors that combine the *now* and the *not yet* and others that separate them. Some aspects of the eschaton reach into our today, while others are achingly distant. Adopted and secure in God's love (1 John 3:1), we nevertheless see only a glimmer of what is to come: "We know that when he appears we shall be like him, because we shall see him as he is" (1 John 3:2). This is the tension. As John puts it, Christ "appeared in order to take away sins, and in him there is no sin" (1 John 3:5). Sin is not merely an internal disordering but also "lawlessness" (1 John 3:4). According to John, this sin or lawlessness can be identified by how it undermines shalom. For example, it often looks like disordered loves: "the desires of the flesh and the desires of the eyes and pride of life" (1 John 2:16). These represent the mistake of loving "the world" more than we love the Father of creation, whereas loving God above all would set our subordinate loves in order. To understand this warning about the world, the flesh, and the pride of life, we must remember that God is the Creator of the material earth, including our physical bodies. He is the one who has given us our breath-induced life. The Creator has not rejected his good creation, but when we elevate a created element above him we also burden it with a load it cannot carry, warping and destroying it and hurting ourselves in the process. These warnings against world, flesh, and pride are spoken not against God's good creation but against the forces that distort that creation—and distort us.

God loves what he made, but he hates the S/sin that distorts that goodness. *World* and *flesh* for John do not simplistically refer to materiality but to cosmic, institutional, and personal forces that oppose God and his goodness. The opposite of the pride of life is not embarrassment or shame about one's life but joyful and humble recognition of healthy dependence on the Creator and of the goodness of interconnection with the rest of humanity (starting with the church) and the earth. The opposite of flesh is not nonflesh but the Spirit: The first designates life in rebellion against the Creator and Sustainer, acting as if Yahweh were unreal or at least ignorable, whereas life in the Spirit is a communion with Yahweh, learning to live in harmony with his desires and purposes that were part of creation's original trajectory. The opposite of *world* is not an ethereal heaven but a rich life under the lordship of the King in his kingdom. We must reject the corrupting ruler of this world and live in the light of the kingdom of Christ.

The world, the flesh, and the pride of life all refer to S/sin and a path away from God; whereas humility, the Spirit, and love-inspired obedience are signs of the human creature once again enjoying life-giving communion with the Holy God. This (re)new(ed) life never moves beyond the truth that "we love because he first loved us" (1 John 4:19). Only in light of this larger relationality is the ego again properly situated. The path of sin undermines shalom, putting the ego in isolation and antagonism rather than in healthy relationships and godly actions. Christian life puts the ego back where it can flourish: in right and loving relations with God, neighbor, and the rest of creation.

Accordingly, the world, the flesh, and the pride of life represent unrighteousness. The one who "practices righteousness is righteous, as he [Messiah] is righteous" (1 John 3:7). In contrast, "Whoever makes a practice of sinning is of the devil, for the devil has been sinning from the beginning" (1 John 3:8). The incarnation—from virgin pregnancy through the ongoing heavenly session—did not merely achieve forgiveness and new life for those in Christ but also destroyed the works of the devil (1 John 3:8). John then turns to the birthing imagery again: One who is "born of God" doesn't "make a practice of sinning," but rather "everyone who practices righteousness has been born of him [God]" (1 John 2:29).

The Scriptures present two contrasting categories of people: There is the "sinner" and the "saint"—in terms of identity and essential being, you are one or the other, not both. *Simul justus et peccator* fairly represents our experience and struggle, *not* our theological identity. As saints, we struggle with temptation and sin (to say otherwise is to lie; 1 John 1:8–10), but that struggle occurs precisely because the root and source of our being is elsewhere, in Christ, and so not in being a "sinner." Paul does not write to the "sinners at Colossae" but to the "saints" (Col 1:2). Saints are not just who believers will be but who we are *now*. This is our individual and collective identity as God's children. It is an eschatological reality that reaches into the now. Like Paul, John writes less in terms of the language *sinner* versus *saint* and more in terms of the family of God: Either you are born again and part of God's family, one of his children enjoying eternal life, or you are outside his family and under the "ruler of this world" (*archon tou kosmou*), who will eventually be judged and cast out (John 12:31; 14:30; 16:11). Again, being a saint is an eschatological reality, but it is also true of us now.

So how are we to navigate the long journey of faith, hope, and love this side of glory? In short, our theology needs a practice, but that practice must also be our theology. So we turn now to ecclesia, thinking first in terms of the place for the various practices of life and then concluding this book by focusing on corporate liturgy as the arc of Christian life.

CHAPTER 8

ECCLESIA I
The Context of Christian Life

> *Practice is the reality of the theory; the theory is the intimate and mysterious nature of the practice.*
> —MAXIMUS THE CONFESSOR[1]

> *So powerful is participation in the church that it keeps us in the society of God.*
> —JOHN CALVIN[2]

> *The formation of Christ is . . . [en hymin, in you], and the plural pronoun requires comment. Formation does not belong to individual believers, as a personal or private possession only. Instead, formation refers to the community of those who are called to faith, what Paul . . . calls the body of Christ.*
> —BEVERLY ROBERTS GAVENTA[3]

> *We know, in fact, that the life of the children of God is simply the life of the Church of God.*
> —KARL BARTH[4]

---

1. Maximus, *Quaestiones ad Thalassium* 63 (PG 90.681), cited and translated by Edward J. Kilmartin, *Christian Liturgy: Theology and Practice*, vol. 1, *Systematic Theology of Liturgy* (Kansas City: Sheed & Ward, 1988), 95.
2. Calvin, *Institutes*, 4.1.3, 2:1015.
3. Beverly Roberts Gaventa, *Our Mother Saint Paul* (Louisville: Westminster John Knox, 2007), 36–37.
4. Karl Barth, *Church Dogmatics* 1.2, *The Doctrine of the Word of God*, ed. G. W. Bromiley and T. F. Torrance, trans. G. W. Bromiley, 2nd ed. (London: T&T Clark, 1956), 453.

> It is in this particular social body—the ecclesia—that the new creation is breaking into the old. What appears now as a political body is in fact a cosmic body coming into being.
> —MATTHEW CROASMUN[5]

Our Christian life includes entering into a fellowship, and church (Gk. *ecclesia*) is the name we give to that fellowship or gathering of God's people. Church is a place of sermons and suppers, singing and sighing, service and sacraments. It is a people and a space given for shaping and living our lives together. This is not merely a sociological phenomenon but a theological one. It testifies to God's ongoing presence and life-giving work. Whether in a large building or secretly as a small group in a home, the ecclesia is the gathered people who give ongoing concrete shape to our theology of Christian life. That people and their shared space have their own peculiar character and dynamics. Therefore, we need to consider what the church is and how it works (a study that we call "ecclesiology"). In particular, we need to examine the function and shape of its corporate worship (which we call "order of worship" or "liturgy"—literally, "the work of the people").

These next two chapters belong together. We begin more generally with the church's importance and the particular significance (and potential dangers) of its shape-giving rituals. In the final chapter we then suggest how the basic elements of corporate worship—which were commonly accepted in the ancient church—appear to inform and reflect the arc of Christian life. Once we articulate these rituals and elements, we will argue that if we weave together the christological, corporate, and personal, we end up with a rich theological vision that is concrete and experientially hopeful. But for now, we must begin by affirming the value of the church.

TEMPTED TO DOWNPLAY ECCLESIOLOGY

Who wants to say anything positive about the church these days? Sometimes, even at our best, believers are pretty unimpressive. At our worst, Christians can make Christianity and even God look repulsive.

---

5. "'Real Participation': The Body of Christ and the Body of Sin in Evolutionary Perspective," in *"In Christ" in Paul: Explorations in Paul's Theology of Union and Participation*, ed. Michael J. Thate, Kevin J. Vanhoozer, and Constantine R. Campbell, Wissenschaftliche Untersuchungen zum Neuen Testament 2, Reihe 384 (Tübingen: Mohr Siebeck, 2014), 138, emphasis original.

Hypocrisy, anger, and arrogance are too often the images that people have of believers. It can be painful to admit how far short we fall, both individually and collectively. Dorothy Day, cofounder of *The Catholic Worker*, nonetheless concluded, "As to the Church, where else shall we go, except to the bride of Christ, one flesh with Christ? Though she is a harlot at times, she is our Mother."[6] Day is right to acknowledge the sin of God's people and, at the same time, to insist that this is *God's* people, *his* bride, *Christ's* body.

First and foremost, the church is a spiritual entity. Yes, it is also an earthly and human organization, so applying sociology and business analysis has its place as they can help us better appreciate various social and economic forces we might too easily devalue or outright ignore. Nevertheless, understanding the church requires theological analysis before we evaluate it by this-worldly standards. We should not ignore abusive Christian leaders and hurtful practices that have crept into the church. Still, we must remember that the holiness and indispensability of the church do not arise from the moral purity of its people but from its connection with God himself. The third stanza of the Nicene Creed declares, "I *believe* in one, holy, catholic, and apostolic Church." Confessing the church's holiness is an act of faith, not empirical science. What we see and experience as part of God's people is often far from holy. Sixteenth-century Reformer John Calvin accordingly comments, "The word 'believe' is used because often no other distinction can be made between God's children and the ungodly, between his own flock and wild beasts."[7] Rarely have people had a difficult case proving that the church is composed of Christians who are serious sinners. In fact, you can't gain entrance without admitting as much.

Despite its shortcomings, the church is central to God's presence and work in his world. Cyprian of Carthage (210–58) coined the startling statement, "Outside the Church there is no salvation" (*extra Ecclesiam nulla salus*),[8] an idea echoed by Protestant voices like Martin Luther and even later Puritans like John Owen.[9] It expresses how God particularly

---

6. She then adds: "We should read the book of Hosea, which is a picture of God's steadfast love." Dorothy Day, "In Peace Is My Bitterness Most Bitter," *The Catholic Worker*, January 1, 1967, 1, 2, https://www.catholicworker.org/250-2/.

7. Calvin, *Institutes*, 4.1.2, p. 1013.

8. Cyprian, *On the Unity of the Catholic Church* vi (CSEL 3.i.214; tr. LCC V. 127f).

9. E.g., Martin Luther, *The Large Catechism of Martin Luther*, "*Of the Creed*," trans. Henry Eyster Jacobs (Philadelphia: United Lutheran Publication Society, 2018), art. 3, esp. pp. 71–72; Martin Luther, *Confession Concerning Christ's Supper*, in *Luther's Works*, vol. 37, ed. Robert H. Fisher

works in and through his church to call, shape, heal, and preserve his people. Calvin, for example, affirmed a version of Cyprian's claim when he wrote that to "those to whom [God] is a Father, the Church may also be a Mother."[10] Eastern Orthodoxy has affirmed a similar sentiment: Aleksei Khomiakov, for example, draws out the strong connection the individual must have to the corporate body of Christ. "No one is saved alone. He who is saved is saved in the Church, as a member of her and in union with all her other members. If anyone believes, he is in the communion of faith; if he loves, he is in the communion of love; if he prays, he is in the communion of prayer."[11] Our faith lives within a worshiping community.

Participation in *God's* church—spread out organically across the world and scattered throughout history, but also locally gathered in particular congregations—plays a central role in the shaping of Christian life. This reflects the *catholic* nature of the faith and is vital to a believer's existence and health. We are a vast and diversified (historically, culturally, and socioeconomically) people of faith who are yet united in worship of the triune Lord.

But is the institutional church really necessary for a theology of Christian life? Can't we live better without the institution?

DOES THE CHURCH AS INSTITUTION MATTER?

One of the challenges that makes valuing the church so difficult in our day is not only that Christians often act sinfully but also that we don't have a positive view of institutions in general. We are keenly aware that those in power have mistreated people and continue to do so. Power structures acquire stability and then fossilize, protecting themselves while neglecting justice for the people they ought to serve. The failures and abuses of government, marriage, news media, religious organizations,

---

(Philadelphia: Muhlenberg, 1961), 368. Cf. Darius W. Jankiewicz, "Martin Luther and *Extra Ecclesiam Nulla Salus* ('Outside of the Church There Is No Salvation'): Did Luther Really Abandon Cyprian?," *Journal of the Adventist Theological Society* 28, no. 2 (2017): 78–96; Owen, *Works*, 15:323. See also Willem van Vlastuin, "John Owen as a Modern Theologian: A Comparison of Catholicity in Cyprian and Owen," in *John Owen Between Orthodoxy and Modernity*, ed. Willem van Vlastuin and Kelly M. Kapic (Leiden: Brill, 2019), 164–85.

10. Calvin, *Institutes*, 4.1.2, p. 1013.

11. Aleksei Khomiakov, "The Church Is One," §9, in Birkbeck, *Russia and the English Church*, 216. Cited by Kallistos Ware, *The Orthodox Way* (Crestwood, NY: St. Vladimir's Seminary Press, 1999), 107–8.

trade unions, and other institutions keep making headlines. Hidden motives, self-serving agendas, and unethical practices all too commonly drive our institutions.

The church is similarly at fault. It is no coincidence that the slogan "Christianity is not a religion, but a relationship" so deeply resonates with so many contemporary people. But maybe that slogan also hurts people by presenting Christian life as consisting simply of the individual Christian's communion with God, even hinting that corporate gatherings for worship don't really matter.

Biblically speaking, Christianity *is* a religion as well as a set of relationships—that is, the Bible presents life with God as both a personal and a communal response to his loving presence. The "religion" is our response in relationship. As we will see, we need that communal activity of life and worship as the context for a holy life. Loving God and neighbor go together, and separating them distorts both. We cultivate love of God and neighbor within the context of God's community and then extend it out to the world. For millennia, the regular gathering of Christians to worship together—whether in a field or a cathedral—has been viewed as a necessary part of spiritual formation. What matters is not so much the size and place but the corporate nature of it in the context of united worship. Is this pattern no longer necessary for us?

We can debate forms of church polity (e.g., whether we are to be governed by bishops or elders or in separate congregations) and other features the institution of the church ought to have, but at a minimum we might all agree at least to have regular gatherings of God's people for corporate worship (Heb 10:25). What happens in that (normally) weekly gathering—no matter the form of church polity, and whatever the order of worship—will help form our vision of Christian life. We will revisit this in the last chapter of this book. For now we must simply recognize that it is partly by these repeated gatherings that the church has acquired the nature of an institution.

The church is an *institution* in the sense that (1) it is bigger than any single person, (2) these people have a wide variety of gifts and functions, (3) the church coordinates those gifts and functions into a stabilized and continuous form, and (4) people in and around the church think of that form and its people as constituting "the church." Here is the home of Christian sacraments, oaths, church discipline, and so on. The details of that form can be debated, but our point here is that the church includes many people. That simple observation is not incidental to Christian life. It values the community as well as individual Christians, honoring our shared adoption by God as our Father, the concrete nature of the body of Christ, and the unifying function of the Spirit. The church as *institution*, with whatever form of government, also points us to a faith *received* rather than manufactured; it expresses the unity of its people in their shared centuries of history, and in it we march together toward the future hope of a united people, not just collected individuals. When it is healthy, the institution of the church honors particular people without allowing any of them besides Jesus Christ to be its center. The person is for the community, and the community is for the person.

But the church as an institution also has periods of sickness when destructive forces (internal or external) try to manipulate God's people. Whether that is a narcissistic pastor who has used charismatic leadership to build a personal empire, or a congregation that has allowed cultural ideology to replace the biblical call to truth, love, and service, all such forces distort Christian faith and life. Does such abuse allow us to renounce the church *as institution*? Not at all. These distortions do not justify abandoning the institutional church. Instead, they are evidence that neglecting it leaves individual believers even more vulnerable to abuse and misshapen visions of Christian life. This combination of neglect and abuse is partly why many are giving up on church, and that in turn weakens the Christian's understanding of real faith and communion with God. Abandoning the church is not the path to freedom and faithfulness but to isolation, instability, and increased vulnerability.

LESSONS FROM AN ANCIENT DEBATE: THE DONATIST CONTROVERSY AND TODAY

We are not the first to question whether the church matters. In AD 303 Emperor Diocletian started a persecution against Christians that swept through the Roman Empire, including the areas in North Africa under Roman governance. When faced with persecution, some ministry leaders denied the faith by symbolically handing in their sacred Scriptures to the governor. These lapsed believers were called *"traditores"* because they "handed over" the received holy words of God rather than keeping and honoring their faith. How were Christians to think about such failure of character? More pointedly, what were they to do about the baptisms and marriages that lapsed priests had performed? Did the priest's compromise (or treacherous action) undermine the promises God made through the marriage and baptism ceremonies they conducted? The short answer is *no*. Why? Because God is faithful and the institution of the church matters.

Debates over that question became known as the Donatist controversy. The church claimed that the marriages and baptisms performed by those priests were valid because *the institution was bigger than the individual* and *God's promises were greater than a particular minister's sins and shortcomings.* God promises that the gates of hell will not prevail over the church (Matt 16:18), even though human sinfulness and failings can often make it seem otherwise. Christians can trust the words of God's kindness and benediction, even if they later learn that those who spoke those words to them were hypocrites. Their lies don't undo God's word or work. Thus the church looked first to the faithfulness of God's word, his presence, and his promises, and only second to the ministers and individuals of the congregations. But both issues were tied to the church-as-institution, where God manifests his ongoing commitment to his people, his family, and the church-as-assembly of believers.

Certainly the church as institution has needed renewal and reformation at times, but there are no circumstances that call for us to abandon the church altogether, because our Lord never abandons the church. Christianity is not and cannot be a religion of autonomous, isolated individuals. Our individual union with Christ entails union with each other in him. Our being in Christ is like the existence of an organ in the body, a picture that Paul uses at least twice (Rom 12; 1 Cor 12) to remind his readers that they are indissolubly linked to each other and sustain each other. So even though God does sustain believers in political, cultural, or ethical conflicts that force them to be isolated and alone, part of the ache of that situation is just how unnatural it is for them. We should not romanticize those situations but rather lament them, praying that believers so isolated will soon be reunited with the gathered community of faith. The center of Christian communion is the church—not just mystically in its spiritual form but especially physically in its local gathered expressions. Ours is an embodied faith.

When speaking about ecclesiology, it is surprisingly easy for us to end up in an abstract world rather than the land of the real experience of actual believers. So for the rest of this chapter we will concentrate on how participation in Christian practices reflects and shapes our theology of Christian life. Later, in the book's final chapter, we will return to the theme of liturgy and corporate worship to tie things together, but for now let us direct our attention to the corporate nature of Christian life, which is deeply driven by practices, even when many participants don't even realize it is happening. This will include a recognition of both potential positives and dangers in light of this phenomenon. Let's begin by examining how being part of a particular church and participating in its corporate worship relates to Christian faithfulness.

CHURCH PRACTICES AS THEOLOGY AND FORMATION

Psychologists and sociologists can make theologians nervous because sometimes they force us to ask hard questions we prefer to avoid. In those disciplines, some version of this precept is often repeated: "Don't tell me what you believe; show me what you believe." It is easy for people to claim beliefs, to nod at socially accepted assertions, but belief is far more complicated than that. Another version of the precept mentioned above says that if you want to know what people really believe or trust, observe their lives, actions, instincts, and intuitions; pay special attention to their checkbooks and day planners. Here one is reminded of James's admonition that faith apart from works is dead (Jas 1:26–2:26): Heartlessness and apathy expose the absence of the kind of "faith" that James was calling people to in the first place. They may have claimed to believe, but neglecting the orphan and widow (1:27), being arrogant toward the materially poor and needy (2:1–17; 5:1–6), and being consumed by selfish desires were all signs of a dead "faith" (4:1–10). James called his readers to be not just hearers of the word, but doers; otherwise, we risk being a person who immediately forgets what they look like right after stepping away from a mirror (1:19–25).

Faith, hope, and love are meant to grow as the children of God enter and then are trained in the household of faith, being repeatedly shaped and sent out to the world. This communal life is vital to a theology and practice of Christian life. Corporate worship plays an especially powerful role in shaping Christians. And, like all activities of nurturing, it will either help or hinder the life it forms. Consequently, in the last chapter I will not just identify key elements of corporate worship but also show how they must be understood christologically, corporately, and personally.

But before we explore the positive place and power of the church's corporate worship, we must admit up front that the malformation of believers can occur even as they engage in Christian practices. Being in the church and participating in the liturgy are not by themselves a guarantee of faith and faithfulness. Here we see how theology and practice are related but not identical. While we must give attention to historical and sociological observations (which I will do below), we ultimately envision the liturgy as not merely a historical or sociological phenomenon but a theological one. Thus the liturgy has often been called the church's "principal" theology—the school of faith for all Christians.

Yet I worry that theologians too often downplay the concreteness and messiness of history and in this way—even if unintentionally—divorce theology from experience. This manifests when we fail to recognize the ways our own stories, cultures, and particularities shape our theological imaginations. Those with an awareness of this complexity too often try to escape it by offering an *abstract* theology, underappreciating the reality and even value of Christian experience. Yes, *theo*logy is about God (*theos*), but we embodied creatures are the ones doing the theologizing, and we should not ignore or belittle this dynamic. Simeon Zahl powerfully laid out this point in his insightful volume *The Holy Spirit and Christian Experience*.[12] I agree with Zahl in his worry that such understandable impulses toward abstraction in our theological proposals often set up a false dichotomy between theology and practice, between the objective and subjective, and between faith and experience. But this move flirts with an imaginary world rather than the real world we inhabit, a world in which God reveals himself and also normally draws us back into his life and love through embodied experiences. So first we begin by acknowledging potential limits and even abuses of Christian practices and experiences but then return full circle to nevertheless confess their theological place and purpose.

---

12. Simeon Zahl, *The Holy Spirit and Christian Experience* (Oxford: Oxford University Press, 2020).

PRACTICES ALONE ARE INSUFFICIENT

Romanticizing church life moves away from realism, and it opens the door to ignoring abuses by leaders and the failures of cherished programs. In her book *The Dangers of Christian Practice*,[13] Lauren F. Winner expresses her appreciation for the role of habits and Christian practices as advocated by the likes of Stanley Hauerwas and others, but she also shows that even good formative practices, like prayer, do not always protect one from deep *mal*formation. Winner and others (including the apostle James) warn us of the perils of mistreating or even excluding people within the church. Because of the reciprocal relationship between faith and action, sin can distort both our practices and theology (see Isaiah 1). Ultimately, the goal will not be to undermine or devalue Christian practices but to ground them theologically in the Christ-event. That is what we tried to do in the previous chapter. But we cannot be naive, treating liturgical practices as if nothing could go wrong.

Beyond providing examples of charismatic leaders who go sideways and damage others through the abuse of their gifts, Winner also draws attention to three central practices that can be hijacked or distorted: Eucharist, prayer, and baptism. Even these foundational practices, on their own, cannot guarantee wisdom, love, and faithfulness. For example, in an attempt to smooth the person's entry into the church, she observes how baptism can be used to deny the particular identity of the one being baptized, as if a person's history, skin color, or other distinctives were of no significance at all in their new life. This can, even if unintentionally, start to strip the convert of concrete aspects of their embodiment, thus compromising their full humanity. However, identity in Christ doesn't mean every natural marker is made invisible or irrelevant, even though they are all rightly relativized in comparison to one's connection to Christ.[14] But you don't have to stop being female or male, tall or short, dark- or light-skinned when you are baptized. Baptism does mean you are joined together with those who worship the triune name. Your ongoing particularity is not lost; instead, it is simply framed within and governed by that larger reality of your connection

---

13. Lauren F. Winner, *The Dangers of Christian Practice: On Wayward Gifts, Charismatic Damage, and Sin* (New Haven, CT: Yale University Press, 2018).

14. For more on how identity in Christ has been misapplied, as well as reflections on its theological and pastoral importance, see Kelly M. Kapic, *You're Only Human* (Grand Rapids: Brazos, 2022), 72–94, esp. 72–73.

to Christ. At other times, the opposite problem can emerge in this ritual: Winner observes how a local church's use of baptism can so elevate the particularity of *this* person or *this* congregation that it loses all sense of connection with the universal church.[15] Extreme forms of isolation or elitism can distort the meaning and impact of this sacrament. One side of this problem risks undermining our concrete humanity, while the other risks undermining our shared union in Christ. In other words, even powerful symbols like baptism and the Lord's Supper can be perverted to excuse or promote distortion and even violence.

Similarly, the vital practice of prayer doesn't guarantee soft hearts but can be used to reinforce hard ones. Winner refers to Keziah Goodwin Hopkins Brevard (1803–86) to exemplify this problem. An owner of two large plantations and more than two hundred slaves, Brevard regularly kept journals of her prayers, and these give painful evidence that following Christian practices does not of itself guarantee a grace-filled heart. At times, Brevard seems to recognize the unchristian nature of chattel slavery and even asks God to forgive her for "unkind thoughts" toward her slaves like Rosanna. Yet her prayer and journaling didn't seem to change her and may even have reinforced her unkind beliefs and actions. According to Winner, too many books on Christian devotion that use historical examples of prayer typically only draw from positive examples that offer what we think God really wants. But this, Winner argues,

> implies that all prayer is rightly formed; that people always pray for the things that . . . please God; that prayer is always in tune with the great Christian virtues; and if prayer arranges power at all, it does so only in a way that fosters peace, concord, and the flourishing of all Creation. But sometimes prayer does not do those things—and then either we must name those prayers as 'not prayer,' or we must account for them.[16]

Brevard prayed for her slaves to be docile and manageable even while she ignored the cruelty they suffered under people like her. She showed how insignificant she thought a slave's life to be when she cried out to God to kill an enslaved person who lied to her, and her prayers indicate

---

15. Winner says that such abuse can "erase wholly the particular; or it can evacuate the ecclesial into the local" (*The Dangers of Christian Practice*, 97).
16. Winner, *The Dangers of Christian Practice*, 61.

that her governing hope for the afterlife was not that there would be a great reconciliation and restored shalom for all God's people but rather that she might be spared from having to be near slaves and abolitionists. That was her vision of glory. Lord, have mercy.

Her prayers, sincerely offered, were ill-formed and had the effect of reinforcing her preconceived notions. She may have been "pious" in many ways, but we see ways her heart was hard and her eyes were blind to the injustice and hatred that she not only witnessed but seems to have perpetuated. This shows that simply engaging in public and private prayer does not protect Christians from their own hatred or injustice or ignorance. This should be sobering for all of us. Therefore, when we encourage prayer, "we should do so knowing its potential for distortion, and do it in such a way that our knowledge informs our practice."[17] This danger is especially potent in settings within Christianized culture, where we don't think twice about prayers offered for sports teams, armies, or other groups, ignoring the often prejudicial assumptions smuggled in.

As sinners, we can use any practice—even prayer—to reinforce unhealthy and wicked desires and habits. How can this happen to a practice? Another contemporary nonreligious example may help explain. Travel is a modern practice that many make into a panacea. We sometimes hear that extensive travel and exposure to different cultures and foreign lands will (automatically) broaden people's attitudes, making them more empathetic, open, and gracious.[18] Travel can do this for some people, but for others, such experiences only reinforce their negative stereotypes rather than breaking them down (e.g., thinking that people are materially poor only because they don't work hard). Too often exposure without proper background and key information can lead to greater misunderstanding rather than genuine discernment. One needs *knowledge* and *practice* together, not one or the other, and when these are rightly engaged, one hopefully ends up with more rightly ordered affections. Too often we pick between these.

---

17. Winner, *The Dangers of Christian Practice*, 61–62.
18. Cf. Agnes Callard, "The Case Against Travel: It Turns Us into the Worst Version of Ourselves While Convincing Us That We're at Our Best," *The New Yorker*, June 24, 2023. For an example of some of the similar challenges in short-term missions, see Kurt Alan Ver Beek, "The Impact of Short-Term Missions: A Case Study of House Construction in Honduras after Hurricane Mitch," *Missiology: An International Review* 34, no. 4 (2006): 447–95.

Similar to the experience of travel, having an orthodox theology doesn't guarantee faithful practice. Part of Christian doctrine is that doctrine must be applied to life and not remain mere information; we might call it *practiced belief.* True faith is embodied faithfulness. Affirming that all humanity is made in the image of God is a far cry from actually loving people. Habitually praying to a merciful God does not guarantee that we will be merciful. Words, after all, are relatively easy. We can expect that continued exposure to God through prayer and the hearing of his word will change hearts, but the Scriptures warn us against hardening our hearts (Heb 3:7–8).

Another example showing that regular corporate worship isn't full protection from cruelty and malformation emerged in early twentieth-century Germany. It reminds us of how the institutional church and its practices can be co-opted for outright evil. I want to admit all of this up front before I later turn to argue for the significance of corporate liturgical practices for a theology of Christian life. My advocacy should not be confused with my ignorance about the abuses.

While we would want to nuance this a bit, it is true that many members of the German Protestant churches in 1933 believed that the goals of the Nazi party were consistent with Christianity. For example, historian Richard Steigmann-Gall has argued that rather than an "anti-Christian movement," what we actually discover is that "many Nazis considered themselves or their movement to be Christian," and while that may make us "uncomfortable" by its "unpleasantness," we cannot duck some of the evidence.[19] Asking, "Who voted for Hitler?" Steigmann-Gall notes how historians looked at various factors but not sufficiently at religion. Earlier historians too often assumed that many in the church were opposed to Hitler and Nazism, which was far from true, since there was a "near total absorption of the Protestant electorate by the Nazi party in 1932 and 1933."[20]

After Hitler became chancellor of Germany at the start of 1933, German Protestant churches were reorganized into the German Evangelical Church.[21] Ludwig Muller was appointed in September of

---

19. Richard Steigmann-Gall, *The Holy Reich: Nazi Conceptions of Christianity, 1919–1945* (New York: Cambridge University Press, 2003), 26, 267.
20. Richard Steigmann-Gall, "Apostasy or Religiosity? The Cultural Meanings of the Protestant Vote for Hitler," *Social History* 25, no. 3 (2000): 267, 284.
21. From 1933 to 1945 this was the successor to the German Protestant Church Confederation.

that year to lead the church as its "bishop of the Reich." The "German Christians" movement (*Deutsche Christen*) consisted of regular participants and leading members within the German Evangelical Church, and yet they believed they could merge National Socialism with Christianity. Though Nazi leadership seems to have doubted the possibility of such a fusion, they played along while calling for greater allegiance to the state.[22] And sadly, it worked, deeply distorting the German church and the faith of its members.

What were the guiding principles of the then "Evangelical Church of the German Nation"? They spoke of their concern for this specific "race, folk, and nation" and made deeply demeaning and dehumanizing comments about the Jews, whom they claimed were jeopardizing their nationality.[23] One such statement reads, "We want an evangelical Church that is rooted in our nationhood."[24] They also avoided or completely rejected the Hebrew Bible (i.e., Old Testament) in an effort to minimize and then eliminate Jewish influences and presence from the Christian faith. This obviously distorted Christianity by detaching the Messiah from Israel, producing a religion that was no longer identifiable as orthodox Christianity.[25] The "German Christian" movement even allowed the "Aryan Paragraph" (which excludes non-Aryans, especially those with "Jewish blood") to take hold in the church. Aryans and Aryans alone could be leaders and members of the congregation.

So even though people continued to gather on Sundays, say their prayers, listen to sermons, sing their hymns, and celebrate the Lord's Supper, non-Christian forces and the spirit of the age had distorted the primary and secondary teachings and practices of the church. Their vision of Jesus and of God's will for his people bore little resemblance to the gospel.

---

22. Ferdinand Schlingensiepen, *Dietrich Bonhoeffer 1906–1945: Martyr, Thinker, Man of Resistance* (London: T&T Clark, 2010), 115–16. See also Doris L. Bergen, *Twisted Cross: The German Christian Movement in the Third Reich* (Chapel Hill: University of North Carolina Press, 1996).

23. James C. Livingston and Francis Schussler Fiorenza, with Sarah Coakley and James H. Evans Jr., *Modern Christian Thought*, vol. 2, *The Twentieth Century*, 2nd ed. (Minneapolis: Fortress, 2000), 99–100.

24. Arthur C. Cochrane, *The Church's Confession Under Hitler* (Philadelphia: Westminster, 1962), 222–23. Found in Livingston and Fiorenza, *Modern Christian Thought*, 2:100, 129.

25. See, e.g., Susannah Heschel, *The Aryan Jesus: Christian Theologians and the Bible in Nazi Germany* (Princeton, NJ: Princeton University Press, 2008).

Some Christians, however, opposed that evil. Known as the "Confessing Church," they stood against the state church, continually asserting that Jesus the Messiah is alone the full revelation of God and is alone worthy of devotion and worship.[26] Martin Niemöller, the Pastors' Emergency League, and vocal resisters like Karl Barth and Dietrich Bonhoeffer pushed back against these powers that were corrupting the church in both belief and practice. In 1934, the Barmen Declaration stated both their opposition to this corruption and their dedication to Jesus Christ. Part of the insight of the Barmen statement was its realization not only that the church influences the world but also that the world could reshape the inattentive church. The only ultimate protection against these forces was a return to Jesus Christ himself, the center of the Gospels and the only hope for the entire world.

Christians, like everyone else, are shaped by countless cultural, social, psychological, and economic forces. While it might be easy for a Western Christian to see how animism can corrupt the church in a distant land, it can be much harder to recognize the distorting forces that come in the air we breathe, the entertainment we consume, and the economy in which we participate. None of us escapes this: no individual, tradition, or location. As a result, believers continually must seek to cultivate faithful practices and to be aware that simply repeating practices of the past is not a guarantee of faithful action, praise, and worship. We have sadly been inundated with true stories from all manner of churches (non-denominational, Presbyterian, Roman Catholic, Baptist, etc.) that did use the standard Christian practices (prayer, word, Eucharist, etc.) and still became places where leaders built communities of narcissism, dysfunction, fear, and abuse.[27] Good liturgical practice is no automatic protection against corruption. Good gifts can be ignored, distorted, or abused.

But the abuse of good gifts is so appalling precisely because *they are good gifts*. A robust theology of Christian life must recognize that doctrine and life are inseparable; belief and practice feed one another.

---

26. See, e.g., Wolfgang Gerlach, *And the Witnesses Were Silent: The Confessing Church and the Persecution of the Jews*, trans. Victoria J. Barnett (Lincoln: University of Nebraska Press, 2000).

27. For examples of work demonstrating some of the distortions that can happen in churches, even those that follow basic Christian liturgical practices, see Diane Langberg, *Redeeming Power: Understanding Authority and Abuse in the Church* (Grand Rapids: Brazos, 2020); Chuck DeGroat, *When Narcissism Comes to Church: Healing Your Community from Emotional and Spiritual Abuse* (Downers Grove, IL: InterVarsity Press, 2020); Scot McKnight and Laura Barring, *A Church Called Tov: Forming a Goodness Culture That Resists Abuses of Power and Promotes Healing* (Carol Stream, IL: Tyndale Elevate, 2020).

God instructs us to worship both corporately and privately. Used well, practices shape our beliefs even as they reflect our beliefs. We engage in these practices because they can help us believe rightly, and believing rightly can shape these practices.

As wonderful and vital as I believe certain Christian practices are, and as much as I would like to see them cultivated, honored, and valued, it is naive to imagine that simply engaging in certain practices guarantees the right beliefs, behaviors, or other results we may want. Christian practices should cultivate love of God and neighbor, and when they don't do both, that is a sign something is wrong in the church and in our Christian lives. And as Winner has forced us to admit, even these good, beautiful, and central Christian practices can be perverted and distorted, thus disordering lives and communities.

Yes, Christian practices are important and commanded and powerful, but they are not a mechanism—magical, spiritual, psychological, or otherwise—that we can manipulate to produce goodness or godliness. Thus, on the one hand, we must employ them, and the history of the church offers a rich variety of ways to use them; on the other hand, even some of those who were most careful to observe God-given practices (e.g., Sabbath keeping) missed Jesus himself when he walked among them because their hearts were closed to the presence and work of their God (e.g., Mark 2:23–3:6). This is why we already addressed the *ego* that is situated within this community: The *I* who must encounter and respond to the living God not merely collectively but personally.

Whereas God has given us laws and practices as means of fostering love and shalom, hard-heartedness and the absence of neighborly love are sure marks of abuse. Such concerns have long been voiced by the "low church" traditions, which have reasonable worries that Christian practices or rituals can become divorced from the vibrant faith of individuals in their communities. We do well to listen to these concerns even as we also must appreciate the theological and pastoral significance of key ecclesial practices, such as the order of public worship (see the next chapter). But to allow practices to be divorced from theology drains them of benefit and turns them into dead religion.

These negative warnings lay a groundwork for a general treatment of the positive role of ritual. This preparatory work is necessary to properly situate what we will later argue when we focus on how corporate liturgy should reflect and inform a theology of Christian life.

RITUALS AND THEOLOGY LINKED

Why does the psalmist tell us to praise God, seek him out, and give him thanks (Ps 69:30–34)? The same passage that provokes the question also provides the answer: It is because our God saves and secures us; he hears the needy and values us as his own. In his righteousness, he establishes order; in his love, he connects us to each other and to himself; and in his creativity, he has invented and made a whole cosmos in which we live. He is not only good but amazingly good. Failure to praise and thank him would be the mark of spiritual blindness; not wanting to praise this amazingly and lovingly good Creator would be the mark of having no grip on reality—indeed, of a kind of insanity.

The Hebrew Bible records that God gave his people rituals to remind them how to be sane, specifically, how to see their relationship with God as the only healthy place to live. These rituals were designed both to reflect and inform their beliefs. But as we are inclined to do, God's people have repeatedly lost sight of the spiritual realities to which the rituals pointed and concentrated instead on the rituals themselves. Consider, for example, Isaiah's opening declarations that God had rejected the offerings, Sabbaths, and even prayers of worshipers (Isa 1:2–20): Their hearts had hardened as they ignored injustice, even abusing or neglecting orphans and widows. God was furious and rejected their liturgical sacrifices, feasts, and prayers. But we must be careful about the deduction we make here. After all, *God* had instituted those rituals in the first place. The point of Isaiah 1 and similar texts is *not* to say that God hates ritual or repetition (one would have a miserable time making sense of the Old Testament and New Testament if that were the case), but rather he had given those rites to his people to reinforce and foster communion with God and neighbor, not to replace them.

Our practices and rituals shape us, both individually and corporately, both daily and weekly, and this is true of both sacred and secular ones. As Old Testament scholar Dru Johnson concludes, "Our entire world—our faith traditions, professions, cultures, and embodied lives—is shot through with ritual."[28] Often we are unaware of their frequency or importance in our lives, maybe even unaware of their existence,

---

28. Dru Johnson, *Human Rites: The Power of Rituals, Habits, and Sacraments* (Grand Rapids: Eerdmans, 2019), 9.

although the increasing literature on habits and structures is starting to give us a renewed appreciation for them.[29]

Rituals and habits can help or hinder, but what is clear is that they shape us. In the case of the Old Testament rituals, Isaiah reminds us that their abuse reinforced bad theology and practice, which is why God distanced himself from them. Continuing to bring sacrifices and prayers to the temple while manipulating the law courts for gain at the expense of the powerless reflects the theological attitude that injustice makes no difference to God. As expressed to Isaiah, God's opinion was that ending the system altogether was better than for God to be seen as not caring for the poor. Sinful actions distort our beliefs, and distorted beliefs corrupt our actions.[30]

For the rest of this chapter we will explain why rituals matter for Christians and then revisit concerns that some, especially Protestants, have had about ways they might go badly. We need to be quick to affirm both the importance and dangers here since the ecclesia must be understood not abstractly but in light of corporate practices and participation.

CHRISTIAN RITUALS: FIVE OBSERVATIONS

Christianity, of course, has its own distinctive practices that are deliberately shaped, carefully performed, and highly symbolic. Baptism and the Lord's Supper are such rituals, and Christians have, in fact, understood these to be more than rituals: They are sacraments that promise God's presence in a special way. We have other rituals that are less symbolic, lack a deliberate or consistent shape, and are so casual that we are hardly conscious of them (e.g., greeting each other). Bernard Cooke and Gary Macy, in their thoughtful volume *Christian Symbol and Ritual*, examine five results that Christian rituals produce.[31] We will unpack the first one more fully than the others since in some ways it provides the foundational understanding for the rest of them. Although much of the wording is mine, this discussion grows directly out of their work.

---

29. For an academic who has made this work more accessible, see Wendy Wood, *Good Habits, Bad Habits: The Science of Making Positive Changes That Stick* (New York: Farrar, Straus and Giroux, 2019).

30. For more on this interrelationship, see ch. 8, "Suffering, Justice, and Knowing God," in Kelly M. Kapic, *A Little Book for New Theologians* (Downers Grove, IL: InterVarsity Press, 2012), 80–92.

31. Bernard Cooke and Gary Macy, *Christian Symbol and Ritual* (Oxford: Oxford University Press, 2005), 52–53. After these pages, the rest of the book fully unpacks this idea.

1. RITUALS AND BELIEFS ARE MUTUALLY INFORMATIVE, GROWING OUT OF AND ALSO SHAPING EACH OTHER. Cooke and Macy write that "every ritual expresses both how a community understands the world and how the ritual itself helps shape that understanding."[32] They use the phrase *hermeneutic of experience*, indicating that ritual is an interpretive action that displays our doctrines to our senses. For example, baptism enacts reminders of our fellowship with each other, our union with Christ, our turning from sin toward God, and other teachings about the nature of the church and salvation. Thus rituals shape and reinforce our beliefs by presenting them to our physical senses. Whether we grow up in the church or come to faith later in life, Christian rituals "gradually come to shape the way Christians see the world, and so the world as it exists for them."[33] For example, as I mentioned in the first chapter, most Christians are Trinitarian not because they have carefully studied the complexities of the doctrine but because they personally experience the life-giving power of the Spirit, trust in the grace of Christ, and rest in the love of the Father, all of which are normally encouraged by the church and her practices. Prayers to the Father are offered in the name of Christ in dependence on the Spirit. The practices shape the beliefs, and the beliefs inform the practices.

Hans W. Frei's book *The Eclipse of Biblical Narrative* argues that the methods and assumptions for understanding life have radically changed for those of us living on this side of the Enlightenment.[34] In earlier years, members of Western society derived much of their understanding of the world from the Bible, interpreting their everyday experiences within the story found there. Nowadays the situation is reversed: Our culture assumes a picture of the world derived from passing news stories and personal observations, all interpreted through our present "social imaginaries," to borrow a phrase from Charles Taylor.[35] Whereas earlier the "real world" was the "biblical world," now the default of what is "real" arises from secular rather than religious assumptions. Instead of trying to fit our experiences into the biblical world, we now try to make the biblical world fit into our present experiences. We end up wondering what the real world actually is, and we keep trying to figure

---

32. Cooke and Macy, *Christian Symbol and Ritual*, 52.
33. Cooke and Macy, *Christian Symbol and Ritual*, 52.
34. Hans W. Frei, *The Eclipse of Biblical Narrative: A Study in Eighteenth and Nineteenth Century Hermeneutics* (New Haven, CT: Yale University Press, 1974).
35. Charles Taylor, *Modern Social Imaginaries* (Durham: Duke University Press, 2004).

out how we relate to it. In the middle of this confusion and misdirection, Christian rituals are an indispensable tool for displaying what our faith actually says and enabling Christians to perceive the substance behind the teaching. Our imaginations need to be lifted, our narratives expanded, our hearts opened.

Formal and informal ecclesial rituals teach so much and so deeply. Since rituals definitely shape our lives, we need to ask, what are those rituals, how are they shaping our brains and bodies, and how should we put them to use? Whether coming from contemporary forms of informal services that emphasize "spontaneity" or more classic concerns of Puritans who were reacting against certain abuses of rituals, the truth is that all of us consistently engage in rituals and repetition. Look for our repeated actions, especially the ones that have become almost automatic. Look at what they accomplish, both in themselves and symbolically. Look at how they orient us toward worship, function in worship, or shape us after worship. From handshakes to confessions of faith, from cups of coffee to baptisms, we move in a series of rituals, inventing new ones while using thousand-year-old traditions as well. Given all this, it makes good sense to employ our corporate worship services deliberately to encourage, reinforce, and shape Christian life. They can do this because the key elements of corporate worship also reflect the arc of Christian life (from calling through benediction) and its underlying theology, thus informing and reforming our beliefs and actions in subtle and powerful ways.

2. CHRISTIANS MATURE THROUGH RITUALS. They are meant to deepen our beliefs and our lives away from the worship service. For example, Cooke and Macy observe that Christians often find that communal prayer "strengthens them so that they gradually, and with fits and starts, actually begin to be the kind of people they want to be: caring, thoughtful, responsible, self-giving—in short, adults!"[36] As the letter to the Hebrews comments, they can move from milk to solid food (Heb 5:12–13). "Solid food is for the mature, for those who have their powers of discernment trained by constant practice to distinguish good from evil" (Heb 5:14). A believer's "discernment" is not merely directed toward ideas; it also gives insight into their life and community. Hebrews warns of those who won't move past the basic rituals and beliefs.

---

36. Cooke and Macy, *Christian Symbol and Ritual*, 105.

Those elementary doctrines and practices are important, but believers should "not be sluggish, but imitators of those who through faith and patience inherit the promises" (Heb 6:12). Rituals are a means of growth into increasing Christlikeness, so if we never move beyond attention to the ritual itself, then its purpose remains unfulfilled and the ritual is in danger of becoming an empty shell.

So, for instance, the ritual of repentance (corporate and individual) leads us to a sober assessment of the complexity and reality of sin in our lives and the stunning depth of God's love and mercy for us. We do not mature out of the need for confession, grace, and forgiveness; we only grow more deeply into awareness of God's kindness, compassion, and transforming love. This serves as an example of the life-giving and reshaping value that a corporate spiritual practice can have: Regular times for corporate confession and repentance push us to remain honest about sin (e.g., Lev 16:21; Num 5:7; Jas 5:16) while also regularly helping us go deeper into God's goodness and love (e.g., Ps 32:5; 1 John 1:8–10). Immaturity imagines sin is a small or passing problem or that the ritual itself solves the problem. Maturity sees the continuing challenges within ourselves while also resting confidently in God's gift of Christ, who "became to us wisdom from God, righteousness and sanctification and redemption" (1 Cor 1:30). Thus maturity does not cease to need practices like prayer, study, and corporate worship, but instead, it has gained a deepened ability to receive God's grace through them.

3. CHRISTIAN RITUALS OF WORSHIP ARE SHAPED AND GOVERNED BY THE RISEN CHRIST. Here we are speaking not merely of the memory of the risen Christ or our doctrines about him but of his personal presence and activity. He is alive now both as our High Priest in the heavenly tabernacle (Heb 3:1; 8:1–13; 9:24) and present to us by his Spirit (Rom 8:9–10; Gal 4:6; Col 1:27). This reality anchors the promise that our worship and lives are a participation in his worship and life. Remember that, as our Mediator, he embodies the grace or gift of God. Again, this is why we are making theological observations here, not simply sociological ones. Trying to ignore either of the aspects or their interplay blinds us to the nature of worship. Chapter 6 on Messiah unpacked this christological link in detail.

Rituals of worship are means by which we cultivate a growing awareness of Christ's presence among us. In other words, "It is in the rituals that Christians believe that they are called, nourished, and challenged by the experience of the risen Christ."[37] Many traditions speak of "means of grace" as the earthly actions and resources through which God works to deepen our knowledge and experience of his love. Though not all agree on what these means of grace are (Only in the sacraments? How many sacraments? What about nonsacramental practices, such as prayer and fellowship, among others?), there is commonly a recognition that some practices and symbols carry special weight. Take, for instance, Passover for the ancient Israelites (Exod 12:1–28; Lev 23:5; Num 9:1–14) and baptism for the emerging church (Matt 28:19; Col 2:12; 1 Pet 3:21; Acts 2:41; 8:12–13; Gal 3:27). While God can work through anyone or anything, repeating some of those activities often enough invests them with a kind of resonance beyond the individual act, and so they become a kind of ritual for us. A healthy view of ritual encourages greater awareness that God's presence brings empowerment, encouraging believers to keep moving forward in faith and life. Roman Catholics, Orthodox, and most Protestants recognize that "the risen Christ somehow empowers the community."[38] As Jesus promised, where more than two are gathered in Christ's name, he is distinctly present with them (Matt 18:20). Further, we affirm that "without this empowerment, and without this way of life, there would be no Christianity at all."[39] The rituals are meant to lift our gaze to the ascended Christ and open us to the work of his Spirit. Once again, rituals, especially sacramental ones, are not given primarily or exclusively to shape our character or guarantee moral performance. Rather, they are given simply as a grace; they offer a way for us to enter into deeper communion with Jesus and invite us into his presence as food for our souls.

4. CHRISTIAN RITUALS IN WORSHIP PROMOTE SERVICE. Because we worship in and through the power of the risen Christ and his Spirit, our worship consists not in mere attempts at moral self-improvement but in continual faith-filled response to the life, death, resurrection, and ongoing work of the ascended Messiah. He has poured out his Spirit on us, and now we are united to the risen King. Remember the discussion in chapter 5 on the distinction between law and gospel. While in some ways the cross reminds us that Christ has once and for all dealt with and forgiven our sins, the resurrection calls us to a joyful life of obedience that works for shalom even in this broken and hurting world.

---

37. Cooke and Macy, *Christian Symbol and Ritual*, 53.
38. Cooke and Macy, *Christian Symbol and Ritual*, 101.
39. Cooke and Macy, *Christian Symbol and Ritual*, 103.

Sacrificial service that is cruciform in nature shapes this resurrection life of ours. Cooke and Macy argue that "service should be the distinguishing feature of the Christian life, and each Christian ritual should remind those celebrating of this calling."[40] This also is a reminder that Christian spirituality is concerned not simply with one's inner psychological world but also with the world of our neighbors. Of course, this is not in any way a form of earning God's favor, but it does serve as an expression of the overarching thesis of this book: Christian life *is a response to the love of God*. When we follow our humble King, Christian rituals (such as bread and wine, foot-washing, bent knees, etc.) do, in fact, prepare and sustain our lives for Spirit-empowered love and service.

5. RIGHTLY ORIENTED, CHRISTIAN RITUALS PRODUCE A DEEPER SENSE OF FAMILY AMONG GOD'S PEOPLE. Although Cooke and Macy use the language of *a celebration of friendship* rather than *family*, I believe the more biblical imagery is that of *adoption* and the *household of God*. This familial language reinforces and strengthens their point. The regular corporate gathering is a fundamental ritual of God's people, whether of fifteen believers in a house church or thousands in a large hall, and "the ritual gathering itself should tell each person attending that others share their concerns, their commitments, their hopes, and their fears."[41] Our worship together before the God and Father of our Lord Jesus Christ strengthens our experience of union with one another, thereby strengthening our doctrine. It connects our love for God to our love for one another (John 12:34–35).

Fellowship among the family of God is in some ways radically different from the world's fellowship, for it is not centered on shared economic status, sporting knowledge, or common hobbies, but it is rooted in the risen Christ who has poured out his Spirit on us and brought us to the Father and to one another. Jew and gentile, male and female, young and old, rich and poor, employed and unemployed, Republican and Democrat. In this way, Christian friendship is both created and celebrated—not because it is easy or natural but because God knits our hearts together through our shared worship of Christ. And we discover we are not just friends but family.

Rituals form and foster such familial relations. One can think, for example, of the "holy kiss" (Rom 16:16; 1 Cor 16:20; 2 Cor 13:12;

---

40. Cooke and Macy, *Christian Symbol and Ritual*, 53.
41. Cooke and Macy, *Christian Symbol and Ritual*, 53.

1 Thess 5:26; cf. 1 Pet 5:14), the "right hand of fellowship" (Gal 2:9), and other biblical expressions that are regularly practiced during corporate worship as a way to both testify to and strengthen divinely given familial links. Weddings in the church bring together not merely two different biological families but the whole congregation, reminding them of their responsibility to encourage this new union. Similarly, infant baptism or "baby dedications" done by different traditions call the community—in response to God's work—to take responsibility for the child through prayer, teaching, and other forms of care. Corporate worship rituals help Christians learn and experience the wonder of their salvation as individuals and as a corporate community. These rituals testify to the family status shared by believers in the church.

Ritual is neither our enemy nor our savior. It is a pattern of human life, and some rituals are explicit gifts of God. We need rituals. We continually make rituals. And rituals, like all patterns in life, need examination, deliberate care, and wise use. Therefore, we ought to look at the rituals and practices of our lives, especially those we use in our worship services, to see both what they *can* do and what they *actually* do, and then use them with care and reverence to pursue maturity, faithfulness, and a deeper awareness of our Lord. Ideally, they both reflect and inform a robust theology of Christian life.

Let's end this chapter by admitting some final stumbling blocks that can cause people to lose their balance as they use Christian rituals, including a regular liturgy. Again, to admit such dangers is not to imply that rituals are bad but to make us wary of abuses, not so we do away with rituals (because we will still be doing them, whether or not we are aware of it) but so that we might more faithfully follow the Messiah, grow in our love for one another, and mature in our Christian lives.

POTENTIAL STUMBLING STONES

Ever since the sixteenth-century Reformation, Protestants have worried about gravely mistaken attitudes toward liturgy and ritual. Many earlier priests and authors had voiced this concern before it became a full-blown crisis.[42] The Reformers and then later groups like the Puritans and evangelicals tended to focus on two abiding concerns: superstition

---

42. Cf. Michael D. Bailey, "A Late-Medieval Crisis of Superstition?" *Speculum* 84, no. 3 (2009): 633–61. He concludes that there was growing and serious concern but not yet a "crisis."

and hypocrisy. Hughes Oliphant Old captures what was behind many of these fears.

> *Superstition* is understood as a failure to recognize the role of the Holy Spirit in worship. It is to attribute the efficacy of a sacrament [for example] to the outward sign rather than to the inner working of the Holy Spirit. *Hypocrisy*, on the other hand, is understood as the performing of a religious act for some other motive than obedience to God. It is worshiping out of some other source of power than the inward working of the Holy Spirit. It must be the Holy Spirit which works faith in the hearts of believers and it must be out of faith that one is obedient to God.[43]

They did not see liturgy or ritual in itself as a problem since, of course, all churches have some kind of liturgy (whether or not they realize it), and the word *ritual* applies to any often-repeated action. The main *theological* problem driving the Protestant concern was that some worshipers ignored or minimized the importance of the Holy Spirit's work among them. When this happens, it reflects not just a logistics or psychological problem but a theological one.

A century after the Reformation, when the Puritan John Owen wrote about a healthy approach to spirituality, he mentioned three particular kinds of people that his readers should avoid lest their faith and life be undermined: rationalists, enthusiasts, and the superstitious.[44] Notice how these groups tie practice and belief together: For example, a rationalist is not simply someone who values reason, but their overly inflated confidence or belief in rationality deforms their ability to recognize God and rightly relate to him. Shaping your life by the practices of rationalism will change who you are, not simply what you believe. While the manifestations of these potential dangers may look different in our day, the problems abide. And so it is well worth listening to this seventeenth-century voice of concern before we turn to the call for personal faith and then advocating for the place and power of liturgy in a theology of Christian life.

---

43. Hughes Oliphant Old, *The Patristic Roots of Reformed Worship*, Zürcher Beiträge zur Reformationsgeschichte (Zürich: Theologischer, 1975), 30, emphasis added.

44. For more unpacking of this material, see Kelly M. Kapic, "John Owen's Theological Spirituality: Navigating Perceived Threats in a Changing World," in *John Owen Between Orthodoxy and Modernity*, ed. Willem Van Vlastuin and Kelly M. Kapic (Leiden: Brill, 2019), 55–82, esp. 55–66.

First, the danger of rationalism was exemplified by Socinianism in Owen's day. The threat from rationalists was not that they didn't value the Bible—many, like John Biddle (1615–62), certainly did.[45] The problem was that such "rationalists" tried to construct a system of reason without an orthodox or confessional foundation as the authority that shaped their interpretation and application of Scripture. In other words, reason stood over rather than under revelation. In particular, this rationalism led them to deny the triune being of God, also denying that his Spirit worked miraculously in producing the Scriptures and continues to work in believers as they read them.[46] While reason is a gift of God, the threat of rationalism turns the gift against the Giver. It often downplays mystery, the transcendent, and the miraculous. Although some lingering stereotypes of the Puritans as hyperrational do have some legitimacy, folks like Owen did honor the aspect of mystery in God's work and our need for the Spirit's enlivening presence and supernatural work in our lives. Rationalists either ignored the phenomenon of revelation or rejected it outright; the orthodox, by contrast, knew that only as God breaks through to us in his self-revelation can we know and worship the God who is and not an idol of our own making. As vice-chancellor of Oxford and a prolific author, Owen obviously respected reason and took for granted that his audience would do so, but he also knew that sin affected people's minds and reasoning as well as their bodies. Any philosophy that tried to start with bare human reason and perception, therefore, doomed itself to failure from the start. Reason can serve our Christian life, but it needs faith to function at its fullest.

Second, Owen drew attention to the opposite concern: "enthusiasts." Not originally a term of endearment, this label emerged in the seventeenth century to refer to those who were led in their religion by their emotions (or "passions") and showed no interest in verifiable knowledge. Whereas many rationalists tend to belittle the subjective or experiential, here the danger is the opposite: grounding theology in pure

---

45. On the general Socinian emphasis on reason (including its positive role) and how it was received by the more orthodox, see Sarah Mortimer, *Reason and Religion in the English Revolution: The Socinian Challenge* (Cambridge: Cambridge University Press, 2010). For more on the political nature of these debates between the likes of Owen and Biddle, see Blair Worden, *God's Instruments: Political Conduct in the England of Oliver Cromwell* (Oxford: Oxford University Press, 2012), esp. 67–85.

46. Paul C. H. Lim traces this out nicely and in great detail in *Mystery Unveiled: The Crisis of the Trinity in Early Modern England*, Oxford Studies in Historical Theology (Oxford: Oxford University Press, 2012).

subjectivity. The risk for enthusiasts is making objectivity the enemy rather than the friend of Christian faith and life. Early seventeenth-century use of *enthusiasts* was drawn from the Greek *enthousiastikos*, meaning "pertaining to possession by a deity," and pointed to the idea of intense rapturous personal experience with God.[47] Groups such as the early Quakers and Shakers took their names from the pejorative labels given by outsiders who mocked them for losing their rational faculties and physical self-control in their worship. Enthusiasts were less concerned with historic revelation and more interested in contemporary revelations or an "inner light" that God could and would give to his people in the present. Simply having strong emotions or affirming the present work of the Spirit, however, isn't what makes one an enthusiast. Emotions are not bad. Enthusiasm is not a problem. According to Owen, this negative term *only applied* to those who (1) belittled their God-given human faculties (mind, will, affections, body), (2) treated the individual's personal subjectivity as primary, and (3) gave priority to their personal emotional impressions over the sacred Scriptures.[48] Sensitivity to the leading of the Spirit is necessary for all believers, but enthusiasts at least appeared not to distinguish the impressions of their own inner spirit from the guidance of God's Holy Spirit, which very naturally worried Owen and other Puritans. Early enthusiasts even went so far as to "cleanse" their corporate gatherings of historic practices or rituals, viewing them as a way to avoid the leading of the Holy Spirit, whereas historically these very practices (e.g., the Lord's Supper, public preaching, prayer, benedictions, etc.) had been the space in which the Spirit so freely moved. As Simeon Zahl has demonstrated, one of the lingering effects of such extreme forms of subjectivism penetrating into Protestantism is that many key later theologians ended up overcorrecting, appearing to completely devalue experience's role in guiding Christian life and theology.[49] However, we can encourage avoiding the imbalance of becoming an enthusiast while still maintaining the good and right role of experience in our embodied faith.

Third, Owen mentioned superstition as a danger to be avoided. While the rationalists and the enthusiasts avoided the sacraments for their

---

47. Etymonline, "enthusiastic (adj.)," https://www.etymonline.com/word/enthusiastic.
48. Kapic, "John Owen's Theological Spirituality," 64.
49. Simeon Zahl, *The Holy Spirit and Christian Experience* (Oxford: Oxford University Press, 2020), esp. 16–35, where Zahl traces this from the later Luther through Barth.

different reasons, Owen recognized that one can affirm and use them wholeheartedly but so wrong-mindedly as to erode the ritual's spiritual benefit. Were the sacraments seen as a way to manipulate the world, the deity, or whatever? Owen proposed that one test of superstitions is whether one sees oneself or Christ as central in it. A healthy use of the ritual requires the believer to look in humility and submission to Christ. Experiences and rituals must be tested against biblical revelation, all of which point to Christ and the outpouring of his Spirit, and all made manifest in love. He worried that some people approached the rituals with hearts hardened toward Christ or neighbor. That is, if one trusts merely in the material aspects of worship or in the rituals themselves rather than looking through them to Christ himself, then there is a genuine possibility of superstition, which allows the ritual to obscure Christ rather than lead to him. This brings the great danger of idolatry. That is not to deny that supernatural realities might occur in and through the sacraments (which many orthodox Christian traditions affirm), but it is to admit that even biblically sanctioned rituals can become superstitions when used in mechanistic, manipulative, or darkly magical ways.

CONCLUSION: ECCLESIAL RITUALS SHOULD REFLECT AND FOSTER COMMUNION WITH GOD

Some Christians have tended to avoid or disparage everything that looks like ritual out of concern that such practices are empty of content, encourage superstition, feed hypocrisy, or are just plain boring and distracting from genuine worship. The criterion for whether they use a given practice is often the presence (or absence) of an internal emotional-spiritual-intellectual response that corresponds to these outer signs and actions. So whether we are talking about making the sign of the cross, kissing an object in worship, moving your body in certain ways, praying, preaching sermons, or baptizing a new convert, this criterion of the internal response in the worshiper has often been given supreme value in deciding what to put into the worship service.

But this criterion isn't enough, and on its own, it can mislead. If a given practice does not produce an appropriately Christ-ward corresponding response in the congregation, then what needs to change? Is it the practice, or is it the hearts of the congregation? The answer to that depends on many factors, and we should be careful in deciding both what those factors are and then how to proceed with the necessary changes.

If we try to build a view of the church simply upon the doctrine of the priesthood of all believers, using each person's personal experience as the test for how to construct a worship service—let alone Christian life—we soon get into serious trouble. Such a method, especially in our highly individualist society, soon elevates contemporary values above historical ones, quick judgment above careful deliberation, and personal experience above church unity. The attempt to make Christianity about "just me and Jesus" becomes little more than a projection of ourselves onto God rather than a matter of hearing and following our Lord.

An example may prove helpful here: In light of this kind of danger, the Reformed Christians of Strasbourg in the early sixteenth century built their view of worship not on a doctrine of equality—though they certainly affirmed the priesthood of all believers—but on the practice of the Eucharist.[50] Private celebrations of the Lord's Supper, performed by an individual rather than with the gathered people of God, undermined what they thought was the biblical image of Christian life: We are part of a living body, the body of Christ, and our self-understanding and mission are inescapably bound together with God's people.

The goal of reviewing our actions is to find those movements and practices that God uses to connect us with himself in worship and to shape our lives into greater faithfulness. This process also connects believers to one another and can even point them out in mission toward a needy world. So we should always be willing to ask questions of our ecclesial practices, which are the context for Christian life.[51]

As the great scholar of liturgy Frank C. Senn once wrote, "The historical study of liturgy bears witness to instances of decay, of superstitious abuse, of heretical malformations, and of flinty incrustations that require reform and renewal. This in itself should tell us that the elements of liturgy can have nothing to do with salvation."[52] Senn and I both believe in the great significance of liturgy; we recognize that the

---

50. Old, *The Patristic Roots of Reformed Worship*, 34.

51. For example, has the congregation become disengaged from some traditional action? If that action is allowed but not prescribed by the Scriptures (e.g., having the choir enter the church at the beginning of the service while singing a traditional hymn), then removing or changing that action might be a good idea. If the action (like the Eucharist or the preaching of the word) is prescribed by the Scriptures, however, then reviewing the manner in which it is done rather than removing it is probably a good idea.

52. Frank C. Senn, *Christian Liturgy: Catholic and Evangelical* (Minneapolis: Fortress, 1997), 43.

patterns of our actions both reflect beliefs and inform them. They can be profoundly helpful, but they can never replace the realities to which they point. The gifts are always meant to take us to the Giver.

It is to be hoped that those who belittle the institutional church and her liturgies will learn afresh to see their value, and that those who ask too much of church practices will be reminded that they are not an end in themselves but are a means to promote living communion with the triune God.

We should also admit that certain hesitations about abuses of liturgy have a legitimate foundation, and we should not think of them as the sole concern of curmudgeonly low-church congregants. Plenty of Eastern Orthodox, Roman Catholic, and high-church Anglican Christians share those concerns. Most Christians don't want empty rituals but want vibrant faith. And this faith and life can ultimately only come as the outflow of a genuinely Spirit-given and Christ-oriented life before the Father. Rightly constructed ecclesial rituals, especially in our corporate gatherings, not only originally invite us into this theological reality but nourish and refashion us in its truth.

Christian spirituality operates like a conversation with God through Christ and by the power of God's Holy Spirit. This dynamic moves through the church and into particular lives. Thus we must not neglect the corporate gathering of God's people in an effort to make things personal. The personal and the corporate depend on each other. Weekly worship gatherings will necessarily use repeated practices or liturgies, some prescribed by the Scriptures and others that have evolved culturally, even if the people enacting them are not fully aware of all that is happening. These practices shape us, whether we call them rituals, liturgies, or habits. In our final chapter we will turn to a more detailed look at how the weekly corporate gathering for worship might helpfully reflect the arc of Christian life. Christian life is our life together, in Christ and by the Spirit. It is personal but always within the body of Christ, under the head who both receives our worship and leads it. Therefore, we must now consider more carefully the significance of corporate worship for a theology of Christian life.

CHAPTER 9

ECCLESIA II
Corporate Worship as the Arc of Christian Life

> *The church is the location where we come to know God, surely not in every possible way, but in the one decisive way, namely as the One who saves us and draws us into the fullness of the divine life—all of this through faith in the crucified and risen Jesus Christ.*
> —REINHARD HÜTTER[1]

> *The worship of the Church is possible only because Jesus Christ in His earthly ministry lived a sufficient and perfect life of worship. . . . The worship of the Church is true and real because Jesus Christ is freely present therein as Lord, abiding with those who are gathered together in his name.*
> —J.-J. VON ALLMEN[2]

> *Because the Word has become human and spoken literally with a human voice, and because he has then, through the holy Spirit, brought believers into an unimaginably intimate relation with himself, as members of his Body, he can present before God completely and truthfully what human beings really feel and think. So in his actual*

---

1. Reinhard Hütter, "The Church: The Knowledge of the Triune God; Practices, Doctrine, Theology," in *Knowing the Triune God: The Work of the Spirit in the Practices of the Church*, ed. James J. Buckley and David S. Yeago (Grand Rapids: Eerdmans, 2001), 23.

2. J.-J. von Allmen, *Worship: Its Theology and Practice* (New York: Oxford University Press, 1965), 32.

> *human life and then again in the life of the worshipping Church, he speaks for us, acts out the part of a human being with comprehensive compassion.*
>
> —ROWAN WILLIAMS[3]

Christian life involves *us* rather than merely *me*. It emphasizes the plural, and the singular operates within that space. This communal character is the presupposition and consistent affirmation of sacred Scripture. Yet when theologians speak of this *we*, we often refer it to an abstract invisible church, not the concrete gathering of believers. While the classic distinction between the *visible* and *invisible* church has its uses, that invisibility is often a hindrance rather than a help in articulating the theology and practice of Christian life. So when I speak of the ecclesia here, I first and foremost have in mind the concrete, particular, gathered existence of God's people localized in space and time: "The Church is the congregation of those who hear and accept God's word."[4] Thus *the church* does not refer to an idealized or romanticized vision of perfect people, nor chiefly to a hierarchical structure, but to everyday believers who come together (as called-out ones) to worship God as he is presented to us in the gospel, the good news that proclaims the Father's love overflowing to us in the gift of the Son who draws us into the life and love of God by the Spirit. Because we are united to the incarnate Son by the life-giving Spirit, we respond to God's love by worshiping him. This reciprocal movement is the heart of a theology and practice of Christian life, a life we do *together*, a shared life that centers on worship.

Whether the *we* includes fifteen or fifteen hundred believers, we are an embodied assembly who worship God together. Because that worship is a response to the Word, carried out in the power of the Spirit, it also becomes a formative setting, shaping our imaginations and instincts more and more into conformity with Christ. Our liturgies—our rituals, practices, and habits—in corporate worship are tools for understanding and practicing our life as given by, sustained through, and leading to God (thus they are of *theological* import). Corporate worship is the generative context for praise and prayer, repentance and faith, promise and comfort. No matter the denomination, tradition, or church polity, what we

---

3. Rowan Williams, *On Augustine* (London: Bloomsbury, 2016), 133–34.
4. Wilhelm Niesel, *Reformed Symbolics: Comparison of Catholicism, Orthodoxy, and Protestantism*, trans. David Lewis (Edinburgh: Oliver and Boyd, 1962), 12.

Christians do together in corporate worship shapes our understanding of God, ourselves, his world, and how we are to live.

Building on the last chapter's emphasis on the general importance of the church and her rituals, we now look at weekly corporate worship because these communal services reflect and inform our theology of Christian life. My great hope for this chapter is that it will lay a groundwork for a theology and practice that are biblically faithful, theologically orthodox, liturgically suggestive, and broadly useful across Christian traditions, even though each tradition will undoubtedly have its distinctive emphasis and approach. Admittedly, each section of material in this chapter deserves volumes and not simply pages; in this setting, I simply have space to lay down some key markers and then indicate several directions for further exploration. However, I am hopeful that others with more energy, time, and expertise will take up the challenge to build upon, revise, correct, or strengthen what they find here.

The first step in explaining my proposal is to look at Augustine's *totus Christus* hermeneutic as he applied it to the Psalms and use it to examine the weekly experience of corporate worship. Then we will outline broad movements and specific elements of corporate worship that have emerged in early Christian history and have persisted for millennia. Finally, I will suggest how to see the corporate worship service in christological, ecclesial, and personal terms.

TOTUS CHRISTUS

As I have noted several times, we too often emphasize one aspect of complex theological themes instead of acknowledging the whole; instead of helpfully simplifying, this habit flattens and distorts both our theology and our lives. Multiple factors can be true at the same time, even when we also need to make distinctions among those factors. For example, when we spoke about the law-gospel distinction, we recognized that if people pick between Christ and us, or faith and obedience, or law and grace, then that typically produces a distorted theology. We regularly need to affirm the conjunction *and* rather than *or* while working out the relationship between different elements. For example, Chalcedonian Christology distinguished the divine and human natures of Christ, yet it requires we neither blend nor separate them even as we honor their unbreakable union. Accordingly, our theology must affirm the primacy of divine agency without denying the significance of human agency. We must value the corporate without discrediting the personal, and we should honor proclamation without belittling action or affections. I would like us to keep this principle in mind as we turn to Augustine's *totus Christus*.

Throughout his extensive *Expositions of the Psalms*, Augustine develops the language and concept of the whole Christ (*totus Christus*). Growing out of his appreciation for both the literal sense (*locutio propria*) and the figurative sense (*locutio figurata*) of Scripture, Augustine drew upon metaphors, similes, allegory, and typology as part of a figurative reading. Given the Spirit's inspiration in the writing and reception of Scripture, Augustine and much of the Christian tradition have made space for reading and applying a text by using a biblical-theological hermeneutic that allows us to hear the multiple resonances of the text without detracting from appropriate historical or literal interpretations.[5] For example, whether speaking of exodus, promised land, or exile, "Augustine frequently returns to the Pauline principle that *All these things happened to them, but with symbolic import (in figura)* (1 Cor 10:11), in order to bring the story of past events to bear on contemporary experience of salvation."[6] He applies this hermeneutic throughout his handling of the Old Testament in general, especially in his treatment of the Psalms. I believe his *totus Christus* method helps make sense of the Psalms because they were written in direct address to God and used in both private and corporate worship, and for Christians in particular, they are read in light of the full canon of Scripture.

Augustine develops the *totus Christus* method as a way to investigate how these ancient songs relate to Christ, to his church, and to contemporary believers rather than just to the historical figures who composed or sang them many centuries before Jesus was born. This does not undermine or cancel out a psalm's original setting or historical significance but instead broadens that significance by relating it to God's

---

5. The leading expert on this material is probably Michael Cameron. See especially Cameron, *Christ Meets Me Everywhere: Augustine's Early Figurative Exegesis* (Notre Dame, IN: University of Notre Dame Press, 2012); Cameron, "The Christological Substructure of Augustine's Figurative Exegesis," in *Augustine and The Bible*, ed. Pamela Bright (Notre Dame, IN: University of Notre Dame Press, 1999), 74–103; Cameron, "*Totus Christus* and the Psychagogy of Augustine's Sermons," *Augustinian Studies* 36, no. 1 (2010): 59–70.

6. Michael Fiedrowicz, introduction to *Expositions of the Psalms*, 1–31, by Augustine, trans. Maria Boulding, III/15 (New York: New City, 2000), 31, original emphasis.

fuller self-revelation in Christ. Just as we need to appreciate the Hebrew Scriptures to make sense of Christ and the gospel in the New Testament, it follows that Christ will help us make sense of the Hebrew Scriptures.[7]

Reflecting and developing patristic exegetical instincts, Augustine treated the Psalms as manifesting various "voices." In the end, he found five complementary voices or words. While it is possible to distinguish between these, they should not be rigidly separated, especially since he believed they were often intermingled:[8]

- *vox ad Christum*: a word *to* Christ
- *vox de Christo*: a word *about* Christ
- *vox Christi*: a word spoken *by* Christ himself
- *vox de ecclesia*: a word *about* the church
- *vox ecclesiae*: a word spoken *by* the church

While scholars often classify the Psalms into various categories (e.g., psalms of lament, thanksgiving, etc.), Augustine's classification is somewhat different. For example, he comments on the opening of Psalm 85 that Christ "prays for us as our priest, he prays in us as our Head, he is prayed to by us as our God."[9] These psalms are Christ's psalms! The intimacy of the *totus Christus* in Augustine assumes a union of God's people (corporate and individual) in the incarnate Son to such a degree that this careful rhetorician happily contorts grammar to emphasize the relationship of Christ, the church, and particular believers. Michael Cameron shows these rhetorical gymnastics when he strings together key quotes from Augustine: "'because in me, they are I'; 'because even we are he'; 'because even he is we.'"[10] Cameron explains, "*Totus Christus* is a training ground for Christian *exercitatio* [exercise] within the comprehensive unity of love, in which the listeners dwell within, not the words of the Bible, but the speaking Ego of the Bible, who is Christ. They learn his words

---

7. In more recent times, Richard B. Hays has made a similar argument. See Hays, *Reading Backwards: Figural Christology and the Fourfold Gospel Witness* (Waco: Baylor University Press, 2014); cf. Hays, *Echoes of Scripture in the Gospels* (Waco: Baylor University Press, 2016).

8. Here I am drawing from the excellent treatment of Fiedrowicz, introduction to *Expositions of the Psalms*, 44–45.

9. Augustine, *en. Ps.* 85:1, quoted in Rowan Williams, *On Augustine* (London: Bloomsbury, 2016), 28–29.

10. Michael Cameron, *Christ Meets Me Everywhere: Augustine's Early Figurative Exegesis*, Oxford Studies In Historical Theology (New York: Oxford University Press, 2012), 288.

as their own words, words they understand with a warm intimacy of the truth, as it were with Christ's own understanding."[11]

Psalm 13, for example, could be read not simply as David's past personal lament but as a lament for other voices throughout redemptive history, including ours: Here we also have a word *to* Christ, *about* Christ, and *by* Christ. As the suffering servant, Jesus is comforted by such promises knowing that his prayers are heard; here we discover our sympathetic High Priest who, by his own experience, knows isolation, pain, and injustice, and so he himself can cry out, "How long, O Lord? Will you forget me forever?" (Ps 13:1).[12] Out of this trial, Jesus emerges as the one who alone can perfectly say, "I have trusted in your steadfast love; my heart shall rejoice in your salvation" (Ps 13:5).[13] Consequently, our confidence in God is now strengthened and even generated by this messianic voice, and we ourselves echo him when we, by his Spirit in us, cry out, "Abba, Father." Suitably, Psalm 13 can also be prayed this way as a word *about* and even *spoken by* the church, since the body of Christ is composed of those who deal with persecution and suffering and who, amid pain, also together cry out in desperate need to the Lord who hears and responds. In this corporate solidarity, God's gathered people in chorus say, "I will sing to the Lord, because he has dealt bountifully with me" (Ps 13:6).[14]

Frank J. Matera concludes that Augustine's suggestions are far more about *praying* the Psalms than about textual-critical analysis (which, on its own, can be a legitimate and helpful enterprise).[15] Augustine makes sense of praying the Psalms for those of us who live in light of the full Paschal mystery: The Son became incarnate, lived, died, rose, and now reigns as the King of Kings and Lord of Lords, the head and leader of the church, who serves as the great representative of God's people.

---

11. Cameron, *"Totus Christus* and the Psychagogy of Augustine's Sermons," 67.

12. This brief rendering of Psalm 13 is not from Augustine, although it is meant to reflect how his *totus Christus* approach could be applied. Augustine himself frames the "how long" in terms of asking how long "will you put me off from spiritually understanding Christ, who is the Wisdom of God and the true end of every intention of the soul?" Augustine, "Exposition of Psalm 12 [13]," in *Expositions of the Psalms*, 173.

13. This is exactly how Augustine reads it: "which obviously means in Christ, the Wisdom of God." Augustine, "Exposition of Psalm 12 [13]," in *Expositions of the Psalms*, 174.

14. Bruce K. Waltke, James M. Houston, and Erika Moore draw from Augustine's framework when they propose this language of *corporate solidarity*, where "the corporate Israel, as the 'I' of the Psalms, has become the 'I' of Christ and his church." Waltke, Houston, and Moore, *The Psalms as Christian Lament: A Historical Commentary* (Grand Rapids: Eerdmans, 2014), 18.

15. Frank J. Matera, *Praying the Psalms in the Voice of Christ: A Christological Reading of the Psalms in the Liturgy of the Hours* (Collegeville, MN: Liturgical, 2023).

> We pray [these psalms] with, to, and in the name of the incarnate Son of God, whom we confess as Messiah and King, Lord and Savior, the One who entered the heavenly sanctuary of the eternal Zion through the sacrifice of himself to the Father. In light of the paschal mystery, we hear his voice praising God and making lamentation on our behalf. In light of the paschal mystery, we hear the voice of the whole Christ: the head praying for the Body, and the Body praying in the name of its Lord. While we hear the voice of Christ and his Body in the psalms, there are times when we also hear a voice addressed to Christ or his Body, or a voice about Christ and his Body.[16]

Knowing our corporate solidarity with each other in Christ enables Christians not only to make sense of the Psalms but also to make sense of corporate worship and Christian life.

Over fifteen centuries after Augustine, Dietrich Bonhoeffer made a similar point. Observing how Jesus used the psalms of David, Bonhoeffer claimed they don't simply inform our view of the Messiah but also should shape our corporate and personal prayers.[17] Since David's words were also the words of the incarnate Son (Heb 2:12; 10:5) and said by the Holy Spirit (Heb 3:7), Bonhoeffer believed that in some mysterious sense the "future Messiah" spoke these original words in and through David.[18] Such a claim does not erase the historical David or the particularity of his personal cries but acknowledges a form of identity and link between David's voice, the Messiah's, and ours (corporate and individual). These are Jesus's prayers that we also hear, benefit from, and then personally express by echoing them ourselves. Thus Bonhoeffer asks the obvious question: "Who prays the Psalter?"

> David (Solomon, Asaph, etc.) prays. Christ prays. We pray. We who pray are, first of all, the whole community of faith in which alone the entire richness of the Psalter can be prayed. But those who pray are also, finally, all individuals insofar as they have a part in Christ and in their congregation and share in the praying of their prayer.

---

16. Matera, *Praying the Psalms*, 178.
17. Dietrich Bonhoeffer, *Prayerbook of the Bible: An Introduction to the Psalms*, trans. James H. Burtness, ed. Geffrey B. Kelly (Minneapolis: Fortress, 1996).
18. Bonhoeffer, *Prayerbook*, 159.

David, Christ, the congregation, I myself—wherever we consider all these things with one another, we become aware of the wonderful path that God follows in order to teach us to pray.[19]

This overlapping of action is central to my own application of *totus Christus*, which illuminates not only the reading of the Psalms but also corporate worship and Christian life. The elements of our church services (e.g., singing, offering, preaching, etc.) must be not simply lyrically grounded in Scripture but also experienced in light of the gospel. Along these lines, while there is a sense of the incarnation connecting *all* of humanity, Kimberly Baker argues that the *totus Christus* is *particularly relevant for the body of Christ*, who have entered the covenant community concretely through baptism, and who then participate in the Eucharist and regular corporate worship.[20] Christ leads his people in worship, and we as his body—composed of particular believers organically connected in the unity of Christ's body—participate in the incarnate Son's worship of God by the action of his Spirit in and among us.

As a Protestant, I recognize that we need to insert some clarifications here to avoid some easily made errors or misunderstandings. The union of Christ with his people is not the exact same as the union of the divine and human natures of Christ, nor the same as the eternal perichoretic union of Father, Son, and Holy Spirit; nor do we want to be heard as saying that the ongoing, earthly church is the actual incarnation of Christ or his replacement.[21] We distinguish the hypostatic union from the mystical union without collapsing either of them, and we maintain the Creator-creature distinction even while affirming the full humanity and full deity of the incarnate Son and affirming that believers are truly united to Christ by faith.[22] Additionally, as John Webster chastens, we should be able to recognize a distinction "between Christ and the objects of his mercy"—if that is lost in one's view of *totus Christus*, then we have

---

19. Bonhoeffer, *Prayerbook*, 160.
20. Kimberly Baker, "Augustine's Doctrine of the *Totus Christus*: Reflecting on the Church as Sacrament of Unity," *Horizons* 37, no. 1 (2010): 14–15.
21. E.g., Polan, the Reformed scholastic quipped, "*Totus Christus* is everywhere, but not the *totum Christi*, i.e. both the natures." Polan (6.16), quoted in Heinrich Heppe, *Reformed Dogmatics*, ed. Ernst Bizer, trans. G. T. Thomson (Eugene, OR: Wipf & Stock, 2007), 443.
22. For further discussion and distinctions surrounding the *totus Christus*, I especially recommend the symposium found in *Pro Ecclesia: A Journal of Catholic and Evangelical Theology*, including contributions from John David Moser, Kevin J. Vanhoozer, Michael Allen, and Michael S. Horton, in *Pro Ecclesia* 29, no. 1 (2020): 3–52. See also John Behr, "Totus Christus: The Perennial Task of Regaining Wholeness," *Pro Ecclesia* 28, no. 4 (2019): 355–61.

real problems.²³ We also do well to remember that a biblical conception of *totus Christus* must admit this is not a statement about all humanity but—to use biblical language—about those "in Christ" who "belong to Christ" and are "found in him" (e.g., Gal 5:24; Phil 3:9). While incarnation links the Son with all humanity, only those united to him by the Spirit are considered within the *totus Christus*, members of his body.²⁴ No version of the *totus Christus* is valid if it replaces the historical and heavenly person of Christ, or undermines a theology of grace, or belittles the significance of faith.²⁵ *Totus Christus* cannot mean the church is in any way contributing to our salvation. No, salvation is in Christ alone (*solus Christus*) by grace alone (*sola gratia*), but having been united to Christ by the Spirit, we are also united to his people, the church. And so with all of these warnings, we should still recognize that a strong view of God's people united to Christ by the Spirit is at the heart of a Protestant view of Christian life, especially for those of us who, like me, are so deeply shaped by the likes of the Puritan John Owen, one of many who happily and strongly affirmed as much.²⁶ But our purpose here is not to further unpack Augustine's ancient position or other related debates; instead, I will assume the version of *totus Christus* noted above and apply it to corporate worship in a way that I hope shows how our theology of Christian life can be reflected and reinforced every Lord's Day.

TOTUS CHRISTUS AND CORPORATE WORSHIP

Let me add to the previous section by more fully describing the proposed connection between the *totus Christus* and the corporate worship service.

Just as Augustine applies a hermeneutic in which one is able to hear the various voices of Christ and his people in the Psalms, I believe we would do well to imagine our corporate worship services in a similar

---

23. John Webster, "On Evangelical Ecclesiology," in *Confessing God: Essays in Christian Dogmatics II* (London: T&T Clark, 2005), 174.
24. Cf. John Webster, "On Evangelical Ecclesiology," esp.167–69, 184.
25. Karl Barth, *Church Dogmatics* 4.2, *The Doctrine of Reconciliation*, ed. G. W. Bromiley and T. F. Torrance, trans. G. W. Bromiley (London: T&T Clark, 1958), §64, p. 60.
26. For more on Owen's view, see R. Robert Baylor, "'One with Him in Spirit': Mystical Union and the Humanity of Christ in the Theology of John Owen," in *"In Christ" in Paul: Explorations in Paul's Theology of Union and Participation*, ed. Michael J. Thate, Kevin J. Vanhoozer, and Constantine R. Campbell (Tübingen: Mohr Siebeck, 2014), 427–52; cf. George Hunsinger, "Justification and Mystical Union with Christ: Where Does Owen Stand?," in *The Ashgate Research Companion to John Owen's Theology*, ed. Kelly M. Kapic and Mark Jones (Surrey: Ashgate, 2012), 199–211.

manner. Below I will briefly survey some historical material and lay out the basic elements or movements of the service. Once this is done, I believe we can start to "read" or "hear" those elements of corporate worship in a similar way to how we handled the Psalms: Each element arises from a particular historical setting, each points to actions and experiences of God's people from the past, and each can be used to engage us corporately and personally in the present. At the same time, the object and chief celebrant of this worship must inevitably be the incarnate Christ.

Corporate worship looks backward and forward, and in the process, it provides us with a gospel reorientation in the present. In corporate worship we can see afresh how Christ is the center of each element, not simply as the one who teaches us what to do, in a sense, but as the one who himself did it or the one to whom it points. Whether we speak of calling, prayer, or offerings, each element of corporate worship works along all three strands of the three-corded rope I introduced earlier: Messiah, ecclesia, and ego. Too often we only analyze the *I*, but that not only misses the larger whole but also misses profound aspects of the small part it concentrates on. I (*ego*) am part of the body of Christ (*ecclesia*), and that placement in the body defines who I am. We are vitally connected to the incarnate Lord (*Christos*) who lived, died, rose, and ascended, who now and forever lives for and in us. So when we gather to sing, we don't just sing *to* the Savior; we join the chorus that he himself leads (Heb 2:12). When we receive the benediction, we don't just hear of God's smiling face; we see it by beholding Christ our Mediator. When we give our offerings to share with those in need, we do so as those who have received the great offering of God himself in and through his Son and by his Spirit.

Each element of corporate worship, therefore, has an ecclesiological, christological, and personal aspect to it, each informing the other. Christ, ecclesia, and me. This is the *totus Christus*, the whole Christ. These three are not separable options but rather are dimensions of an organic whole. This doesn't mean they are equal: Clearly, Christ is the key and center and head—but head of what? He is the head of a body, his church, in which he unites us not only to himself but also to each other. Together we worship Christ and serve our King, forming communities that are enabled and commanded to show the fruit of the Spirit. "In [Christ] you [plural] also are being built together into a dwelling place for God by the Spirit" (Eph 2:22). Individuals matter to God, but these individuals are secured together "in the Beloved" (Eph 1:6). *Totus Christus*. Here oneness and distinction dwell together under the umbrella of worship: "There is one body and one Spirit—just as you were called to one hope that belongs to your call—one Lord, one faith, one baptism, one God and Father of all, who is over all and through all and in all" (Eph 4:4–6). *Together* we come to see our life in Christ and his body with special power and clarity. As a gathered people, we are regularly reminded of who Jesus is and what he has done for us, his people—the daughters and the sons of God.

Corporate worship reminds us that *God first loved us* as well as, from the human side, *Jesus first loved God for us*. Grace upon grace; love upon love. This is the love that flows from the triune God to humanity and then flows back to God through the human Savior, Jesus of Nazareth, our Priest, our King, our Prophet.

Now that we have described the *totus Christus* and started to consider its application to our weekly corporate worship services, we need to consider which elements or movements in those services can be supported biblically, historically, and theologically. My goal here is obviously not to provide a full historical treatment of how the elements arose or were decided upon, nor to argue extensively for one particular tradition. Instead, I am interested in looking at the most fundamental movements of a corporate worship service along with foundational elements in those movements and seeing how they emerge in Scripture, are supported by the ancient church, continued by most early Protestant communities, and are still held to be generally catholic. My hope is that whatever one's denominational background, these considerations will generally resonate with all readers despite the idiosyncrasies of various liturgical vocabulary and expressions.

The broad, fundamental movements (namely, calling, proclamation, Eucharist, sending) of corporate worship are made up of several elements (e.g., prayer, word, song, offering, etc.). We can appreciate the significance and effects of all these by using the *totus Christus* hermeneutic: That is, in my particularity I also worship in community with my brothers and sisters in Christ, all of us being members of the body of Christ, united with him and enjoying all the benefits of his faithfulness. We do not bring this worship to God in our own power, but it arises as the overflow of our unity with Christ, who draws us in by his Spirit to participate in his action of loving the Father.

CONSIDERING CORPORATE WORSHIP

Although there is far more biblical and historical material than I can review here, a fair-minded and generous handling of the sources can allow us to recognize some general patterns that have occurred in corporate worship through history and across traditions. We can delineate key elements of corporate worship that are roughly recognizable to just about all Christian traditions and people. While the exact expression, emphasis, and vocabulary will certainly change, we aim to highlight critical elements that in some form are found across the breadth of Christian churches. Many of the key elements (e.g., baptism) may not happen every week, but we can consider an element vital to corporate worship if it fits within one of the regular movements (e.g., calling) and is necessary for Christian practice and identity.

The list of common elements of corporate worship, as given later, takes into account the differences of expression and doctrine that different communities have. Even with those differences, there is a significant level of agreement that honors Christ and his kingdom. Thus we can honor both the differences and the reasons for them and at the same time be aware that there are recognizable analogies between *this* element of worship in one community and *that* element in another, so much so that we use the same name for both.

Before I lay out what I believe are key movements and elements of corporate worship, I would like to offer some preliminary historical comments.

Preliminary Comments on Determining Corporate Practices

First, one cannot appreciate early expressions of corporate Christian worship without appreciating the Hebrew Scriptures and the importance of Jewish practices. The regular gathered worship times of the earliest Christians normally occurred against the backdrop of a synagogue framework.[27] Synagogues began more like schools for scriptural study

---

27. While in recent decades some scholars have raised serious questions about "synagogues" before the temple's destruction, there remains good reason to affirm that Jesus and those who followed him attended synagogue settings and engaged in synagogue practices. See James D. G. Dunn, "Did Jesus Attend the Synagogue?," in *Jesus and Archaeology*, ed. James H. Charlesworth (Grand Rapids: Eerdmans, 2006), 206–22. However, it is more than fair to raise questions about how many later synagogue practices can be dated back to the first century. This remains an ongoing debate.

and fellowship before eventually becoming places of ceremonial worship.[28] For instance, Luke 4 describes Jesus reading from the scroll and proclaiming that the day of the Lord is at hand, while other texts describe postresurrection events of conversion (e.g., Acts 13:13–52) in synagogues in response to sermons citing the Hebrew Scriptures. It is reasonable to recognize that emerging Christian conceptions of corporate worship grow out of the Scriptures of the Old Testament (2 Tim 3:16) and have some links to contemporary synagogue services.[29]

In the Diaspora, the scattered Jews used these gathering spaces to center their lives on the Torah while they were far from the temple. Such places continued to increase in importance after the temple's destruction. Thus, while it is hard to date exactly when particular ceremonial practices started, we do know that eventually something like a synagogue liturgy often took this basic form:[30] (1) the invocation, (2) the *Shema Israel* and its blessings, (3) the Eighteen Benedictions (sometimes known as the central prayer or the standing prayer), (4) the priestly or Aaronic blessing, (5) readings from the Torah and Prophets, (6) a homily by a rabbi (local or visiting), (7) psalms (normally sung), and (8) since the thirteenth century, the *Aleinu leshabei'ach* or the obligation to praise God at the conclusion of services. It is not hard to see possible liturgical parallels with expressions of corporate worship in emerging Christian churches.

As Christianity spread, small churches in their own diaspora surfaced, far from the land where Jesus lived, died, and rose, but the early Christians remained connected to their Savior as they gathered with his people in the Spirit around the sacred texts. Like the (later?)[31] synagogue gatherings, early Christians read and explained the Scriptures, offered invocations and prayers, sang Psalms and hymns and spiritual songs, and pronounced benedictions and blessings. Early Christian corporate worship gatherings read the earlier Hebrew Scriptures as well as the more recent writings of the apostles, and they were likely influenced in

---

28. Cf. John S. Kloppenborg, "The Theodotos Synagogue Inscription and the Problem of the First-Century Synagogue Buildings," in Charlesworth, *Jesus and Archaeology* (Grand Rapids: Eerdmans, 2006), esp. 278–79.

29. Cf. C. W. Dugmore, *The Influence of the Synagogue upon the Divine Office* (Westminster: Faith, 1964).

30. Here I am drawing directly from Frank C. Senn, *Christian Liturgy: Catholic and Evangelical* (Minneapolis: Fortress, 1997), 68–70. He more fully unpacks some of these practices, but I cannot do so here. Again, we are only making modest claims about how early to date these liturgical elements.

31. Some believe this reflects later synagogue material; for those interested in more on that debate, see sources noted above that mention synagogues as a way into this controversy.

many ways by Jewish practices. Their use of these practices, however, inevitably took on a distinctive interpretation in light of the gospel. While we should not overstate the level of agreement on details, we nonetheless can see general patterns emerging, and some of those have clear links to the Hebrew Bible and even later synagogue services.

Second, we should admit that the New Testament does not lay out any precise Christian order of worship. We furthermore must keep in mind Paul F. Bradshaw's warning against concluding that in the earliest church there was any form of "panliturgism" in which everyone simply took Jewish rituals and slightly modified them, or that all Christian congregations followed any kind of common lectionary or agreed-upon service.[32] That is far too mechanical and less organic than what must have been the case. Of course, the New Testament informs our understanding of a Christian service, but it doesn't, in any straightforward or simple manner, lay out a church polity or an order of worship.

Adaptation and contextualization have always been part of the church's corporate experience, for good and for ill. At their best, the church's methods grow out of the authoritative Old and New Testaments, and are implemented only after careful (and critical) observation of how the ancient and later church received those Scriptures and sought to put them into practice. Out of this pattern we gain liturgical guidance. But we must admit that none of us exposit or apply the Scriptures in a vacuum. As Stephen Holmes memorably said, "Tradition is what both links us to, and separates us from, the prophets and apostles who wrote the Scriptures."[33] Therefore, we look to Scripture and tradition not because we treat the former as authoritative as the latter but in recognition that we cannot approach the Bible apart from the gift (and hindrance) of tradition—or more accurately, *traditions*! This is true of all of us, no matter our denomination, polity, or hermeneutic. We should be keenly aware of this dynamic when discussing the pattern or shape of corporate worship services.

We must avoid both romanticizing church history and treating it so selectively that it perfectly supports our particular tradition and no other. Learning to appreciate genuine and reasonable disagreement within the

---

32. Paul F. Bradshaw, *The Search for the Origins of Christian Worship: Sources and Methods for the Study of Early Liturgy* (New York: Oxford University Press, 1992), e.g., 30–40.

33. Stephen R. Holmes, *Listening to the Past: The Place of Tradition in Theology* (Grand Rapids: Baker Academic, 2002), 5.

family of God is essential for the global church. Becoming more aware of the breadth and depth of the Christian tradition(s) often deepens our faith, even if it also complicates it. While we may believe that our particular conclusions are clearly drawn from Scripture, we do well to recognize that our application of particular texts to corporate worship is often based on a centuries-old (or sometimes just decades-old) received reading that has been passed along to us, often without our awareness that we are receiving a particular tradition. This process is so powerful yet so subtle that we may think our interpretation is utterly obvious when in fact it is simply what we have been taught. Yet not all godly believers see the same things we see in Scripture. In our interpretation, we often feast on the meals prepared long ago by brothers and sisters we don't even know. But just because one doesn't know the name of the chef who prepared our banquet doesn't mean the food just magically appeared on a plate.

Our ignorance of the past doesn't mean we are not dependent upon it. Other believers who also hold to Scripture's authority might view the same texts and their implications differently, often because different interpretive traditions shape them. When Scripture is our ultimate source and authority for Christian worship and life, that principle also must remind us to appreciate the work of others who have wrestled with and rested in those Scriptures long before us. This includes many who come from different Christian traditions than our own. And since we want to be as catholic as possible in our formulation of corporate worship, the more universally accepted our basic conclusions are, the greater confidence we can have that we are understanding and applying Holy Scripture faithfully. Again, I am aiming here to outline a broad and foundational approach to the task of studying Christian worship, not trying to specify the results of that task. The approach lays out some tools and methods and attitudes for a scripturally based, Spirit-led enterprise.

Third, significant aspects of worship cannot receive here the attention they deserve, so we should be aware of how our omissions can create blind spots. For example, years ago, C. F. D. Moule warned about determining the various "components of worship" in the earliest church and throughout history and yet ignoring how embodied these practices were and why that matters so much. Physicality, for example, connects the "outward" with the "inward" in our theology and practice of corporate worship. When we ignore the body, physical movement, volume, tone, and so on, our conclusions likely will not fit the constraints that those factors impose on practice.³⁴ "Whether for Judaism or for Christianity, the absence of scope for rhythmic movement, for choral chanting, for the throwing of the whole body into the expression of worship, is going to make a considerable difference—perhaps both for better and for worse—in the whole manner of worship."³⁵ Similarly, the garments that were worn and the physical spaces of worship that were inhabited—all of these deeply matter. So even though I cannot draw attention to all these physical, spatial, and related factors, I want to acknowledge that the absence of that attention does impoverish what could have been a more robust treatment if this study had not been so restricted. Yet I will say that a strong theological emphasis on (1) the incarnate Christ, (2) the localized gathered people of God, and (3) activated personal agency in such worship-oriented spaces lays the groundwork for an even more practicable appreciation of corporate worship and its larger significance.

With these preliminary remarks in mind, we are finally ready for an all-too-brief biblical and historical survey.

Biblical and Historical Background

All of the Hebrew Bible puts a strong emphasis on worshiping only Yahweh, avoiding idolatry, and obeying the creator God: Each of these is framed corporately and applicable individually.³⁶ There is only one God worthy of Israel's worship, and Israel should look to him as governor and guide for every area of life. It necessarily follows that directing praise to, showing dependence upon, or expressing reverence toward other so-called gods is a rebellious violation of trust, compromising those made in God's image, distorting their loves and values, and wrecking shalom. God's redemptive response to that human rebellion and the failure of their worship follows a distinct pattern: The exodus precedes Sinai (i.e., rescue

---

34. Cf. Frank C. Senn, *Embodied Liturgy: Lessons in Christian Ritual* (Minneapolis: Fortress, 2016). More recently, see W. David O. Taylor, *A Body of Praise: Understanding the Role of our Physical Bodies in Worship* (Grand Rapids: Baker Academic, 2023).

35. C. F. D. Moule, *Worship in the New Testament* (Richmond: John Knox, 1961), 12–13.

36. For more on worship in the Hebrew Scriptures, see esp. the classic and important newer treatments in Roland de Vaux, *Ancient Israel: Its Life and Institutions*, trans. John McHugh (London: DLT, 1961), esp. 269–517; Hans-Joachim Kraus, *Worship in Israel: A Cultic History of the Old Testament*, trans. Geoffrey Buswell (Oxford: Blackwell, 1965); John Eaton, *Vision in Worship: The Relation of Prophecy and Liturgy in the Old Testament* (London: SPCK, 1981); Samuel E. Balentine, *The Torah's Vision of Worship* (Minneapolis: Fortress, 1999); Walter Brueggemann, *Worship in Ancient Israel* (Nashville: Abington, 2005); Andrew Hill, "Old Testament and Worship," in *Theological Foundations of Worship: Biblical, Systematic, and Practical Perspectives*, ed. Khalia J. Williams and Mark A. Lamport (Grand Rapids: Baker Academic, 2021), 3–19.

before law). This pattern occurs in several God-given covenants with more details in each. The pattern also dominates the warnings that address the hard hearts and covenant-breaking tendencies of Israel. God also established priests and prophets, sacrifices and prayers, kings and laws to teach Israel the nature of his holiness and his determination to purify an impure people. Both the explicit worship described in Leviticus and the implicit worship of obedience and faithfulness described in Deuteronomy shape the whole relation between God and his people: Love, faith, repentance, and obedience were the appropriate human responses to Yahweh's character, provision, compassion, righteousness, and love. The temple stood at the center of Israel's imagination of this movement.

With this backdrop, the New Testament identifies Israel's Messiah in the opening half of the first century as the unique Word of God who came and tabernacled (Gk. *eskēnōsen*) among God's people (John 1:14). He alone is the visible image of the invisible God (Col 1:15), always dependent upon the Father in the power of the Spirit, perfectly loving God and neighbor (John 3:34; cf. Matt 22:36–40; Mark 12:30–32). Continuity from the Old Testament to Jesus is illustrated in his fulfillment (Gk. *plērōsai*)—not rejection—of God's good and perfect law, which, along with the writings of the prophets, acted to protect shalom and foster love (Matt 5:17). The Messiah's obedience to and fulfillment of the Law and the Prophets, as the perfect embodiment of love, constitutes the complete and appropriate human response to God—worship!

Yet Jesus also willingly takes on Israel's failings and covenantal unfaithfulness (cf. Jesus's baptism). Specifically, as covenant keeper, he binds himself to the covenant breakers. He announced himself to be the King who was ushering in God's kingdom, prophetically calling people to repentance and faith. Climactically, in and through his crucifixion, Jesus absorbs the judgment and exile of his people on their behalf: On the cross he not only embodies divine love but also demonstrates himself to be exactly who John the Baptist said he was—the very Lamb of God who takes away the sin of the world (John 1:29, 36). Jesus's life, death, resurrection, and ascension not only execute divine judgment against the disruption of shalom and true worship but also accomplish divine forgiveness and new life, giving rise to a new creation where shalom and worship are freely actualized by bringing God's people into communion with God and neighbor. The New Testament thus proclaims Jesus to be the fulfillment of the Law, Wisdom, and Prophets that constitute the Hebrew Scriptures. In this way his unique person, position, and actions shape Christian approaches to worship.[37] Hebrews, for example, traces the threefold nature of Christ's priestly work, including his past earthly life and once-for-all sacrifice (*ephapax*; e.g., Heb 10:10), his present ongoing heavenly work as exalted Lord (*eis to diēnekes*; Heb 7:26), and his action as the one who will come again to rescue and save (*ek deuterou*; Heb 9:28; 10:9).[38] Jesus is both the leader of our praise to God and the appropriate object of our worship and praise. The ecclesia, therefore, eventually became the people and location for this worship to be concretely expressed in corporate gatherings.

How clearly can we identify and assess the corporate worship practices that emerged in the post-Pentecost church? This question becomes especially pressing since we are sometimes reminded that there is no Leviticus in the Newer Testament.

Detailed discussions and debates would take us well beyond the scope of this study, but we can give samples of key findings. Oscar Cullmann, for example, observes that from the beginning of Christian worship as recorded in the New Testament (e.g., Acts 2:42, 46; 20:7), elements of corporate worship included instruction and/or preaching, prayer, and breaking of bread.[39] These gatherings often included full meals, which could occasionally lead to too much drinking, chaos, offense, and other problems (cf. 1 Cor 11:17–34; 14:27–33). As these assemblies began to pop up, they had strong similarities to other first-century "associations" connected to different deities or trades;[40] in other words, such gatherings were familiar to people in the first century.

From early on, Christian meetings were marked by a shared meal. Many believe that the Lord's Supper mentioned in Paul's correspondence to the Corinthian church had been happening from a fairly early date. Such events are often understood as the tradition behind Luke's rendering of the Last Supper and then combined with a "symposium" by about

---

[37]. For good examples of trying to cover both the Old and New Testament accounts of worship, I recommend beginning with Allen P. Ross, *Recalling the Hope of Glory: Biblical Worship from the Garden to the New Creation* (Grand Rapids: Kregel, 2006); and Daniel I. Block, *For the Glory of God: Recovering a Biblical Theology of Worship* (Grand Rapids: Baker Academic, 2014).

[38]. Oscar Cullmann, *The Christology of the New Testament*, rev. ed., trans. Shirley C. Guthrie and Charles A. M. Hall (Philadelphia: Westminster, 1963), 103–4.

[39]. Oscar Cullmann, *Early Christian Worship*, Studies in Biblical Theology (London: SCM, 1969), 12–20.

[40]. See John S. Kloppenborg, *Christ's Associations: Connecting and Belonging in the Ancient City* (New Haven, CT: Yale University Press, 2019).

AD 85 (Acts 20:7–12).[41] Valeriy A. Alikin follows the Corinthian material to trace these practices: (1) blessings over cup and bread, (2) Lord's Supper, (3) singing, (4) teaching, (5) revelations, (6) speaking in tongues, and (7) interpretations.[42] Even here, however, the available material does not establish a clear, distinct order of worship.

As these early gatherings took shape, the worship reflected a Christ-centered nature. Yet the material gives no sense of worship being directed to a new or foreign god because the participants treat the God of Abraham and Malachi and the God of Mary and Paul as one. Here different deities are not worshiped, but the same God, who is now fully revealed in the resurrected Son by his Spirit (cf. 1 Thess 1:9–10). Thus worship is *to* and *through* Christ. Notice, however, that unlike in contemporary parlance, the word *church* is not primarily about a physical building but about a community of believers who come together—usually in homes or other agreed upon spaces (e.g., Acts 20:7–8)—to worship the God and Father of the Lord Jesus Christ.

A repetition of basic worship elements does begin to surface, providing some guidance for our examination. Larry Hurtado's work helpfully shows the distinctly christological orientation of the earliest Christian worship. The general devotional practices that emerge early on are marked by "reverence given as part of the cultic pattern of early Christian groups," which demonstrates how Jesus was central to their corporate worship in these elements: (1) prayer, (2) invocation and confession, (3) baptism, (4) the Lord's Supper, (5) hymns, and (6) prophecy (often linked with teaching).[43] Examining both the continuities and discontinuities, Charles H. H. Scobie sees much in common between patterns of corporate worship in the Old Testament and the patterns that emerge in the New Testament. According to Scobie, both sets of patterns involve (1) "preparation" (OT: circumcision and purification practices; NT: circumcision and then baptism), (2) prayer, (3) praise, (4) Scripture

---

41. See Valeriy A. Alikin, *The Earliest History of Christian Gathering: Origin, Development and Content of the Christian Gathering in the First to Third Centuries*, Supplements to Vigiliae Christianae (Leiden: Brill, 2010), 293. Drawing on the work of Kathleen E. Corley, *Private Women, Public Meals: Social Conflict in the Synoptic Tradition* (Peabody: Hendrickson, 1993), 17, this combination is further explained: "A supper with an ensuing symposium was the setting in which the followers of Jesus, Pauline groups as well as other Christian communities, came together for sharing their beliefs, their joys and their concerns." Alikin, *The Earliest History of Christian Gathering*, 30–31.

42. For a helpful chart, see Alikin, *The Earliest History of Christian Gathering*, 294.

43. Larry Hurtado, *At the Origins of Christian Worship: The Context of Earliest Christian Devotion* (Grand Rapids: Eerdmans, 1999), esp. 74–94. For Hurtado's exhaustive treatment of this topic, see *Lord Jesus Christ: Devotion to Jesus in Earliest Christianity* (Grand Rapids: Eerdmans, 2003).

reading, (5) preaching, (6) almsgiving, and (7) sacrifice (OT: offerings; NT: Lord's Supper).[44] Additionally, there is some real continuity (despite some discontinuity) with later second- and third-century practices. All of these patterns show key movements and common elements.

Although we find similarities between the patterns in both testaments and from place to place around the Mediterranean, we do not find evidence that everyone used exactly the same elements, nor should we think, as an earlier generation of scholars appeared to believe, that the earliest churches neatly and consistently followed one particular order.[45] We find variation and flexibility alongside similarity and continuity. In the relevant debates, I find Robert E. Webber's three summary statements to be both accurate and helpful as a starting point for considering New Testament worship:[46]

1. Christ superseded the temple cult and Jewish ritual.
2. The common source of Christian worship is rooted in the Christ event.
3. The New Testament does not provide a complete picture of worship.

We do well to make sure our visions of corporate worship and Christian life grow out of the soil of the Hebrew Bible, for Christians are dependent upon the root of Jesse. Additionally, the absence of a *Book of Church Order* in the New Testament doesn't mean that it gives no guidance for our corporate worship, nor that Leviticus is no longer relevant—we can't understand Jesus or the Gospels without the Hebrew Scriptures. It is because God's people now worship the Messiah, the very one to whom Moses, the prophets, all the ancient rituals and sacrifices, and the temple pointed (cf. Luke 24:25–27), that we can understand those elements of Old Testament worship better and gain wisdom from them.

Jesus's life, death, resurrection, and ongoing heavenly life now frame our theology of worship as well as its practice. As a result, we recognize that Christian worship has Jesus not only as our object of worship but as

---

44. Charles H. H. Scobie, *The Ways of Our God: An Approach to Biblical Theology* (Grand Rapids: Eerdmans, 2003), ch. 14, esp. 578–82, 597–602. He goes into much more detail (e.g., when and where), but this also is the context for what makes up the heart of the corporate gathering.

45. E.g., Gregory Dix, *The Shape of the Liturgy* (London: Dacre, 1945).

46. Robert E. Webber, *Worship Old and New: A Biblical, Historical, and Practical Introduction*, rev. ed. (Grand Rapids: Zondervan, 1994), 48–49.

the leader of our worship. This has been vital to Christ-followers from the beginning, and it also helps make more sense of why groups like the Ebionites (an early form of adoptionism) surface.[47] Ebionites happily affirmed Jesus was a faithful Jew who worshiped God without fault or failure, but *they stopped there*. Orthodox Christians become known as those who echo Thomas, who looked into the eyes of the resurrected Jesus and declared, "My Lord and my God!" (John 20:28). Jesus is thus both the faithful worshiper and the object of our worship. A theology of Christian life requires that we declare both!

The noncanonical *Didache*—which some scholars date as early as the late first century[48]—displays at least five movements in corporate worship: (1) confession of sins, (2) eucharistic prayers, (3) eucharistic meal, (4) thanksgiving prayers, and (5) teaching and other activities.[49] Valeria Alikin notes evidence of similar aspects in corporate gatherings recorded in other noncanonical, pseudepigraphal writings.[50]

All around the Mediterranean basin, early Christian corporate worship regularly included common elements, despite some genuine differences.[51] From North Africa we have evidence from Tertullian, Cyprian, and later Augustine; from Egypt, we have Clement of Alexandria's early notes, then more in Origen, and the classic fuller material found in the fourth-century *Apostolic Church Order Canons of Hippolytus*; Syria is the location of the early material from the *Didache* as well as second-century material from Ignatius and the *Epistle of Barnabas*, and in the fourth century we have the important *Apostolic Constitutions*; out of Asia Minor we learn from Pliny's early second century report, but later the most

---

47. See Andrew Gregory, ed., *The Gospel According to the Hebrews and the Gospel of the Ebionites*, Oxford Early Christian Gospel Texts (Oxford: Oxford University Press, 2017).

48. NB, others argue for a second-century setting. Either way, it is very early!

49. *Didache*, 9–10. Again, cf. Alikin, *The Earliest History of Christian Gathering*, 294, whose wording and arrangement I find so helpful I am drawing on her throughout.

50. For example, the Acts of Paul mentions prophetic discourse, a eucharistic meal, and singing (ch. 9); the Acts of Peter in one place highlights the eucharistic meal, admonition, and intercessory prayer (ch. 1–2), and then later highlights the reading of Scripture, giving of a sermon, intercessory prayer, healings, and then the eucharistic meal (chs. 20–22); the Acts of John observes the practices of a sermon, prayer, eucharist, imposition of hands, and healing (ch. 46, cf. chs. 106–10, which is a slightly less complete); and finally, the Acts of Paul and Thecla simply note prayer, eucharistic meal, and sermon (ch. 3.5). Because I found Alikin's single-word summaries both accurate and helpful, I am here following the language and lists from *The Earliest History of Christian Gathering*, 294–95.

51. For a quick overview of the global nature of where this material is gathered from, see James F. White, *Documents of Christian Worship: Descriptive and Interpretive Sources* (Louisville: Westminster John Knox, 1992), 6, 8, 10–11. For a more recent massive gathering of such sources, see Lawrence J. Johnson's four-volume set, *Worship in the Early Church: An Anthology of Historical Sources* (Collegeville, MN: Liturgical, 2010). Together, the four volumes cover from the first through the sixth century.

important records of worship appear in Basil, Chrysostom, Theodore, and the *Testamentum Domini*; from later in Jerusalem we have Cyril and the female pilgrim Egeria (fourth century); and in Milan, Ambrose (fourth century) and Cassian (fifth century) produced similar material; all of this in addition to the literature on worship coming out of Rome, which includes the late first century material in *1 Clement*, the crucial Justin Martyr discussions in the second century, the *Apostolic Tradition* in the third century, Jerome in the fourth, and Benedict and Gregory I in the sixth century. While corporate worship clearly was not uniform from place to place, two other points emerge even more clearly: (1) *As the gospel of Christ and his kingdom spread across the Mediterranean world, believers regularly gathered for corporate worship directed toward Christ*, and (2) as we might reasonably expect, given that their object of worship was the same and their understanding of him was remarkably similar, *the actions and words involved in that worship were remarkably similar from place to place.* Different places had different degrees of emphasis on the various elements (e.g., Scripture, Eucharist, prayer). Some sources mention many elements, while others mention only a few. Of course, we must remember that just because something isn't explicitly stated, that doesn't mean it didn't happen. Likewise, we should not assume that the lists are complete, nor can we say that just because something is listed in one location, it must have been practiced everywhere Christians gathered. For example, we are not told if the extended reading of Scripture was interspersed with the singing of psalms, yet in later synagogue settings, this was the case; consequently, many scholars assume that, even if not mentioned, the congregations sang.[52] Going through each and every relevant patristic passage and other key material from ancient, medieval, Reformation, early modern, and contemporary church gatherings is beyond our scope here. From a general survey, however, we can acknowledge the practice of basic movements of corporate worship (e.g., gathering, sending, etc.) and the most basic elements (e.g., prayer, singing, offerings, etc.).

The fact that second- and third-century expressions of worship take a certain shape doesn't necessarily mean we can read that shape back into the New Testament, nor does it necessarily mean that these sources represent the practice of the church in all locales and cultural settings. My claim is somewhat more modest: I am only looking for the practices

---

52. E.g., Bard Thompson, ed., *Liturgies of the Western Church* (New York: Meridian, 1961), 4.

of corporate worship that both are widely used and reflect a basically biblical and catholic consensus.

At this point, let us narrowly focus on a classic passage that is dated somewhere between AD 155 and 157. In his *First Apology*, Justin Martyr patiently introduces the outsider or newcomer to some basic Christian thought and practice, without getting overly detailed. We could compare this to what we commonly find on many church websites these days, under the "What to expect" heading. One difference is that, for Justin and the early church, the Eucharist services were not always public since they required not merely intellectual assent but also the mark of baptism.[53] We will focus here only on the regular gatherings that took place on Sunday. As leading liturgical scholar Maxwell E. Johnson observes, while there is some debate about how this service described by Justin was related to earlier Jewish synagogue-style services, it is generally agreed that "the ritual skeleton provided by Justin is discernible in every Christian Eucharistic tradition thereafter."[54] In other words, while the passage does not imply a universal uniformity, it does indicate patterns that appeared in much of the church throughout its history. Given this passage's importance, let me quote extensively from it:

> On the day which is called Sunday we have a common assembly of all who live in the cities or in the outlying districts, and the memoirs of the Apostles or the writings of the Prophets are read, as long as there is time. Then, when the reader has finished, the president of the assembly verbally admonishes and invites all to imitate such examples of virtue. Then we all stand up together and offer up our prayers, and, as we said before, after we finish our prayers, bread and wine and water are presented. He who presides likewise offers up prayers and thanksgivings, to the best of his ability, and the people express their approval by saying "Amen." The Eucharistic elements are distributed and consumed by those present, and to those who are absent they are sent through the deacons. The wealthy, if they wish, contribute whatever they desire, and the collection is placed in the custody of the president. [With it] he helps the orphans and widows, those who are needy because of sickness or any other reason, and the

---

53. E.g., Justin Martyr, *First Apology*, §66.
54. Maxwell E. Johnson, "Worship, Practice, and Belief," in *The Early Christian World: Vol. I–II*, ed. Philip F. Esler (London: Routledge, 2000), 481.

captives and strangers in our midst; in short, he takes care of all those in need. Sunday, indeed, is the day on which we all hold our common assembly because it is the first day on which God, transforming the darkness and [prime] matter, created the world; and our Savior Jesus Christ arose from the dead on the same day. For they crucified Him on the day before that of Saturn, and on the day after, which is Sunday, He appeared to His Apostles and disciples, and taught them the things which we have passed on to you also for consideration.[55]

While there are some legitimate cautions about claiming that this statement from Justin reflected every Sunday gathering of Christians in all parts of the Mediterranean world, his outline does anticipate much of what we find in the later church universal, with most of the basic elements continuing across Christian traditions to this day. The details may look and sound different, and the emphases will certainly change between the communities of faith, but something like the following elements often remains:

- weekly corporate worship in a meeting place
- statement-and-response action between the leader(s) of the service and the congregation (e.g., "Amen")
- reading of Scripture (e.g., apostles, prophets)
- exposition and application of those biblical texts (by a president or pastor)
- prayers offered
- Eucharist (Lord's Supper and expressions of thanksgiving)
- offerings collected (with special focus on the care of the vulnerable and the materially poor)
- all done in light of Jesus the Messiah's cross and resurrection, dependent upon the apostle's explanation of the Christ event's significance, and in connection with God's original creation
- kiss of peace (not in the material here, but noted earlier)[56]
- baptism (not mentioned here, but noted earlier)[57]

---

55. Justin Martyr, *The First Apology, The Second Apology, Dialogue with Trypho, Exhortation to the Greeks, Discourse to the Greeks, The Monarchy or The Rule of God*, trans. Thomas B. Falls, Fathers of the Church: A New Translation 6 (Washington, DC: Catholic University of America Press, 1948), 105–7.
56. Justin Martyr, *The First Apology*, §65, p. 105.
57. Justin Martyr, *The First Apology*, §65, pp. 104–5.

A few quick observations of Justin's writing can help us. First, *the theological context was the worship of the triune God.* Justin considered that God's people received everything they had as a gift from God, and this God was explicitly and specifically the triune God. In the line immediately before the material quoted above, Justin observes that "we make a blessing to the Creator of all things, through his Son Jesus Christ and through the Holy Spirit." Second, *the triune shape of responding to God did not exclude Christocentrism but rather anchored it.* All blessings come from this God, and all responses in worship and life are to this God. Thus the believers gathered and worshiped on Sunday because the first day—Sunday—was both the first day of the creation of the world and the day of Jesus's resurrection and the renewal of that creation. Jesus's life, death, and resurrection shaped the corporate gathering, from *when* they met to *what* they believed to *how* they responded. Their practices—from prayers and praises to calls for growth in virtue—all point to the life and work of Christ. Finally, *social and economic factors of the kingdom shaped the gatherings.* Justin begins by saying that their community is one in which "the rich among us come to the aid of the poor, and we always stay together," and on the special day of Sunday those living in the "cities or in the countryside gather together in one place."[58] In and through corporate worship and practice, the kingdom of heaven and its shalom invade this present divided and disordered world, making the church a light on a hill for all to see (Matt 5:14–15).

While we could look further at this historical background, we also must recognize just how much variety there really was and admit how limited our understanding of the specifics remains. It is easy for us to group things together that actually might not have always been done together or to imagine everything was in a "sacramental" setting, when in fact that may not have been the case.[59] Not all preaching or hymn singing appears to be accompanied with Eucharist or baptism, and it appears that some settings might have included one or both of these even if they were not treated sacramentally. Eventually, some strong patterns seem to have solidified, but let us not overstate them.

---

58. The quotes from Justin in this paragraph all come from *The First Apology of Justin Martyr,* §67, in Thompson, *Liturgies of the Western Church,* 8–9.
59. E.g., C. F. D. Moule, *Worship in the New Testament* (Richmond: John Knox, 1961), 61–66.

US TO GOD

General Consensus? Key Movements and Elements

Building upon this all-too-brief survey of texts from the Scriptures and ancient church history, let's jump to the general consensus that I see emerging from those documents. By the middle of the twentieth century, scholars argued that at least a basic fourfold movement or structure of liturgy is identifiable from early in the church: *gathering, word, meal,* and *dismissal*.[60] Having roots in the Scriptures and developing its expression in the ancient church, this basic outline shows up across the breadth of Christian traditions, from Lutheran to Roman Catholic, Presbyterian, Episcopal, and Methodist.[61]

Different traditions tend to focus more on one movement than another. For example, many congregational churches emphasize the proclamation of the Word, while Anglicans center their worship gathering around celebrating the Eucharist. Both, however, wholeheartedly aim to worship the triune God in and through Christ, in response to the incarnate Son's provision. Both traditions value, in their own way, the importance of the corporate gathering, the life-giving power of the Word, the celebration of the Eucharist, and the power of God's sending love and guidance.

In addition to affirming these basic movements, some traditions also push us to recapture an aspect of worship that we inadvertently may have ignored or even lost. For example, Pentecostals encourage us to value congregational participation in worship,[62] Anabaptists and Mennonites help us value the "visibility" of the worshiping community,[63] and Methodist and Wesleyan churches encourage us to appreciate the relationship between worship and sanctification,[64] while the Reformed

---

60. Frank C. Senn, *Christian Liturgy: Catholic and Evangelical* (Minneapolis: Fortress, 1997), 645.

61. A detailed side-by-side chart comparing the particular liturgical elements of these traditions can be found in Senn, *Christian Liturgy*, 646–47. In this format the general overlap is obvious even amid the distinctives and disagreements among those traditions.

62. J. Kwabena Asamoah-Gyadu, "Pentecostal and Charismatic Practices of Worship," in *Historical Foundations of Worship: Catholic, Orthodox, and Protestant Perspectives*, ed. Melanie C. Ross and Mark A. Lamport (Grand Rapids: Baker Academic, 2022), 267–80, esp. 274–76. See also Steven Félix-Jäger, *Renewal Worship: A Theology of Pentecostal Doxology* (Downers Grove, IL: IVP Academic, 2022).

63. Valerie G. Rempel, "Anabaptist and Mennonite Practices of Worship," in Ross and Lamport, *Historical Foundations of Worship*, 225–39, esp. 229–30.

64. Matthew Sigler, "Methodist and Wesleyan Practices of Worship," in Ross and Lamport, *Historical Foundations of Worship*, 223.

often stress the holiness of God and the glory of Christ.[65] Roman Catholic corporate worship highlights Christ's solidarity with us and his suffering on our behalf, while the Orthodox remind us that we are not the ones who begin the worship but that our worship joins the great cloud of witnesses who are continually praising our God. Baptist sisters and brothers may push us to recognize how worship relates to the conscience and freedom.[66] We all do well to listen to other Christians and examine our own practices to make sure they reflect Scripture and the theological wisdom and practice of the church through the ages. Karl Barth reminds us that recognizing the *totus Christus* means not only looking to heaven but also valuing the small communities of Christ's body on earth:

> Although [Christ] lives also and primarily as the exalted Son of Man, at the right hand of the Father, in the hiddenness of God (with the life of Christians), at an inaccessible height above the world and the community, He does not live only there but lives too (in the power of His Holy Spirit poured out from there and working here) on earth and in world history, in the little communities at Thessalonica and Corinth and Philippi, in Galatia and at Rome.[67]

Christ lives in our local communities and inhabits our particular praises. Even when we don't all agree about theology or practice, we must be willing to identify our Lord among his diverse people. We don't want to pull up the wheat, which we mistakenly mistook for tares (Matt 13:24–30).

Another almost-universal feature of worship is its character as a kind of dialogue between God and his people. Worship is not self-generated but occurs in response to the triune God's self-revelation and the work of salvation he has accomplished. In corporate worship, we find a localized

---

65. See the work of reformedworship.org. Also see the helpful background in Jonathan Gibson and Mark Earngey, *Reformation Worship: Liturgies from the Past for the Present* (Greensboro: New Growth, 2018); Hughes Oliphant Old, *Worship That Is Reformed According to Scripture* (Atlanta: John Knox, 1984).

66. The "four fragile freedoms" of a Baptist ecclesiology, as laid out by Jennifer W. Davidson, include Bible freedom, soul freedom, church freedom, and religious freedom, with each of these influencing their practices of corporate worship. Davidson, "Baptist Practices of Worship," in Ross and Mark A. Lamport, *Historical Foundations of Worship*, 240–52, esp. 244–48.

67. Karl Barth, *Church Dogmatics* 4.2, *The Doctrine of Reconciliation* (New York: T&T Clark, 2004), 658–59.

expression of the body of Christ, a body in which each person is a vital member. As I argued earlier in the book, God not only exercises his divine agency of love, grace, and fellowship in coming to us, but also exercises human agency through Jesus's worship, obedience, and love. This twofold action is the framework for *Christian* worship: Jesus is the center, the triune God is worshiped and glorified, and together as Christ's body, God's people respond in faith, hope, and love.

So even though it is probable that not everyone will affirm my proposal, I suspect that most readers will agree that the basic structure below (in its simplest form on the left) occurs in corporate worship across the ages and still around the world today. At the same time, most readers will also agree that different communions use that basic structure in different ways. For example, some may have the minister carry out almost all the functions, while others give far more opportunity to congregational voices. Although almost all denominations administer the Eucharist, they have many different views of the bread and wine's relationship with the presence of Christ. Some communities set aside extended time for sermon exposition, while others keep homilies extremely brief. Such variety can be found across time (historically) and space (geographically). The point is not that all conduct worship services the exact same way, nor even are all agreed upon which aspects of corporate worship should be emphasized. My claim is simply that even "nonliturgical" churches usually have a basic pattern they follow, and that pattern tends to reflect a four- or fivefold movement; some will not include the Eucharist or baptism in their weekly gatherings, but most churches still view these elements as a formative communal ritual to honor and practice regularly.

It is now time to lay out the key movements and related common elements. An extremely clear, generous, and deeply helpful chart has been put together by Carrie Titcombe Steenwyk and John D. Witvliet and their team as part of *The Worship Sourcebook*.[68] A few things to note immediately: First, they see a general five-movement pattern (in the left column below) in corporate worship. Second, those movements

---

68. With permission (via John D. Witvliet) I am drawing directly from the chart found on page 25 of *The Worship Sourcebook*, 2nd ed. (Grand Rapids: Calvin Institute of Christian Worship; Faith Alive Christian Resources; Baker, 2013). I suggest this invaluable over-eight-hundred-page resource to those interested in helping construct and support weekly corporate worship. For another list that similarly lays out the flow and particular elements of corporate worship but focuses more on contemporary church expressions, see Bernard Cooke and Gary Macy, *Christian Symbol and Ritual* (Oxford: Oxford University Press, 2005), 97–98.

often have several elements in them (right column), although one should not expect all of the elements in every service. Third, they use arrows to indicate how those elements are normally understood in terms of direction: from God to us (↓), from us to God (↑), and from people to people (↔). Please review this chart, but then also try to consider how it can be interpreted in light of the *totus Christus*, or the three-corded rope I have been advocating, with Christ as our Priest, Prophet, and King:

Key Movements	Elements
	↓ = FROM GOD TO THE PEOPLE ↑ = FROM THE PEOPLE TO GOD ↔ = AMONG THE PEOPLE
Gathering [Calling]	Call to Worship ↓ Greeting ↓ Prayer of Adoration or Prayer of Invocation ↑ Call to Confession ↓ Prayer of Confession and Lament ↑↔ Assurance of Pardon ↓ Passing the Peace ↓↔ Thanksgiving ↑ The Law ↓ Dedication ↑↔
Proclamation [Word]	Prayer for Illumination ↑ Scripture Reading ↓ Sermon ↓
Response to the Word	Profession of the Church's Faith ↔ ↑ Prayers of the People ↑ Offering ↑ [Psalms, Hymns, and Spiritual Songs here and throughout]
The Lord's Supper	Declaration of God's Promises and Invitation ↓ Prayer of Thanksgiving ↑ Breaking of the Bread ↓ Communion ↓↔ Response of Thanksgiving ↑
Sending	Call to Service or Discipleship ↓ Blessing/Benediction ↓

US TO GOD

The movement of corporate worship (also known as "the liturgy") reflects God's action of shaping us in our Christian life. God calls his people, and we hear and encounter the Word and respond in faith, regularly celebrating the action of Christ in giving himself for us, that we might give ourselves back to God and others, liberated to return to the watching world as those secure in God's kind benediction and grace. God calls; believers come. God speaks; believers confess, praise, and pray. God gives life in Christ (Eucharist); believers give—especially to their neighbors (in offering and almsgiving). God gives his benediction; believers go out to be a blessing to the world.

This leads to what I might call a soft rather than hard claim: From early on in the Christian church, worship follows a basic dialectic that parallels the reciprocal actions of divine and human agency, as we have noted in this book. And so I here reiterate what I proleptically noted in our opening chapter: *Christian life reflects and is shaped by the basic contours of corporate worship, which moves in the rhythm of call and response*:

- calling invites coming;
- proclamation provokes faith, prayer, and praise;
- Eucharist grounds and enables our gratitude made manifest in offerings;
- the peace of Christ enables us to live in peace with our neighbor; and
- benediction frees and sends us out in love to sacrificially serve a broken and hurting world.

In this liturgical and theological conversation, God reveals himself through the calling, proclamation, Eucharist, passing of the peace, and benediction. Our union with Christ includes being joined to Christ's human response of attending to God; of faith, prayers, and praises; of peace making; of offerings; and even in going out into the world. This theological and liturgical flow of Christian life works along the threefold dynamic we laid out: It is christologically driven (the centrality of the Messiah), emphasizes the corporate (God's people, ecclesia, both ancient Israel and the universal church), and includes the particular and personal (me, ego). Christ both presents God to us and presents us to God. Only *in him* by the Spirit do we have new life. In this way, God in Christ, by his Spirit, envelops us in his love, grace, and fellowship, bringing the fresh waters of forgiveness, reconciliation, and purpose as he enables us to participate in his loving work in the church and world.

Corporate worship is "possible only because Jesus Christ in His earthly ministry lived a sufficient and perfect life of worship. . . . [and such worship] is true and real because Jesus Christ is freely present [in corporate worship] as Lord, abiding with those who are gathered together in his name."[69] In this way, corporate worship has the sense of the *totus Christus*: The movements or elements can be heard in a multi-dimensional manner—here is a word spoken *by* Christ, *about* Christ, and *to* Christ, as well as a word spoken *about* the church and *by* the church. Following in the Irenaean tradition, we affirm that Jesus's life, death, resurrection, ascension, and heavenly intercession are the means of saving fallen people, summing up all things, bringing new life and hope where they were absent because of sin, death, and the devil. As Prophet, Priest, and King, Jesus brings new revelation (he is the revelation!). He not only offers sacrifices, but becomes the sacrifice, and as the Servant-King he both brings his commandments and is the embodiment of faithfulness to them.[70] Just as Jesus's earthly life recapitulated all the stages of human life, so Christian worship services reflect the life of Jesus and the salvation he achieved for his people. And in this way, corporate worship also reflects the pattern and content of Christian life (e.g., calling, word, confession, praise, prayer, Eucharist, offering, and blessing). If we had the time, we could examine the pattern of recapitulation found in each element of worship, especially when approached christologically, corporately, and personally. Elsewhere I have written more fully along similar lines when dealing with the benediction[71] and lament.[72] But here I will simply mention how this might work with "calling."

"Called" as a Test Case

Worship services, certainly from the time of Moses onward, respond to God's *calling*. The word *ecclesia* comes from *ek* and *kaleō*, which means "to call forth," thus "to assemble" (e.g., Acts 9:31) in response to that

---

69. Von Allmen, *Worship*, 32.
70. For more on this, see von Allmen, *Worship*, 21–41, esp. 38 for the threefold office comments.
71. Kelly M. Kapic, "Receiving Christ's Priestly Benediction: A Biblical, Historical, and Theological Exploration of Luke 24:50–53," *Westminster Theological Journal* 67, no. 2 (2005): 247–60.
72. Kelly M. Kapic, "Psalm 22: Forsakenness and the God Who Sings," in *Theological Commentary: Evangelical Perspectives*, ed. Michael Allen (London: T&T Clark, 2011), 41–56.

calling, just as Israel's religious gatherings (cf. Heb. *qāhāl*) did. Just as the synagogue (Gk. *synagōgē*) was the location where Jews gathered to hear God's word and honor Yahweh (e.g., Matt 4:23; Luke 4:16; Acts 9:20; 15:21; Jas 2:2), Christian believers gathered as the church to worship, share gifts, and be sanctified by God (e.g., 1 Cor 14:33; 16:1; 2 Cor 1:1; 8:1–9:15, etc.). While such gatherings included the reading of scrolls, the sharing of resources, and other elements, Christian communions came into being first and foremost because they are a called-together group, called by God himself and to one another. As we already noted, *church* for the earliest Christians did not indicate a building but a gathering for worship. And this is where the language of *liturgy* comes from.[73] In Acts 13:1–2, we are told about happenings in Antioch "among the existing church [*ecclesia*]," when the Spirit moved while they were "worshiping" (*leitourgeō*). The *liturgy* was their activity in this gathering and shared worship. As Peter declares to the elect in *diaspora* in Pontus, Galatia, Cappadocia, and Bithynia: The one who "called you" (plural) is the Holy One who calls you (i.e., his people) to be holy (1 Pet 1:15). As a worshiping people "chosen and precious in God's sight," God's people are like "living stones" who are to be "built into a spiritual house, to be a holy priesthood" and a people who "offer spiritual sacrifices acceptable to God *through* Jesus Christ" (1 Pet 2:4–5 NRSVue).

While many traditions reflect the "calling" in corporate worship through explicit verbal and visual cues at the beginning of a gathering (e.g., "Come, all who are weary and heavy laden"; see Matt 11:28), even those who do not employ a formal "call to worship" still inevitably enact the sense of this element by their very gathering. So how might this work biblically, theologically, and experientially? One passage of Scripture will demonstrate the *totus Christus* or three-corded dynamic.

In Hosea 11:1 we read, "When Israel was a child, I loved him, and out of Egypt I called my son." The prophet warns that even as God

---

73. Many Christians (e.g., nondenominational) are nervous about or sometimes even repelled by the word *liturgy*. For example, they occasionally (mis-)understand it to refer to empty rituals handed down over the centuries. Thus they see Anglican and Lutheran churches as being "liturgical" while their own churches are not. Readers should understand that this book (like much of the Christian world) uses the word *liturgy* simply to mean "what we do in worship at church" and nothing else. Consequently, *every* worship service has a liturgy, even if it wasn't planned beforehand. Consequently, *liturgy* can refer to spontaneous pew-jumping as well as a confession of the Apostles' Creed; it can refer to snake-handling every bit as much as prayers in Latin or Greek or Hebrew. If you did it in a worship service, it was liturgy.

called them, the people were tempted to idolatry and unfaithfulness. Hosea then directs God's people to recognize God's faithfulness toward them. Hosea extends the picture of Israel as God's firstborn son (cf. Exod 4:22) by writing that God was the one who lifted them by their arms and taught them to walk, even healing them when they didn't know it (Hos 11:3). God was leading them "with cords of kindness, with the bands of love, and I [the LORD] became to them as one who eases the yoke on their jaws, and I bent down to them and fed them" (Hos 11:4). Yahweh was calling to Israel, to his people, to his corporate "son," calling them to respond in worship and love so they could live in healthy dependence on God and flourish in loving obedience. Yet as Hosea and the rest of the Hebrew Scriptures make clear, Israel's response was inconsistent rather than faithful, and their worship was at times mechanistic rather than sincere.

Centuries later, Matthew 2:15 applies this text from Hosea directly to the Messiah, signaling that the earlier promise to corporate Israel was embodied and fulfilled in the coming of the incarnate Son, Jesus the Christ. Although God called his people out of Egypt and all it represented, they kept turning back to idolatry and disobedience. Christ, by contrast, is the faithful Son who, filled with the Spirit beyond measure, lives in constant communion with the Father and embodies perfect obedience and love. Further, when he was "called out of Egypt," Jesus did not act simply as an individual but also as a representative for Israel, as the one who brought an eternal deliverance.

As God's people continue to be called "out of Egypt," they themselves are organically and firmly held in the person and work of Christ. Thus their calling is not vague or merely general, but effectively includes the specific, the personal, gathering you and me. As a shepherd calls his sheep (Isa 43:1; John 10:3) so God calls us by name: Lydia, John, Mary, and Kelly. Called out from my slavery to sin, death, and the devil, I (ego) am enlivened by the Spirit, who secures each of us in the grace of Christ as we enter the communion of the saints, all the while being able more and more to rest in the love of God.

This threefold dynamic of the corporate, christological, and personal thus characterizes the shape, content, and action of the call to worship God. This calling is a word to Christ, about Christ, and for Christ. It is also necessarily a word to and about the church, those united to him. Finally, it is a word to and for me—for each child of God. God calls his people, all of us, and this call moves all the way to the individual. He knows and calls us by name.

Thus, as we receive the call to worship, it empowers us to lift our gaze to the One who came to love and honor his Father when we would not, offering himself not only for our deliverance but also to lead us in worship and in communion with God. As his people, we now come together as one family, called from every tribe and tongue, called by name to be one in Christ.

God is calling his people out of the world and to himself, calling women and men to be his "sons" and to receive the fullness of his inheritance, which ultimately is to receive God himself. While we were unfaithful in responding, the incarnate Son, *the* elect or chosen one called by God (Isa 42:1, Luke 9:35; 1 Pet 2:4; Luke 23:35) came and responded not only on our behalf but also in such a way as to include us in his response. He is the covenant keeper who replaces our idolatry, rebellion, and hard-heartedness with his faithful worship.[74] So we by faith and trust in him enter the movement of worship and love.

While we cannot unpack this more fully here, much less go into every movement or element of corporate worship, I am hoping this sample will spark imagination and conversation regarding how our corporate worship might more faithfully reflect the arc of Christian life, and how we must understand the movements of worship in a christological, ecclesiological, and personal manner: the three-corded rope.

CONCLUSION

First and foremost, a theology of Christian life is about Christ, the anchor and perfecter of our faith. Jesus lives the liturgy. He embodies the worship service. He is the head worshiper and the one we worship. Israel and the church derive their meaning, life, and identity from the Messiah by means of their participation in him. To live by faith is to trust—personally and corporately—in the faithfulness of God, as did the list of people in Hebrews 11. From the time we were born again

---

74. Cf. John Webster, who ably and powerfully summarizes Karl Barth's view that election must be "christologically determined. This entails that the agent of election is none other than Jesus Christ himself (not some 'unknown God' (II/2, p. 147) and that the means of election is Christ's sharing of our humanity in the incarnation. It also involves an affirmation that election is to that form of human life which Jesus Christ himself establishes." Webster, *Karl Barth: Outstanding Christian Thinkers* (London: Continuum, 2000), 91–92.

by God's Spirit (John 3:3), we have been in the process of learning this new life and are being shaped by it (Gal 4:19). Our faith—and the shape and movement of our Christian life—consists of references to and connection with the King and his kingdom. In Christ, I am part of his body; I am secure in him who lived, died, rose, and ever lives for us, for me. There is no other way.

CONCLUSION

This volume has led us on a long journey with many twists and turns, so it is appropriate that we turn around at the trail's end to see the terrain we have covered. The path was marked by the same sign found at every step: Christian life is a response to the love of God.

As we walked, it became clear that to get to God we must go straight to the incarnate Son; he not only comes from God but also leads us back to God. Jesus's central place is so much more profound than anything captured by a bumper sticker or contained in a single idea. Even those who have been Christians for a long time may fail to appreciate how their Christian life is fully found in Christ.

We have seen that a theology of Christian life must be built in terms of divine and human agency, acknowledging not only that the triune God first loved us but also that the incarnate Son first loved God for us. God first comes to us in our weakness and sin, and in Christ he leads our return to himself. This is the heart of the gospel, the good news that we discover is centered on Christ, who becomes ours by the Holy Spirit. Believers, those who have been united to Christ by his Spirit, are called to participate in the Son's love for the Father in the power of the Spirit.

Guided by the Pauline benediction in 2 Corinthians 13:14, we discover not only that God is love but also that we encounter God's love in the grace of Christ, and we experience God's love by the fellowship of the Holy Spirit: from the Father, through the Son, and in the Holy Spirit. The triune God is the very source and telos for Christian life.

God's love has overflowed to us, and this God—the one Creator, Redeemer, and Sustainer—shapes and reshapes how we understand the law-gospel distinction. God's law was not arbitrary, cruel, or useless. It functioned more like a map than an engine—it was not meant to give humans the power of righteousness and love, but it does help us understand where we stand before God and others. The law reveals our sin to us so that we might turn to find our refuge in Christ, who did not abolish the law but perfectly fulfilled it. Because we are united to Christ, we then use a right understanding of the law to shape our imaginations regarding what it means to love God and neighbor and navigate life in this world.

Grateful, we now understand that the holy God did not leave us in our sin. The basis of Christian life is not a theory of self-improvement, nor first and foremost a doctrine or idea, but a person—the incarnate Son, our Lord Jesus Christ, who was the unique servant of God, like us in all ways yet without sin. He lived as the faithful Adam, the human who always rightly worshiped God and loved his neighbor. This singular Messiah, through his life and sacrificial death, his life-giving resurrection, empowering ascension, and ongoing heavenly intercession—this Messiah alone is the living source of our response to God.

Jesus is both worthy of our worship and the lead worshiper. Accordingly, Christian life is always our life in Christ by his Spirit. This is the life that I, a particular person, live as part of the larger body of Christ, his church.

Because the personal and corporate are woven together, we learn to navigate this life as members of this great cloud of witnesses who live together in particular places and times as God's people. We gather weekly to worship the living God, participating in Christ's life, while he as our great Priest, King, and Prophet not only receives our worship but is also the leader of our prayers, laments, and corporate worship. We observed that corporate worship appears to follow the arc of Christian life. From calling to benediction, worship displays a life of word and prayer, song and sacrament, offering and peacemaking, all with the eschatological confidence that God will manifest his shalom on earth as it is in heaven.

This is our *theologia viatorum*, our theology of pilgrimage: In response to the triune God's love, our gaze is lifted from our own sins and challenges to the wonder of the gospel; we now run this race with confidence because we look to Jesus, the "founder and perfecter of our faith" (Heb 12:2). Wonder of wonders, not only did the triune God first love us, but the incarnate Son also first loved God for us. Christian life is thus reflected in our response to God's love as we have been united to Christ by the Spirit. May we live freely within this very life that has been given to us.

SCRIPTURE INDEX

Genesis
1 . . . . 69, 70, 94
1–2 76
1:2 43
1:27 . . . . .73, 95
1:28 69
1:28–31 198
2:7 225
3 . . . . 126, 226
3:8 69
4:7 . . . . 226, 227
6:18 196
9:8–17 196
9:12–17 198
12:1–9 196
15:1–21 196
15:6 . . . . 98, 238
15:9–10, 17–18 197
16:13 212
17:7 203
17:1–14 196
22:8 197
22:15–18 .196
32:30 46

Exodus
3:3–4 46
4:22 315
12:1–28 274
19:3 197
19–24 197
19:4–5 197
19:5 197
19:8 197
20:2 203
20:3 46
20:6 197
20:45 203
32:1–35 226
33:17–23 .212

Leviticus
16:21 273
23:5 274
26:12 204
26:45 203

Deuteronomy
4:1–8 197
5:3–5 46
5:10 197
6:4 132
6:20–25 197
10:12–13 .137
11:1 197

Joshua
1:7–8 160
8:34 166

Judges
17:6 171
21:25 171

1 Samuel
8:4–7, 19–88 198

2 Samuel
7:8–16 198
7:12–14 201
7:14 198
22:15 198
23:5 198

1 Kings
12:28–33 .226

CHRISTIAN LIFE

2 Kings
21:1–18 226

1 Chronicles
16:23–30 46
21:1 227

2 Chronicles
13:5 198
21:3–20 226
21:7 198
23:3 198

Nehemiah
9:13–14 160

Job
1:6–2:7 227
33:4 43
42:1–6 46

Psalms
1:2 160
8:4–5 208
13 288
13:1, 5, 6 288
17:15 212
19 159
19:7 160
22 209
27:4 212
32:5 273
33:12 242
34:8 46
36 150
37:31 160
40:8 160
45:6–7 .207n56
47:6–7 204
51:16–17 100
65:4 242
69:30–34 269
85 287
85:10–11 179
89:3–4 198
89:30–37 198
104:30 43
106:5 242
110:1 217
115:8 . . . . .46, 95
119 160
132:1–18 198
135:18 . . . . .46, 95
139:1–18 215
147:5 215

Proverbs
15:3 215

Isaiah
1 . . . . .262, 269
1:2–20 269
1:11 100
6 . . . . .43, 45
6:1 . . . . .46, 212
7:14 204
8 209
8:8 204
25:8 187
40:13–14 215
41:10, 13 203
42:1 . . . . .78, 316
43:1 315
43:25 114
46:10 215
57:15 . . . . .42, 43
63:10–11 43
63:11 43

Jeremiah
7:5–7 201
7:23 204
17:5–8 199
18:18 157
30:22 203
31:31–37 198
31:33 204
31:34 46

Ezekiel
1–2 116
11:20 203
20:6–8 226
36:25–28 198
36:27 43
37:23 204
43:5 212
47 150

SCRIPTURE INDEX

Daniel
7. 116

Hosea
6:6 100
6:7 196
7:14 226
8:12 157
11:1 314
13:14 187

Joel
2:28–32. .148
2:32 39

Habakkuk
3:9 198

Zephaniah
3:17 209

Haggai
2:23 242

Zechariah
3:1–2 227
6:13 208
8:8 203
10:6 203
13:1–3, 6, 7, 9 95

Matthew
1. 76
1:18–20. 43
1:23 204
2:15 315
3:11 43
3:17 .64, 78
4:1–11 227
4:9–10 46
4:10 .46, 227
4:23 314
5:8 212
5:14–15. .307
5:17 .161, 299
6:10 118
10:30 215
11:28 314
12:32 43
13:24–30. 309
13:39 227
16:18 259
17:5 78
18:20 . . . . 209, 274
22:31–32. .39
22:32 197
22:36–40. 299
24:14 39
25:41 227
26:30 209
28:18 109
28:19 . . . . 43, 47, 274

Mark
2:23–3:60 268
6:46 .207n56
7:20–23. .226
12:26–27. 197
12:30–32. 299
14:26 209
14:35 . . . . 207n56
16:19 217

Luke
3:8 197
3:21–22. .207
4. 295
4:7–8 46
4:16 314
5. 44
5:4, 5, 8 44
5:16 207
6:12–13. .207
9:18, 28–29 207
9:28 .207n56
9:35 316
10:21 207
11:1 207
16:16 . . . . 166n33
19:9 197
22:20 198
22:31–32. 207
22:42 114
23:34, 46. 207
23:35 316
24:25–27. 302
24:30 207
24:47 39

24:50–53 . . . . 207, 313n71
25:25–27 39

John
1:1 . . . . .207n56
1:12 243
1:14 299
1:17 161
1:18 47
1:29 . . . . 119, 299
1:36 299
2:27 43
3:3 . . . . .212, 231, 317
3:5–6 231
3:7 231
3:16 137
3:19 229
3:20 229
3:34 . . . . 141, 299
3:35 78
4:1, 2 121
6:37 211
7 150
8:12 . . . . 229, 230
8:31–47 210
8:34 228
8:36 229
8:39 197
8:44 227
8:48–58 200
9:5 229
10:1–18 95
10:3 315
10:14–15 47
10:18 109
10:27–28 233
10:30 . . . . 38, 47, 135
11:51–53 243
12:31 . . . . 227, 252
12:32 81
12:34 275
14 128
14:6 . . . . 81, 96, 143, 230
14:8–9 212
14:15 172
14:16 . . . . 103, 147
14:16–17 129
14:21 172
14:23 . . . . 38, 138
14:23–26 136
14:26 43
14:27 125
14:30 252
15 . . . . 138, 212
15:1–11 103
15:4–5 233
15:10 172
15:26 147
16:7 147
16:8 147
16:10 135
16:11 252
16:13 135
16:14–15 135
16:19–20 . . . . .230n28
17 . . . . 184, 207n56
17:11 . . . . 38, 47
17:21 . . . . 38, 47, 149
19:30 145
20:17 . . . . 207, 207n56
20:22 43
20:28 . . . . 45, 46, 187
21:17 215

Acts
1:5, 8 43
2:4, 33 . . . . 43, 148
2:21 148
2:33–34 217
2:36 148
2:38 . . . . 43, 44
2:41 274
2:42, 46 300
3:25 196
4:8–12, 31 .148
7:55–56 217
7:56 212
8:4–25 . . . . .200n47
8:12–13 271
8:15 . . . . .200n47
8:26–40 39
9:20 314
9:31 . . . . 147, 313
9:36–43 39
10 39
13:1–2 314
13:13–52 295
13:17 242

SCRIPTURE INDEX

13:39	165
13:52	148
15:21	314
16:14–15	39
17:28	43, 63
20:7	300
20:7–8	301
20:7–12	301
27:3	101
28:2	101

Romans

1–7	141n30
1:7	38
1:18–23	159
1:20–28	67
1:21–32	226
1:23	95
2:12	165
2:15	204
3:21–4:25	158
3:25	238
3:28	238
3:31	161
4:1–5	200
4:1–9	238
4:1–16	197
4:3	238, 243
4:5	99, 238
4:6	243
4:9–11	238
4:9	243
4:11	243
4:22	238, 243
4:22–24	238
5	244
5:5	82, 137, 214
5:10	126
5:11	120
5:12	244
5:12–21	196
5:12–8:3	228
5:14	244
5:17	196, 244
5:20	244
5:21	244
6	200
6:1–2	156
6:1–11	140
6:2	240
6:4	241
6:6	240, 244
6:13	246
6:16–18	229
6:17, 20	244
6:18	229n27
7:4	244, 247
7:5	140
7:11	228
7:12	161
7:14	140, 228
7:14–25	231
7:18	140
7:22	161
8	140, 142, 146
8:1	167
8:2	167
8:4	140
8:6	84
8:7	140
8:9	43, 141
8:9–10	273
8:9–11	44, 47
8:11–15	43
8:11	142
8:13	142, 145
8:15–16	128
8:15–17	243
8:17	145, 146
8:22	72
8:23	247n66
8:24–25	146
8:28	146
8:30	146
8:32–39	200
8:33	236, 242, 247
8:34	105
8:38–39	233
9–16	141n30
9:11	242
10:9–10	39
11:28	242
11:36	84, 87, 136, 162
12	234, 246, 259
12:1–2	178, 246, 247
12:3–9	246
12:4–8	138
13:10	171

CHRISTIAN LIFE

14:7–8 240
14:8 233
15:6 208
15:17–12 . . . . .209n62
15:9 209
16:16 275
16:23 248

1 Corinthians
1:10 248
1:30 233
2:2 139
3:16 . . . . 38, 43
5:7 119
6:19 43
7:22–23 . . . . 229n27
8:6 47
10:11 286
10:20 227
11:17–34 300
11:25 198
12 . . . . .234, 259
12:3 148
12:4–6 149
12:12–31 138
12:25 149
12:26 234
13:1–13 148
14:27–33 300
14:33 314
15 146
15:3 39
15:3–5 139
15:13–14 139
15:22–23 233
15:33 248
15:45 200
15:45–47 . . . . 103, 121
16:1 314
16:20 275

2 Corinthians
1:1 314
1:3 208
1:24 248
2:1–4 248
3:12 248
4:4 . . . . 47, 73
5–11 248
5:5 141
5:14–15 . . . . 114, 233
5:17 . . . . 187, 231
5:20 38
5:21 . . . . 55, 188, 216, 233, 235
6:1 248
6:16 . . . . 43, 204
7:12 248
8:1–9:15 314
11:31 208
12:12 39
13:12 275
13:14 . . . . 53, 133, 136, 169

Galatians
1:4 208
2:9 276
2:19–20 167
2:20 . . . . 62, 139, 233
3 22
3:5–8 200
3:6 . . . . 238, 243
3:6–9 238
3:6–18 197
3:13 167
3:13–14 . . . . 200, 235
3:14 55
3:27 274
3:28 241
3:29 233
4:4 114
4:5 233
4:6 . . . . 44, 47, 273
4:6–7 144
4:19 317
5:16–17 84
5:16–26 143
5:24 . . . . 139, 291
6:15 . . . . 187, 231

Ephesians
1:3 208
1:3–5 38
1:3–23 200
1:4 242
1:6 . . . . 200, 293
1:14 141
1:20 109
1:20–21 217

1:22	103
2:1	166
2:4–5	233
2:4–8	208
2:5–7	114
2:6	139, 208, 242
2:10	50, 233
2:15	241
2:18	135
2:19–21	38
2:19–22	38
2:20	39
2:22	292
3:16–17	233
3:19	55
4:4–6	48, 293
4:6	208
4:11–12	39
4:22	241
4:22–24	142, 239, 240
4:30	142
5:23	103
5:25–27	38
6:12	227

Philippians

1:6	145
1:19	47
1:29	146
2	110
2:7	208
2:9	109
2:10	40
3:3	47
3:8–9	233
3:9	291
3:10	146
4:20	208

Colossians

1:2	252
1:15	299
1:15–17	47, 73
1:15–19	140
1:16	227
1:18	103, 232
1:21	126
1:27	273
1:29	145

2:9	241
2:10	103
2:12	139, 241, 274
2:18	46
2:20	241
3:1	139, 217, 233, 241
3:1–4	146
3:2	88
3:3	62, 125, 139, 240
3:4	233
3:5–11	143
3:8–10	239, 240
3:10	95
3:12	242
3:12–14	143

1 Thessalonians

1:3	208
1:4	242
1:5	147
1:9–10	301
3:11, 13	208
4:16	233
4:16–17	233
5:26	276

1 Timothy

1:8	161
2:5	47, 97, 107
4:1	227

2 Timothy

1:10	99, 187
1:14	43
2:3	146
2:10	242
3:16	39, 295
4:1–6	39

Titus

1:1	242
3:4	101

Philemon

3, 7, 8	249
8–11	249
10	249
15–16	249
16–17	249

CHRISTIAN LIFE

19. 249
23. 249

Hebrews
1. 80
1:3 . . . . 48, 73, 194, 217
1:6 . . . . .207n55
1:9 207
2:5–10 120
2:7–9 208
2:10 216
2:11 . . . . 47, 216
2:11–12. 102
2:12 . . . . 209, 210, 289, 292
2:13 209
2:14 216
2:14–15. . . . . 102, 200
2:17 . . . . 102, 238
2:18 216
3:1 273
3:7 289
3:7–8 265
4:12–13. 215
4:14–16. 148
4:15 . . . . 188, 193, 215, 216, 218
5:12–13. 272
5:14 272
6:12 273
6:15 197
7:16 212
7:26 300
7:27 212
8:1 217
8:1–2 . . . . .217n77
8:1–13 273
8:2 204
8:10 204
8:27 146
9:12 212
9:14 169
9:15 198
9:24 . . . . 217n77, 273
9:25–28. . . . . .217n77
9:26 212
9:28 300
10:1 .166n33
10:5 289
10:9 300
10:10 . . . . 212, 240, 300

10:25 257
11. 316
11:1 146
11:8 197
11:16 204
11:17 197
11:26–27. 212
12:1 . . . . 143, 147, 168
12:2 . . . . 118, 187, 320
12:6 198

James
1:13–15. 226
1:17 87
1:17–18. 230
1:19–25. 260
1:22 174
1:26–2:26 260
1:27 260
2:1–17 260
2:2 314
2:14–26. 174
2:18–12. 161
2:21–23. 197
2:23 238
4:1–10 260
4:8 217
5:1–6 260
5:16 273

1 Peter
1:1–2 242
1:2 169
1:10–12. .39
1:11 47
1:15 314
1:19 119
1:23 231
2:4 316
2:4–5 314
2:8–9 242
2:9–10 . . . . 38, 121
2:22 . . . . 188, 193, 216
2:24 200
3:18 200
3:21 274
3:22 217
4:12–19. 146
5:10 233

SCRIPTURE INDEX

5:13 242
5:14 276

2 Peter
2:19 229

1 John
1:8–10 . . . . 231, 252, 273
2:1 105
2:2 238
2:14 47
2:16 . . . . 226, 250
2:27 43
2:29 251
3:1 250
3:1–2 243
3:2 250
3:4 250
3:5 . . . . 216, 250
3:7 251
3:8 . . . . 200, 251
3:20 215
4:2 47
4:7 133
4:7–8 81
4:7–21 134
4:8 . . . . 58, 60
4:10 238
4:10–11 134
4:11 82
4:13 134
4:16 . . . . 55, 58, 60, 133
4:19 . . . . 62, 251
4:19–21 82

Jude
1 169

Revelation
1:4 115
1:5 232
1:5–6 121
1:6 . . . . 121, 208
1:17 . . . . 46, 118
1:17–18 119
1:18 187
2–3 . . . . 119, 242
3:21 121
4 . . . . 117, 121
4:1 . . . . 121, 122n87
4:2 121
4:11 115
4–5 . . . . 95, 109, 115, 116, 117, 122
5 . . . . 117, 118, 119, 121
5:2 119
5:3–4 119
5:5 119
5:6 119
5:8–9 121
5:8–13 209
5:9–10 . . . . 115, 121
5:10 121
5:12 121
5:13–14 121
7:9–10 209
11:15 175
12:10 200
13:4–8 118
13:11–15 119
14:1–5 209
14:6–7 119
14:9–12 119
14:13 233
15:4 119
16:2 119
16:14 227
17:14 242
19:4 119
19:7–9 39
19:10 118
19:19–20 119
20:4 121
20:6 121
20:10 227
21:2 118
21:4 187
21:5 118
21:6 119
21:10 118
22 150
22:2 39
22:5 121
22:8–9 . . . . 46, 118
22:13 . . . . 118, 119
22:17 39
22:20 115

SUBJECT INDEX

Adam, 73–74, 192, 193, 204. *See also* Jesus Christ, Adam typology
Alexander of Hales, 74
Alikin, Valeriy A., 301, 303
Ambrose, 105–106
Anselm, 77
Anderson, Gary A., 199
anthropology, 92–93, 95–96, 189–90. *See also* sin
apocalypse, 116
Apostles' Creed, 38, 314n73
Aquinas, Thomas, 9, 25, 62, 74, 77, 130, 169
Athanasius, 91, 101, 109–12
Atonement, 48–49, 100, 105, 200, 228
Augustine, 25, 55, 65, 67, 103–104, 112, 129, 133–34, 150, 153, 169, 184, 258
  City of God, The, 96–99
  totus Christus, 285–91
  triadic nature to love, 59–62
  uti and *frui*, 82–87
Baker, Kimberly, 290
Barclay, John M. G., 161, 162
Barmen Declaration, 267
Barth, Karl, 21, 25, 136n26, 163, 164, 173–74, 183–84, 253, 267, 309, 316n74
Basil the Great, 131, 136n25
Bates, Matthew W., 169
Bauckham, Richard, 25, 119
Baylor, Timothy, 74n47, 75
Beale, G. K., 121, 232
Behr, John, 186
being human. *See* human being
Berkouwer, G. C., 13
Biddle, John, 278
Boethius, 77
Bonhoeffer, Dietrich, 267, 289
Bradshaw, Paul, 116–17, 296

Brevard, Keziah Goodwin Hopkins, 163
Bruner, Emil, 183
Bultmann, Rudolph, 224, 243
Burton, Tara Isabella, 171, 221
Calvin, John, 21, 74, 92, 102, 104–105, 142, 144, 158–60, 163, 164, 172, 210–11, 236–37, 253, 255–56
Cameron, Michael, 287
Chalcedonian Christology, 285
Christ. *See* Jesus Christ
Christianity. *See also* church, the; rituals
  catholic nature of, 37–41
  definition, 257
  historic faith, 13, 35–36, 127–28
Christian life. *See also* Messiah
  argument concerning, 27–28, 230–31
  center of a, 106–109, 188, 193–94
  forgiveness, 99–100
  living a, 81, 84–85, 200–201, 267. *See also* love; sin
  obedience to a, 172–74
  theology of, 23–24, 27–28, 30, 45, 93, 182–84, 285, 316. *See also* dichotomies; human response
  threefold dynamic of, 29, 312, 315. *See also* christological; ecclesiological; ego
  transformation of a, 247–48. *See also* ego; Holy Spirit
  questions concerning, 21–24
Christian practices. *See* rituals
christological, 29, 107, 181–82, 185, 220, 292. *See also* Irenaeus; worship
church, the. *See also* worship
  definition of, 284
  as institution, 257–58
  four characteristics of, 37–40, 254
  function of, 257–58
  rituals of. *See* rituals

SUBJECT INDEX

understanding, 254–56
value of, 256–58
Cole, Graham A., 179
compassion, 214–17
Cooke, Bernard, 270–75
Cranfield, C. E. B., 163
creation. *See also* Jesus Christ
   beginning of, 77–78
   disruption of, 71–73. *See also* sin
   God's love and, 63–69
   reflection of God, 69–70
Croasmun, Matthew, 244–45, 247, 254
Cullmann, Oscar, 115–16, 145, 300
Cyprian of Carthage, 255
Cyril of Alexandria, 112
Dahl, N. A., 219
Day, Dorothy, 255
Decalogue, 167, 171
De Moor, Bernadinus, 75
Derrida, Jacques, 162
Descartes, Rene, 224
Diaspora, 295, 314
dichotomies. *See also* Irenaeus
   catholic and particular, 37–41
   false, 30–31, 184
   objective and subjective, 31–37
   representation and imitation, 48–51
   transcendence and immanence, 41–46
   Trinitarian and Christ-centered, 46–48
Didache, 230–31, 303
DiVito, Robert A., 71n40, 234
dogmatic theology, 13, 71n39
Donatist controversy, 258–59
Eastman, Susan, 223–25, 231
ecclesia, 29. *See also* church, the; three-corded rope
   called by God, 313–16
ecclesiology, 39, 189, 254–60
Edwards, Jonathan, 150
ego. *See also* Christian life, threefold dynamic
   Christian life and, 222–25
   definition of, 219–22
   fallen, 225–32, 238–39, 250–52
   response to God, 237–38, 268, 284
   transformation of, 248–50
   united to others, 239–41, 244, 246–48
   with Christ, 233–37, 239–40, 242–43
   worship and, 292–93

eschatological view, 115–23, 144–45
eschatology, 144, 189–93, 216
eternity, 77
Eucharist. *See also* rituals; worship
   reason for, 29, 64, 182
   distorted, 262, 267, 281
faith
   abandoning, 258–59
   cultivating, 127–28, 267
fellowship
   with God, 27–28, 126–28, 178. *See also* Holy Spirit
   with others, 275–76
Ferguson, Sinclair, 195
Fitzgerald, John T., 248, 249
forgiveness, 99–100, 188. *See also* Jesus Christ
Franklin, Benjamin, 224
Frei, Hans W., 271
French Confession of Faith (1559), 169
Freud, Sigmund, 222, 224
Gaventa, Beverly Roberts, 228, 244, 253
God
   centeredness, 47–48
   characteristics of, 42–43, 198, 269
   church and, 255–56
   compassion of, 214–17, 269
   creator, 191–92
   fellowship with, 128, 172–75, 199–200. *See also* Holy Spirit
   holiness of, 42
   love of, 58–63, 88–89, 126–27, 150. *See also* love
   revealing of, 28
   worship of, 205–18. *See also* worship
Goodwin, Thomas, 217–18
gospel. *See also* law
   foundation of the, 106–107, 178
   overuse of the, 155–57
   promise of the, 175–78
grace
   Christ embodiment of, 154
   from sin, 93–95
   law and, 161–64
   through mediator, 95–101, 105–106
Gregory of Nazianzus, 25
Gunton, Colin, 42–43
Heidelberg Catechism, 202–203
Heron, Alasdair I. C., 125

Hoekema, Anthony A., 233
Holmes, Stephen, 296
Holy Spirit. *See also* Trinity
  presence of hope, 145
  reason for, 125–28
  role of: bond of love, 129–35; convicts and comforts, 147–50; connection to Christ, 137–40; gift of grace, 135–37; in our lives, 140–42; spiritual counselor, 142–45
Hooker, Richard, 91
Horton, Michael, 100
human being, 80, 95–96, 186, 189–90. *See also* anthropology; Irenaeus
human response
  subjective vs. objective, 183–84
  to God. *See* law-gospel distinction; response
Hume, David, 64
Hurtado, Larry, 25, 117, 122, 301
Hütter, Reinhard, 283
Irenaeus, 189–95
Jesus Christ
  Adam typology, 93, 110, 196, 200, 234–35, 241, 244
  as a mediator, 96–98, 104–105. *See also* Athanasius
  as a prophet, 119–20, 188, 202–205
  as our priest, 101–106, 202–205
  center of life, 106–109
  death of, 200–202
  God's delight in, 200
  humanness of, 102–104, 112, 127, 193, 194, 206, 313
  incarnate Son, 45–46, 100–101, 109–14, 154, 185–86
  Gospel identity, 111–12
  King, 202–205, 313
  life as example, 185–86, 193–94, 205
  love of, 64, 73–79, 214–17
  loving, 79–81
  Messiah, 103–104, 107, 315. *See also* Messiah
  salvation through, 79, 96, 101–102, 154–55, 235
  threefold anointing of. *See* Heidelberg Catechism
  totus Christus, 285–91, 313–14
  Trinitarian foundation, 28–29
  union with, 233–36
  worship of, 46–47, 106, 115–23, 299–300, 313
John of Damascus, 42, 96, 181, 203
Johnson, Dru, 269
Johnson, Maxwell E., 305
Julian of Norwich, 82
Jungmann, Josef, 107–108, 119, 122
justification, 146, 159, 173n53, 223, 235n44, 237–38. *See also* gospel
Justin Martyr, 305–307
Kant, Immanuel, 83
Karlstadt, Andreas Bodenstein, 183
Khomiakov, Aleksei, 256
Kieser, Ty, 112
knowledge
  of God, 92–95
  of self. *See* human, being
law, the
  in Christian theology, 157–59
  ministerial use of, 170–78. *See also* gospel
  negative context of, 160–61
  obedience to, 167–69
  reason for, 161–64
  role of, 165–67
law-gospel distinction, 28, 58, 139–40, 285–86, 319–20. *See also* gospel; law
Leithart, Peter J., 63, 162
Lewis, C. S., 68, 86n81
liturgy. *See also* worship
  definition, 254, 261, 308
  first church's, 116, 131, 182
  Jesus as, 107, 316
  used today, 314, 314n73
Lord's Supper, the. *See* rituals
love
  Christian life and, 56–58
  creation and, 66–70. *See also* love, toward others
  distortion of, 86–87. *See also* sin
  divine, 58–63, 88–89
  Jesus is, 73–79
  law and, 170–72
  ours to God, 71–73, 79–81, 94. *See also* worship
  source of, 82, 150
  toward others, 81–87, 148–49
  within the Trinity, 63–66

SUBJECT INDEX

Luther, Martin, 33–35, 160, 164, 183–84, 241, 255
Macy, Gary, 270–75
Magnus, Albertus, 74
man, old and new, 142, 239–41. *See also* Christian life, transformation
Martin, Dale B., 243–44
Martyn, J. Louis, 248
Mary (mother of Jesus), 76. *See also* Jesus Christ, humanness of
Matera, Frank J., 288
Maximus the Confessor, 253
McDonald, Suzanne, 213
McGuckin, John Anthony, 93
Mediator, 79, 96, 101–102, 154–55, 235. *See also* Jesus Christ
Meek, Esther Lightcap, 153
Meeks, Wayne, 219
Melanchthon, Philip, 92, 142, 172
Messiah. *See also* Jesus Christ; worship
  foundation to Christian life, 182–85
  leader of God's people, 185–89, 202–205
  promises concerning, 195–201
Miller, Patrick, 187
Moffitt, David M., 212
"moral influence theory," 48
mortification, 142, 145, 241
Moule, C. F. D., 297
Mowry, Lucetta, 122–23
Murray, John, 170–72, 208
Naldini, Mario, 83
Nicene Creed, 38, 43, 114, 131, 255
Niemöller, Martin, 267
Nietzsche, Friedrich, 67
Norris, Thomas, 55
Nygren, Anders, 83
Oepke, Albrecht, 234
Old, Hughes Oliphant, 277
Olevianus, Caspar, 100, 101, 102
Osiander, Andreas, 74, 236–37
Otto, Rudolf, 44, 45
Owen, John
  Christian life theology, 79–81, 145, 174, 277–80
  divine love view, 68, 73–79, 255
  sacraments and Trinity, 47, 64–66, 213
  view of sin, 174, 228
Paddison, Angus, 219

Pickavance, Tim, 67
Pitkin, Barbara, 159
Polanyi, Michael, 26
prayer, 107–109, 236–65. *See also totus Christus*; worship
Primasius, 120
Protestant Reformation, 202, 243
Proctology. *See* Irenaeus
reconciliation, 29, 49, 79, 98–101, 111n60. *See also* Jesus Christ
Reformed tradition, 39–40, 157, 164, 172–73, 178
response to
  God's love, 154–56, 181–82, 187–89, 220. *See also* Christian life; ego; worship
  others, 28, 61, 81–88
  us from God, 195–201
Ridderbos, Herman, 239–41
righteousness. *See also* Mediator
  definition, 98, 160
  Christ's, 34, 95, 142, 175, 236–38
  gift of, 158–60, 189–90, 196, 269
  incomplete, 176–77
rituals
  beliefs and, 271–72
  dangers of: baptism, 262–63; corporate worship, 265–66; Lord's Supper, 263, 281; prayer, 263–65
  negative influences toward: enthusiasm, 278–79; rationalism, 265–67, 278; superstition, 276–77, 279–80
  positive nature of: fellowship in, 275–76; maturation through, 272–73; shapes theology, 260–62, 268
  reason for, 269–70, 280–82
  worship: Lord's Supper, 64, 263, 270, 301–302, 306; promote service, 274–75; shaped by Christ, 273–74
Rohls, Jan, 156, 169n43, 172, 173n53
Rotelle, John E., 85
Rupert of Deutz, 74
Sayers, Dorothy L., 130–31
Schleiermacher, Friedrich, 104n39, 183
Scobie, Charles H. H., 301
Scotus, Duns, 74
Senn, Frank C., 281
shalom, 57, 69–70, 80–81

333

sin. *See also* ego; Holy Spirit; Irenaeus
  definition of, 245–46
  disrupts love, 71–73
  disrupts relationships, 95–96, 192–94
  freedom from, 231–32
  need for Mediator, 98–101, 138–40. *See also* Jesus Christ
Slater, Lauren, 66
Solzhenitsyn, Alexander, 13
Steenwyk, Carrie Titcombe, 310
Stump, Eleonore, 77
Sweet, J. P. M., 120
Tanner, Kathryn, 133
Taylor, Charles, 63, 221, 271
Tertullian, 208, 303
theology. *See also* dichotomies
  atonement, 49
  Christian life, 92–94, 267–68. *See also* Christian life; Owen, John
  covenant: Abrahamic, 196–97; Adamic, 196; Christ as, 200–201; Davidic, 198–99; Mosaic, 197–98
  doctrine overview, 189–90
  dogmatic, 13
  Protestant, 182–85
  Trinitarian, 25–26, 47–48, 131, 134–35. *See also* Trinity
theory
  atonement, 48–49
  Christian, 26, 129, 320
  "moral influence," 48
  worship, 107–108
three-corded rope, 182–85
threefold confession, 202–203
Torrance, Thomas F., 91, 113, 125, 153
totus Christus, 285–91, 313–14
transcendence, 43–45
Treier, Daniel, 15, 181
Trinitarian
  becoming, 25–26, 271
  Christ-centered and, 46–48
  questions concerning, 25
Trinity. *See also* God; Holy Spirit; Jesus Christ; love, divine
  as one, 43, 60–61, 133–35, 154–55. *See also* Owen, John
  description of, 65, 130–31
  need for, 111, 128, 187
  uti and *frui*, 82–87. *See also* Augustine
Van Bavel, Tarsicius J., 62
Vanhoye, Albert, 181
vivification, 142
von Allmen, J.-J., 16, 106–107, 283
Webber, Robert E., 302
Webster, John, 44, 59, 68, 290, 316n74
Weinandy, Thomas, 112–14
Wesley, John, 35
Westminster Larger Catechism, 167
Willard, Dallas, 176
Williams, Rowan, 284
Wingren, Gustaf, 193
Witvliet, John D., 310
Wolter, Michael, 249
worship. *See also* church, the; prayer; rituals
  corporate, 29, 181–82, 291–93
  elements of, 293, 301–307, 310–12
  example from Christ, 187, 206–14, 217–18
  history of, 294–96, 298–99, 303–304. *See also* Justin Martyr
  New Testament, 296–97, 299–300
  of Jesus, 115–23, 301–302, 313. *See also* Jesus Christ; *totus Christus*
  reason for, 284–85, 309–10
  sin and, 95–96
  theology and, 93–94, 260–62
  three-corded rope of, 316
  traditions of, 308–309
Zahl, Simeon, 182–84, 261, 279
Zizioulas, John, 94
Zwingli, Huldrych, 165–68